The Changing Geography of International Business

THE ACADEMY OF INTERNATIONAL BUSINESS

Published in association with the UK Chapter of the Academy of International Business

Titles already published in the series:

The Changing Geography of International Business

Edited by

Gary Cook
University of Liverpool Management School, UK

and

Jennifer Johns
University of Liverpool Management School, UK

First published 2013 by
PALGRAVE MACMILLAN

Palgrave Macmillan in the UK is an imprint of Macmillan Publishers Limited,
registered in England, company number 785998, of Houndmills, Basingstoke,
Hampshire RG21 6XS.

Palgrave Macmillan in the US is a division of St Martin's Press LLC,
175 Fifth Avenue, New York, NY 10010.

Palgrave Macmillan is the global academic imprint of the above companies
and has companies and representatives throughout the world.

Palgrave® and Macmillan® are registered trademarks in the United States,
the United Kingdom, Europe and other countries.

ISBN 978–1–137–27749–7

This book is printed on paper suitable for recycling and made from fully
managed and sustained forest sources. Logging, pulping and manufacturing
processes are expected to conform to the environmental regulations of the
country of origin.

A catalogue record for this book is available from the British Library.

A catalog record for this book is available from the Library of Congress.

10   9   8   7   6   5   4   3   2   1
22 21 20 19 18 17 16 15 14 13

Contents

Figures and Tables

Figures

Tables

Foreword

The 39th Annual AIB UK & Ireland Conference took place from 29–31 March 2012 at the University of Liverpool. This book contains a selection of the contributions to the conference and takes its title from the conference theme 'New Global Developments and the Changing Geography of International Business'.

The first chapter in the volume is the text of the keynote address by Prof. Ram Mudambi of the Fox School of Business, Temple University, who spoke on the theme of 'Flatness'. Prof. Mudambi's many distinguished contributions to the field have spanned the domains of International Business and Economic Geography. This was a distinctive theme of the 39th Conference, which sought to explore the interface between International Business and Economic Geography. Indeed, the UK & Ireland Chapter was pleased to welcome delegates from the Economic Geography Research Group of the Royal Geographical Society, to whom an invitation and call for papers had been sent. Prof. Henry Yeung of the National University of Singapore, a world-leading Economic Geographer, gave the second keynote address 'Global Production Networks: The Economic Geography of International Business'. This contained many perceptive insights into how the perspective of Economic Geography can sharpen the analytical focus of International Business.

The chapters in Part I of the book all explore the importance of institutions in framing the context within which firms make their strategic decisions and which are an essential influence on the processes of International Business and economic performance more generally. The careful analysis of the role of institutions in economic processes represents one important area where International Business scholars and Economic Geographers find common ground.

The chapters in Part II likewise represent a common interest in the issue of space. Each presents a vista on the subtle ways in which processes that operate at a range of spatial scales from the very local to the broadly global influence the requirements for successful firm strategies and condition the prospects for individual firms and, indeed, particular regions and countries. International Business scholars have contributed much to understanding the strategic and practical challenges of managing across borders, just as Economic Geographers have developed a rich understanding of the subtle interplay of processes which operate at a range of spatial scales as they frame economic processes in particular locations.

The complexities of place are explored by the chapters in Part III. Interest in International Business has come to focus increasingly on the choice of location at the sub-national scale by MNEs. Likewise, how firms chose to place themselves in networks has also become a central interest. The issues of how firms best adapt to requirements for local responsiveness and how policymakers interested in capturing spillovers from MNEs can promote this are of longer standing. These chapters provide varied and fresh perspectives on these themes, old and new, where there is scope for fruitful interdisciplinary work between International Business scholars and Economic Geographers.

There were 189 delegates at the conference. In all there were delegates from 25 different countries and from as far afield as New Zealand. The explorations of the interface between International Business and Economic Geography, together with a high standard of papers and discussion in the plenary and paper sessions, provided much stimulating food for thought. The Academy of International Business is the main forum for International Business and International Management research in the United Kingdom and Ireland, and its federated position within the wider Academy of International Business links to work advancing worldwide. Our website (www.abi-uki.org) provides details and links.

Heinz Tüselmann
Chair, Academy of International Business
UK and Ireland Chapter

Acknowledgements

Many thanks to the University of Liverpool Management School for hosting the 39th Annual Conference of the Academy of International Business, UK and Ireland Chapter. Particular thanks are expressed to Katie Neary, the Conference Coordinator, for organizing the Conference and the Gala Dinner in an efficient and professional manner and the support of the events team. Thanks are also expressed to Joseph Cook for his careful copyediting of the manuscript and to Virginia Thorp and Keri Dickens at Palgrave for overseeing the smooth production of the volume.

Contributors

Maria L. Aldred is Senior Lecturer in International Business at Manchester Metropolitan University Business School. She has studied the development of firms and institutional systems in Central and Eastern Europe. She has also recently examined the role of trade unions in influencing firm-level policies, such as profit-sharing schemes and equal-opportunity policies.

Matthew M.C. Allen is Senior Lecturer in Organisation Studies at Manchester Business School. His research covers comparative institutional analysis. He is particularly interested in the links between institutions and organizational capabilities. His research has examined these associations within the areas of employment relations and innovation.

Björn Ambos is Chaired Professor of Strategic Management and Director at the Institute of Management, University of St. Gallen. He previously held positions at the University of Edinburgh, the WU Vienna and the University of Hamburg. Björn's research interests revolve around strategy and innovation in the global firm. Recent papers have looked at the role of parenting advantage and how MNCs control but also learn from their foreign affiliates.

Ulf Andersson is Professor of Strategy and International Management at the Department of Strategic Management and Globalization, Copenhagen Business School, and Editor of the *Journal of International Business Studies*. He has been a Professor of International Business at Uppsala University where he also earned his doctoral degree. His research focuses on subsidiary development, knowledge governance and transfer, network theory, strategy and management of the MNC. Ulf's research is published in, among others, the *Journal of International Business Studies*, *Strategic Management Journal*, *Journal of World Business*, *International Business Review*, *Management International Review* and *Organization Studies*.

Martin T. Bohl is Professor of Finance and Monetary Economics at the University of Muenster. Martin has published in highly ranked finance and monetary economics journals. His current research interests are the implications of short-selling restrictions, speculative bubbles in agricultural products and the implications of passive investing. One of his primary goals in teaching is to bridge the gap between theory and practice so that investors better understand the functioning of financial markets, financial products and how to manage their own wealth. Martin worked as consultant and analyst for central banks and institutional investors.

Peter J. Buckley is Professor of International Business and Director of the Centre for International Business, University of Leeds. He is author of 26 books and over

175 refereed journal articles and Fellow of the Academy of International Business, the British Academy of Management, the Royal Society of Arts. He is a Fellow and President of the European International Business Academy and was President of the Academy of International Business (2002–2004). He was awarded the OBE for services to 'higher education, international business and research' in the New Year's Honours list 2012. His current research includes the analysis of 'The Global Factory', Chinese outward foreign direct investment and international mergers and acquisitions by Indian companies.

Chris Carr is Professor of Corporate Strategy at the University of Edinburgh Business School and Research Leader for the International Business Group. He has spent over 30 years researching strategic approaches to globalization, comparing 21 countries worldwide through extensive field research, in over 300 companies including particularly the automotive sector. Prior to this he worked in industry for over ten years with British Aerospace and then GKN, Britain's two largest engineering companies.

Pi-Chi Chen is Research Associate at the School of Business, Economics and Informatics, Birkbeck, University of London. Her research focuses on strategy and strategy change of multinational enterprises and the role of foreign subsidiary, with a particular interest in the IT industry in emerging markets.

Gary Cook is Senior Lecturer in Applied Economics and Head of Economics, Finance and Accounting at the University of Liverpool Management School. His principal areas of research are industrial clusters, with particular emphasis on media industries and financial services, multinational location, innovation and internationalization. He also researches in the area of law and economics, focusing on the insolvency and turnaround of small firms.

Mike Crone is Senior Lecturer in International Business at Sheffield Business School, Sheffield Hallam University, UK. Since completing his Ph.D. in Economic Geography at the University of Sheffield, he has worked at the Northern Ireland Economic Research Centre and Queen's University Belfast and the University of Strathclyde, Glasgow. Mike's research interests lie at the interface of business and management studies (especially international business and entrepreneurship) and economic geography/regional studies. Previous research has been published in journals such as *Regional Studies, Environment & Planning C: Government & Policy* and the *British Journal of Management*.

Peter Enderwick is Professor of International Business at AUT University, Aukland. He is a founder member of the Australia and New Zealand International Business Academy. His research interests are in globalization and labour, service sector multinationals, large emerging markets, particularly China and India, and the competitiveness of small, open economies. He is the author of eight books and numerous book chapters and articles in professional journals.

Nicolas Forsans is Associate Professor in International Strategic Management at Leeds University Business School, University of Leeds. He is also Director of the James E Lynch India and South Asia Business Centre. His research interest is centred on three main areas: (i) the impact of regional trade agreements on the foreign market servicing strategies of multinational firms (exports, licensing, FDI), in particular in North America, (ii) corporate strategies of multinational firms with regard to emerging economies such as India, and (iii) the emergence of 'third world' multinationals, the increasing importance of Indian business groups and their internationalization strategies.

Mia Hsiao-Wen Ho has a Ph.D. in Management Research from King's College London with specialization in International Business and Strategy. She completed her doctoral studies in 2012. Her thesis title was 'Knowledge Transfer, Organisational Learning, and the Performance of International Strategic Alliances: A Co-evolutionary Perspective'. She has held research and teaching positions in King's College London and in Queen Mary, University of London. Her research interests lie in the co-evolution of international strategic alliances, cross-border knowledge transfer and acquisition, innovation in the knowledge-intensive industries and international entrepreneurship in small and medium-sized enterprises. Prior to her doctoral studies, she was awarded a Distinction for M.Sc. in Business Studies at Aston University in 2009 and obtained BA in Economics at National Chengchi University in Taiwan in 2007.

Odile E. M. Janne is Lecturer at the School of Business, Economics and Informatics, Birkbeck, University of London. Her research interests are in the fields of international business, geography and technological innovation, including corporate technological strategy, the geography of innovative activities, multinational networks and subsidiaries, regional innovation and development, multinationals and industrial policy and intellectual property rights.

Jennifer Johns is Senior Lecturer at the University of Liverpool Management School. She works on research issues of inter-disciplinary interest including globalisation, the agglomeration of economic activities and global trade and production networks.

Caleb C. Y. Kwong is a Senior Lecturer in entrepreneurship and small business management at Essex Business School, University of Essex, UK. His research interests include entrepreneurship, management education and international business and human resource management.

Frank McDonald is Professor of International Business at Bradford University School of Management and Director of the Bradford Centre in International Business. He is the former Chair of the Academy of International Business United Kingdom & Ireland Chapter. His research focuses on strategic issues connected to the subsidiaries of MNCs and internationalization strategies. He has authored or edited 13 books and 40 journal articles.

Ram Mudambi is Professor and Perelman Senior Research Fellow at the Fox School of Business, Temple University. Previously he served on the faculties of Case Western Reserve University, the University of Reading (UK) and the University of North Carolina – Chapel Hill. He is a Fellow of the Academy of International Business. He is a visiting Professor at Henley Business School, University of Reading, and Honorary Professor at the Centre for International Business, University of Leeds (CIBUL), and a member of the advisory council of the University of Bradford Centre in International Business (BCIB). He has served as a Visiting Professor at a number of universities including Bocconi (Italy), Uppsala (Sweden), Sydney (Australia) and Copenhagen Business School. He holds a Masters Degree from the London School of Economics and a Ph.D. from Cornell. His current research projects focus on innovation and governance of knowledge-intensive processes. He has published over 80 peer-reviewed articles, including work in the *Strategic Management Journal, Journal of International Business Studies, Journal of Political Economy* and *Journal of Economic Geography.* He serves on the editorial boards of the *Journal of International Business Studies, Journal of International Management, Journal of World Business, Management International Review, Asia-Pacific Journal of Management* and *Industry and Innovation.*

Surender Munjal is Lecturer, Centre for International Business, University of Leeds. His key research interests are mergers and acquisitions and internationalization strategies of emerging country multinationals.

Phillip C. Nell is an Assistant Professor at the Department of Strategic Management and Globalization at Copenhagen Business School. Phillip holds a European Master of Business Sciences (EMBSc) degree and a Diplom-Kaufmann from the University of Bamberg. He received his Ph.D. from WU Wien (Vienna University of Economics and Business) and joined Copenhagen Business School subsequently. Before joining academia, Phillip gained considerable industry experience as a consultant with Roland Berger Strategy Consultants and conducted projects in Germany, the United States and France in several industries such as construction, white goods, glass products, non-profit and hospitals. His research interests are centred on the organization of the multinational corporation, the management of subsidiaries and the role headquarters play in large and complex organizations.

Ellis Osabutey is Lecturer in International Business and Strategic Management in the Department of Business and Management at Middlesex University. His key research interests are International Management and Strategy, Foreign Direct Investment and Technology Transfer, Innovation and Technology Transfer Management, Cross-cultural Management and International Human Resource Development and Management. His research interests primarily focus on Africa and seek to promote evidence-based policymaking in Africa. He entered academia from a corporate background with managerial working experiences with private- and public-sector organizations in domestic and multinational firms.

Naresh R. Pandit is Professor of Management and Director of Learning and Teaching at Norwich Business School, University of East Anglia. His main research interests are on the linkages between business clustering and economic performance, location decisions of multinational enterprises and corporate insolvency and turnaround.

Paz Estrella Tolentino is Lecturer in International Business at the School of Business, Economics and Informatics, Birkbeck, University of London. Her research interests include theory of the multinational enterprise, multinational enterprises based in emerging markets, international business history and international business strategy.

Heinz-Josef Tüselmann is Professor of International Business and Director of the Centre for International Business and Innovation at Manchester Metropolitan University Business School. He is Chair of the Academy of International Business United Kingdom and Ireland Chapter. His current research interests include national institutions and labour relations in MNCs, intra- and inter-organizational relationships of MNCs and their impact on subsidiary performance.

Svitlana Voronkova worked as a lecturer in finance at the School of Business at Trinity College Dublin and as a researcher in international finance at the Centre for European Economic Research (ZEW) in Germany. Her research interests include international finance, emerging European financial markets and pension funds in Central and Eastern Europe. Svitlana's research has been published in a number of international peer-reviewed journals, including *Emerging Markets Review, Journal of International Money and Finance* and *Journal of Business Finance and Accounting*. Svitlana is currently working at a major insurance company.

Sigrun M. Wagner is a Teaching Fellow in International Business at Royal Holloway, University of London. She completed her Ph.D. at Loughborough University Business School on corporate political activities of multinational enterprises in the EU, specifically in the area of environmental regulations for the automotive industry. She holds a BA in European Studies from the University of Osnabrück (Germany) and an M.Sc. in International Management from Loughborough University. She has presented at various International Business conferences (EIBA and AIB UK & Ireland) and won the Neil Hood and Stephen Young Prize for Most Original New Work at the AIB UK & Ireland conference in Portsmouth. Her current research and teaching interests include European business, lobbying and environmental sustainability.

Paul Windrum is Associate Professor in Strategy at Nottingham University Business School. His key research interests are in the areas of strategic management of innovation, innovation in services (public and private sector) and health innovation.

Alessa Witt is a Ph.D. candidate at the University of Edinburgh Business School. Her research concerns hidden champions and she has authored a book on the subject *Internationalisation of Hidden Champions*.

Yong Yang is Senior Lecturer in Strategy at the School of Business, Management and Economics at the University of Surrey. He was previously Lecturer in International Business and Entrepreneurship at the University of Essex. Before joining Essex, he worked on a FP7 project funded by the European Commission at Brunel University, UK, for one year. He obtained his Ph.D. in Business and Management from Queen Mary University of London. He holds an M.Sc. in Business Management from University of East Anglia and a BA in Accounting from China. His research interests include the internationalization process of firms, location choice of foreign direct investment, international knowledge transfer and exporting and firm performance.

Introduction: The Changing Geography of International Business

Gary Cook and Jennifer Johns

The theme for the AIB (UK&I) 2012 Conference was *New Global Developments and the Changing Geography of International Business*. This theme had two distinct, but interconnected motivations. First, the world economic order has changed markedly over recent years, epitomized by the rapid growth of China, on course to become the largest economy in the world in the near future and exerting increasing influence through its overseas ventures. Several other countries have experienced rapid rates of growth, including some other populous countries such as India and Indonesia. These countries have caused demonstrable anxiety in the West on several grounds, some of which are redolent of fears which arose with the emergence of Japan as a significant economic power. There are concerns regarding the ability of Western companies to compete with aggressive, low-costs MNEs from emerging economies. These fears are compounded by the spectre of jobs being exported to such regions as Western MNEs are compelled to locate in emerging economies to maintain competitiveness in the face of this heightened competition. There are also fears of threats to economic and political influence, exemplified by concerns regarding the increasing indebtedness of the United States to China. Moreover, as governments in developed economies generally struggle with the aftermath of the financial crisis and burgeoning fiscal deficits, greater reliance is being placed on emerging economies as motors of the global economy. The emergence of the 'Arab Spring' has brought mixed feelings in the West. On the one hand, there is hope at the welling up of a desire for individual liberty and democracy, as well as joy at seeing feared and despised potentates unseated. On the other, there are fears regarding the possible ascendancy of militant Islam, which may bring in its wake greater hostility to the West, and regarding possible chaos in the face of power vacuums, as tyranny is displaced without strong democracy and democratic institutions being established. There are also acute dilemmas regarding how best the West ought to respond, exemplified at the time of writing by debate about how best to confront the brutal attempts of President Assad to cling to power in Syria. From the narrower perspective of business, these epochal changes may have profound, yet uncertain, effects on prospects for international business (IB) in that region.

Second, the spatial organization of IB has witnessed profound shifts. One is the rise of the 'global factory' and the fine-slicing of where value is added in production and distribution and which parts are internalized and which outsourced. R&D activity has been internationalized at an accelerating rate by multinational enterprises from the 1990s. Emerging economies are growing in importance both as locations for and as sources of FDI. Rapidly internationalizing new ventures and micromultinationals have come sharply into view as important elements in the world economy. As with the broader economic and political context, these changes create both opportunities and threats for established firms. At the levels of the firm, city-regions, the nation and regional blocs, there is again uncertainty regarding the appropriate response. Already some firms have learned the hard way that the death of distance has been greatly exaggerated, as they start to reverse some of the geographic dispersion of their activities. Likewise, exaggerated claims regarding the homogenization of consumer tastes are being revealed as unduly simplistic. As this dispersal of activity, in production, consumption and R&D takes place, firms and academic observers are coming to a deeper understanding of the importance of institutions and culture in IB. Somewhat paradoxically, given fears about the impotence of national governments to find effective policy responses in a turbulent and rapidly changing global economic system, a reappraisal of the significance of the nation state and of political borders is under way within IB.

An important element of the 2012 Conference was the invited presence of the Economic Geography Research Group (EGRG) of the Royal Geographical Society. Valuable contributions from the geographers, including keynote speaker Henry Yeung and EGRG chair Andrew Jones, spoke powerfully of the need for IB scholars to engage more widely in interdisciplinary research. This is imperative to achieve greater analytical grip, in terms of both theory and empirical evidence, on the complex and rapidly evolving phenomena outlined above.

The papers

Keynote address

Mudambi's keynote address explores the concept of 'flatness', which he defines as parity between units in terms of their economic outcomes. A convergence of the income distribution either within or between countries, for example, would be examples of increasing flatness. Mudambi paints on a broad canvass to consider what has been happening, as a general trend, to flatness across three historical epochs. First he characterizes the pre-industrial world, where there were substantial disparities in income within countries, with a tiny wealthy elite and a mass living at subsistence level. This period, he also argues, saw a high degree of localization in production and consumption. Second comes the Industrial Revolution up to roughly three decades ago. This period saw increasing flatness within industrialized countries, which we might nowadays think of as a rise of a middle class, escaping the poverty afflicting the vast majority in the pre-industrial era. Production remained largely localized, but trade became increasingly significant. Most importantly, this era saw the emergence of a close correspondence between the interests of individuals, firms and the state within particular countries. Per capita incomes between the richest and poorest countries widened. Third comes the current era, beginning in approximately 1980. What is conspicuous about the current era is the significant fall in transport and communication costs. This has enabled the disaggregation and geographic dispersal of the value chain to create sometimes highly elaborate global value chains. What has emerged are clusters of activity which are more interconnected with the global value chains in which they are embedded than with their immediate hinterland. Clusters and the labour employed within them are becoming more equalized in their economic outcomes, regardless of where they are located. This has seen greater income disparities within advanced countries, counterpoised by a convergence in per capita GDP among *some* developing countries. In the current era Mudambi identifies a flattening across countries, which is particularly evident within particular skill levels or occupational categories.

Part 1 – institutional perspectives on international business

The papers in Part 1 of the book all exemplify the importance of institutions for understanding IB activity and reflect the growing influence of the institutional perspective within the domain of IB.

Tüselmann et al. examine the question of whether institutional rigidity in Germany led to a flight of capital through higher levels of outward FDI by German MNEs in the case of a variety of external shocks to the German economy over the period 1976–2008. They identify that there is a prima facie case for such a strategic response, within the institutional perspective. They identify that Germany is a coordinated market economy (CME), within the Varieties of Capitalism framework due to Hall and Soskice (2001). The argument is made that CMEs may have a weakness in being slow to adapt in the face of shocks, due to their complexity and lack of flexibility. They test this hypothesis using time series data on ten mature German manufacturing industries, applying augmented Dickey–Fuller, KPSS and Zivot–Andrews tests. The weight of evidence is overwhelmingly *against* capital flight by MNCs caused by institutional rigidity, implying that institutions in Germany were capable of adapting to shocks. As they identify, this evidence is based on aggregate data at the two-digit NACE level; more fine-grained analysis, particularly at the firm level, may find exceptions to this general case.

Allen and Aldred examine the influences on GDP growth rates in Central and Eastern European countries. They set this in the context of a comparison between the institutionally focused 'comparative capitalism' approach and the conventional lens of IB, which is heavily influenced by economics, particularly the transaction cost approach of Williamson. The paper provides an excellent exposition of Ragin's fuzzy set qualitative comparative analysis approach, which is used to tease out both necessary and sufficient conditions for an economy to achieve superior GDP growth. A range of factors are included in the analysis, brigaded under the broad categorizations of corporate governance, labour market institutions and business regulation. Some important results emerge which challenge the conventional wisdom. First, and perhaps the least surprising, is that there is no single recipe for success. Indeed, they find four distinct combinations of factors which lead to superior growth rates. This underscores the criticism which has been levelled at the 'Washington consensus' as a definitive recipe for economic development. Second, they find that the only factor which is common to all four constellations is the *difficulty* of enforcing contracts, which is directly opposed to what conventional economic analysis would predict. Third, *greater* difficulty of doing business is positively associated with higher growth in three of the four constellations. Fourth, *greater* employment protection is sometimes associated with higher growth.

Wagner explores the reasons why MNEs enter into relations with government, an under-researched area in IB. Her context is the original equipment manufacturer automotive industry in the EU, an important and instructive case given the economic importance of the industry and the extent of national and supranational regulation to which it is subject. Her analysis is based on 71 interviews with manufacturers, policymakers and non-governmental interest groups. Thus the perspectives of the industry, the state and civil society are represented. Wagner argues that the motivations for MNEs to enter into government–business relationships fall into five broadly defined dimensions: information and communication, to be informed of policy developments and to keep policymakers advised of corporate views; business interest, which is more sharply focused on influencing policy with commercial interests in mind; predictability and fairness, aimed at ensuring feasibility, solid assumptions for planning and a level playing field; avoiding, weakening or postponing legislation; positive motivations, which reflect the desire to ensure legislation is the best solution from a wider perspective and being seen to be a good corporate citizen. Of these, Wagner identifies information and communication and the promotion of business interests as the most important motivations.

Part 2 – international business activities across different spatial scales

The papers in Part 2 consider questions regarding the influence on MNEs of processes operating at a variety of spatial scales and the ways in which MNEs fashion responses to them. They provide a rich perspective on international strategy, probing some subtleties in the requirements for effective international strategy and going beyond a simple homogenization of 'international' as that which occurs outside the home country.

Buckley et al. examine the importance of economic–political relationships between countries on the pattern of FDI activities. They examine this question with a data set of 841 foreign acquisitions made by firms headquartered in India over the period January 2000 to December 2007. They use two dependent variables, the number of acquisitions by the country and the value of these acquisitions. The three economic–political alliances within the scope of their analysis are the Commonwealth, the G15 and the G20. They develop a theoretical argument that such alliances will be apt to encourage FDI flows by reducing transaction costs, raising potential economic and strategic benefits (particularly learning and knowledge flows), lowering political risk and supporting development within member countries. Their principal conclusions are that 'North–South' linkages such as the Commonwealth and the G20 do have a statistically significant influence, encouraging FDI flows from India, whereas the 'South–South' linkage, the G15, does not. The paper also presents evidence that knowledge-based assets in host countries and openness to trade also encourage FDI, whereas geographic distance plays no statistically significant role.

Witt and Carr focus on the characteristics and internationalization strategies of so-called Hidden Champions. These are defined as medium-sized companies which establish top three positions in terms of global or regional market share in particular niche activities. These companies are important as they achieve a high degree of success in IB, but they are 'hidden' in the sense that, due to their relatively small absolute size compared to major MNEs, they have mainly passed unremarked in the academic literature. Witt and Carr present new evidence on 26 Hidden Champions based in Germany, which is an important example of a country where small and medium-sized enterprises which succeed in IB flourish. In popular and academic writing the focus has typically been on how such companies contribute to the success of Germany in manufacturing exports compared to other countries. A key contribution of Witt and Carr's chapter is that they demonstrate that both on theoretical and on empirical grounds there is no simple categorization of the internationalization strategies of such firms. Many have substantial overseas operations; therefore the traditional emphasis on exports is misleading. They do not comply in a straightforward way with either the 'stages' model of the Uppsala school or the 'born global' model. One distinctive feature they identify is a preference for using licensing as a basis for internationalization. Witt and Carr conclude with a challenge to extend analysis of such companies to other countries to tease out the influence of institutional context on the tendency for such companies to arise and on the characteristics of their growth and internationalization strategies.

Yang and Kwong examine the role of language in the process of MNEs promoting innovation and the development of firm competencies through the strategic use of foreign direct investment. Using a sample of 3,712 overseas subsidiaries of 1,514 MNEs drawn from the Orbis database, they first demonstrate that the subsidiaries are more likely to develop innovation and new competencies the more knowledge-oriented is the parent (both variables proxied by total factor productivity). They then go on to show that the effect of higher knowledge orientation of the parent is mediated in a positive way when parent and subsidiary are located in countries sharing a common language. They articulate reasons why this should be so, in particular the cost and difficulty of translating complex and tacit knowledge effectively from one language to another. Their conclusions discuss the merits for both MNEs and nations of investing in the development of language skills.

Ho addresses the question of what, if anything, is distinctive regarding the ability of firms to acquire knowledge *across borders*. In the process, she includes a wide set of influences on knowledge acquisition which have typically been investigated in only a piecemeal fashion in the literature, possibly causing misleading results. She applies structural equation modelling to survey data derived from a sample of 207 Taiwanese firms operating in ICT industries. Her principal conclusion is that knowledge protectiveness is the distinctive feature of cross-border knowledge acquisition, which mediates the effect of other variables such as the type of knowledge being acquired, relational capital or institutional distance. Knowledge protectiveness in this research has two dimensions: the extent to which an alliance partner deliberately restricts access to its knowledge and the difficulty a firm has in absorbing 'acquired' knowledge. In particular, knowledge protectiveness mediates the linkage between institutional distance and knowledge acquisition, with institutional distance remaining a significant influence. Another important finding is that investment in 'relational capital' can mitigate the negative impact on cross-border knowledge acquisition.

Part 3 – placing multinational enterprise activities

The papers in Part 3 provide a range of perspectives on the issue of where MNEs place themselves: in geographic space; in particular positions within international networks and with respect to the degree of responsiveness to local institutions. They thus provide valuable insights into the complexity of answering questions about where MNEs place themselves.

Cook and Pandit examine the question of what, principally, attracts MNEs to strong clusters and what, if anything, distinguishes the benefits they derive from such a location compared to uninational enterprises (UNEs). They take as their case the media cluster in London, which, after the City in Financial Services, is the United Kingdom's most significant cluster within the context of its global industry. The evidence is based on questionnaire surveys returned by 187 media companies located in London, 37 of which were MNEs. Their literature review identifies a tension between Porter's argument in *The Competitive Advantage of Nations* that domestic clusters benefit primarily domestic firms and the contrary argument made by Enright, Porter's Ph.D. student, that *overseas* MNEs are better placed to capitalize on the positive spillovers that exist within clusters. They further identify that MNEs may be *less* reliant on these localized spillovers than UNEs, as they are likely to have substantial internal resource strengths. They first extract seven factors, which group items in the questionnaire into readily recognizable constructs. A logit analysis is then used to identify which factors distinguish in a statistically significant way between MNEs and UNEs. In line with expectation, MNEs are significantly less reliant on social capital and local institutions within the cluster. MNEs perceive a significantly higher benefit of access to a deep, skilled labour pool, which speaks of a strategic asset-seeking motive for locating in London. MNEs also view the ability to garner intelligence as a significant advantage compared to UNEs.

Nell et al. explore the phenomenon of both subsidiaries and HQ of MNEs being involved in the same network, something which has attracted recent academic interest. This they term 'network redundancy' and they develop theoretical links between this phenomenon and both organizational and environmental factors. The term redundancy indicates a puzzle as to why an MNE would establish a subsidiary, presumably to benefit from the extent to which that subsidiary embeds itself in networks overseas, yet also itself builds a direct relationship with the same network. This appears to be an unnecessary duplication of effort. The central idea is that high degrees of subsidiary embeddedness in overseas networks, whilst they may promote deep learning and other benefits for the subsidiary, may make it more difficult for the HQ to control the subsidiary and, in particular, ensure that the benefits accrued by the subsidiary are made more widely available within the MNE itself. The right degree of redundancy is argued to be contingent on the environmental and organizational context, with higher levels of 'fit' leading to superior performance. The evidence is based on survey responses of 193 subsidiaries based in Europe. In only 12 per cent of cases was the HQ of the subsidiary strongly embedded in the same network. Higher degrees of environmental turbulence are found to be positively and significantly related to higher network redundancy, which conforms with expectation, as rapid information flows within the MNE are at a premium and control problems apt to be more acute. Somewhat contrary to expectation, *greater* resilience of the local economy to the business cycle was also positively and significantly associated with higher levels of redundancy. Other environmental influences, including competition, were not significant.

Tolentino et al. examine the emergence of higher levels of strategic complexity in the strategic configuration of MNE subsidiaries, using the overseas subsidiaries of US IT firms in Taiwan as the evidentiary base. They probe the under-researched question of the relationship between subsidiary strategy and the configuration of their functional activities. The comparison is longitudinal, based on the years 1997 and 2007. The paper works within the Integration–Responsiveness framework, yet goes down to probe the differences between functional areas, rather than limiting the perspective to some overall composite picture using the subsidiary or the MNE as the key unit of analysis. The paper also espouses the Resource-Based View. The core functions examined are R&D, production, marketing, sales and services. The subsidiaries of 16 US MNEs are analysed. Three broad types of strategy are identified at the MNE level: Globally Integrated (high integration, low responsiveness – four MNEs), Locally Responsive (low integration, high responsiveness – four MNEs) and Multifocal (high integration, high responsiveness – seven MNEs). Within each broad strategic type of subsidiary, there are differing degrees of emphasis in integration and responsiveness in each of the functional areas analysed. The authors conclude that over the period 1997 to 2007 there was a move in the direction of greater strategic complexity. This complexity is manifested in MNEs establishing increasingly differentiated networks of activities. The authors conclude, however, that the subsidiary remains a meaningful unit of analysis in IB and strategy, notwithstanding the emphasis increasingly given to particular functions and activities in the light of increasing 'fine-slicing' of activities by MNEs.

Osabutey sheds light on a neglected area in IB: knowledge and technology transfer in sub-Saharan Africa. As he notes, this region, like many others which have moved onto a path of rapid economic development, has turned away from import substitution policies and is now looking to encourage inward direct investment.

Such investment is occurring and these are no longer 'bypassed places' in the global economy. Reviewing the literature, Osabutey identifies that what little we know about inward direct investment in sub-Saharan Africa points to two critical conclusions: inward direct investment is at a sub-optimally low level from the point of view of economic development and knowledge and technology transfer to local enterprises is also unsatisfactory. Osabutey identifies four key areas where governments can improve policy and the institutional environment to encourage both higher levels of inward investment and knowledge and technology transfer. A more strategic approach needs to be taken by governments on these issues. Local firms should be encouraged to invest more in R&D, human resource development and knowledge management/organization learning. Education, particularly higher education, needs to be better resourced to produce higher numbers of good-quality graduates, particularly in science, technology and engineering. Lastly, governments need to foster stronger institutions, including for tackling corruption, still a significant deterrent to inward investment, and making property rights more secure.

Crone takes a geographical and historical perspective on the evolution of the indigenous software industry in Ireland, with particular emphasis on the internationalization of new ventures within it. As he notes, the substantial literature which has grown up around rapidly internationalizing new ventures has largely ignored the question of the importance of place in providing a context within which such companies could emerge and be successful in their growth and internationalization strategies. He explicitly introduces the concept of a cluster life cycle as an important analytical lens within which to frame his analysis. One of his key conclusions is that the speed and scope of internationalization was far greater in the more mature phases of the cluster life cycle than in its embryonic stage. During the latter the cautious and incremental internationalization of new ventures was more akin to the 'stages' model of internationalization. As Crone identifies, the key benefits of being in a cluster stem from superior access to critical resources and knowledge, which are more abundant in developed clusters. Those which were particularly important in supporting rapid internationalization in the Irish software case were access to venture capital, skilled labour and experienced senior managers, and specifically managers and entrepreneurs with accumulated know-how about internationalization. Also important was the maturing of the policy environment, supporting entrepreneurship.

1
Flatness: The Global Disaggregation of Value Creation

Ram Mudambi

Introduction

At the most general level, the idea of 'flatness' in the context of economic development has to do with parity. This is the property whereby different individuals or areas of the world are roughly similar in terms of their levels of economic outcomes. Thus, in comparing one individual or area to another, the observer perceives similarity in terms of measurable outcomes like standards of living and incomes.

Academics see the approach to flatness as a part of the process of convergence. Theoretically convergence is occurring if the relationship between a measure of the level of economic outcome and the rate of growth of economic outcome is downward sloping. Thus, if we use gross domestic product (GDP) as the measure of economic outcome, a situation where high GDP countries witness relatively slower rates of growth than low GDP countries is associated with convergence. The greater the difference in growth rates, the more rapid the convergence (Figure 1.1).

On the other hand, popular writers see flatness more anecdotally in terms of the 'see, touch, feel' of locations. Thus, convergence is seen as occurring when the nature of consumption and service availability becomes similar across locations, regardless of the extent of diffusion of these within the mainstream economy (Friedman, 2005).

The nature of the world economy and the extent of parity across countries and regions has been changing dramatically over the last few decades. In this essay, I will argue that this can be best understood by considering three worlds. The first is the pre-industrial world of the distant past characterized by an extreme lack of parity both across and within countries and regions. The second is the world of yesterday, a period beginning with the Industrial Revolution, during which rough parity or flatness was established *within* certain regions and countries of the world. The third is the evolving world of today and the future, a period beginning about three decades ago, when large new economies began to emerge in the sense of becoming integrated in the world economy.

The world of today is one where the flatness that was established within many wealthy industrial countries (Pomfret, 2011) is under threat, as many

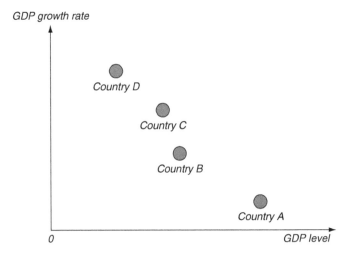

Figure 1.1   Convergence

economic activities, especially those involving low knowledge inputs, migrate to emerging economies. At the same time, emerging economies are seeing the appearance of large and rapidly growing middle classes springing from their formerly homogeneous or 'flat' poverty-stricken masses. These new moneyed classes are being nurtured by the same economic activities that are migrating out of wealthy, advanced economies, some of which are even expanding the local (previously tiny) wealthy elites. A new form of parity or flatness is appearing that is not based on geography or location, but rather on human capital and skill levels.

The distant past – a local world

The world before the Industrial Revolution was made up of economies dominated by agriculture and craft manufacture. It was a world where all economies were composed of very small leisure classes and where the vast majority of the population of even the wealthiest economies of China and India lived in abject poverty (Maddison, 2007). There was a large gap between the miniscule population of 'haves' and the vast population of 'have-nots' in every location on the globe. Most of humanity was mired in a subsistence existence. It would be fair to say that this parity or flatness was a sub-optimal state of affairs for most, if not all of humanity.[1]

Both production and consumption were largely local. Few individuals travelled beyond their immediate neighbourhoods and all were completely dependent on indigenous systems for their needs. The international transport of luxury items through desert caravans and long, risky sea voyages has been celebrated in song and story (Mark, 1997; Wellard, 1977), but it made up a tiny proportion of total consumption of even the very wealthiest individuals.

The world of yesterday – trade in goods

The first two centuries after the advent of the Industrial Revolution were characterized by urbanization, that is, the growth of cities as industrial centres. These industrial cities were connected to their immediate hinterland, and over time, to a national production and innovation system by both physical and institutional infrastructure. Systems of production remained largely local as illustrated by the classic von Thünen (1827) model.

International trade increased by fits and starts over the two-century period between the mid-eighteenth and the mid-twentieth centuries. To a large extent, the Ricardian principles of comparative advantage prevailed throughout this period. Thus, countries specialized in the production of particular goods and services and the trade that occurred was largely in terms of final (finished) goods. These goods were mostly produced in local systems of production (Belussi, 1999). They were local in the sense that most of the industrial or manufacturing activities, both those with high- and low-knowledge intensity, were undertaken within concentrated geographical spaces, mostly in advanced industrialized countries.

Further, in these advanced industrialized counties, local redistribution of wealth (eventually) occurred through trickle-down and more formal redistributive schemes like taxation. The dominance of local systems of production (and in particular, local labour markets and unions) ensured that low-skill individuals in high-productivity countries could enjoy disproportionately high standards of living due to the prevailing high level of spatial transaction costs (Beugelsdijk et al., 2010; Dunning, 1998; McCann and Shefer, 2004; Storper and Scott, 1995).[2] To some extent they could free-ride on the knowledge and value created in the jurisdictions within which they lived (a) directly through wages that were high relative to their skills; and (b) indirectly through enjoying public goods and services created from tax revenues on high local productivity. Thus, for most advanced economies, the twentieth century became the 'age of equality' (Pomfret, 2011).

The cohesion of these local and national production and innovation systems (Lundvall, 2007) led to a convergence of local, corporate and national interests. Workers, stockholders and taxpayers all felt a common bond of shared self-interest based on their geographical colocation. Improved performance of locally based corporate entities increased local employment and wages, increased the wealth of local stockholders and boosted local tax revenues, enabling the provision of more and better public services. Thus, it was possible and even essentially correct for General Motors chairman Charles Erwin Wilson to say at a Senate hearing on his confirmation as Secretary of Defense in the Eisenhower administration in 1953 that he faced no conflict of interest since 'what's good for General Motors is good for the country'.

These local systems of production and national systems of innovation came into being due to high spatial transaction costs and were reinforced over time by layers of national institutions (Mudambi and Navarra, 2002). As intra-country income and standards of living grew more 'flat' in most of the developed or so-called 'first' world, the gap between industrialized and agrarian and primary goods-producing countries grew.[3] Corporate entities in industrialized countries had little interest in the knowledge resources in these developing countries, since the cost of leveraging them was just too high.

The consequences of the world of high spatial transaction costs and consequent locational aggregation of economic activities were unambiguous. Incomes and standards of living were determined by geography and location than by human capital and skills. It was a world of global disparities and the division of the world into 'rich' and 'poor' countries. In the world of yesterday, it was considered the norm for an assembly line worker in Detroit with an eighth-grade education to earn more and enjoy a higher standard of living than a brain surgeon in New Delhi.

The world of today – trade in activities

The key change that has been occurring over the last three decades is the inexorable decline of spatial transaction costs. This is a process that has been unfolded over several decades and is made of too many different factors, advances and innovations to examine each in detail. Suffice it to say that they are concentrated in the areas of logistics and information and communications technologies (ICT) and include:

- Improved international shipping and logistics including containerization
- Just-in-time systems involving increased and improved buyer–supplier coordination
- ICT beginning with facsimiles and continuing through email and web-based enterprise resource planning systems.

The best way to understand the evolving modern economy and the transformation from the world of yesterday dominated by trade in goods into the world of today based on trade in activities is through the tool of global value chains (GVCs).

Global value chains

Value chain analysis is an innovative tool that views the economy in terms of activities instead of its constituent industries and firms (Mudambi, 2008). A value chain for any product of service consists of a number of interlinked activities extending from ideation and upstream R&D to raw materials and component supply, production, through delivery to international buyers, and often beyond that to disposal and recycling.[4]

Modern value chain analysis enables us to pinpoint the relative contributions to value creation associated with each activity, from basic raw materials to final demand. This approach helps us to understand that as far as geographic location is concerned, success in terms of creating prosperity is based on the local activities performed rather than the identity of local firms or industries.

Drastically reduced spatial transaction costs make it feasible to disaggregate the firm's business processes into progressively finer slices. Firms are able to specialize in increasingly narrow niches, which need not even be contiguous in the value chain (Mudambi, 2008). This makes it crucial for the firm to identify the process activities over which it has competitive advantage, since these are the basis of the firm's core competencies that enable it to generate rents (Hamel and Prahalad, 1990).

The importance of fragmented production and intermediates trade has been widely documented in academic research (e.g., Baldwin, 2006). When trade is disaggregated and geographically dispersed across national borders, a GVC exists. GVCs incorporate all the activities related to producing a good or service and delivering the product or service to the end user.

The implications of GVCs

Viewing the world economy through the lens of GVCs makes it possible to make analytical comparisons between yesterday's 'trade in goods' and today's 'trade in activities'. Coasian transaction costs determine the boundaries of the firm, that is, they underpin the control decision in terms of activities that are retained in-house versus those that are outsourced. In the same way, spatial transaction costs determine the location of activities in terms of concentration versus dispersion. As spatial transaction costs fall, the optimal level of dispersion of economic activities over geographic space rises. In other words, the lower the spatial transaction costs, the more likely activities are to be performed in their most efficient locations.

In yesterday's world of high spatial transaction costs, the optimal strategies for firms, including multinational enterprises (MNEs), involved a significant concentration of economic activities in their home countries, with trade carried out largely in terms of finished goods. This is the world of Ricardo and it persisted more or less intact through most of the twentieth century. However, beginning about three decades ago, spatial transaction costs began to fall, slowly at first as regional trade agreements in Europe and North America increased the attraction of moving activities rather than finished goods from the home country to the host country.[5]

This activity dispersion began to accelerate as technology made it possible for outsourcers as well as a firm's foreign subsidiary units to undertake increasingly sophisticated activities while remaining closely embedded within the parent firm's corporate network (Anderson, Forsgren and Holm, 2002; Meyer et al., 2011). The movement of knowledge activities to high-skill, low-cost labour MNE subsidiaries set in train a virtuous cycle of value creation in many of today's emerging economies. Knowledge spillovers from these MNE subsidiaries into the local economy occurred through numerous channels, including labour force turnover and the training of suppliers and local partner firms. In time, these spillover processes spawned populations of local firms intent on catching up with the global industry leaders based in market economies. Finally, pressure from these new and aggressive emerging market MNEs, the so-called EMNEs, is a factor in the increased pressure to innovate and develop new industries in advanced market economies. These three processes of spillover, catch-up and industry creation are driving the changing geography of value creation in the world of today and the coming decades (Mudambi, 2008).

Concluding remarks – flatness today

The flatness of yesterday consisted of rough parity at a high standard of living in advanced market economies along with rough parity at a low standard of living elsewhere. In other words, it was largely an intra-country phenomenon. Today we are witnessing the rise of a different variety of flatness. Global value creation is increasingly arising from GVCs. These GVCs are based on activities largely located in economic centres or clusters. The GVC connects these clusters, not with their immediate geographical hinterland, but with the global knowledge network associated with the particular product or service being orchestrated.

Sub-national clusters are becoming progressively more tightly connected with each other, very often across national frontiers. Their prosperity depends not on their local environs, but on their connectivity with their global network (Lorenzen and Mudambi, 2010; Saxenian and Hsu, 2001). A new flatness is arising, levelling the differences between leading economic centres around the world. Software engineers in Silicon Valley, Bangalore and the Hsinchu-Taipei region are converging in terms of their incomes and standards of living. Indeed, this underlies much of what influences populist writers and commentators (e.g., Friedman, 2005).

At the same time, GVCs are increasing the intra-country disparities and inequalities. As wages increasingly represent human capital and skills, low-knowledge and low-skill workers in advanced market economies are seeing their incomes and standards of living fall to levels more commensurate with their human capital and skills (Freeman, 1995). In many advanced market economies, the old national convergence of interests among workers, shareholders and taxpayers is beginning to fray and in some cases it is degenerating into open conflict.

Viewed in this light, the rise of GVCs and the increasingly knowledge-intensive, asset-light global economy represent nothing less than an economic revolution. The Industrial Revolution shifted the source of value creation from land to physical capital and machinery and this slowly but surely destroyed the power of the landed aristocracy, as the assets they controlled declined in value. In the same way, declining spatial transaction costs are shifting the source of value appropriation from mere geographical location to human capital and skills. Unions in advanced market economies representing low-skill workers can no more resist the power of these global processes than the Luddites were able to resist the spread of industrial machinery. The inevitable outcome of these processes is an inexorable increase in the premium on skill acquisition and lifelong learning in *all* countries, advanced, emerging and poor.

Notes

1. This is evident from the quantitative and qualitative date presented by Maddison (2007), who integrates a wide variety of sources to paint this picture of the worldwide pre-industrial economy.
2. Spatial transaction costs may be defined as the costs of controlling and coordinating economic activities that are dispersed over geographic space.
3. Many of this latter group were colonies and later ex-colonies of the wealthy nations.
4. Value chain analysis can be traced to early work focused on disaggregating the individual business firm into its constituent activities with the objective of identifying its sources of competitive advantage (Porter, 1985). The firm-centric focus of this work has been extended and generalized in recent years to analyse the overall creation of value.
5. Spatial transaction costs have political drivers as well. Thus, the US-imposed 'voluntary export restraints' on Japanese automobile manufacturers in the 1980s lowered the costs of undertaking foreign direct investment in the United States, moving a large swathe of economic activities from Japan to the United States.

References

U. Anderson, M. Forsgren and U. Holm, 'The strategic impact of external networks: subsidiary performance and competence development in the multinational corporation', *Strategic Management Journal*, 23(11) (2002) 979–96.

R. Baldwin, 'The great unbundling(s)', Working Paper, Prime Minister's Office, Economic Council of Finland (2006).

F. Belussi, 'Policies for the development of knowledge-intensive local production systems', *Cambridge Journal of Economics*, 23(6) (1999) 729–47.

S. Beugelsdijk, P. McCann and R. Mudambi, 'Place, space and organization: economic geography and the multinational enterprise', *Journal of Economic Geography*, 10(4) (2010) 485–93.

J. H. Dunning, 'Location and the multinational enterprise: a neglected factor?', *Journal of International Business Studies*, 29(1) (1998) 45–66.

R. B. Freeman, 'Are your wages set in Beijing?', *Journal of Economic Perspectives*, 9(3) (1995) 15–32.

T. Friedman, *The World Is Flat: A Brief History of the Twenty-First Century*, (New York: Farrar, Straus and Giroux, 2005).

G. Hamel, and C. K. Prahalad, 'The core competence of the corporation', *Harvard Business Review*, 68(3) (1990) 79–93.

M. Lorenzen and R. Mudambi, 'Bangalore vs. Bollywood: connectivity and catch-up in emerging market economies', *AIB Insights*, 10(1) (2010) 7–11.

B. A. Lundvall, 'National innovation systems – analytical concept and development tool', *Industry and Innovation*, 14(1) (2007) 95–119.

A. Maddison, *Contours of the World Economy 1–2020 AD: Essays in Macro-Economic History*, (Oxford: Oxford University Press, 2007).

S. Mark, *From Egypt to Mesopotamia: A Study of Predynastic Trade Routes*, (London: Chatham Publishing and Texas A&M University Press, 1997).

P. McCann and D. Shefer, 'Location, agglomeration and infrastructure', *Papers in Regional Science*, 83(1) (2004) 177–96.

K. E. Meyer, R. Mudambi and R. Narula, 'Multinational enterprises and local contexts: the opportunities and challenges of multiple embeddedness', *Journal of Management Studies*, 48(2) (2011) 235–52.

R. Mudambi, 'Location, control and innovation in knowledge intensive industries', *Journal of Economic Geography*, 8(5) (2008) 699–725.

R. Mudambi and P. Navarra, 'Institutions and international business: a theoretical overview', *International Business Review*, 11(6) (2002) 635–46.

R. Pomfret, *The Age of Equality: The Twentieth Century in Economic Perspective*, (Boston, MA: Harvard University Press, 2011).

M. E. Porter, *Competitive Advantage*, (New York: The Free Press, 1985).

A. Saxenian and J-Y. Hsu, 'The Silicon Valley – Hsinchu connection: technical communities and industrial upgrading', *Industrial and Corporate Change*, 10(4) (2001) 893–920.

M. Storper and A. J. Scott, 'The wealth of regions', *Futures*, 27(5) (1995) 505–26.

J. von Thünen, *The Isolated State in Relation to Agriculture and Political Economy*, re-released 2009 edition, (Basingstoke: Palgrave Macmillan, 1827).

J. H. Wellard, *Samarkand and Beyond: A History of Desert Caravans*, (London: Constable, 1977).

Part I

Institutional Perspectives on International Business

2
Outward Foreign Direct Investment and the Adaptive Efficiency of the German Institutional System

Heinz-Josef Tüselmann, Frank McDonald, Martin T. Bohl, Svitlana Voronkova and Paul Windrum

Introduction

There have been calls to incorporate comparative institutional literature, such as the Varieties of Capitalism (VoC) (Hall and Soskice, 2001) and National Business Systems (NBS) (Whitley, 1999), into research in international business, including the investigation of FDI (Mudambi and Navarra, 2002; Redding, 2005). Outward FDI is considered in terms of such factors as political risk, market size, and cultural and geographical proximity (Buckley et al., 2007; Butler and Domingo, 1998). There has, however, been limited consideration of the role of institutional factors for outward FDI trends, especially in the light of rapid changes in the external environment. Consensus-based institutional systems in developed countries may lead to incentives for multinational corporations (MNCs) to escape home countries (Witt and Lewin, 2007). As global conditions change MNCs requirements in their home base need adjusting to maintain competitive advantages. This issue connects to the concept of adaptive efficiency of institutional systems. Adaptive efficiency is the ability of institutions to evolve to adjust to new conditions such that transaction costs and risks are low enough to permit firms to successfully respond to changing conditions (North, 1990a, 1990b). In consensual institutional systems, adjustments of institutions can be slow, leading to increases in outward FDI as MNCs seek to avoid loss of competitive edge in their home base. In such cases the institutional system has ineffective adaptive efficiency leading to institutional systems that hinders the necessary strategic adjustment process of MNCs to external shocks.

There is considerable debate in Germany about whether its institutional systems encourage flight of MNCs by outward FDI (Financial Times, 2004; Franz, 2001). In the VoC context, Germany is a stereotypical coordinated market economy (CME) (Hall and Soskice, 2001) and in the NBS approach Germany is a prime example of a collaborative institutional system (Whitley, 1999). A common thread in the critique of the German model of capitalism is that the highly integrated and complex institutional infrastructure results in a high degree of regulation and a strong requirement for the consensual co-ordination of policy by decision-makers to adjust to changes in the external environments. This can lead to slow

19

adjustment to institutional systems resulting in a misalignment of these systems with the requirements of MNCs (Witt and Levin, 2007). If the German institutional system suffers from this problem it is likely to affect the trend of German outward FDI. Given the large number of often large exogenous shocks in the world economy in the last 30 or so years it is likely that institutional systems that encourage MNCs to escape will have had significant changes in outward FDI that will lead to changes in the trend of such investment. In other words, outward FDI trends will have experienced structural breaks.

The contribution of this chapter is to provide tests on whether outward FDI of German manufacturing industries have been shock persistent in the face of turbulence in the global economy. The absence of structural breaks would indicate that there is no evidence that the German institutional system suffers from adaptive efficiency problems that are encouraging German MNCs to escape to other locations. The test for structural breaks uses the trend of the German outward FDI stock for manufacturing industries in the period 1976–2008. The study focuses on mature manufacturing industries because there is long-run data available for these industries permitting robust tests for shock persistence. Moreover, manufacturing FDI constitutes the bulk of outward German FDI, accounting for 87 per cent of the total in 2008 (Statistisches Bundesamt, 2011). These investments also capture the large German export industries, which are the backbone of the German economy. If shock effects were not evident there would be a persistence of the trend on the stock of outward FDI. In other words, the time series would be shock persistent with external shocks leading to only temporary deviation from long-term trends. Industry-specific factors are often neglected in studies on the impact of exogenous shocks on FDI. There have been studies on total and manufacturing FDI (Agarwal et al., 1991; Lipsey, 1999, 2001), but there have been no studies that investigate industry trends in outward FDI. Aggregate FDI figures may mask industry-specific impacts; therefore an industry-level analysis is required. If German outward FDI trends are not shock persistent, at least for some industries, this provides indications that the German institutional systems may have incentivized escape activities by MNCs by use of outward FDI.

This chapter examines German FDI outflows in ten mature manufacturing industries to assess if there is evidence of industry-level shock persistence. The following section of the chapter sets out the main tenets of the comparative institutional literature with particular reference to the German model and considers the background of German economic conditions in the period 1976–2008. This is followed by an overview of German outward manufacturing FDI and an overview of studies on shock persistency. Next, the econometric methods used to test for shock persistence are presented. A section describing the data sources is followed by discussion of the results. In light of the results, the final section considers the implications of the findings and sets out some avenues for future research.

The German institutional system and exogenous shocks

The comparative capitalism literature highlights the ways in which home country institutions inform the behaviour of MNCs (Hall and Soskice, 2001; Whitley,

1999). The literature suggests that the institutional setting of countries influences the strategies pursued by firms. A number of interlinked complementary institutional domains, including financial, education and skills formation, innovation systems, corporate governance, interfirm collaboration and industrial relations systems play an important role in this process (Hall and Soskice, 2001; Whitley, 1999). A result of these institutional influences is that firms that operate in different national institutional settings develop distinctive policies and routines to coordinate and control their activities, leading to varying behaviour by firms across different institutional settings. The comparative institutional approach postulates that comparative advantage can arise from institutional structures that provide firms with advantages of engaging in specific kinds of activities (Jackson and Deeg, 2006). These advantages can arise from the encouragement of trust-based societies that lead to low costs because of reduced conflict in economic and business transactions and a reduction in costs connected to battles over the distribution of surpluses from economic transactions (Hall and Soskice, 2001; Whitley, 1999). The institutional change dynamics in such systems are path-dependent and tend to be stable because consensus is required to change institutions and this normally leads to slow and cautious change (Allen et al., 2006). These institutional systems therefore require large exogenous shocks before significant changes emerge in institutional systems, and these changes tend to be made slowly and to be incremental (Hall and Gingerich, 2009).

Systems that follow a path of slow and incremental institutional adjustment to external shocks while maintaining the competitive advantages arising from the trust-based nature of their systems should not experience outward FDI flight in the face of large-scale external shocks. In cases, however, where countries are unable to retain the competitive advantages of a consensual institutional system, because change is too slow and incremental, then external shocks are likely to induce MNCs to engage in increases in outward FDI that lead to change in the trend of such investments. The ability to secure effective institutional change in the face of external shocks connects to the New Institutional Economics concept of adaptive efficiency (North, 1990a).

Adaptive efficiency is the ability to modify institutional systems to keep transaction costs and risk low in the face of economic, social, political and technological changes. Institutional change is a complex process requiring the resolution of institutional contradictions arising from failure to meet the needs of changing conditions. Institutional change processes must, however, accommodate the perceptions, preferences and power of agents within institutional systems (Seo and Douglas Creed, 2002). The multifaceted process of adaptive efficiency that emerges from institutional contradictions can lead to slow and incremental or fast and radical institutional change. Slow and incremental change may not be adequate to permit agents to adjust to external shocks. Fast and radical change may, however, destroy trust and consensus and thereby undermine key characteristics of the institutional system that provides agents with key advantages. The 'correct' adaptive efficiency is therefore that which achieves low transactions costs and risks in human interactions without destroying the requirement for balance between institutional contradictions and the interests and powers of agents within the system.

The adaptive efficiency issue also connects to the path-determined nature of institutional systems. Sustaining a balance between formal and informal institutional systems in the face of significant changes in conditions is a difficult process. The path-determined nature of institutional systems often constrains the speed and the radical or incremental nature of such changes (North, 1990b). Institutional systems with appropriate adaptive efficiency therefore permit agents (including firms) to attain their objectives in the face of changing conditions. Mobile agents that cannot attain their objectives with their institutional system can move to other, more preferable institutional systems. In the context of MNCs this relates to the ability to engage in outward FDI to escape the constraints of institutional systems (Witt and Lewin, 2007).

The German business system is often portrayed as being at the opposite end to that of Liberal Market Economies (LMEs), such as the United States and the United Kingdom. The latter are characterized by lightly regulated systems with institutional frameworks that place markets in a dominant role for coordinating economic behaviour (Hall and Soskice, 2001). They tend to have short-term finance, deregulated labour markets that place emphasis on general non-vocational education, strong intercompany competition and corporate governance systems that are heavily influenced by stock markets. These types of institutional systems normally require adaptive efficiency that is rapid and often involves radical institutional changes in the face of external shocks. These adaptive efficiency characteristics permit firms to retain competitive advantages in the face of external shocks. In contrast to LMEs, the institutional system in Germany is of the CME variety of capitalism and has a high degree of regulation with much economic behaviour coordinated by non-market mechanisms. The German NBS has long-term industrial finance, cooperative labour relations, high levels of vocational training, corporate governance systems that are not heavily connected to stock markets, and cooperation in technology and standard setting across companies. This type of institutional system requires adaptive efficiency that retains consensual practices within institutional systems while permitting firms to maintain competitive advantages in the face of external shocks. The configuration of the German institutional setting has enabled a large section of German manufacturing to compete successfully in international markets based on a diversified quality production strategy (Streeck, 1992).

The German economy, however, experienced a variety of exogenous shocks in the period 1976–2008. In this period there was reunification in October 1990, followed by the collapse of communism in the early 1990s. The German economy also experienced economic, financial and monetary shocks in this period. These included crises and eventual collapse of the currency 'snake' in 1979, the subsequent creation of the European Monetary System (EMS) in the same year, the crises of EMS in 1992 and 1993, the end of deutschemark and the introduction of euro in 1999 and the global financial crisis since 2007/08. The period also includes the enlargement of the European Union (EU) from 9 to 15 members in 1995 with subsequent enlargement to 27 members by 2007, the implementation of the Single European Market programme in the 1990s and extensive privatization programmes in Germany and among many of her main trade partners. In the 1990s, trading and FDI significantly increased with the Asian Tigers and later the reforms in China and India led to significant changes to trade and investment levels with these and other emerging economies. There were also a number of technology shocks in this period. New and often radical technologies, particularly new IT systems and processes, were introduced and led to the restructuring of the international activities of many firms (Dunning, 2000), and the reconfiguration of national and international supply chains (Tavares and Young, 2006). Shocks caused by oil price increases were also experienced; notably the 1979 oil crisis that occurred in the wake of the Iranian Revolution and the 2007/08 oil price shock. These economic, monetary, political and technological shocks led to considerable incentives for the development and rationalization of many German industries.

There has been a series of reforms in the Germany institutional system in response to these external shocks but they have tended to be cautious and to remain largely within the parameters of the existing institutional systems (for an overview see Allen et al., 2006; Tüselmann and Heise, 2000). In other words, institutional change has been slow and incremental. These changes have broadened the scope for more flexibility and strategic choice in German firms, whilst keeping the fundamentals of the German VoC intact. In relation to German FDI, however, there is debate about whether the rate of institutional adjustments in CMEs, such as Germany, has been sufficient to avoid severe misalignments between firms' needs and home country institutional conditions (Berthold and Stettes, 2001; Witt and Lewin, 2007). If the incremental reform process in Germany has led to such misalignments, this should result in flight of outward FDI by those German MNCs most affected by external shocks. In these circumstances exogenous shocks should have had a lasting effect on the long-term trend of outward investment of German manufacturing industries and structural breaks should emerge in outward FDI trend data. A test for structural breaks in outward FDI in manufacturing industries therefore provides insight into the adaptive efficiency of the German institutional system with regard to maintaining the competitive advantages of German MNCs.

German manufacturing FDI

The level and development of German manufacturing outward FDI stocks exhibits several distinctive features in terms of both regional and sector patterns. With regard to the former, outward manufacturing FDI stocks have been traditionally focused on Western industrialized countries and have become increasingly concentrated in these countries, accounting for nearly 85 per cent of German FDI stocks in 2008, compared to 75 per cent in 1976 (Deutsche Bundesbank, 1978, 2011). Furthermore, a handful of these countries account for a large share of German FDI as it has become increasingly concentrated in these host destinations, albeit with varying growth rates and changing shares within this country group. In 2008 over 65 per cent of German manufacturing FDI stock was concentrated in the United States, Belgium, the United Kingdom, France and the

Netherlands (in descending order). This compares to 48 per cent in 1976 (Deutsche Bundesbank, 1978, 2011). The industry pattern of German manufacturing FDI displays a similar and growing concentration. Germany's four large export industries dominated German manufacturing FDI. The motor vehicle, chemical, mechanical engineering and electrical engineering industries accounted for over 65 per cent of all German manufacturing outward stock in 1976. This figure rose to 87 per cent by the end of 2008 (Deutsche Bundesbank, 1978, 2011). There is also some evidence, at the aggregate level, that suggests inertia and shock persistence of German outward FDI in general, and of the manufacturing sector in particular (Agarwal et al., 1991; Hubert and Pain, 2002; Jost and Nunnenkamp, 2002).

Studies on exogenous shocks

There are several studies on the relative stability of inward FDI to developing countries, compared with other financial flows and portfolio investments in the face of external shocks such as the Latin American debt crisis of the 1980s, the Mexican currency crisis of 1994–95 and the financial crises of 1997–98 in East Asia (Lipsey, 1999, 2001). These studies find that inward flows of FDI were not as volatile as other forms of inward financial investment in these countries during these particular periods. A theoretical explanation for this relative stability has been put forward by Goldstein and Razin (2003). This theory postulates that principal agent issues leads to transaction costs differences between these forms of investment resulting in asymmetric information, which leads to better information for FDI, resulting in a more stable trend. Most of these studies do not consider sufficiently whether shocks have affected the trend of outward FDI at the industry level. German FDI is of particular interest in this regard because Germany is not only the third largest source of outward FDI, in terms of global stock (UNCTAD, 2006), but the development of German FDI, and in particular, manufacturing FDI are often ascribed country-of-origin specific patterns in responding to changes to global and host country investment conditions (Agarwal et al., 1991).

Another literature that is of interest is that on hysteresis related to sunk costs (Baldwin, 1989; Krugman, 1989). Roberts and Tybout (1997) examined the decisions by Colombian manufacturing plants in four key sectors for the period 1981–89. They found that exports increased following an initial shock from a favourable change in the exchange rate. They further discovered that these decisions to export remain persistent even when the exchange rate returned to its previous purchasing power parity value. In other words an external shock led to a structural break in the time series trend. Roberts and Tybout (1997) provide an explanation for such structural breaks in terms of the lumpiness of the decision to export caused by sunk cost incurred in the investment decision. Clearly, FDI decisions are also lumpy because of the high sunk costs associated with this type of investment. This view on the lumpiness of FDI is challenged by those who argue that the financial sophistication of MNCs makes FDI similar to portfolio investment (Albuquerque, 2003; Hausmann and Fernandez-Arias, 2000). Thus, the ability of MNCs to finance and refinance FDI from a multitude of sources, in terms of countries and types of financial instruments, reduces the lumpiness of FDI (Fernandez-Arias and Hausmann, 2001).

The literature that connects to the likely stability of outward FDI is mixed. On balance the evidence favours a stable trend suggesting that external shocks will only lead to temporary deviations from trend. This literature has not, however, focused on industry time series data or on advanced developed economies with consensual institutional systems that responded slowly and incrementally to external shocks. This study centres on looking for evidence of outward FDI flight in response to inadequate adaptive efficiency of institutional systems. Thus, although FDI outflows may or may not be trend stable in general, they are likely to display structural breaks in the face of large external shocks in institutional systems that cannot continue to provide competitive advantages for their MNCs.

Econometric methods

Augmented Dickey–Fuller and Kwiatkowski unit root tests

Trend stability can be tested for using unit root tests. These tests provide evidence on whether a time series is trend-stationary or difference-stationary. In the case of stationary time series there is a deterministic linear time trend and fluctuations around the linear trend are temporary and due to the transitory character of shocks; therefore the time series system will return to its long-run trend. These time series trends are shock persistent. In contrast, random walk processes are a difference-stationary time series. The important property of these time series is that shocks have a permanent character. When the time series is shocked it does not completely return to its trend and the series is not shock persistent. Unit root processes reveal the existence of shock persistence (Kennedy, 2003).

This study applies the augmented Dickey–Fuller (1979, 1981) test and the approach proposed by Kwiatkowski, Phillips, Schmidt and Yongcheol (1992), hereafter ADF and KPSS tests. The ADF test is implemented using the regression:

$$\Delta y_t = \alpha_0 + \alpha_1 y_{t-1} + \alpha_2 t + \sum_{i=1}^{l} \gamma_i \Delta y_{t-i} + \varepsilon_t. \tag{2.1}$$

Δ denotes the first difference operator, y_t the time series under investigation, t a linear time trend and ε_t the error term. The ADF test analyses the null hypothesis of a unit root in the (log) level of the time series, that is, $H_0 : \alpha_1 = 0$, versus the alternative hypothesis of trend stationarity. The critical values are MacKinnon's (1991) response surface estimates. The lag length l is determined implementing the general-to-specific procedure suggested by Hall (1994) starting with the lag $l = 3$.

In contrast to the ADF test, the KPSS test investigates the null hypothesis of trend stationarity against the alternative of a unit root. Let $\hat{u}_t$, $t = 1, 2, \ldots, T$, the estimated residuals from the regression:

$$y_t = \beta_0 + \beta_1 t + u_t. \tag{2.2}$$

The KPSS test statistic is defined as:

$$LM = \sum_{t=1}^{T} S_t^2 / \hat{s}_{Tl}^2,$$ (2.3)

where $S_t = \sum_{i=1}^{t} \hat{u}_t$, $t = 1, 2, \ldots, T$ and

$$\hat{s}_{Tl}^2 = T^{-1} \sum_{t=1}^{T} \hat{u}_t^2 + 2T^{-1} \sum_{\tau=1}^{l} (1 - \frac{\tau}{l+1}) \sum_{t=\tau+1}^{T} \hat{u}_t \hat{u}_{t-\tau},$$ (2.4)

where l is a truncation lag. Sephton (1995) provides response surface estimates of approximate critical values for the LM test statistic. The maximum truncation lag is set to $l = 2$.

Due to the different null hypotheses of the ADF and the KPSS test, we can implement a simple confirmatory analysis, to confirm our conclusions about unit root (Choi, 1994; Kwiatkowski et al., 1992; Maddala and Kim, 1995). It is generally agreed that using both tests gives the most reliable results (Amano and van Norden, 1992). If the ADF test cannot reject the null hypothesis of a unit root in the log level of the time series and the KPSS test rejects the null hypothesis of trend stationarity, we have found confirmation for the difference stationarity and the persistence of shocks of the FDI time series.

Zivot and Andrews unit root test

The occurrence of an exogenous shock may have a permanent effect on the level of variables. In statistical terms, this may result in under-rejection of the null hypothesis of a unit root (Perron, 1990; Zivot and Andrews, 1992), when a trend-stationary process with a break in its parameters is erroneously concluded to be a unit root (non-stationary) process. The likelihood of occurrence of a structural break increases with the data span. Since our data set covers 28 years of data, we perform an additional unit root test suggested by Zivot and Andrews (1992), which assumes a trend-stationary process with a break under alternative hypothesis.[1] The advantage of this test over the one of Perron (1990) is that the break point is endogenous, that is, it is estimated from the data rather than assumed based on the history of macroeconomic effects. This feature of the Zivot–Andrews test avoids a potentially erroneous assumption regarding the date of the break.

The Zivot–Andrews unit root test is formulated as follows. Under the null hypothesis of a unit root the time series is assumed to follow a process given by:

$$y_t = \mu + y_{t-1} + u_t.$$ (2.5)

Under the alternative hypothesis, the series is assumed to follow a trend-stationary process with a structural break in parameters. Since the break may occur both in intercept and in slope of the data, Zivot and Andrews suggest three model specifications under the alternative hypothesis:

$$y_t = \mu^A + \theta^A DU_t(\lambda) + \beta^A t + \alpha^A y_{t-1} + \sum_{j=1}^{k} c_j^A \Delta y_{t-j} + u_t, \tag{2.6}$$

$$y_t = \mu^B + \beta^B t + \gamma^B DT(\lambda) + \alpha^B y_{t-1} + \sum_{j=1}^{k} c_j^B \Delta y_{t-j} + u_t, \tag{2.7}$$

$$y_t = \mu^C + \theta^C DU_t(\lambda) + \beta^C t + \gamma^C DT(\lambda) + \alpha^C y_{t-1} + \sum_{j=1}^{k} c_j^C \Delta y_{t-j} + u_t, \tag{2.8}$$

where $\lambda = \frac{T_B}{T}$ is the estimated time of the break (measured as a fraction of a sample), $DU_t(\lambda) = 1$ if $t > T_B$ and 0 otherwise; $DB_t(\lambda) = t - T_B$ if $t > T_B$ and 0 otherwise, and k is the lag length. Dummy variables DU_t and DT_t model break in intercept and slope, respectively.

The estimation of an endogenous timing of the break λ is performed by running a series of regressions with different date T_B. Namely, T_B is set to all the sample dates and regressions (2.6)–(2.8) are estimated with all the possible break points. For practical purposes, however, T_B is assumed to belong to the interval $[0.1T; 0.9T]$. As a result, a series of t-statistics for α^i coefficient is obtained, where $i=A, B, C$. The ultimate test statistic for a given model specification is the one constituting the strongest evidence against the null hypothesis, that is, the smallest statistic in this series:

$$t_{\alpha^i}[\lambda_{\inf}^i] = \inf_{\lambda \in [0.1T; 0.9T]} t_{\alpha^i}(\lambda). \tag{2.9}$$

The asymptotic distribution and critical values for the statistic (2.9) for the models A, B and C are provided in Zivot and Andrews (1992).

Data

The data used in this study is on German outward FDI, measured across ten industries. The study extracted annual data on the stock of German industrial FDI from the Deutsche Bundesbank publications *Kapitalverflechtung mit dem Ausland*, for the period 1976–2008. Prior to 1995, the Bundesbank defined industries using the German industrial classification. After 1995 it adopted the EU NACE (Rev. 1) industrial classification. The identification of industry in official Bundesbank data uses the two-digit NACE classification. Consistent identification for the sample required reclassification of the FDI data prior to 1995 using the NACE (Rev. 1) classification. Amalgamation of some industries was necessary to achieve consistency because reclassification was not always possible. The final sample includes ten manufacturing industries (NACE codes in brackets)[2]:

1. Food and Beverages (15)
2. Textiles (17)
3. Clothing and Leather (18, 19)
4. Wood, Paper, Publishing Printing (20, 21, 22)

5. Chemicals (24)
6. Rubber and Plastics (25)
7. Glass, Ceramics and Cement (26)
8. Metals and Metal Products (27, 28)
9. Machinery and Equipment (29)
10. Motor Vehicles (34)

The sample accounted for 87 per cent of all German manufacturing outward stock in 2008, 77 per cent in 1976 (Deutsche Bundesbank, 1978, 2011). With the exception of the pharmaceutical industry, which is contained in the two-digit chemical industry, the sample consists of mature industries. The Bundesbank does not provide industry data for FDI stocks at the three-digit NACE code; therefore it was not possible to separate out this industry from the chemical industry.

In the Deutsche Bundesbank publications the FDI data prior to 1999 is reported in millions of deutschemarks and in millions of Euro afterwards. The data therefore were converted into euro using the fixed exchange rate between euro and deutschemark as provided by the European Central Bank (http://www.ecb.int/home/html/index.en.html). To account for the impact of inflation on FDI valuation, the data has been deflated using the German consumer and producer price indices (CPI and PPI, respectively). The data on CPI and PPI have been extracted from the Deutsche Bundesbank *Monatsbericht*.

Empirical results and discussion

Table 2.1 shows the results of the unit root tests for the FDI time series deflated by the producer price index.[3] For all time series the ADF tests cannot reject the null hypothesis of a unit root. The findings of the KPSS tests are broadly in line with this result. With only a few exceptions the KPSS tests reject the null of trend stationarity. Hence, the empirical evidence on the stochastic properties of German FDI supports the view of a shock persistence property.

Table 2.2 presents the results of the Zivot–Andrews unit root test that assumes stationarity with a structural break under the alternative hypothesis.[4] For all the series of industrial FDI, the null hypothesis of a unit root cannot be rejected. This result is generally in line with the findings of both ADF and KPSS tests. It provides additional evidence in favour of shock persistence and this evidence is robust to the possible presence of structural break of the parameters of the underlying process.

The results support the view that German FDI displays shock persistence and therefore confirm studies that find this outcome for total German FDI and for the manufacturing sector as a whole (Agarwal et al., 1991; Hubert and Pain, 2002; Jost and Nunnenkamp, 2002). This study provides evidence that there is no industry-specific differential response to shocks in the period 1976–2008. Mature German manufacturing industries, not including manufacturing industries that could

Table 2.1 Results of unit root tests

	ADF		KPSS		
	τ_τ	l	$l=0$	$l=1$	$l=2$
Food and beverages	−2.57	0	0.49***	0.29***	0.21**
Clothing and leather	−2.26	0	0.19**	0.12*	0.09
Pulp paper and paper products; publishing and printing	−1.09	0	0.74***	0.40***	0.29***
Rubber and plastic products	−2.38	3	0.18**	0.12*	0.10
Non-metallic mineral products: glass, ceramics, and so on	−1.99	0	0.32***	0.19**	0.15*
Metals and metal products	−1.50	3	0.17**	0.12*	0.11
Machinery and equipment	−2.62	0	0.32***	0.19**	0.16**
Vehicles and vehicle parts	−2.69	3	0.29***	0.16**	0.12*
Textiles	0.85	0	0.62***	0.35***	0.26***
Chemicals	−1.31	0	0.60***	0.34***	0.26***

Notes: ***, ** and * denote significance at 1, 5 and 10 per cent, respectively. τ_τ denotes the value of the ADF test statistics and l denotes the number of lags used for estimation of equations (2.1) and (2.4). Critical values for the ADF tests are from MacKinnon (1991) and for the KPSS tests from Sephton (1995).

Table 2.2 Results of Zivot–Andrews unit root test

Industry	Minimum t-statistics	Lag (k)	Estimated date of the break ($\hat{\lambda}$)
Food and beverages	−4.25	0	1990
Clothing and leather	−3.80	0	1999
Pulp paper and paper products; publishing and printing	−3.48	0	1988
Rubber and plastic products	−2.82	0	2005
Non-metallic mineral products: glass, ceramics, etc.	−3.83	0	1999
Metals and metal products	−4.42	0	2005
Machinery and equipment	−4.28	0	1989
Vehicles and vehicle parts	−3.98	0	1997
Textiles	−1.83	0	2000
Chemicals	−4.14	0	2000

Notes: The table reports test statistics for Zivot and Andrews (1992) unit root test. The null hypothesis of a unit root is tested against the alternative of stationarity with a structural break of unknown timing. Zivot and Andrews (1992) allow three model specifications: break in intercept only; break in a trend and break in both intercept and trend. We estimated all three model specifications. Reported results are for model allowing for the break in both intercept and trend, since this model is least restrictive:

$$y_t = \mu + \theta DU_t(\lambda) + \beta t + \gamma DT(\lambda) + \alpha y_{t-1} + \sum_{j=1}^{k} c_j \Delta y_{t-j} + \varepsilon_t,$$

where DU and DT are dummy variables modelling break and λ is the assumed date of the break. The number of lags k is chosen based on the values of the relevant t-statistic.

not be included in this sample, constitute roughly three-quarters of all German manufacturing FDI stock (Deutsche Bundesbank, 2011). This study therefore confirms that mature German manufacturing industries display shock persistence in outward FDI.

The results challenge, at least for most German mature manufacturing industries, those studies that support the view that FDI is not shock persistent (Aizenman and Marion, 2004; Albuquerque, 2003; Hausmann and Fernandez-Arias, 2000; Levchenko and Mauro, 2006). The findings support the view, at least for mature manufacturing industries, that there has been no significant flight by German MNCs from an institutional system due to the lack of good adaptive efficiency. The results do not provide a direct link between high transaction and sunk costs leading to shock persistence in outward FDI trends. Nevertheless, failure to find structural breaks in any of the industries indicates a lack of evidence for the view that FDI is not shock persistent, thereby indirectly supporting the view that high transaction and sunk costs are likely to make FDI shock persistent. Likewise, the study does not provide direct evidence linking the institutional system to shock persistence of outward FDI. The results provide no direct evidence that the adaptive efficiency of German institutions is ineffective and thereby limits the ability of MNCs in mature manufacturing to retain and develop competitive advantages in their home base. If such poor adaptive efficiency were present at least some industries should display structural breaks and thereby indicate that some German MNCs were fleeing from the German business system. It seems that there is no evidence that Germany provides severe institutional system problems for these industries. The findings therefore help to shed light on the view of Witt and Lewin (2007) that consensual institutional systems in developed economies may encourage escape by outward FDI.

Care is needed before drawing firm conclusions that adaptive efficiency in Germany is sufficient to prevent flight by German MNCs. Data on newer manufacturing industries and on the service industries is also required to assess if the adaptive efficiency of the German institutional system extends to these more dynamic sectors. As these sectors are likely to provide much of the future growth in developed economies such as Germany, research in these areas is important to assess if there are problems with adaptive efficiency in Germany. This, however, requires long-run time series of disaggregated data and such data is not easy to acquire. These data problems are likely to require extensive data gathering and in the case of newer industries, consideration of appropriate data analysis techniques that can cope with limited length of time series data. Less strong evidence on the extent of structural breaks in outward FDI at the disaggregated level and in new manufacturing industries and in the services sector may emerge from case studies and surveys of firms. Indeed, evidence from firm-level studies would be most useful to discover if industry-level data is concealing important shifts in outward FDI in advanced developed economies with consensual institutional systems.

Conclusion

This study finds that although the German economy experienced a variety of external shocks in the period 1976–2008, including fundamental structural change, the industry level of this study confirms, for mature German manufacturing industries, the general view of existing national-level studies that outward German FDI is shock persistent. It seems that despite a series of significant external shocks, German MNCs in mature manufacturing industries have continued to follow their long-term trend of outward FDI. The study does not allow direct linkage to the German institutional setting, but it is reasonable to postulate that at least in mature manufacturing industries, the relationship between the institutional system and company FDI strategies seems to have worked well. In short, the study found no evidence that the Germany institutional system has poor adaptive efficiency. It is possible that such is not the case for the entire mature manufacturing sector. Greater disaggregation of industry data is, however, required to examine this issue. It is also possible that new manufacturing industries and the services sector may not have the same match between the institutional system and MNC strategy in the face of external shocks. Examination of this area is important because much of future growth is likely to come from these areas.

To shed more light on the shock persistence of FDI and to substantiate the issues raised in this paper requires further longitudinal studies based on more fine-grained industry classifications or ideally firm-level data on FDI outward stocks. Investigation of new manufacturing and service industries is also required. These types of studies will, however, be difficult to undertake given the lack of publically available time series data. Assessing the likelihood that MNC escape from institutional systems because of inadequate adaptive efficiency requires examination of structural breaks in time series outward FDI data for other institutional systems. This should include countries with different types of institutional systems, economic sizes and levels of development. To assess how institutional system contradictions interact with agents to influence MNC escape requires incorporation of institutional variables that adequately proxy national institutional systems and their dynamics into tests for structural breaks or other measures of MNC flight. Such research poses numerous data and conceptual challenges. Nevertheless, such research is important to enhance our understanding of the links between institutional systems and FDI strategies in the face of external shocks.

Notes

1. Related work includes studies by Rappoport (1990) and Banerjee et al. (1990). However, it is not the purpose of this paper to exploit the variety of unit root tests available and we choose the Zivot–Andrews test based on its popularity in empirical financial research. The latter resulted in the full version of the Zivot and Andrews (1992) original article being reprinted in the 20th anniversary issue of the *Journal of Business and Economic Statistics* (2002) (see Vol. 20(1) pp. 25–44).
2. Time series for tobacco was not included in the calculations because of missing values.

3. In addition to the producer price index we used the consumer price index to deflate the time series. The findings (not reported but available on request) are qualitatively the same.
4. Estimations were performed using RATS6.01 statistical software.

References

J. Agarwal, A. Gubitz and P. Nunnenkamp, 'Foreign direct investment in developing countries – the case of Germany', *Kieler Studien 238*, (Kiel: Institute of World Economics, 1991).

J. Aizenman and N. Marion, 'The relative merits of horizontal versus vertical FDI in the presence of uncertainty', *Journal of International Economics*, 62 (2004) 125–48.

R. Albuquerque, 'The composition of international capital flows: risk sharing through foreign direct investment', *Journal of International Economics*, 61 (2003) 353–83.

M. Allen, L. Funk and H. Tüselmann, 'Can variation in public policies account for differences in comparative advantage?', *Journal of Public Policy*, 26(1) (2006) 66–80.

R. A. Amano and S. van Norden, 'Unit root tests and the burden of proof', *Bank of Canada Working Paper*, (1992) 92–7.

R. Atkins and R. Milne, 'How a Rhineland behemoth changed course', *Financial Times*, 22 November (2004) 8.

R. Baldwin, 'Hysteresis in import prices; the beachhead effect', *American Economic Review*, 78(4) (1989) 773–85.

A. Banerjee, J. Dolado and J. Galbraith, *Recursive Tests for Unit Roots and Structural Breaks in Long Annual GNP Series*, Unpublished Manuscript, University of Florida, Department of Economics (1990).

N. Berthold, and O. Stettes, 'Der Flächentarifvertrag – Vom Wegbereiter des Wirtschaftswunders zum Verursacher der Beschäftigungsmisere', in C. Ott and H.-B. Schäfer (eds), *Ökonomische Analyse des Arbeitsrechts*, (Tübingen: Mohr-Siebeck, 2001), pp. 1–29.

P. Buckley, J. Clegg, A. Cross, X. Liu, H. Voss and P. Zheng, 'The determinants of Chinese outward foreign direct investment', *Journal of International Business Studies*, 38(3) (2007) 499–518.

K. Butler and C. Domingo, 'A note on political risk and the required return on foreign investment', *Journal of International Business Studies*, 29(3) (1998) 392–401.

I. Choi, 'Residual-based tests for the null of stationary with application to US macroeconomic time series', *Econometric Theory*, 10 (1994) 720–46.

Deutsche Bundesbank, *Kapitalverpflechtung mit dem Ausland*, (Frankfurt a.M., 1978).

Deutsche Bundesbank, *Kapitalverpflechtung mit dem Ausland*, (Frankfurt a.M., 2011).

D. Dickey and W. Fuller, 'Distribution of estimators for autoregressive time series with a unit root', *Journal of the American Statistical Association*, 74(366) (1979) 427–31.

D. Dickey and W. Fuller, 'The likelihood ratio statistics for autoregressive time series with a unit root', *Econometrica*, 49(4) (1981) 1057–72.

J. Dunning, *Regions, Globalization, and the Knowledge Economy*, (Oxford: Oxford University Press, 2000).

E. Fernandez-Arias and R. Hausmann, 'Is foreign direct investment a safer form of financing?', *Emerging Markets Review*, 2(1) (2001) 34–49.

W. Franz, 'Das Betriebsverfassungsgesetz ist komplett überflüssig', *Handelsblatt*, 26 (2001) 12.

I. Goldstein and A. Razin, 'An Information-Based Trade Off Between Foreign Direct Investment and Foreign Portfolio Investment: Volatility, Transparency, and Welfare', *NBER Working Papers*, 9426 (2003).

A. Hall, 'Testing for a unit root in time series with pre-test data-based model selection', *Journal of Business and Economics Statistics*, 12(4) (1994) 461–70.

P. Hall and D. Gingerich, 'Varieties of capitalism and institutional complementarities in the political economy: an empirical analysis', *British Journal of Political Science*, 39(3) (2009) 449–82.

P. Hall and D. Soskice (eds), *Varieties of Capitalism: The Institutional Foundations of Comparative Advantage*, (Oxford: Oxford University Press, 2001).

R. Hausmann and E. Fernandez-Arias, 'Foreign Direct Investment: Good Cholesterol?', Paper presented at seminar: *The New Wave of Capital Inflows: Sea Changes or Just Another Tide*, Annual Meeting of the Board of Governors, Inter-American Development Bank and Inter-American Investment Corporation (2000).

F. Hubert and N. Pain, 'Fiscal Incentives, European Integration and the Location of Foreign Direct Investment', *NIESR Discussion Papers*, (London: National Institute of Economic and Social Research, 2002).

G. Jackson and R. Deeg, 'How Many Varieties of Capitalism?', *Max-Planck-Institut für Gesellschaftsforschung Discussion Paper 06/2*, (Cologne: Max-Planck-Insititut, 2006).

T. Jost and P. Nunnenkamp, 'Bestimmungsgründe deutscher Direktinvestitionen in Entwicklungs- und Reformländern – Hat sich wirklich was verändert?', *Kieler Arbeitspapier 1124*, (Kiel: Institut für Weltwirtschaft, 2002).

P. Kennedy, *A Guide to Econometrics*, 5th Edition, (Cambridge, MA: MIT Press, 2003).

P. Krugman, *Exchange Rate Instability*, (Cambridge, MA: MIT Press, 1989).

D. Kwiatkowski, P. Phillips, P. Schmidt and S. Yongcheol, 'Testing the null hypothesis of stationarity against the alternative of a unit root', *Journal of Econometrics*, 54(1/3) (1992) 159–78.

A. Levchenko and P. Mauro, 'Do some forms of financial flows help protect from sudden stops?', *IMF Working Paper*, WP/06/2002, Washington DC, (2006).

R. Lipsey, 'The role of foreign direct investment in international capital flows', *NBER Working Paper*, 7094 (1999).

R. Lipsey, 'Foreign direct investors in three financial crises', *NBER Working Papers*, 8084 (2001).

J. MacKinnon, 'Critical Values for Cointegration Tests', in R. F. Engle and C. W. J. Granger (eds), *Long-Run Economic Relationships*, (Oxford: Oxford University Press, 1991), pp. 267–76.

G. Maddala and K. In-Moo, *Unit Root, Cointegration and Structural Change*, (Cambridge: Cambridge University Press, 1995).

R. Mudambi and P. Navarra, 'Institutions and international business: a theoretical overview', *International Business Review*, 11(6) (2002) 635–46.

D. C. North, *Institutions, Institutional Change, and Economic Performance*, (Cambridge: Cambridge University Press, 1990a).

D.C. North, 'A transactions cost theory of politics', *Journal of Theoretical Politics*, 2(4) (1990b) 355–67.

P. Rappoport, 'Testing for the frequency of permanent shifts in time series', unpublished manuscript, Department of Economics, Rutgers University.

P. Perron, 'Testing for a unit root in a time series with a changing mean', *Journal of Business & Economic Statistics*, 8(2) (1990) 153–62.

G. Redding, 'The thick description and comparisons of societal systems of capitalism', *Journal of International Business Studies*, 36(2) (2005) 123–55.

M. J. Roberts and J. R. Tybout, 'The decision to export in Colombia: an empirical model of entry with sunk costs', *American Economic Review, American Economic Association*, 87(4) (1997) 545–64.

M. Seo and W. E. D. Creed, 'Institutional contradictions, praxis, and institutional change', *Academy of Management Review*, 27(2) (2002) 222–47.

P. S. Sephton, 'Response surface estimates of the KPSS stationarity test', *Economics Letters*, 47 (1995) 255–61.

Statistisches Bundesamt, *Zahlungsbilanzstatitik*, (Stuttgart: Metzler Poeschel, 2011).

W. Streeck, *Social Institutions and Economic Performance*, (London: Sage, 1992)

A. Tavares and S. Young, 'Sourcing patterns of foreign-owned multinational subsidiaries in Europe', *Regional Studies*, 40(6) (2006) 583–99.

H. Tüselmann and A. Heise, 'The German model of industrial relations at the crossroads: past, present and future', *Industrial Relations Journal*, 31(3) (2000) 162–76.

UNCTAD, *World Investment Report 2006*, (Geneva and New York: United Nations, 2006).

R. Whitley, *Divergent Capitalisms: The Social Structuring and Change of Business Systems*, (Oxford: Oxford University Press, 1999).

M. Witt and A. Lewin, 'Outward foreign direct investment as escape response to home country institutional constraints', *Journal of International Business Studies*, 38(4) (2007) 579–94.

E. Zivot and D. Andrews, 'Further evidence on the great crash, the oil-price shock, and the unit-root hypothesis', *Journal of Business and Economic Statistics*, 10(3) (1992) 251–70.

3
The Impact of Institutions on Economic Growth in Central and Eastern Europe

Matthew M. C. Allen and Maria L. Aldred

Introduction

Within the international business literature, the importance of locational differences has recently come to the fore in many studies (Dunning, 2009; Meyer et al., 2011; Rugman et al., 2011). However, in contrast to studies that are underpinned by a more comparative sociological perspective, many of these analyses within the international business literature adopt a relatively narrow definition of 'institutions' when examining the consequences for commercial activities of any locational differences. For instance, within the international business literature, many studies focus on a relatively narrow range of formal, regulatory institutions that shape arm's length contracting within markets (Khanna and Rivkin, 2001; Meyer, 2001; Meyer et al., 2011). This definition of institutions is favoured over broader ones that can encompass a greater range of regulation-based ones as well as more informal or, indeed, para-public institutions (Jackson and Deeg, 2008). A corollary of this conceptualization of 'institutions' is that several prominent studies in the international business literature refer to 'institutional voids' (Khanna and Palepu, 2006; Kim et al., 2010; Tan and Meyer, 2010; compare, Peng et al., 2008). By this, such analysts often mean the lack of strong legal rules that can be enforced, for example, to uphold the terms of a contract (Khanna and Palepu, 2006, p. 62; Tan and Meyer, 2010).

However, in studies that adopt a more sociological perspective that is common within the 'comparative capitalisms' literature, a term such as 'institutional void' would be anathema, as other institutions or 'rules of the game' that are enforceable either legally (Streeck and Thelen, 2005) or in some other way (Crouch, 2005; Whitley, 1999) would be present. Whilst this latter approach does not preclude the possibility that the rule of law is so weak that the only people you can trust in business are family members or those with whom you have close personal ties, it does take into consideration a more wide-ranging set of institutions that can potentially influence firm behaviour (compare Khanna and Rivkin, 2001; Puffer et al., 2010). In short, in analyses of the ways in which locational differences, including institutional ones, influence firms' activities and competitiveness, international business scholars are likely to privilege regulatory as well as other institutions that support market-based activities; by contrast, those who adopt a more sociologically informed perspective are likely to encompass a broader range of institutions, such as dominant patterns of corporate financing, labour market systems and interfirm networks (Allen and Aldred, 2011; Casper and Matraves, 2003; Hall and Soskice, 2001; Liu and Tylecote, 2009; Whitley, 1999, 2007).

This difference between the two perspectives is important for three main reasons. Firstly, international business scholars tend to downplay the influence that other institutions may have on firm behaviour, including the ways in, and extent to, which they internationalize. In other words, and simplifying greatly, there is, within the international business literature, a tendency to assume that the only institutional resource that all firms need to rely on to help their competitiveness is the rule of law that is strictly upheld. Secondly, and consequently, in contrast to the international business literature, the comparative capitalisms perspective seeks to explain how the organizational capabilities that are required by firms to be competitive in different sectors are created and maintained (Allen and Whitley, 2012; Casper and Matraves, 2003; Casper and Whitley, 2004; compare, Peng and Meyer, 2011). These differences lead to a third key variation in the analytical foci of the two perspectives. In the international business literature, a corollary of the emphasis on the rule of law is that there is a proclivity to emphasize a convergence on this privileged institutional dimension in different countries, if firms located in any particular country are to be successful and, indeed, if countries are to attract foreign firms to invest there (see, for instance, Globerman and Shapiro, 2003; Meyer et al., 2011, pp. 237–39). In contrast, the comparative capitalisms literature assesses the conditions under which countries are likely to continue to have divergent sets of institutions, as there is no one institutional regime that is associated with superior firm or country performance across all sectors of the economy and across all measures (Allen and Aldred, 2011; Allen et al., 2006; Amable, 2003; Hall and Soskice, 2001; Lane and Wood, 2011; Whitley, 1999, 2007).

It is this issue of divergence and convergence that this chapter assesses. Drawing on country-level data, it analyses the extent to which there is any one set of institutions that is clearly associated with superior macroeconomic performance. From the perspective of the international business literature, it can be expected that a strong legal framework will consistently and primarily be associated with superior macroeconomic performance. By contrast, the comparative capitalism perspective leads to expectations that there are likely to be a number of clusters that lead to good macroeconomic performance. Whilst the rule of law is also expected to be of significance from a comparative capitalisms perspective, it will be one institutional factor amongst many.

Central and Eastern Europe (CEE) provides an ideal location to examine the extent to which convergence around a common regulatory model is likely. The reasons for this are threefold. Firstly, the new European Union (EU) member states in the region are highly dependent upon foreign direct investment (FDI) (Bohle and Greskovits, 2006; Nölke and Vliegenthart, 2009). Secondly, the competition between the new member states for such investment is likely to lead to pressures to create regulations that foreign firms find most attractive (Hansmann and Kraakman, 2000; Lane, 2007; McCahery et al., 2004). Finally, the collapse of communism in the region created an opportunity to implement changes at a time when restrictions on the extent to which change could occur were reduced (Vaughan-Whitehead, 2003).

The next section sets out the theoretical differences between the two perspectives examined here. This is followed by sections on the research design, data and variable calibration, methodology and results. This chapter concludes with a discussion of the results, and draws out some of the study's implications for future research.

Theoretical background

The emphasis on organizational capabilities in the comparative capitalisms literature leads to a broader definition of institutions compared to that in international business. In the former, as formal and informal rules, both constitute and regulate strategic actors (Morgan and Whitley, 2012). By contrast, institutions in the international business literature are often viewed as being wholly external to firms that constrain companies' behaviour (Meyer, 2001; Peng and Meyer, 2011; Peng et al., 2008). This, consequently, leads to a research focus within the comparative capitalisms literature on the conditions under which firms from different institutional regimes are able to become and remain competitive. By contrast, the international business literature tends to look at the impact of the presence of market-supporting or market-hindering institutions on firms.

For instance, within the international business literature, the dominant approach to institutions and firm behaviour tends to privilege formal regulations that impact upon arm's length, impersonal market-based activities. As a result, analyses within the international business literature have sought to explain the most appropriate entry mode into foreign markets with weak or inchoate regulations (Brouthers, 2002; Meyer, 2001). The focus of such studies is to examine the ways in which a relatively narrow range of formal institutions shape the type of commercial entities that firms establish and operate in foreign markets. The discussion of the role(s) that the subsidiaries will be carrying out, in terms of the types of activities that the foreign establishment will be conducting, and the integration of such activities into the firm's value chain, is relatively 'thin' (compare Erramilli et al., 2002). Consequently, in-depth assessments of the ways in which the necessary organizational competencies and capabilities will be created and developed within the subsidiaries are downplayed.

Those studies within the international business literature that do take into consideration the ways in which home country institutions shape the development of firm capabilities tend to treat institutions in a relatively limited way that emphasizes narrow, market-related regulations. As a result of inefficient or 'missing' institutions, domestic firms, if they are to be successful, will have to develop managerial capabilities to overcome these deficiencies (see, for example, Cuervo-Cazurra and Genc, 2008; Peng et al., 2005). In short, ownership control or managers' personal networks are often regarded in the international business literature as substitutes for a relatively narrow set of 'inadequate' market-supporting institutions (Jackson and Deeg, 2008). Such institutions are not assessed in terms of their influence over the firm's specific capabilities and, hence, competitiveness.

What is lacking from the international business literature, therefore, is a detailed treatment of the ways in which institutional diversity across a number of areas can impact upon either the types of organizational capabilities that companies can successfully develop or the dominant forms that innovation within companies is likely to take as a result of the institutional context within which they operate (Jackson and Deeg, 2008). It is these areas that form a key part of the analytical focus within the comparative capitalisms literature (Allen and Aldred, 2011; Allen et al., 2011; Casper, 2009; Crouch and Voelzkow, 2009; Hall and Soskice, 2001; Liu and Tylecote, 2009; Whitley, 1999, 2007). Within this latter perspective, the development of organizational capabilities is strongly shaped, but not determined, by the institutional regime within which companies operate.

A corollary of this emphasis is that sectoral characteristics, such as the need for different types of employee as well as the volume and duration of funding that firms require, become part of the analytical focus (Allen and Whitley, 2012; Allen et al., 2011; Casper and Whitley, 2004; Keizer, 2005; Tylecote et al., 2010). Consequently, the comparative capitalism literature pays closer attention to the particular institutional context within which firms operate, as it seeks to explain how the resolution of organizational challenges associated with a particular sector are helped or hindered by firms' specific institutional environment (Allen, 2004; Crouch and Voelzkow, 2009; Lane and Wood, 2009, 2011; Lange, 2009; Schneiberg, 2007). Similarly, the approach also assesses the ways in which firms may attempt to overcome domestic institutional constraints by accessing structurally conditioned resources that are based abroad (Allen and Whitley, 2012; Casper, 2009; Lange, 2009).

An important theme within the comparative capitalism literature, and one that further differentiates it from much of the international business literature, is 'institutional complementarity' (Crouch, 2005; Crouch et al., 2005; Hall and Soskice, 2001). Although there has been much discussion over the meaning of this term, it will be defined here to mean that the presence of one institution increases the efficiency of another. This highlights the ways in which individual institutions may interact with one another to reinforce pressures on senior managers and others within firms to take particular decisions. For instance, the presence of relatively strict employment laws that make it difficult for employers to lay off workers may be viewed by companies as 'beneficial constraints' (Streeck, 1997) that encourage firms to invest in the skills of their workers to a greater extent than might otherwise be the case (Harcourt and Wood, 2007). If these employment regulations are coupled with a financial system that is characterized by long-term funding, companies may find it easier to pursue strategies that require a focus on medium- to long-term growth at the potential expense of increases in short-term profitability. This, in turn, is likely to lead to firm success in those sectors of the economy that require a longer-term approach to investments and employees (Casper and Whitley, 2004; Hall and Soskice, 2001).

Research design

This chapter examines the pressures for convergence by assessing the links between a broad range of institutions and gross domestic product (GDP) growth rates in CEE. If it can be shown that higher GDP growth rates are consistently and primarily associated with regulations that facilitate activities contracted through the market, this would indicate that countries in the region need to adopt a relatively standard set of measures if they wish to attract foreign investors and grow. Indeed, for international business scholars, the main expectation is that narrow, market-promoting institutions are likely to be the primary influence behind higher GDP growth rates in CEE. For comparative capitalisms scholars, there is likely to be an expectation of greater diversity between countries as well as the anticipation that a number of institutions will shape GDP growth rates in the region.

The analysis uses fuzzy-set qualitative comparative analysis (fsQCA) (Ragin, 2000, 2006, 2008) that is increasingly being used in related studies to identify the complex institutional configurations of both sufficient and necessary causes of various outcomes (Allen and Aldred, 2011; Boyer, 2004; Jackson, 2005; Pajunen, 2008; Schneider et al., 2010). The use of fuzzy sets has several advantages. Firstly, the technique enables the identification of any potential patterns in both necessary and sufficient causal conditions that promote higher GDP growth rates. This, in turn, will help to establish the extent to which institutional regimes are likely to converge across the region to a common model that includes regulations that lower the transaction costs of doing business. Secondly, fuzzy sets are particularly appropriate for research designs that are limited to a relatively small number of observations, which is often the case with cross-country analyses (Jackson, 2005). Finally, fuzzy sets facilitate a more nuanced examination of 'causal complexity' to put it one way (Ragin, 2008) or 'institutional complementarities' as others have put it (Hall and Soskice, 2001; Whitley, 2007).

Building on the arguments presented above, it is necessary to include issues of corporate governance into the analysis. Within the comparative capitalisms literature, the issue of corporate governance is a central one, and it has been ascribed an important role in capitalism in CEE (Bohle and Greskovits, 2006; Hall and Soskice, 2001; Nölke and Vliegenthart, 2009; Whitley, 2007). As a result of the large amount of foreign investment in CEE and as a result of formerly state-owned enterprises being privatized and then taken over by overseas companies, there have been important changes to the corporate governance systems of enterprises in the region, as many CEE firms are now controlled by others outside the region (Lane, 2007; Nölke and Vliegenthart, 2009).

The influence of those based outside the region does not stop there: the corporate governance codes of the region have been strongly shaped by transnational entities (Nölke and Vliegenthart, 2009), banks in CEE are often foreign owned (Bohle and Greskovits, 2006) and overseas investors own a large proportion of equities that are listed on the region's stock markets (Allen and Aldred, 2009). If foreign investors wish to have a more direct influence over CEE companies, they will own outright their overseas subsidiaries. This, in turn, will mean that they are not listed on local stock markets and, hence, will not have to adhere to the relevant host country regulations. Consequently, host country stock markets will be of little relevance to them (Lane, 2007; Myant, 2007). Additionally, wholly owned subsidiaries may be less likely to be reliant on banks in the region for funding. If FDI is, indeed, the preferred route for foreign companies to coordinate and control their subsidiaries in CEE, then those countries that attract the most FDI can be expected to be the ones to post the strongest GDP growth rates. If FDI is the main route to higher economic growth levels, then domestic banks and stock markets are likely to contribute less to increases in GDP rates in the region.

Another key element analysed within the comparative capitalisms literature is the employment system, which covers various forms of employment regulations, such as employment protection, wage bargaining and workplace representation. This is an area where there is a clear distinction between the two perspectives covered here, as the analytical focus is narrower in the international business literature than it is within the comparative capitalisms approach. Much of the transaction cost-inspired international business literature would see employment regulations as a burden for the firm, whilst the comparative capitalisms approach contends that, under certain conditions, they can be beneficial to firms (Harcourt and Wood, 2007; Whitley, 2007).

Regulations surrounding market-based activities are deemed to be of great significance in many analyses within the international business literature in assessments of firms' overseas expansion, as they can alter transaction costs (Meyer, 2001; Meyer and Peng, 2005). The inclusion of this factor is important, as, given the emerging nature of the economies in CEE, overseas investors who are considering establishing subsidiaries in a foreign country may be deterred from doing so if that country is deemed to place too great a burden on the companies that operate there. This may be the case even if employment regulations are viewed favourably by those potential investors. The inclusion of a variable that measures the ease of doing business in a country is an appropriate way to capture these more general aspects of a country's business environment.

Another factor that is likely to increase GDP growth rates is the availability of well-educated employees. In order to capture this possibility, this research includes the percentage of the labour force that has successfully completed a tertiary-level qualification. Tertiary education covers university undergraduate degrees. The inclusion of this variable is in line with related studies (Schneider et al., 2010). It will also help to shed light on the extent to which this factor is important to foreign investors and, hence, the extent to which states in CEE will have to not only promote the establishment of markets, but also increase workforce skills, by, for instance, increasing the numbers of those going to university.

Data and variable calibration

In order to assess the extent to which the desire to increase GDP growth rates is likely to create pressures for economies in CEE to converge around a model that privileges strong regulations that facilitate commercial transaction, all ten countries from CEE that joined the EU in either 2004 or 2007 have been included in the analysis. In order to ensure that the results are not biased by, for instance, large one-off investments by foreign firms, mean annual values for the five-year period (2005 until 2009, inclusive) have been used for most of the variables in this study. The year 2009 is the latest for which most measures are available. The data on employment and business regulations are only available for one year; these values do not, however, suffer from large annual variations.

The outcome variable is GDP growth rates. Data for this factor along with those for six of the causal conditions were collected from the World Bank's World Development Indicators data set, which itself draws on a number of sources; data for the seventh on 'participation' are from the European Trade Union Institute (ETUI). These data are for 2006; once again, this measure is not subject to significant fluctuations. The 'raw data' for all of the variables used in this analysis are shown in Table 3.1; the sources and definitions for that data are set out in Table 3.2.

In order to use the data as part of a fuzzy-set analysis, the figures had to be transformed. To establish the set membership values, three anchor points are required: two extreme points defining full membership and full non-membership and a crossover point at which the country is neither in nor out of the set (Ragin, 2000, pp. 158–59). These anchors are assigned set membership values of 1, 0 and 0.5, respectively. A value of 1 was assigned to the country with the highest GDP growth rate; 0 to the country with the lowest. The crossover point was calculated as the arithmetic mean for all of the countries. Given these three anchor points, the set membership values for all cases were calculated by using the log odds method described by Ragin (2008). Using this measure, five countries are members of the 'high GDP growth rate' set (Bulgaria, the Czech Republic, Poland, Romania and the Slovak Republic). The procedure that was used to calculate the set membership for high GDP growth rates was used for all of the causal conditions. This results in countries having varying membership for each institutional variable.

In order to examine the links, if any between corporate funding and GDP growth rates in the region, three variables that cover financing from different sources are included in the study. These are FDI, domestic bank credit and domestic stock market capitalization as a percentage of GDP. In order to measure labour market factors, two measures are included in the analysis. The 'employment rigidity' index captures general employment legislation, whilst the other, the European Participation Index, measures workplace and board-level employee representation, collective bargaining coverage rates and trade union density. The general regulatory environment is captured by the ease of doing business index – expressed in the analysis as the rigidity of doing business in order to aid the interpretation of the results. The ease with which legal agreements between corporations can be upheld in the courts is measured by the ability to enforce contracts.

Methodology

Developed by Ragin (2000) and drawing on Boolean algebra, fsQCA provides a means to assess the relationship between combinations of 'causal conditions'

Table 3.1 Data used in the analysis prior to transformation

Country	GDP	FDI	Domcred	Stockmkt	Labforce	Diffbus	Diffcontract	Emprigidity	Participation
Bulgaria	4.1	19.6	59.2	26.4	24.1	51	87	19	0.08
Czech Republic	3.5	4.7	46.8	31.5	13.9	63	82	11	0.44
Estonia	1.8	12.3	91.0	22.3	33.3	17	49	51	0.06
Hungary	0.6	24.1	61.8	27.0	19.9	46	14	22	0.40
Latvia	2.0	5.0	88.4	10.4	21.8	24	15	43	0.06
Lithuania	2.6	4.0	56.9	22.2	28.9	23	17	38	0.04
Poland	4.7	4.2	40.9	34.4	18.8	70	75	25	0.25
Romania	3.8	6.5	34.8	20.6	12.2	56	55	46	0.43
Slovak Republic	5.1	3.4	40.2	6.8	14.4	41	61	22	0.44
Slovenia	2.6	1.8	60.4	33.6	20.5	42	60	54	0.57
Mean	3.1	8.6	58.0	23.5	20.8	43.3	51.5	33.1	0.28

Notes: All data are the annual averages for the five-year period 2005–2009 (inclusive), except 'domcred' for the Slovak Republic, for which the four-year mean from 2005 until 2008 has been used because of missing data; 'labforce', for which the five-year mean from 2003 until 2007 has been used because of missing data; and the data for 'diffcontract' and 'emprigidity' which are for 2010 only.

Table 3.2 Causal conditions: definitions and sources

Variable	Definition	Source
GDP	GDP growth (annual %)	World Bank national accounts data, and Organization for Economic Cooperation and Development (OECD) National Accounts data files. The five-year mean (2005–09, inclusive) has been used.
Corporate Governance		
FDI	FDI, net inflows (% of GDP)	International Monetary Fund, International Financial Statistics and Balance of Payments databases, World Bank, Global Development Finance, and World Bank and OECD data. The five-year mean (2005–09, inclusive) has been used.
Domcred	Domestic credit to private sector (% of GDP)	International Monetary Fund, International Financial Statistics and data files and World Bank and OECD data. The five-year mean (2005–09, inclusive) has been used, except for Slovakia as data for 2009 are missing.
Stock	Market capitalization of indigenous listed companies (% of GDP)	Standard & Poor's, Emerging Stock Markets Factbook and supplemental S&P data. The five-year mean (2005–09, inclusive) has been used.
Labour Market		
Emprigidity	Rigidity of employment index (0 = less rigid to 100 = more rigid)	World Bank, Doing Business project (http://www.doingbusiness.org/). Data are for 2010.
Participation	European Participation Index, measuring employees' plant-level, board-level, collective bargaining coverage and trade union density (1 = highest level; 0 = lowest level)	ETUI, http://www.worker-participation.eu/About-WP/European-Participation-Index-EPI. Data are for 2006.
Labforce	Labour force with tertiary education (% of total)	International Labour Organization. The five-year mean for the latest available years (2003–07, inclusive) has been used, except for Estonia, Romania and Slovenia (four-year mean, as data are missing).
Business Regulation		
Diffbus	Ease of doing business index (1 = most business-friendly regulations)	World Bank, Doing Business project (http://www.doingbusiness.org/). Data are for 2010.
Diffcontract	Ease of enforcing contracts (rank; a higher value denotes greater difficulties)	World Bank, Doing Business project (http://www.doingbusiness.org/). Data are for 2010.

and the outcome in question. In short, fsQCA examines how the membership of cases in the set of causal conditions is linked to membership in the outcome set. In common with conventional statistical methods, fsQCA enables researchers to examine a higher number of cases than might be possible using many qualitative methods. However, unlike conventional statistical analytical techniques, such as multivariate analysis, fsQCA is based on the logic of set relations. This means that cases are considered differently in the two methods (Braumoeller and Goertz, 2000; Ragin, 2000, 2008). For instance, conventional statistical techniques would assess, in various ways, the correlation between two variables. However, the logic behind such a technique would lead to certain values being considered as errors (Ragin, 2006). Yet, fsQCA considers the cases, at least in some instances, to be causally linked (Ragin, 2000, 2006).

An advantage of using fsQCA here is that it enables potential clusters of institutional configurations and, hence, countries to be identified. If any such clusters are found, this would, potentially, reveal strong convergence tendencies amongst countries in the region. If, on the other hand, there are no clusters of either necessary or sufficient causal conditions, such tendencies will be less. An additional advantage of the fsQCA approach is that it allows for the possibility that more than one combination of causal conditions may be linked to the same outcome. In other words, there may be more than one way for countries to achieve high GDP growth rates (Fiss, 2007).

Finally, unlike conventional statistical techniques which are based on examinations of sufficiency (Ragin, 2000, 2006), fsQCA can examine the links between various combinations of causal conditions and the outcome as both necessary and sufficient conditions. This is important here, as it is yet to be established whether certain institutional features are either necessary or sufficient for countries in CEE to achieve strong GDP growth rates. The use of fsQCA means that causal conditions that are necessary and that are sufficient can be explored. These findings may, in turn, lead to clearer policy implications than would be the case from an analysis of the marginal effects obtained from regression analyses (Fiss, 2007, p. 1195; Schneider et al., 2010).

Results

Necessary conditions and functional equivalents

A necessary causal condition is one for which the instances of the outcome constitute a subset of the instances of the causal condition (Ragin, 2006, p. 297). In other words, a *necessary* cause, as Ragin (2000, p. 91) has noted, is one that 'must be present for the outcome in question to occur'. Its presence does not, however, 'automatically' lead to the outcome. This means that, for each case, the values of the set membership for the outcome will be lower than the values for the set membership for the necessary cause. However, as the data do not, normally, conform to that specification, fsQCA draws on consistency measures, which are calculated using probabilities, to enable assessments of the degree to which observations meet the requirement of necessity. Following the consistency rule suggested by

Ragin (2006, pp. 296–97), the analysis views near misses favourably, but sees those cases in which the scores for the causal membership greatly exceed those for the outcome membership negatively.

A consistency score of 1 denotes that the causal condition or combination of causal conditions meets the necessity rule across all cases. Consequently, values closer to 0 indicate either that many cases fail to conform to that rule or that there are a large proportion of cases that are a long way from meeting that rule. If a causal condition or a combination of them has a consistency score of 0.9 or above, this is, conventionally, deemed to be a 'necessary' or 'almost always necessary' condition. Table 3.3 shows the results of the analysis of causal conditions for all eight of the factors included here. Following convention, conditions that are written in lower case denote 'non-membership' of that set; those in upper case represent membership. Individually, none of the causal conditions exceeds the threshold of 0.9. In other words, not one of the causal conditions countries examined here creates the necessary conditions for high GDP growth rates. This, as is discussed below, is an important finding, as it suggests that there is no single factor that countries in the region can change in order to promote higher GDP growth rates.

Sufficient conditions

In set-theoretic reasoning, a sufficient cause is one that, in a strict interpretation, leads to the outcome if, for all cases, the fuzzy-set membership value of the causal condition does not exceed the fuzzy membership value of the outcome (Ragin, 2006). Combinations of factors can be considered in the same way and are denoted by a logical 'AND' (*). As individual cases or combinations of them are unlikely to

Table 3.3   Analysis of necessary conditions

Condition tested	Consistency	Coverage
Domcred	0.878	0.801
DIFFCONTRACT	0.856	0.780
DIFFBUS	0.796	0.783
Fdi	0.774	0.586
Labforce	0.749	0.702
Emprigidity	0.741	0.760
STOCKMKT	0.660	0.582
PARTICIPATION	0.622	0.616
Stockmkt	0.434	0.535
Participation	0.402	0.430
LABFORCE	0.325	0.369
EMPRIGIDITY	0.322	0.331
Diffbus	0.282	0.304
FDI	0.281	0.449
DOMCRED	0.235	0.276
Diffcontract	0.224	0.264

Notes: Outcome variable is GDP; the use of upper case denotes the presence of a condition, and lower case, its absence.

satisfy the strict criterion for sufficiency across all cases, a consistency measure, as specified in Ragin (2006), is needed.

Those causal combinations that exceed a certain consistency score are categorized as sufficient. This leads to such cases being assigned a value of 1 in the truth table for the outcome (GDP). Those causal combinations that have a consistency score below the cutoff point are not deemed to be sufficient, and they receive a score of 0 for the outcome. Using 0.80 as the cutoff point for sufficiency leads to the combinations of causal conditions and outcome shown in Table 3.4. Out of the 258 possible logical combinations of causal factors, 10 are observed. The fact that there are not fewer observed combinations suggests that there is little complementarity between the various institutions. In other words, having higher levels of, for instance, stock market capitalization does not mean that, say, employee participation levels will be comparatively strong or weak. This evidence indicates that there has been little convergence around any particular institutional model or models amongst the CEE countries.

In order to examine the sufficiency of the causes for strong GDP growth rates, a truth table algorithm is applied. The 'intermediate' solution is shown, which is recommended by Ragin (2008, pp. 160–75) for interpretation. Each line in Table 3.5 represents a combination of sufficient conditions that lead to the outcome. As can be seen, all sufficient causes consist of more than one condition. In short, there is no one condition that is, by itself, sufficient to account for high GDP growth rates.

Four ways to achieve high GDP growth rates emerge from the sufficiency analysis. The scores for 'raw coverage' and 'unique coverage' that are shown in the table help to assess the empirical importance of these four routes to success in advanced technology markets (Ragin, 2006). Raw coverage refers to the extent of the overlap between the causal combination set and the outcome set relative to the size of the outcome set (Ragin, 2006, p. 301). The measure for unique coverage controls for overlapping explanations by drawing on the raw coverage data. For any particular causal combinations, it is calculated by subtracting the raw-coverage score for all the other causal combinations (excluding the one of interest) from the raw-coverage score for all causal combinations (including the one of interest). As there are four causal combinations that explain strong GDP growth rates, the unique coverage score for each combination is relatively modest. This indicates a relatively high degree of diversity amongst those CEE countries that have strong economic growth records.

The four sufficient combinations of conditions have one factor in common. That factor is, from a comparative capitalisms and, *a fortiori*, from an international business perspective somewhat surprisingly, the difficulty in enforcing contracts. In other words, the more onerous it is to ensure compliance with the terms and conditions of a legal agreement between two companies, the higher the GDP growth rate is likely to be. In addition, the general difficulty in doing business in a country is, in three of the four combinations, a factor that helps to explain higher GDP growth rates. This does not conform to many of the expectations within the international business literature. The finding that, in three of the four combinations of conditions, more deregulated employment standards promote

Table 3.4 Truth table and assignment of countries to institutional configurations (logical remainders not listed)

Country	fdi	Domcred	Stockmkt	Labforce	Diffbus	Diffcontract	Emprigidity	Participation	GDP	Consist
Poland	0	0	1	0	1	1	0	0	1	0.998
Romania	0	0	0	0	1	1	1	1	1	0.998
Slovak Republic	0	0	0	0	0	1	0	1	1	0.997
Bulgaria	1	1	1	1	1	1	0	0	1	0.995
Czech Republic	0	0	1	0	1	1	0	1	1	0.861
Lithuania	0	0	0	1	0	0	1	0	0	0.465
Slovenia	0	1	1	0	0	1	1	1	0	0.418
Latvia	0	1	0	1	0	0	1	0	0	0.295
Estonia	1	1	0	1	0	0	1	0	0	0.168
Hungary	1	1	1	0	1	0	0	1	0	0.074

Table 3.5 Sufficient combinations of conditions for high GDP growth rates

Intermediate solution	Raw coverage	Unique coverage	Consist
emprigidity*DIFFCONTRACT*DIFFBUS* labforce *STOCKMKT*domcred*fdi	0.310	0.293	0.894
PARTICIPATION*emprigidity* DIFFCONTRACT*diffbus*labforce* stockmkt*domcred*fdi	0.129	0.108	0.997
PARTICIPATION*EMPRIGIDITY* DIFFCONTRACT*DIFFBUS*labforce* stockmkt*domcred*fdi	0.140	0.119	0.998
participation*emprigidity*DIFFCONTRACT* DIFFBUS*LABFORCE*STOCKMKT* DOMCRED*FDI	0.120	0.107	0.995
Solution coverage: 0.654			
Solution consistency: 0.947			

Notes: The use of upper case denotes the presence of a condition, and lower case, its absence.
'*' indicates that the combination of the conditions indicated are sufficient for the outcome.
Calculation with fsQCA 2.0 software (www.fsqca.com).

higher levels of economic growth is more in line with the expectations of the international business literature.

The lack of consistency in the combinations of sufficient causes is at odds with some of the arguments within the comparative capitalisms perspective: if institutions do complement one another, this will reduce the number of combinations of causal conditions that explain higher GDP growth rates (Hall and Gingerich, 2009). However, the fact that a wide range of causal conditions are needed to explain stronger economic growth rates is more in keeping with the expectations of the comparative capitalisms literature than those of the international business literature. This is because greater emphasis is attached to the creation and development of organizational capabilities and, hence, the ways in which these are institutionally structured in the former perspective compared to the latter.

Discussion and implications for future research

One of the important findings of this research is that there is a great deal of institutional diversity within CEE. As the results show, there are no clusters of countries around a specific variety of capitalism or an economic model that, in order to attract foreign investment, must adopt market-promoting policies. This, in turn, suggests that the pressures for convergence are not as great as some have argued (Globerman and Shapiro, 2003; Meyer et al., 2011). Indeed, the differences between the empirically important causal combinations of factors that are sufficient to explain stronger GDP growth rates have important implications for the prospects of institutional convergence in CEE. This is clearly apparent in some of the labour market institutions: low levels of employee participation are not, for instance, universally sufficient to explain higher economic growth levels. In two of the four combinations of sufficient conditions that explain higher GDP growth rates, employee participation levels are above average. In the other two, they have below-average values.

Although in three of the four combinations, relatively low employment regulations help to explain better economic growth levels, in the fourth combination, it takes an above-average value. These results, which indicate the importance of diversity, are also corroborated by the findings that relate to necessary conditions, as low employee participation levels and employment protection regulations were not consistently associated with higher economic growth levels. This acts as a warning against arguments to dismantle employment protection and forms of employee representation in companies (Harcourt and Wood, 2007). A reduction in these factors will not, in terms of either necessity or sufficiency, lead to stronger GDP growth rates. Indeed, if changes were to be made this could have a detrimental effect on existing comparative advantages.

The results here, furthermore, indicate that the impact of institutions may not be as straightforward as some theoretical frameworks expect; this is especially true for some of the international business analyses. For instance, one of the differences between Bulgaria and Hungary is that contracts are appreciably more difficult to enforce in Bulgaria than they are in Hungary; yet the former country has a superior record on economic growth during the period covered than the latter. In contrast to theoretical expectations, then, the more difficult it is to enforce contracts, the higher the levels of GDP growth are likely to be. Indeed, this is the only causal condition that is present in all four combinations of factors that explain higher GDP growth rates. This poses a significant challenge to the international business literature, as the presence of 'institutional voids' or 'institutional hazards', such as the lack of strong legal framework that facilitates market-based activities, is, in that perspective, generally associated with lower levels of economic growth.

Although it would appear that companies may be able to surmount the problems associated with weak or nascent regulatory environments by relying on trusted partners, the ways in which the use of informal institutions, such a trust amongst relatively tightly knit networks, shapes organizational capabilities and, hence, firms' competitiveness have not, within the international business literature, been addressed. Similarly, although there have been some analyses of firms in weak regulatory environments within the comparative capitalisms literature (see, for example, Wood and Frynas, 2006; Wood et al., 2011), these have not measured directly the competitive competencies that firms have developed. As firms, in the aggregate, contribute to economic growth, a key part of the explanation between narrow, market-supporting institutions and economic growth is, consequently, underspecified. However, it would appear that the comparative capitalisms literature would offer a richer framework to assess the impact of institutions on firms, their capabilities and economic growth.

Therefore, future research could attempt to assess the specific capabilities that firms, both domestic and foreign, are able to develop when operating in countries where the rule of law is either weakly enforced or too costly for many companies to use or too unpredictable. The inability of companies operating in such environments may reduce the number and variety of organizations with which they can cooperate (Whitley, 2007). However, this might not prevent them from becoming competitive within that economy. Indeed, as this research has shown, countries may still be able to post comparatively good GDP growth rates despite the generally weak ability of companies to enforce contracts. The capabilities that firms that operate in such institutional environments develop, therefore, requires greater scrutiny. This issue is of importance not just in CEE, but in other transition and developing economies, too.

References

M. M. C. Allen, 'The varieties of capitalism paradigm: not enough variety?', *Socio-Economic Review*, 2(1) (2004) 87–107.

M. M. C. Allen and M. L. Aldred, 'Varieties of capitalism, varieties of innovation? A comparison of old and new EU member states', *Journal of Contemporary European Research*, 5(4) (2009) 581–96.

M. M. C. Allen and M. L. Aldred, 'Varieties of capitalism, governance, and high-tech export performance: a fuzzy-set analysis of the new EU member states', *Employee Relations*, 33(4) (2011) 334–55.

M. M. C. Allen and R. Whitley, 'Internationalization and Sectoral Diversity: The Roles of Organizational Capabilities and Dominant Institutions in Structuring Firms' Responses to Semiglobalization', in C. Lane and G. T. Wood (eds), *Capitalist Diversity and Diversity within Capitalism*, (London: Routledge, 2012), pp. 97–120.

M. M. C. Allen, L. Funk and H.-J. Tüselmann, 'Can variation in public policies account for differences in comparative advantage?', *Journal of Public Policy*, 26(1) (2006) 1–19.

M. M. C. Allen, H.-J. Tüselmann and M. L. Aldred, 'Institutional frameworks and radical innovation: an analysis of high- and medium-high-technology industries in Germany', *International Journal of Public Policy*, 7(4/5/6) (2011) 265–81.

B. Amable, *The Diversity of Modern Capitalism*, (Oxford: Oxford University Press, 2003).

D. Bohle and B. Greskovits, 'Capitalism without compromise: strong business and weak labor in Eastern Europe's new transnational industries', *Studies in Comparative International Development*, 41(1) (2006) 3–25.

R. Boyer, 'New growth regimes, but still institutional diversity', *Socio-Economic Review*, 2(1) (2004) 1–32.

B. F. Braumoeller and G. Goertz, 'The methodology of necessary conditions', *American Journal of Political Science*, 44(4) (2000) 844–58.

K. D. Brouthers, 'Institutional, cultural and transaction cost influences on entry mode choice and performance', *Journal of International Business Studies*, 33(2) (2002) 203–21.

S. Casper, 'Can new technology firms succeed in coordinated market economies? A response to Herrmann and Lange', *Socio-Economic Review*, 7(2) (2009) 209–15.

S. Casper and C. Matraves, 'Institutional frameworks and innovation in the German and UK pharmaceutical industry', *Research Policy*, 32(10) (2003) 1865–79.

S. Casper and R. Whitley, 'Managing competences in entrepreneurial technology firms: a comparative institutional analysis of Germany, Sweden, and the UK', *Research Policy*, 33(1) (2004) 89–106.

C. Crouch, *Capitalist Diversity and Change: Recombinant Governance and Institutional Entrepreneurs*, (Oxford: Oxford University Press, 2005).

C. Crouch and H. Voelzkow (eds), *Innovation in Local Economies: Germany in Comparative Context*, (Oxford: Oxford University Press, 2009).

C. Crouch, W. Streeck, R. Boyer, B. Amable, P. A. Hall and G. Jackson, 'Dialogue on "institutional complementarity and political economy"', *Socio-Economic Review*, 3(2) (2005) 359–82.

A. Cuervo-Cazurra and M. Genc, 'Transforming disadvantages into advantages: developing-country MNEs in the least developed countries', *Journal of International Business Studies*, 39(6) (2008) 957–79.

J. H. Dunning, 'Location and the multinational enterprise', *Journal of International Business Studies*, 40(1) (2009) 20–34.

M. K. Erramilli, S. Agarwal and C. S. Dev, 'Choice between non-equity entry modes: an organizational capability perspective', *Journal of International Business Studies*, 33(2) (2002) 223–42.

P. C. Fiss, 'A set-theoretic approach to organizational configurations', *Academy of Management Review*, 32(4) (2007) 1190–98.

S. Globerman and D. Shapiro, 'Governance infrastructure and foreign direct investment', *Journal of International Business Studies*, 34(1) (2003) 19–39.

P. A. Hall and D. W. Gingerich, 'Varieties of capitalism and institutional complementarities in the political economy: an empirical analysis', *British Journal of Political Science*, 39(3) (2009) 449–82.

P. A. Hall and D. Soskice, 'Introduction', in P. A. Hall and D. Soskice (eds), *Varieties of Capitalism: The Institutional Foundations of Comparative Advantage*, (Oxford: Oxford University Press, 2001), pp. 1–68.

H. Hansmann and R. Kraakman, 'The end of history for corporate law', *Georgetown Law Journal*, 89 (2000) 439–68.

M. Harcourt and G. Wood, 'The importance of employment protection for skill development in coordinated market economies', *European Journal of Industrial Relations*, 13(2) (2007) 141–59.

G. Jackson, 'Employee representation in the board compared: a fuzzy sets analysis of corporate governance, unionism and political institutions', *Industrielle Beziehungen*, 12(3) (2005) 252–79.

G. Jackson and R. Deeg, 'Comparing capitalisms: understanding institutional diversity and its implications for international business', *Journal of International Business Studies*, 39(4) (2008) 540–61.

A. B. Keizer, *The Changing Logic of Japanese Employment Practices, A Firm-level Analysis of Four Industries*, (Rotterdam: Erasmus Research Institute of Management, 2005).

T. Khanna and K. G. Palepu, 'Emerging giants: building world-class companies in developing countries', *Harvard Business Review*, 84(10) (2006) 60–9.

T. Khanna and J. W. Rivkin, 'Estimating the performance effects of business groups in emerging markets', *Strategic Management Journal*, 22(1) (2001) 45–74.

H. Kim, H. Kim and R. E. Hoskisson, 'Does market-oriented institutional change in an emerging economy make business-group-affiliated multinationals perform better? An institution-based view', *Journal of International Business Studies*, 41(7) (2010) 1141–60.

D. Lane, 'Post-State Socialism: A Diversity of Capitalisms?', in D. Lane and M. Myant (eds), *Varieties of Capitalism in Post-Communist Countries*, (London: Palgrave Macmillan, 2007), pp. 13–39.

C. Lane and G. Wood, 'Capitalist diversity and diversity within capitalism', *Economy and Society*, 38(4) (2009) 531–51.

C. Lane and G. T. Wood (eds), *Capitalist Diversity and Diversity within Capitalism*, (London: Routledge, 2011).

K. Lange, 'Institutional embeddedness and the strategic leeway of actors, the case of the German therapeutical biotech industry', *Socio-Economic Review*, 7(2) (2009) 181–207.

J. Liu and A. Tylecote, 'Corporate governance and technological capability development: three case studies in the Chinese auto industry', *Industry and Innovation*, 16(4) (2009) 525–44.

J. A. McCahery, L. Renneboog, P. Ritter and S. Haller, 'The Economics of the Proposed European Takeover Directive', in G. Ferrarini, K. J. Hopt, J. Winter and E. Wymeersch (eds), *Reforming Company and Takeover Law in Europe*, (Oxford: Oxford University Press, 2004), pp. 575–646.

K. E. Meyer, 'Institutions, transaction costs, and entry mode choice in Eastern Europe', *Journal of International Business Studies*, 32(2) (2001) 357–67.

K. E. Meyer, R. Mudambi and R. Narula, 'Multinational enterprises and local contexts: the opportunities and challenges of multiple embeddedness', *Journal of Management Studies*, 48(2) (2011) 235–52.

K. E. Meyer and M. W. Peng, 'Probing theoretically into Central and Eastern Europe, trans-actions, resources, and institutions', *Journal of International Business Studies*, 36(6) (2005) 600–21.

G. Morgan and R. Whitley (eds), *Capitalisms and Capitalism in the Twenty-First Century*, (Oxford: Oxford University Press, 2012).

M. Myant, 'The Czech Republic: From "Czech" Capitalism to "European" Capitalism', in D. Lane and M. Myant (eds), *Varieties of Capitalism in Post-Communist Countries*, (London: Palgrave Macmillan, 2007), pp. 105–23.

A. Nölke and A. Vliegenthart, 'Enlarging the varieties of capitalism: the emergence of dependent market economies in East Central Europe', *World Politics*, 61(4) (2009) 670–702.

K. Pajunen, 'Institutions and inflows of foreign direct investment: a fuzzy-set analysis', *Journal of International Business Studies*, 39(4) (2008) 652–69.

M. W. Peng and K. E. Meyer, *International Business*, (London: Cengage Learning, 2011).

M. W. Peng, S.-H. Lee and D. Y. L. Wang, 'What determines the scope of the firm over time? A focus on institutional relatedness', *Academy of Management Review*, 30(3) (2005) 622–33.

M. W. Peng, D. Wang and Y. Jiang, 'An institution-based view of international business strat-egy: a focus on emerging economies', *Journal of International Business Studies*, 39(5) (2008) 920–36.

S. M. Puffer, D. J. McCarthy and M. Boisot, 'Entrepreneurship in Russia and China: the impact of formal institutional voids', *Entrepreneurship Theory and Practice*, 34(3) (2010) 441–67.

C. C. Ragin, *Fuzzy-Set Social Science*, (Chicago: Chicago University Press, 2000).

C. C. Ragin, 'Set relations in social research: evaluating their consistency and coverage', *Political Analysis*, 14(3) (2006) 291–310.

C. C. Ragin, *Redesigning Social Inquiry, Fuzzy Sets and Beyond*, (Chicago: University of Chicago Press, 2008).

A. Rugman, A. Verbeke and W. Yuan, 'Re-conceptualizing Bartlett and Ghoshal's classification of national subsidiary roles in the multinational enterprise', *Journal of Management Studies*, 48(2) (2011) 253–77.

M. Schneiberg, 'What's on the path? Path dependence, organizational diversity, and the problem of institutional change in the US Economy, 1900–1950', *Socio-Economic Review*, 5(1) (2007) 47–80.

M. R. Schneider, C. Schulze-Bentrop and M. Paunescu, 'Mapping the institutional capital of high-tech firms: a fuzzy-set analysis of capitalist variety and export performance', *Journal of International Business Studies*, 41(2) (2010) 246–66.

W. Streeck, 'Beneficial Constraints: On the Economic Limits of Rational Voluntarism', in J. R. Hollingsworth and R. Boyer (eds), *Contemporary Capitalism: The Embeddedness of Institutions*, (Cambridge: Cambridge University Press, 1997), pp. 197–219.

W. Streeck and K. Thelen (eds), *Beyond Continuity: Institutional Change in Advanced Political Economies*, (Oxford: Oxford University Press, 2005).

D. Tan and K. E. Meyer, 'Business groups' outward FDI: a managerial resources perspective', *Journal of International Management*, 16(2) (2010) 154–64.

A. Tylecote, J. Cai and J. Liu, 'Why is Mainland China rising in some sectors and failing in others? A critical view of the Chinese system of innovation', *International Journal of Learning and Intellectual Capital*, 7(2) (2010) 123–44.

D. Vaughan-Whitehead, *EU Enlargement versus Social Europe? The Uncertain Future of the European Social Model*, (Cheltenham: Edward Elgar, 2003).

R. Whitley, *Divergent Capitalisms: The Social Structuring and Change of Business Systems*, (Oxford: Oxford University Press, 1999).

R. Whitley, *Business Systems and Organizational Capabilities: The Institutional Structuring of Competitive Competences*, (Oxford: Oxford University Press, 2007).

G. Wood and G. Frynas, 'The institutional basis of economic failure: anatomy of the segmented business system', *Socio-Economic Review*, 4(2) (2006) 239–77.

G. Wood, P. Dibben, C. Stride and E. Webster, 'HRM in Mozambique: homogenization, path dependence or segmented business system?', *Journal of World Business*, 46(1) (2011) 3.

4
Why Do MNEs Engage in MNE–Government Relations? Empirical Evidence from the European Union and the Automotive Industry

Sigrun M. Wagner

Introduction

> As the world economy becomes more integrated, MNC cooperation with host governments grows increasingly critical yet more complex.
>
> (Luo, 2001, p. 416)

Whilst much of the literature on multinational enterprise (MNE)–government relations focuses on initial entry, political risk and host governments within a conflictual, bargaining context, little attention has been given to subsequent operations within a cooperative context, involving not only host but also home governments (Dahan et al., 2005; Luo, 2001, 2004a, 2004b).

National governments are also facing regulatory competition from organizations such as the European Union (EU) (Grosse, 2005), which has complicated the monitoring of the political environment for MNEs (Brewer and Young, 2001). With regard to regional economic integration, Dunning and Lundan (2008) point out that, as MNEs become more prominent as political actors, they might seek regional rather than multilateral fora to use and build their influence (see also Scherer et al., 2009). Dahan et al. (2005) also underline that research in international business (IB) on MNEs and their international political environment has overlooked the rise of international organizations such as the EU.

This provides the background and motivation for the chapter at hand, focusing on MNE–government relations within the EU, which with its institutions embodies both host and home governments for MNEs from the Triad regions.[1] The chapter investigates the reasons why MNEs engage in MNE–government relations, in this case, the EU institutions, as the literature has provided only partial explanations as will be discussed in the following section. It then goes on to frame the study within the context of the car industry and EU environmental regulations before discussing the methodology of interviews within the societal triangle. Findings and discussion present the empirical evidence. The chapter concludes with some reflections on limitations and future research.

Literature background

The IB literature on MNEs can be traced to two interrelated strands of literature. The first strand of literature has examined determinants of ownership, sectoral pattern and geographical scope of MNE activity (Dunning, 2001[2]). The second strand of literature is concerned with changes in the external technological, economic and political environment (Dunning, 2001). Within this second strand, Boddewyn and Brewer (1994, p. 137) stress that political behaviour is intrinsic to international business as the crossing of borders means introducing companies into other sovereignties. These authors assert that IB research is much more concerned with political factors than research in domestic business.[3] Governmental policies differ from country to country and thus distinguish international from domestic business (Boddewyn and Brewer, 1994, pp. 123–25; see also, Grosse and Behrman, 1992, p. 119; Toyne and Nigh, 1998). Boddewyn (1988) anticipates this notion in claiming that the distinction between international and domestic business is fundamentally political (see also, Boddewyn, 1997; Grosse, 2005a). Grosse (2005a) implicitly defines international business–government relations as the relations between national governments and multinational firms. Moon and Lado (2000) confirm that an important issue in IB is the interaction between multinationals and host governments, among which strategic interdependence often exists (Ring et al., 1990). Blumentritt and Nigh (2002) argue for more integration between MNE literature and literature on international business–government interactions. Dunning (2002) also stresses the need for a reappraisal of the significance of governments for MNE activities.

In order to bring political aspects into MNE theory, Boddewyn (1988) expands Dunning's eclectic OLI paradigm of Ownership, Location and Internalization advantages to include political dimensions, which were missing from the framework until then. The environment of a firm can, thus, be dichotomized into market and non-market components. Enriching Dunning's paradigm requires that non-market factors such as the government should be endogenized instead of being taken as exogenous 'givens' (Boddewyn, 1988, p. 357), which involves interdisciplinary borrowings. One borrowing this author would like to stress is the notion that 'public policy (...) is not developed in a vacuum but is usually the outcome of power plays by interested parties' (Boddewyn, 1988, p. 344). Political activities of MNEs (and other corporations) thus take part in shaping legislation. Boddewyn (1988) criticizes previous work for an economic bias, taking government policies as givens, which may not be internalized by MNEs. He furthermore emphasizes that even though MNEs' goals might still be economic, they can use political means to achieve economic ends.[4] Markusen (1995) also urges further research to consider making the relationship between policy and foreign ownership, that is, between governments and MNEs, endogenous. It is this relationship that is examined in this chapter, asking why MNEs engage in government relations in order to shed light on the nature of the relationship, whether this is exogenous, or indeed internalized by MNEs. The main research question is therefore what are the motivational factors for MNEs to engage in business–government relations?

This is in line with Getz's (2001) point that, for example, literature on political strategy provides inconsistent explanations of why MNEs become politically engaged.

In the context of firm–state interaction in IB, Kobrin (1997) alludes to the political risk[5] and bargaining power literatures (see, for example, Brewer, 1992; Grosse and Behrman, 1992; Kobrin, 1987; Poynter, 1982; Vernon, 1971). These two streams of research have dominated the IB scholarship dealing with MNE host government relations (Dahan et al., 2005). The bargaining model, the dominant MNE–government relations paradigm (Ramamurti, 2001), has been predominantly conflictual[6] (Lecraw, 1984; Luo, 2001, 2004a, 2004b). Dunning (1993) discusses bargaining with respect to the OLI paradigm and points out that home country–MNE bargaining relationships have been given less attention than relationships with host countries (Dunning and Lundan, 2008; see also, Ramamurti, 2001, on MNEs targeting home and host countries). It is within this context the chapter is set, investigating MNE–host government relations in the EU and why MNEs in the automotive industry choose to engage with policymakers.

Research context: car industry and environmental regulations in the EU

> Of all the areas of public policy, it is the environment where the European Union has probably the greatest daily impact on the way companies go about their business.
>
> (FT, 2002)

Environmental regulations in the EU have grown immensely in number over the past two decades and pose new challenges for policymakers and industry (Wagner, 2009, see also Figure 4.1 below). Areas generally covered under environmental legislation include waste, noise, air, soil, nature, water and chemicals (DG Environment, 2007; Krämer, 1997). The EU is considered an international environmental leader – its environmental regulations are among the world's strictest and most ambitious ones (Kelemen and Vogel, 2010).

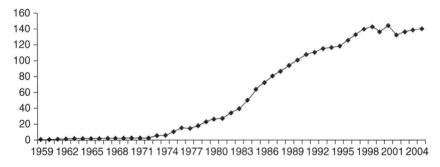

Figure 4.1   EU environmental legislation in force 1959–2005, directives only (Lenschow and Sprungk, 2010, p. 138)

According to Rugman and Verbeke (1998b), research on MNE environmental strategies is vital as MNEs dominate in pollution-intensive industries such as petroleum and chemicals (see also, Levy, 1995). Environmental legislation in the EU is most costly for manufacturing and energy production industries (EEA, 2003). As MNEs are faced with regulations that vary from country to country they have to choose between differentiated or standardized responses (Levy, 1995). For this research this argument can be translated into an expectation that MNEs in the EU would work (or would have worked) towards single European environmental standards, which would make their operations 'easier' and more consistent across this bloc of regional economic integration. MNEs as larger firms also have more resources to utilize corporate political activities (Lenway and Rehbein, 1991; Levy, 1995). Thus, it is more advisable to analyze MNEs' political behaviour rather than smaller firms' political activities.

The regulatory environment is one of the major determinants of competitiveness of the automotive industry as it affects almost all aspects of doing business (European Commission, 2004). It particularly faces significant market and technological challenges on account of climate change (Levy and Egan, 2003) and other environmental regulations both in voluntary and legally binding form. All major global car companies operate in Europe, that is, they not only sell but also produce in Europe. This makes it possible to compare European MNEs with US and Japanese subsidiaries in one location. Furthermore, the majority of the companies in the industry are represented politically in the EU, that is, in Brussels, as well as in several member states, thus providing an opportunity to research their business–government relations comparatively in one location. In the European context, the automotive industry, more than most industries, illustrates the significant irreversible shift of decision-making power from member states to the regional EU level (McLaughlin and Maloney, 1999).

The focus is on the vehicle manufacturers (OEMs – Original Equipment Manufacturers) as these are the most important players, being more visible and less fragmented than the supplier side.[7] Fragmentation brings with it smaller sizes of companies, which tend to be politically represented at a collective rather than individual level (see, Schuler, 1996). As the focus is on individual MNE–government relations, the major car producers as MNEs offer the best possibility to research this field – 11 OEMs have representative offices in Brussels, all of which have been interviewed directly (ten cases) or indirectly (one case); thus the whole population of politically active automotive MNEs from all Triad regions at the point of data collection has been covered.

Methodology

As research design, a case study approach using qualitative methods was chosen. The complex and potentially sensitive nature of the subject of MNE–government relations, the small number of companies involved and the exploratory nature of the research influenced this choice of qualitative instruments. These comprised semi-structured interviews, supported by primary and secondary sources such as reports, policy and legal documents from the companies and industry associations involved, and from the EU institutions. Data sources as well as interview sources were triangulated: all three corners of the so-called societal triangle (Van Tulder and Van der Zwart, 2006) were included in the investigation, that is, state, market and civil society, to give a holistic representation of the complex reality involved in MNE–government relations. Figure 4.2 conceptualizes this framework:

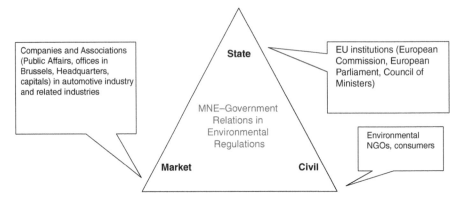

Figure 4.2   The societal triangle – triangulating MNE–government relations

The stakeholders were identified by investigating contributions to the consultation process of EU legislation as well as by following up references in organizational documents and academic and professional publications related to the regulatory areas. In those situations where the initial contact felt they were not able to offer helpful information, they recommended alternative respondents in their stead. Importantly, the author was also given recommendations by interviewees.

In total, 71 interviews were conducted, most of them face to face in Brussels, complemented by telephone interviews and some interviews in Berlin. On the market side this process resulted in 37 respondents from firms and industry associations represented in Brussels in both the automotive industry and related industries (such as component and supplier industries, raw material industries, recycling industry). On the state side, 26 interviews were conducted with officials in the European Commission and members or officials in the European Parliament (EP). On the civil society side, eight respondents were interviewed from (mostly) environmental non-government organizations (NGOs) that are involved in pre-legislation discussions due to their interest in environmental protection.

The respective interview sections concerning this question – which was part of a larger study – were coded on paper, with codes developed during data analysis (Harrison, 2003) as *in vivo* codes or closely fitting ones, thus resulting in data-driven codes (Gibbs, 2002) or open coding (Corbin and Strauss, 2008). Sets of codes resulted for each area and research question examined. In order to arrive at a smaller number of analytic units (Miles and Huberman, 1994), clusters were formed and defined by the author to subsume the codes into higher-level subcategories or concepts and themes (Corbin and Strauss, 2008), allowing the identification of key themes in the responses (see Crotty, 2006). Quotes are used to provide evidence and to make sense of the analysis (Corbin and Strauss, 2008), according to themes and concepts arising out of the data. An iterative process of presenting the data and writing about them and going back to the data was followed which helped clarify thoughts and logic (see Corbin and Strauss, 2008).

A note regarding the use of language in the interview quotes is necessary at this point: as many interviewees are non-native speakers of English, some quotes are grammatically wrong. However, in order to preserve the original nature and authenticity of the spoken word, all quotes from the interviews have been left unedited (verbatim quotes) in terms of language and grammar.

As triangulation is applied throughout, the results are presented accordingly, and interviewees are identified by the societal triangle and type of organization. Companies are referred to by their region of origin and a number (e.g., EU1, US1 and JP2). Company representatives are identified by their company code and a letter (e.g., EU1-A, US2-B) in order to protect their anonymity. Other interviewees are referred to by societal triangle and organizational type (e.g., Rel1, Com10, MEP4, NGO1-A). In the cases of more than one respondent per organization, these are differentiated by letter, for example, US2-A and US2-B or NGO1-A and NGO1-B. The codes and abbreviations used are summarized in Table 4.1.

Table 4.1 Key to codes of companies and interviewees

AA1 to AA3	Respondent from automotive association (interview key), Market side:
	AA1 to AA2 – European Automotive Associations
	AA3 – Japanese Automotive Association
Com1 to Com13	Respondent from European Commission (interview key), state side:
	Com1 – DG Employment
	Com2 to Com8 – DG Environment
	Com9 to Com13 – DG Industry and Enterprise
EU1 to EU6	European Automotive Company
EU1-A/B to EU6-A	Respondent from European Automotive Company (interview key), market side
JP1 to JP3	Japanese Automotive Company
JP1-A to JP3-A	Respondent from Japanese Automotive Company (interview key), Market side
MEP1 to MEP13	MEP, respondent (interview key), state side:
	MEP1 to MEP5 – Conservative Party
	MEP6 to MEP9 – Labour/Social Democrat Party
	MEP10 to MEP12 – Green Party
	MEP13 – Liberal Party
NGO1-A to NGO6	Respondent from non-governmental Organization (interview key), civil society side:
	NGO1 to NGO5 – Environmental NGO
	NGO6 – Consumer NGO
Rel1 to Rel14	Respondent from related industry (interview key), market side:
	Rel1 to Rel9 – related industry association
	Rel10 to Rel14 – related industry company
US1 to US2	American Automotive Company
US1-A to US2-B	Respondent from American Automotive Company (interview key), Market side

Findings and discussion

The results are presented according to the categories of the societal triangle (market, state, civil society) and by organizational type (companies, association, Commission, EP, NGOs), thereby triangulating responses.

During the coding, key themes were drawn out and identified from the initial codes, and thus a smaller number of analytic units (than the individual codes) emerged (Miles and Huberman, 1994). The following five key themes emerged in the data analysis process, each consisting of several individual subthemes or codes, which will be discussed below:

- *Information and communication*, which concern the need to be informed by policymakers (passive aspect) and to inform policymakers (active aspect), characterized by flows of information between policymakers and firms, which includes relational aspects and therefore social capital.
- *Business interest*, which states the impact of legislation on firms and the desire to influence legislation according to business interests as motivation to get involved with policymakers.
- *Predictability and fairness* which stress the importance of ensuring feasibility and predictability for planning purposes as well as a level playing field for companies.
- *Avoiding, weakening or postponing legislation* and 'preventing the worst'. These are summarized as *defensive motivators*.
- *Positive motivators* include elements such as working for the best solution, better regulation and being a good corporate citizen.

The market side

The market side was interviewed through automotive companies (15 interviews – IVs), automotive industry associations (7 IVs) as well as companies (5 IVs) and industry associations (9 IVs) from related industries who were included to triangulate responses.

Firstly, *automotive companies* are discussed. For these, the main motivation to engage in MNE–government relations is *to inform policymakers and to be informed*. While informing policymakers is the active side of *information and communication*, being informed could be seen as the complementary passive side to it. The active side of this key theme includes codes such as the *provision of expertise, information and data* (being a source of information), the *promotion and creation of understanding* as well as the *informing of consequences* (EU1-A, EU3-A, EU3-B, EU6-A, US1-B, US2-B, JP1-A, JP2-A). The following quotes are indicative of this active side of information and communication:

> The decisive factor is always to transmit the factual information in the right form to the right person. We are trying to advise politics by good factual information.
>
> (EU3-B)

(…) contribute expertise for legislation in the sector and beyond; information.

(JP2-A)

The overlap between the passive and active side can be seen that companies want to be informed in order to inform as in the following quote (see also EU2-A):

Firstly you need to know, which scenarios to prepare for. Then, when you know it, then you have to point out what it could mean in consequence.

(EU1-A)

This quote also illustrates an overlap between information and communication and *predictability and fairness* as there is a desire to be informed for *planning purposes* (EU2-A, JP1-A, EU4-A). In the following quote, information and communication is also related to *ensuring technical feasibility* (see US2-B as well):

EU civil servants as well as particularly MEPs don't have the know-how at all to fulfil certain regulations in their details, that means, to a certain extent they need us as well in order to pass a law in a reasonable way. So they need the technical input, our experts in order to polish legislation in the end; legislation which accordingly comprises technical opportunities, but also technically clean requirements.

(US1-B)

Although the literature discusses the influences and effects that government decisions and policies may have on business enterprises and their competitive environment as justification for MNE–government relations and corporate political activities (e.g., Keim and Hillman, 2008), the *business interest* is much less observed in the actual responses given by automotive companies (though still more prevalent than predictability and fairness). It is a surprising result that the main motivation seems to be to inform policymakers, while the actual impact on the companies, the business case and interest, plays a lesser role. This raises question as to whether there is an element of social desirability (as in serving policymakers by informing them) in these replies and whether the business case is taken for granted as a reason for lobbying. The elements or codes mentioned as part of this key theme include the *business impact of legislation* and the *avoidance of cost* (US2-A, EU1-B, EU5-B), *safeguarding the economic framework*, *widening business options* (EU3-B), *impact on products and design, depending on product portfolio* (JP1-A, EU1-A), *staying competitive* (US1-A) and *protecting or advancing the business or interests of the company* through influencing the policymaking process (JP2-A, US1-B, EU5-B, EU4-A). The following two quotes illustrate these:

(…) political decisions definitely influence corporate operations and also investment decisions. And that's why one tries to influence these decisions as early as possible as adjustments afterwards are much more cost-intensive than trying to prevent it from the start. So cost avoidance through influencing certain decisions.

(EU1-B)

That's very clearly the business case: If we don't adhere to certain requirements in the area of environmental policy, then we're out of the market, we are no longer competitive, our products won't be bought anymore.

(US1-A)

The two themes that receive least attention by car manufacturers are the complementary factors of *positive* and *defensive* motivators. Only two interviewees mention positive reasons for engaging with policymakers:

To be a good European corporate citizen: that is our working premise; it's also in our mission statement.

(JP2-A)

(...) to support all the institutions to build up a technical dossier and to find out political solutions for the best for the industry, for the society, for the competitiveness and for the environment as well.

(EU6-A)

These two companies constitute a minority, which is also true for the three companies stressing defensive reasons for engaging with governments:

(...) to prevent the worst.

(EU1-A)

I could maliciously say, we try to prevent the worst.

(US2-B)

To (...) defend the interest of the company.

(EU4-A)

The last quote also shows an overlap with the business case as motivation, which, together with information and communication, is the main reason stated by automotive companies in the interviews to engage in business–government relations.

Automotive associations show a similar result with the emphasis on *information and communication*, albeit with a pronounced tendency towards the active side of this key theme, where typical responses are:

In particular cases we bring up certain positions and supply technical information that is needed to draft the technical parts, e.g. test procedures.

(AA1-B)

(...) we need to promote understanding of the automobile industry for the European economy.

(AA3)

Unlike automotive companies, however, respondents from the associations stress *predictability and fairness* in terms of *ensuring technical feasibility* as much as information and communication as main motivation for automotive firms and associations to engage with policymakers:

That creates a motivation of course, to communicate their uniqueness with respect to different characteristics, and perhaps also give as a result that they might have a very different view as to what is feasible and what is not feasible to comply with it.

(AA1-D)

In this respect, association respondents, more than corporate respondents, also stress *harmonization of standards* (AA3) and the creation of a *common playing field* for manufacturers, which might be due to the nature of their activities as associations, trying to put across a unified industry view with regard to regulations:

(...) to make sure that all of the manufacturers face a common playing field across the EU.

(AA1-C)

The *business interest* for companies to engage in MNE–government relations features prominently among association interviewees. This includes codes such as the *dependence of corporate political activities on product portfolios* (AA1-A, AA1-D), *influencing* and *remaining competitive* (AA1-C), *reducing costs* (AA3) and *protecting the products and the business* (AA1-E) as motivation to engage with policymakers.

As in corporate responses, *positive* and *defensive* motivators can hardly be observed within association responses. Only one respondent points to attaining *better regulation* (AA1-D) as a positive reason for engaging with policymakers, while two association representatives mention defensive reasons. The first respondent stresses the need to cope with the problems the industry is faced with, whilst the second points to engineers influencing the defensive nature of MNE–government relations:

One reason for that is (...) we are faced with the same problems.

(AA3)

It is rather seen defensively than perceived as a chance. It's often like that development engineers are saying, by all means keep it away from me; keep it at arm's length.

(AA1-A)

Interestingly, respondents from *related industries* do not mention *defensive* motivators. A possible explanation for this is that related industries are less in the limelight of policymakers and observers than the automotive industry, which is a very visible industry (Rel9). *Positive* motivators are observed by one interviewee each (association and company):

> To act as a credible and trustful source.
>
> (Rel7)

> Then, it's hot air, but actually to enable the industry to make a contribution to society so it can be seen as doing so (it's linked to image), a sincere attempt to make a positive contribution.
>
> (Rel12)

Stakeholders from related industries stress *predictability and fairness* and the *business interest* equally, although companies emphasize the former and associations the latter. The following examples are typical for responses in related industries, firstly, for predictability and fairness where a level playing field and feasibility played a role for associations and companies:

> (...) a good regulatory environment so that your markets can be developed and done in the proper way, that there is no discrimination.
>
> (Rel6)

> (...) to make sure that the proposals become as realistic as possible.
>
> (Rel9)

> (...) to have a picture of what level of playing field we expect to act at.
>
> (Rel11)

Secondly, for the business case, associations mention the *interests of companies* (Rel1), the *impact of legislation, profitability* (Rel5), the *development of business and markets* as well as *maintaining good conditions* for the industry (Rel9) as reasons to engage in MNE–government relations. For related companies, the *protection of industry interests* (Rel12) and the *impact of legislation* (Rel14) are observed. The following two quotes represent the business case for related industries:

> (...) that determines their profitability as well.
>
> (Rel5)

> There is a lot of legislation, which directly or indirectly refers to the automobile industry; this alone is already motivation and justification to engage in government relations.
>
> (Rel14)

As with automotive companies and association, the most important motivational factor, as stated by related industries (associations and firms), is *information and communication*, both *to inform policymakers* and *to be informed*. Unlike the automotive industry, however, respondents in related industries also include elements of *promoting and improving* the *image and reputation* of the industry as motivational factors (Rel6, Rel8, Rel10, Rel12). These responses might be influenced by the less visible position of related industries compared to the automotive industry[8]:

> Of course we want to do something about the image or reputation of [the material] so that we can do business in a proper way.
>
> (Rel6)

> On a secondary level it's to improve the image of the industry and to maintain a dialogue with key stakeholders with government at every level.
>
> (Rel12)

The second quote reveals a relational aspect of information and communication in addition to improving the image of the industry – to be in contact and in dialogue with governmental stakeholders:

> (…) our purpose is really to have those relationships (…)
>
> (Rel4)

This motivation could be interpreted as building up social capital, especially in its bridging form, to facilitate access to power, decision-making and policy formulation (Serageldin and Grootaert, 1999), which is crucial in MNE–government relations.

To summarize, the main reason for respondents from the market side – across industries and organizational types – to engage in MNE–government relations is information and communication, *to inform policymakers* and *to be informed*, followed by the business case and predictability and fairness, while positive and defensive motivators play a rather negligible role.

In triangulation, the responses of the market side differ markedly to the responses from the state side, that is, the Commission and the EP, which are now discussed in turn.

The state side

Interviews from the state (EU) included respondents in the Commission (12 IVs) and the EP (13 IVs) plus one respondent who had experienced both sides as well as the Council side (Com13). As the Commission is normally the first point of contact in policymaking and therefore MNE–government relations in the EU, **Commission** responses are discussed first.

Unlike the market side responses, *information and communication* hardly feature as a key theme in how Commission respondents view the industry's motivation to engage with them. One respondent mentions the active side of information and communication, *to inform the Commission of what is at stake* (Com9), the second mentions the passive side, *to be informed* (Com5), while the third brings in *marketing reasons* (Com2) which is related to the improvement of image as discussed for the market side above:

> And perhaps another reason is maybe for marketing reasons, they want to appear as proactive in certain fields like safety and environment, they will be seen as involved with policy makers to say what we should do.
>
> (Com2)

This could also be interpreted as a *positive motivator*, which is only mentioned once in the Commission as a reason for companies to engage in relations:

> (...) going beyond that, there are indeed individual companies, individual persons that also have a political vision, who want to contribute their ideas, who have a European vision, but I think, we shouldn't cherish an illusion here, the driving force is very clearly the economic interest.
>
> (Com10)

This respondent acknowledges such positive reasons whilst also clearly being very realistic about the actual reason, the economic interest or *business interest* that receives the heaviest emphasis for key themes among Commission respondents. This includes various elements, among them the *cost factor*, that is, *to save or reduce costs* (Com2, Com11, Com3), *the impact of legislation* (Com1, Com4, Com10) and *the influence of political decisions according to interests* and for a *beneficial environment for industry* (Com5, Com7, Com8). Representative of these responses are the following two quotes, typical for this key theme:

> The main reasons I see in the effort to create, foster, and maintain an environment that is beneficial for the industry.
>
> (Com7)

> Well, I think the motor industry, probably, of all industries, are one of the most affected by regulation at European level, especially now in the context of the fight against climate change. I think that will become even more and more the case.
>
> (Com1)

The business case overlaps with *defensive motivators*, illustrated by the following quote:

> I think the main motivation is of course to influence political decisions in a way that they either benefit the corporation or burden it with as little cost as possible.
>
> (Com8)

Whilst acknowledged by very few market side respondents, defensive motivators play a larger role within Commission respondents and are more emphasized than information and communication. Companies are seen as engaging in MNE–government relations *to avoid legislation* (Com6) and *to minimize the economic impact* or *postpone legislation* (Com4), engaging in a *defensive stance* (Com4, Com12) – this is summed up by this respondent:

> My experience is, that the automotive industry, its sole purpose in engaging in discussions with regulators was to minimize the economic impact and there is, no, I never experienced any discussions with the automobile industry where it has been anything other than a damage limitation defensive posture.
>
> (Com4)

The business case also overlaps with *predictability and fairness* as emphasized by the following respondent:

> Cost and predictability of planning new products, they are sort of related factors, really. But ultimately what we do results in higher costs and so that is obviously an important factor for the industry.
>
> (Com11)

Predictability for planning purposes is related to *regulatory certainty* (Com2), while the other elements include the *guarantee of a level playing field* (Com12) and the *harmonization of standards* (Com5) for companies to engage with policymakers in the eyes of Commission respondents.

Among respondents from the *EP*, which is the second point of contact for companies in their corporate political activities, *predictability and fairness* in the form of a *level playing field* (competitive equality) as a motivational factor are only observed by two members who were both involved in the CARS 21 process[9] (MEP6, MEP7) and in the EP's Forum for the Automobile and Society (European Commission, 2006). Interestingly, one of them relates both an equal playing field and defensive motivators as being behind the motive of the business case for MNE–government relations:

> The attempt of exerting influence is certainly the main motive. And I think driven by two motives behind it. One is partly to organise competitive equality and secondly of course is also to reduce regulatory density that goes against individual interests or to prevent regulation.
>
> (MEP7)

Defensive motivators, similarly to the Commission, are more emphasized among MEPs than among market side respondents and include desires *to keep costs down, to avoid legislation* (MEP10), *to weaken or postpone* it (MEP1) or even *to stop* it (MEP12). Depending on the wording, the cost factor can be placed or interpreted as defensive motivators (MEP10) or as the *business interest*, which – unlike the other themes – is mentioned by every single EP respondent, and therefore appears to be the most important key theme among these respondents:

> (…) for motor vehicle manufacturers the legislative environment is a major strategic input into the business. And legislation represents a significant cost for them in terms of product development.
>
> (MEP3)

While most EP respondents observe mixed motivational factors (i.e., more than one key theme), the business interest as sole reason is observed by 5 of the 13 EP respondents. Typical responses in this category are:

> The motivation is to enforce individual interests in political decisions. (…) A firm can be massively affected by a proposal. (…) For the companies it's about safeguarding favourable conditions for their corporate operations, costs accordingly.
>
> (MEP2)

> (…) they want to protect the interests of their business.
>
> (MEP11)

> Influence on legislation, of course. (…) I think that is the most decisive, it all comes to this in the end.
>
> (MEP4)

Beyond *influence*, the *cost factor* and the *impact of regulation* (see also MEP6, MEP3, MEP13), the other responses for business case include elements and codes such as *profitability* and *creating beneficial conditions* for the industry (MEP1, MEP5).

As with the Commission, only one *positive motivator* is mentioned, overlapping with the business interest:

> Whereas I think there are hopefully a growing number of enterprises and inter-est organizations who actually want to be part of the change and who also feel there is something to be gained in terms of business and new opportunities.
>
> (MEP12)

Lastly, *information and communication*, as one of the five key themes, seems to have a more relational aspect among EP respondents, in addition to the already mentioned elements of *being informed* and *to inform policy makers* (MEP13, MEP8, MEP9, MEP12). The following quotes illustrate this relational aspect (emphasis added):

> In order *to accompany* legislative *procedures*.
>
> (MEP8)

I think the main motivational factors are to *participate* in the drafting of policy/policy-making or to influence it (...).

(Com13)

I think that it is the policy makers after all who are going to change the law and make emissions tougher, or safety conditions tougher, or whatever, and it is in the interests of the manufacturers *therefore to stay in touch* with policy makers and to try and, well frankly, to influence them. Or at least educate them about the reality of car manufacturing.

(MEP9)

Whilst acknowledging the business case as motivational factor, the third respondent heavily stresses the relational aspect later in the interview:

In the essence of good public affairs and the essence of good lobbying is to know their client long before there is something to lobby them about. So the contacts have got to *be* there. You shouldn't be making the contacts once you have a proposal for the commission, you should already have the contacts and be able to use them.

(MEP9)

It can therefore be said that the building up of social capital is an important reason why firms engage in MNE–government relations, in order to be then able to influence policymakers based on the business case. It is the bridging form of social capital as the contacts are built up between members of different groups (Grix, 2002; Putnam, 2000).

To summarize, respondents from the state side (Commission and EP) see the business interest as the main reason for companies to engage in relations with policymakers.

The civil society side

Lastly, interviews were also triangulated with respondents from the civil society side, which is now discussed. This included seven interviews with environmental NGOs and one interview with a consumer organization.[10] As could almost be expected from this side of stakeholders, no *positive motivators* are identified and only the respondent from the consumer organization acknowledges the desire *to be informed* within *information and communication* as a reason for companies to engage in MNE–government relations (NGO6). Two respondents recognize the creation of a *level playing field* (NGO1-A) and the provision of *clarity and certainty* (NGO1-B) and therefore *predictability and fairness* as motivational factors. The *business interest* is more prevalent in the civil society responses where the *extension of business strategy* and the *creation of market opportunities* are mentioned (NGO1-A) in addition to *influencing legislation* as mentioned by other stakeholders above (NGO3, NGO5, NGO6), where a typical response is:

If you can't prevent it, then to influence it according to your own interest, to optimize it.

(NGO3)

Here the business interest overlaps with *defensive motivators*, which, overwhelmingly, the majority of civil society respondents (six out of eight) refer to as main reasons for automotive companies to engage with policymakers. Given that the relationship between the market side and the civil society is often portrayed as antagonistic, this should not come as a surprise. Companies are perceived to engage in MNE–government relations with a *defensive posture in principle* (NGO2-B), for which the following respondent uses the strongest language:

'To keep those damned politicians off our backs', this motivates most political action. (...) The main motivation is keeping off everything.

(NGO1-A)

A more elaborate example of this key theme is provided by the following respondent:

I would say, controlling the regulatory output. With other words, to try that the state intervenes in market processes as little as possible. So that the autonomy of producers is held up as much as possible and of course that costly measures are avoided.

(NGO4)

Other elements and codes of this key theme of defensive motivators have been mentioned above already, such as *preventing or avoiding legislation* and *avoiding or minimizing costs* (NGO2-A, NGO3, NGO1-B), exemplified by the following quote:

(...) to minimize costs, to minimise the requirement for future investment, to allow from an industry perspective a free hand as to what their financial resources can be invested in, what part of the product their investments can go towards.

(NGO1-B)

To summarize, respondents from the civil society side (environmental NGOs, consumer organization) see defensive motivators as main reasons for firms to engage in MNE–government relations.

Conclusion and outlook

Five key themes emerged from the analysis of why MNEs engage in government relations. The two main motivators were, firstly, the *business interest*, that is, the legislative impact on operations, which makes companies desire to influence legislation according to their interest. Secondly, it was *information and communication* – the wish to inform policymakers about the industry and its needs as well as the wish to be informed about legislative developments. Other reasons to engage in MNE–government relations included *predictability and fairness* (to create a level playing field), *defensive* (to avoid, weaken or postpone legislation) and *positive motivators* (to contribute to the best solution).

How do these findings for the research question of why MNEs engage in government relations relate to previous studies? Compared with the literature, the findings address the gap of providing a more consistent explanation of why MNEs become politically engaged (Getz, 2001). Yoffie (1987) stresses high strategic salience of an issue as a reason for companies to become politically active which would be in line with Markusen's (1995) call to internalize MNE–government relations. Baysinger (1984) also cites the attainment of public policy results favourable to the firm's success as the overall objective of MNE–government relations. This clearly relates to the findings of the *business interest* as main reason for companies to engage in these relations (see also Keim and Hillman, 2008; Salorio et al., 2005).

Gale and Buchholz (1987) distinguish between two goals of corporate involvement in the political process – pursuit of legitimacy and pursuit of competitive advantage. Looking at the findings, the pursuit of legitimacy only emerges in the key theme of *positive motivators* whereas competitive advantage is strongly linked to the *business interest* as a motivation for MNE–government relations, as well as to the key theme of *defensive motivators*. What Gale and Buchholz (1987) term competitive advantage is in line with what Baysinger (1984) terms public policy results favourable to the success of an organization. What the findings add to the literature is the motivation to inform and communicate with policymakers as well as to be informed – the key theme of *information and communication*. Furthermore, the desire for *predictability and fairness* is added to this typology of reasons for engaging in MNE–government relations. These results underline the significance of policymaking for MNE activities, thus reappraising them as Dunning (2002) called for.

The findings support the proposition that government policies are not seen as exogenous factors by firms, but that government relations and policies are indeed an endogenous factor for MNEs, and thus an important part or even extension of strategy as one respondent put it (NGO1-A) that firms can indeed influence.

Limitations and future research

This study investigated a single industry where producers and states are powerful. The generalizability beyond one industry is therefore somewhat limited and further research could and should thus extend to other industries as political behaviour and resources may differ among industries and issue areas (see, for example, Boddewyn and Brewer, 1994; Brewer, 1992; Frynas et al., 2006; Héritier and Eckert, 2009).

The study was constricted to a single geographic location of MNE–government relations. The research could be extended to the other two major political locations where MNE–government relations are rooted within this industry. The location of Brussels could be compared to the locations of Washington, DC, where most major car companies have offices or use lobbyists, and Tokyo, where the European automotive association opened an office in 1995 (ACEA, 2008). Loewenberg (2001) points out stark differences between the United States and the EU with respect to interest representation, which was also highlighted by the respondent who had experienced both (EU2-B; see also Mahoney, 2007). As an increasingly important and emerging political location, Beijing could be an interesting place to investigate MNE–government relations – the European Auto-mobile Manufacturers' Association opened offices there in 2004 (ACEA, 2008). The increasing importance of Beijing, and thus China, in the political automotive landscape is illustrated by the fact that the new head of the EU2 office in Brussels spent three years in Beijing as the General Manager, North-East Asia Government affairs (Public Affairs News, 2009).

A related possibility for further research in the same area is the investigation of automotive subsidiaries in EU member states or globally in terms of integration or dissimilarities of their MNE–government relations (see, for example, Blumentritt and Nigh, 2002; Wan and Hillman, 2006).

Acknowledgements

The author would like to thank all interviewees for their valuable contribution to this research.

Notes

1. It is an 'institutional reality' that governments do not unambiguously represent either a home or a host country (Rugman and Verbeke, 1998a, p. 130).
2. See, for example, Hymer (1976); Vernon (1966) (Product cycle and international invest-ment); Buckley and Casson (1976); Hennart (1982); Dunning (1981) (OLI paradigm of ownership, location, internalization). For overviews on the theoretical foundations in IB, see also Buckley (1990); Grosse and Behrman (1992); Dunning and Lundan (2008).
3. Their argument of distinguishing domestic from international business is as follows: nations are typified by physical, economic, social and cultural characteristics whereas states are typified by political characteristics. Technically, this would mean that inter-national business is in fact 'inter-state' business. However, to be consistent with other writings, this chapter will use the established term 'international' business.
4. Wilkins (1997) argues similarly, and advocates against the separation of the political from the economic in providing analytical frameworks.
5. Boddewyn (1988, p. 347) criticizes that non-market factors have been perceived as risks rather than opportunities 'as if there were not also "political opportunities"'. Political risk is generally defined as 'home or host government intervention in international business activities' (Ring et al., 1990, p. 143).
6. Luo (2001), furthermore, mentions transaction cost theories as underpinning conflict-based views of MNE–host government relations. See Gomes-Casseres (1990) for an attempt to integrate both bargaining and transaction cost approaches. Grosse's edited book (2005b) gives an overview of the history and theories in the analysis of interna-tional business–government relations.
7. The ten biggest companies account for approximately 70–80 per cent of the car production market (McLaughlin and Maloney, 1999; Wells, 2010).

8. PR and image reasons are mentioned by one automotive industry respondent (EU1-B); their response might, however, be influenced by the fact that they left the company to pursue research in global climate policies and protection.

9. CARS 21 stands for 'A Competitive Automotive Regulatory System for the 21st century', a report issued by the CARS 21 High Level Group. It was launched in 2005 and mandated to make recommendations for the 'short, medium and the long-term public policy and regulatory framework' for the European car industry, integrating competitive, environmental, safety, employment and affordability aspects (European Commission, 2006, p. 2). The group consisted of key stakeholders in the automotive field: Commission, Member States, EP, Industry, Trade Unions, NGOs and Users (ibid.).

10. While trade unions as a civil society stakeholder of the automotive industry were contacted, they did not reply to any contact attempts by this author.

References

ACEA, *European Automobile Manufacturers Association, Website*, (2008), available at http://www.acea.be (31.07.2008).

B. D. Baysinger, 'Domain maintenance as an objective of business political activity: an expanded typology', *The Academy of Management Review*, 9(2) (1984) 248–58.

T. P. Blumentritt and D. Nigh, 'The integration of subsidiary political activities in multinational corporations', *Journal of International Business Studies*, 33(1) (2002) 57–77.

J. J. Boddewyn, 'Political aspects of MNE theory', *Journal of International Business Studies*, 19(3) (1988) 341–63.

J. J. Boddewyn, 'The Conceptual Domain of International Business: Territory, Boundaries, and Levels', in B. Toyne and D. Nigh (eds), *International Business: An Emerging Vision*, (Colombia, SC: University of South Carolina Press, 1997), pp. 50–61.

J. J. Boddewyn and T. L. Brewer, 'International-business political behavior: new theoretical directions', *Academy of Management Review*, 19(1) (1994) 119–43.

T. L. Brewer, 'An issue-area approach to the analysis of MNE–government relations', *Journal of International Business Studies*, 23(2) (1992) 295–309.

T. L. Brewer and S. Young, 'Multilateral Institutions and Policies: Their Implications for Multinational Business Strategy', in A. M. Rugman, and T. L. Brewer (eds), *The Oxford Handbook of International Business*, (Oxford: Oxford University Press, 2001), pp. 282–313.

P. J. Buckley, 'Problems and developments in the core theory of international business', *Journal of International Business Studies*, 21(4) (1990) 657–65.

P. J. Buckley and M. Casson, *The Future of the Multinational Enterprise*, (London: Macmillan, 1976).

J. Corbin and A. Strauss, *Basics of Qualitative Research: Techniques and Procedures for Developing Grounded Theory*, 3rd Edition, (London: Sage, 2008).

J. Crotty, 'Greening the supply chain? The impact of take-back regulation on the UK automotive sector', *Journal of Environmental Policy & Planning*, 8(3) (2006) 219–34.

N. Dahan, J. P. Doh and T. Guay, 'The role of multinational corporations in transnational institution building: a policy network perspective', *Human Relations*, 59(11) (2005) 1571–600.

DG Environment, *Directorate General Environment of European Commission, Website*, (2007), available at http://ec.europa.eu/dgs/environment/index_en.htm (12.07.2007).

J. H. Dunning, *International Production and the Multinational Enterprise*, (London: Allen & Unwin, 1981).

J. H. Dunning, *Multinational Enterprises and the Global Economy*, (Harlow: Addison-Wesley, 1993).

J. H. Dunning, 'The Key Literature on IB Activities: 1960–2000', in A. M. Rugman and T. L. Brewer (eds), *The Oxford Handbook of International Business*, (Oxford: Oxford University Press, 2001), pp. 36–68.

J. H. Dunning, 'Perspectives on international business research: a professional autobiography, fifty years researching and teaching international business', *Journal of International Business Studies*, 33(4) (2002) 817–35.

J. H. Dunning and S. M. Lundan, *Multinational Enterprises and the Global Economy*, 2nd Edition, (Cheltenham: Edward Elgar, 2008).

EEA (European Environment Agency), *Europe's Environment: The Third Assessment, Environmental Assessment Report*, (Luxembourg: Office for Official Publications of the European Communities, 2003).

European Commission, *European Competitiveness Report*, Commission staff working document, SEC(2004)1397, Brussels, (2004).

European Commission, *CARS 21 – A Competitive Automotive Regulatory System for the 21st century*, Final Report, (2006), available at http://ec.europa.eu/enterprise/sectors/automotive/files/pagesbackground/competitiveness/cars21finalreport_en.pdf (16.03.2010).

J. G. Frynas, K. Mellahi and G. A. Pigman, 'First mover advantages in international business and firm-specific political resources', *Strategic Management Journal*, 27(4) (2006) 321–45.

Financial Times (FT), *Europe's green-fingered legislators*, 15.08.2002.

J. Gale and R. A. Buchholz, 'The Political Pursuit of Competitive Advantage: What Business can Gain from Government', in A. A. Marcus, A. M. Kaufman and D. R. Beam (eds), *Business Strategy and Public Policy: Perspectives from Industry and Academia*, (New York: Quorum Books, 1987), pp. 31–41.

K. A. Getz, 'Public affairs and political strategy: theoretical foundations', *Journal of Public Affairs*, 1/2(4/1) (2001) 305–29.

G. R. Gibbs, *Qualitative Data Analysis: Explorations with NVivo*, (Maidenhead: Open University Press, 2002).

B. Gomes-Casseres, 'Firm ownership preferences and host government restriction: an integrated approach', *Journal of International Business Studies*, 21(1) (1990) 1–22.

R. Grosse, 'Introduction', in R. Grosse (ed.), *International Business and Government Relations in the 21st Century*, (Cambridge: Cambridge University Press, 2005a), pp. 1–21.

R. Grosse (ed.), *International Business and Government Relations in the 21st Century*, (Cambridge: Cambridge University Press, 2005b).

R. Grosse and J. N. Behrman, 'Theory in international business', *Transnational Corporations*, 1(1) (1992) 93–126.

J. Grix, 'Introducing students to the generic terminology of social research', *Politics*, 22(3) (2002) 175–86.

A. Harrison, 'Case Study Research', in D. Partington (ed.), *Essential Skills for Management Research*, (London: Sage, 2003), pp. 158–80.

J.-F. Hennart, *A Theory of Multinational Enterprise*, (Ann Arbor, MI: University of Michigan Press, 1982).

A. Héritier and S. Eckert, 'Self-regulation by associations: collective action problems in European environmental regulation', *Business and Politics*, 11(1) (2009) Article 3.

S. H. Hymer, *The International Operations of National Firms: A Study of Foreign Direct Investment*, (Cambridge, MA: MIT Press, 1976).

G. D. Keim and A. J. Hillman, 'Political environments and business strategy: implications for managers', *Business Horizons*, 51(1) (2008) 47–53.

R. D. Kelemen and D. Vogel, 'Trading places: the role of the United States and the European Union in international environmental politics', *Comparative Political Studies*, 43(4) (2010) 427–56.

S. J. Kobrin, 'Testing the bargaining hypothesis in the manufacturing sector in developing countries', *International Organization*, 41(4) (1987) 575–607.

S. J. Kobrin, 'Transnational Integration, National Markets, and Nation-States', in B. Toyne and D. Nigh (eds), *International Business: An Emerging Vision*, (Colombia, SC: University of South Carolina Press, 1997), pp. 242–56.

L. Krämer, *Focus on European Environmental Law*, 2nd Edition, (London: Sweet & Maxwell, 1997).

D. J. Lecraw, 'Bargaining power, ownership, and profitability of transnational corporations in developing countries', *Journal of International Business Studies*, 15(1) (1984) 27–43.

A. Lenschow and C. Sprungk, 'The myth of a green Europe', *Journal of Common Market Studies*, 48(1) (2010) 133–54.

S. A. Lenway and K. Rehbein, 'Leaders, followers, and free-riders: an empirical test of variation in corporate political involvement', *Academy of Management Journal*, 34(4) (1991) 893–905.

D. L. Levy, 'The environmental practices and performance of transnational corporations', *Transnational Corporations*, 4(1) (1995) 44–67.

D. L. Levy and D. Egan, 'A neo-Gramscian approach to corporate political strategy: conflict and accommodation in the climate change negotiations', *Journal of Management Studies*, 40(4) (2003) 803–29.

S. Loewenberg, 'Lobbying, Euro-style', *National Journal*, 33(36) (2001) 2742–46.

Y. Luo, 'Toward a cooperative view of MNC–host government relations: building blocks and performance implications', *Journal of International Business Studies*, 32(1) (2001) 401–19.

Y. Luo, 'A coopetition perspective of MNC-host government relations', *Journal of International Management*, 10(4) (2004a) 431–51.

Y. Luo, *Coopetition in International Business*, (Copenhagen: Copenhagen Business School Press, 2004b).

C. Mahoney, 'Lobbying success in the United States and in the European Union', *Journal of Public Policy*, 27(1) (2007) 35–56.

J. R. Markusen, 'The boundaries of multinational enterprises and the theory of international trade', *Journal of Economic Perspectives*, 9(2) (1995) 169–89.

A. M. McLaughlin and W. A. Maloney, *The European Automobile Industry: Multi-Level Governance, Policy and Politics*, (London: Routledge, 1999).

M. B. Miles and A. M. Huberman, *Qualitative Data Analysis: An Expanded Sourcebook*, 2nd Edition, (Thousand Oaks, CA: Sage, 1994).

C. W. Moon and A. A. Lado, 'MNC–host government bargaining power relationship: a critique and extension within the resource-based view', *Journal of Management*, 26(1) (2000) 85–117.

T. A. Poynter, 'Government intervention in less developed countries: the experience of multinational companies', *Journal of International Business Studies*, 13(1) (1982) 9–25.

Public Affairs News, (…) takes top [EU2] EU role after (…) departure, 01.12.2009.

R. D. Putnam, *Bowling Alone: The Collapse and Revival of American Community*, (New York: Simon & Schuster, 2000).

R. Ramamurti, 'The obsolescing "bargaining model"? MNC–host developing country relations revisited', *Journal of International Business Studies*, 32(1) (2001) 23–39.

P. S. Ring, S. A. Lenway and M. Govekar, 'Management of the political imperative in international business', *Strategic Management Journal*, 11(2) (1990)141–51.

A. M. Rugman and A. Verbeke, 'Multinational enterprises and public policy', *Journal of International Business Studies*, 29(1) (1998a) 115–36.

A. M. Rugman and A. Verbeke, 'Corporate strategies and environmental regulations: an organizing framework', *Strategic Management Journal*, 19(4) (1998b) 363–75.

E. M. Salorio, J. J. Boddewyn and N. Dahan, 'Integrating business political behavior with economic and organizational strategies', *International Studies of Management & Organization*, 35(2) (2005) 28–55.

A. G. Scherer, G. Palazzo and D. Matten, 'The business firm as a political actor: a new theory of the firm for a globalized world', *Business and Society*, 48(4) (2009) 577–80.

D. A. Schuler, 'Corporate political strategy and foreign competition: the case of the steel industry', *Academy of Management Journal*, 39(3) (1996) 720–37.

I. Serageldin and C. Grootaert, 'Defining Social Capital: An Integrating View', in P. Dasgupta and I. Serageldin (eds), *Social Capital: A Multifaceted Perspective*, (Washington, DC: The World Bank, 1999), pp. 40–58.

B. Toyne and D. Nigh, 'A more expansive view of international business', *Journal of International Business Studies*, 29(4) (1998) 863–76.

R. Van Tulder and A. Van der Zwart, *International Business-Society Management: Linking Corporate Responsibility and Globalization*, (London: Routledge, 2006).

R. Vernon, 'International investment and international trade in the product cycle', *Quarterly Journal of Economics*, 80(2) (1966) 190–207.

R. Vernon, *Sovereignty at Bay: The Multinational Spread of US Enterprises*, (New York: Basic Books, 1971).

S. M. Wagner, 'The Automotive Industry and Environmental Regulations: Challenges to Corporate Political Activities of Multinational Enterprises in the European Union', in K. Ibeh and S. Davies (eds), *Contemporary Challenges to International Business*, (Basingstoke: Palgrave Macmillan, 2009), pp. 269–84.

W. P. Wan and A. J. Hillman, 'One of these things is not like the others: what contributes to dissimilarity among MNE subsidiaries' political strategies', *Management International Review*, 46(1) (2006) 85–107.

P. Wells, *Whatever happened to industrial concentration?*, available at www.AutomotiveWorld.com (20.04.2010).

M. Wilkins, 'The Conceptual Domain of International Business', in B. Toyne and D. Nigh (eds), *International Business: An Emerging Vision*, (Colombia, SC: University of South Carolina Press, 1997), pp. 31–50.

D. Yoffie, 'Corporate Strategies for Political Action: A Rational Model', in A. A. Marcus, A. M. Kaufman and D. R. Beam (eds), *Business Strategy and Public Policy: Perspectives from Industry and Academia*, (New York: Quorum Books, 1987), pp. 43–60.

Part II

International Business Activities Across Different Spatial Scales

5
Country Linkages and Firm Internationalization: Indian MNEs within Economic–Political Alliances of Nations

Peter J. Buckley, Peter Enderwick, Nicolas Forsans and Surender Munjal

Introduction

The theory of alliances between nations has been primarily studied in the field of politics from the point of view of defence and foreign policy whereas the economic theory of alliances is widely studied in the context of public goods (Olsen and Zeckhauser, 1966). However, the role of inter-country alliances in promoting economic development, trade or investment has attracted less interest. This chapter builds on the economic theory of alliances to argue that economic–political alliances between nations, such as the Commonwealth grouping, contribute to promoting foreign direct investment (FDI).

In a rapidly globalizing world, economic–political alliances among nations are becoming increasingly important. Such alliances can take a variety of forms and may, as in the case of bilateral treaties, regional trade agreements, and custom unions, be forged by national and regional governments with the aim of enhancing trade and investment relationships among member countries (Gao, 2005; Medvedev, 2006; Raff, 2004). In the same way, international businesses develop cross-border alliances and networks with suppliers, buyers and competitors to improve the efficiency of their operations (Shi and Gregory, 1998). In many cases there is strong interaction between the two types of linkages with multinational firms tapping into the associations established by their home country with other countries as a platform for expanding their global value chains. This has occurred within the European Union (EU) and the North America Free Trade Agreement (NAFTA), both of which promoted trade between firms located in member countries and encouraged intra-bloc investments among member countries (Buckley et al., 2003; Motta and Norman, 1996).

We can also observe groupings of nations which have been established to achieve broader goals than simply trade and investment promotion. An historical example is provided by the League of Nations established at the conclusion of the First World War. At its height, the League had a membership of 58 nations. While its primary purpose was to ensure continuing peace and stability, the League did undertake other roles, for example, providing extensive humanitarian aid to Turkey in 1923. The United Nations with its various component bodies provides a contemporary example of a multination grouping that seeks to pursue a range of goals. Similarly, in economic policy terms the former G7 and current G8 and G20 groupings play a dominant role. Broadly, these groupings aim for the advancement of individual members within the ambit of the group. One of the most enduring examples of cross-national union with a wide remit is provided by the British Commonwealth association of nations.

Unlike bilateral treaties and regional trade agreements which have a very narrow scope, the Commonwealth is an economic–political organization which aims to promote development among member countries. Established in 1870, the Commonwealth is a voluntary association of 54 countries (formerly under British rule) including the United Kingdom and encompasses a population of two billion. The Commonwealth aims to promote democracy, facilitate international negotiations between member countries and support economic and social development. The Commonwealth plays a crucial role in policy, political, social and developmental aspects for member countries.

Under the ambit of economic objectives the Commonwealth seeks to promote economic development within member countries. Among its members only the United Kingdom, Canada, New Zealand and Australia are considered developed states with the rest still developing. The G20[1] is another eco-political alliance which was established in 1999 to coordinate economic policies and strengthen economic growth within member (developed and developing) countries. Similarly, the rationale for setting up the G15,[2] in 1989, was to promote cooperation among developing countries for mutual commercial and economic benefits. Hence, the economic role of these international eco-political alliances among nations in promoting development is an important one.

Political economists have also argued the case for free trade between member nations (Cameron, 2005) as these organizations are 'well-placed to provide support through collaborative actions....' (Milner, 2008, p. vii). Extending such arguments forward this study identifies the importance of these economic–political alliances in promoting FDI. We do this by investigating outward FDI though foreign acquisitions by Indian multinational enterprises (MNEs) within and outside such eco-political alliances of nations. For comparative purposes both South–South and North–South alliances are included, particularly the G15 as an example of South–South cooperation and the Commonwealth, and the G20 as an example of North–South cooperation.

India is a good test case for a number of reasons. First, India is an important and one of the fastest growing economies in the world. Second, Indian MNEs have made significant outward FDI through acquisitions in a cluster in some countries. Third, the recent spurt in the internationalization of Indian firms is expected to be related to its membership of the G20 and the Commonwealth. This could be the case because of existing close trade and economic relations with other member countries, preferential market access, and a high level of familiarity – cultural and economic – with some other Commonwealth countries.

The chapter is organized as follows: the next section provides the setting of the study by highlighting recent trends in the internationalization pattern of Indian

MNEs, in particular in member countries of the G20, G15 and Commonwealth. The following section reviews the role of country-specific linkages in the form of eco-political alliances[3] in the foreign expansion of MNEs. We then explain the methodology employed in this study and discuss the results. Finally, we conclude by drawing policy implications.

Acquisitions by Indian MNEs

Indian MNEs made some 841 acquisitions valued over US$50 billion during the period 2000–07 (see Table 5.1). Of these, about a quarter of acquisitions by number, and about one-sixth when measured in value terms, took place within the G15 countries. The share of the G20 is noteworthy, where about three-quarters of acquisitions by number, and about 80 per cent of their value was conducted. The share of the Commonwealth countries is also relatively high, accounting for 43 per cent of the total number of India's acquisitions abroad and 47 per cent of its value. All three groupings have seen India's share of their acquisitions increase since the turn of the century.

Economic–political alliances within the countries of the G20, Commonwealth and G15 not only attract firms embedded within these countries but also smooth their overseas market entry by bridging institutional and cultural distances. The next section examines the role of economic–political linkages in influencing these deals.

Country-specific linkages and MNEs

As cross-country linkages expand in the ever-globalizing world, so does the firm's geographical reach with its boundaries becoming more porous (Buckley, 2009). The increasing importance of MNEs linkages and alliances is described by Johanson and Mattson (1988) who suggest that alliances, networks and linkages can create internationalization capabilities as members within a network often provide complementary activities and cooperative cross-border relationships. Quite often linkages between firms are initiated as a result of the presence of linkages between countries where these firms are based.

Complementarity and cooperative behaviour at the macro level, where different forms of linkages among countries such as bilateral treaties and trade agreements

Table 5.1 Acquisitions by Indian MNEs in eco-political alliances, 2000–07

Country alliance	Number	Per cent (No.)	Value (in '000 USD)	Per cent (value)
CW	364	43.28	23,773	47.25
G20	642	76.33	40,645	80.79
G15	220	26.16	7,589	15.08
Total	841	100.00	50,307	100.00

Source: Author's compilations from TOB database.

may bring about common policies across countries, can encourage cooperative cross-border relationships among firms embedded in these countries. This can affect the motivations and internationalization strategies of indigenous firms (Murtha and Lenway, 1994).

We can identify five key benefits that cross-border acquisitions within an alliance of countries can offer the investing firm. These are: (i) a pool of attractive resources; (ii) the opportunity to exploit factor price differences; (iii) as a source of managerial and technical assistance; (iv) an opportunity for rapid learning; and (v) as a means for overcoming or minimizing the 'liability of foreignness' (Zaheer, 1995).

First, a group of countries can provide a pool of resources and market access to its member country firms. For example, if country 'A' is characterized by a large domestic market while country 'B' has production capabilities then firms from country 'B' may seek to serve the market in country 'A'. Similarly, if country 'C' is well endowed with natural or physical resources, the firm can incorporate such inputs in the production undertaken in country 'B'. From this perspective, within the Commonwealth and G15 countries, India and African member countries offer a vast market and the availability of cheap labour. Advanced countries within the G20 and the Commonwealth can attract firms seeking ownership advantages in technology, management skills, distribution networks and established brand names.

There are many international country-level forums which pool resources and markets, for example, the EU provides a vast common market to EU firms. Members of the G15 produce about a quarter of global crude oil output and may facilitate resource-seeking FDI among member countries (www.G15.org). Firms from the G20 countries may undertake market-seeking FDI in other member countries since members of the G20 account for about 90 per cent of global gross national product, 80 per cent of world trade (including EU intra-trade) and two-thirds of the world's population (www.G20.org). Thus, country-specific linkages can bring complementarities and synergies amongst member states and their firms.

A second way in which linkages between countries can positively influence internationalization of a firm's activities can be through the establishment of production facilities across borders to take advantage of factor price differences. This is called the 'factor-proportion hypothesis' (Samuelson, 1948). The rising importance of the 'Global Factory' (Buckley, 2009) is a reflection of the growing ease with which discrete value-adding tasks can be geographically separated but effectively managed using advanced information technology. Such task dispersal enables a more efficient distribution of activities and the exploitation of differences in factor price, quality and availability.

Within cross-country alliances such a 'Global Factory' configuration of MNEs is highly feasible. The MNE can allocate activities to different countries in the alliance to take advantage of factor price differences in different locations. For instance, cheap and ample labour supply characterizes a number of Asian member countries of the Commonwealth, including Bangladesh, Malaysia and India.

These countries have attracted labour-intensive MNE activities, whereas more knowledge-intensive activities are located in more advanced countries in the Commonwealth, specializing in 'knowledge hubs'. A recent example from India is Tata Motors' acquisition of Jaguar and Land Rover (JLR) from Ford Motors in the United Kingdom. Following the acquisition, manufacturing of labour-intensive parts of JLR has been transferred to India while the knowledge-intensive activities, such as design and research and development functions, have been retained within the United Kingdom.

Third, international groupings, particularly where member nations enjoy differing levels of economic and technical development, provide firms with opportunities for acquiring managerial and technical knowledge and raise production quantity, quality or facilitate innovation (Helpman and Krugman, 1985; Lall, 1980; UNCTC, 2001). There are different ways through which such knowledge can be sourced by firms embedded within alliances of nations, such as intra-alliance trade.

Knowledge or technical assistance through the import of intermediate or capital goods enables firms to produce at a lower cost while accessing foreign technology. These can contribute positively to the competitiveness of firms (Desai et al., 2005). Thus, knowledge sharing within networks has the ability to facilitate firms in their internationalization ventures (Dunning, 1997; Dunning and Boyd, 2003). This phenomenon has been particularly observed in the case of firms originating from non-TRIAD countries; these firms often seek access to knowledge resources to facilitate their internationalization process.

North–South trade among Commonwealth and the G20 nations could be noteworthy in this respect (Cameron, 2005; Milner, 2008). It is argued that many software firms from India have benefited from exposure to foreign knowledge and resources that they have accessed through outsourcing (Athreye, 2005; Elango and Pattnaik, 2007).

Fourth, cross-national linkages, often forged through trading relationships, also offer means for rapid learning facilitating foreign expansion by the member country MNE. Firms engaged in exporting are likely to make forward expansion by undertaking FDI for directly serving the market (Hatonen, 2009; Korhonen et al., 1996). FDI may be undertaken by importing firms for reasons such as securing the supply of inputs, lowering transaction costs or extending control over operations. Some early studies (Johanson and Mattson, 1988; Korhonen et al., 1996) recognized sourcing and importing, that is, supply side transactions of firms, as an important form of internationalization. Korhonen et al. (1996) found that more than half the Finnish MNEs that internationalized during the 1970s and 1980s did so through importing and sourcing. Intra-Commonwealth trade has grown in recent years and there is a considerable heterogeneity in terms of endowment differences across Commonwealth countries providing scope for trade expansion (Milner, 2008). Learning helps firms internalize operations by switching from exporting/importing to a FDI-based approach to internationalization (Buckley and Casson, 1976, 1985). Besides learning, the attractiveness of a foreign market can further motivate a firm's investment decision (Dunning, 1977, 1980) leading to a switch from export to FDI in the firm's foreign market servicing strategy. Thus, firms often invest in countries where exporting and importing relations already exist. Such trading experience helps the firm better understand the foreign market (Buckley and Pearce, 1979; Dunning, 1980).

The nature of economic–political alliances, with their broad political, social and developmental purposes provides other opportunities for rapid learning. The extent of political and cultural interactions as well as sporting and educational links means that market and cultural familiarity between members may be high. For instance, a distinctive feature of the Commonwealth in its early years was the transfer and imposition of institutional norms from Britain to member nations. Examples include the parliamentary political system in New Zealand, the civil service in India and the Singaporean legal system. The imposition of English language was also widespread.

Fifth, another way in which an economic–political alliance of nations could facilitate international acquisitions is through their ability to reduce the so-called liability of foreignness (Zaheer, 1995). The liability of foreignness describes the disadvantages that foreign firms experience when competing against local firms in overseas markets. Because indigenous firms enjoy greater familiarity with local business conditions through better understanding of consumers, political connections and relationships with competitors and suppliers and so on, foreign producers lack such familiarity and are at a competitive disadvantage (Miller and Richards, 2002; Zaheer, 1995). However, the literature recognizes that MNEs can use their ownership advantages to compensate for the disadvantages of foreignness (Zaheer and Mosakowski, 1997).

In the case of Indian MNEs venturing overseas we might expect their liability of foreignness to be high for at least two reasons. First, Indian MNEs may not possess significant firm-specific advantages. Their limited experience and levels of internationalization and their apparent desire to undertake outward FDI to acquire such advantages suggest that they may possess only limited compensating advantages. Second, the international business experience of Indian firms is not significant. High levels of protectionism characterized the Indian economy during the second half of the twentieth century. This limited opportunities for international expansion and exposure to international competitors. There is some evidence to suggest that the liability of foreignness is likely to be higher for firms with little international experience relative to more experienced firms (Petersen and Pedersen, 2002). For these reasons we would expect Indian MNEs to direct their international expansion efforts to countries where they are most familiar, have more experience or enjoy preferential access.

One important resource that Indian MNEs might utilize to reduce the liability of foreignness is the global presence of the Indian diaspora. The 'Overseas and Non-Resident Indian' (NRI) population is globally dispersed and estimated to total some 25 million. Only China has a larger diaspora. While migration from India has a considerable history, its characteristics are particularly pertinent to our study. A major wave of Indian migration occurred during the nineteenth century when poorly skilled workers migrated to other British colonies under the indenture system. Significant numbers settled in Fiji, Mauritius and East Africa, providing vital labour in tea plantations, for rubber extraction and sugar cane production. This early wave of outward migration ensured a strong Indian presence within the Commonwealth by the twentieth century. While a large number of NRI were displaced following Africa's independence during the 1960s, many resettled in more developed economies including those of the United States, the United Kingdom and Canada. More recently, the oil price boom in the 1970s attracted huge numbers of Indians to the Gulf countries and the Middle East. Many highly skilled Indians – mostly engineers and managers – migrated to the United States during the software boom and the period of strong economic growth in the United States during the 1990s (Commander et al., 2004).

The result of such a migration is a highly dispersed Indian diaspora present in many of the major economies of the world and strongly represented within the Commonwealth. NRI represent an excellent resource for Indian MNEs seeking overseas acquisitions (Enderwick et al., 2011).

Tapping into the knowledge and connections of migrants offers a number of potential benefits to home-based firms wishing to internationalize their operations. First, migrants can provide knowledge of trade, investment and acquisition opportunities – such knowledge can contribute to effective due diligence in the case of international acquisitions. Second, local knowledge can provide valuable insights into environmental understanding and adaptability to changing circumstances. This has the potential to contribute to effective decision-making with regard to the commercial feasibility of a target acquisition (Enderwick, 2011). Third, the pooling of knowledge drawn from a variety of sources can increase the force of decision-making as the volume of available information increases and its validity is subject to greater scrutiny.

Members of a diaspora can also assist country-of-origin firms through a reduction in transaction costs and liability of foreignness (Enderwick et al., 2011). Linkages can lower transactions costs through superior understanding of the local culture and increasing levels of trust between parties. Furthermore, involvement within an ethnic network can be useful in contract enforcement and dispute settlement given the value of reputational effects. Finally, overseas-based migrants can provide valuable insights into consumer behaviour and likely market developments. One direct way in which they affect demand is through so-called nostalgic trade, the demand for goods and services that have particular appeal to the immigrant population but which may 'cross-over' into the mainstream. The Mexican Corona beer brand in the United States is an example of such a product.

To summarize, bilateral agreements, free trade agreements and custom unions are positively associated with the volume of international trade and FDI flows (Gao, 2005; Raff, 2004). Similarly, economic–political linkages which are broader in scope such as the Commonwealth, the G20 and the G15 can also facilitate foreign expansion of firms. The formation of such linkages not only reduces tariff barriers and encourages preferential treatment and common policies for member states' firms which has a direct impact on the transaction cost for these firms, but also facilitates knowledge transfer, provides complementary resources, reduces factor prices, facilitates learning and reduces the liability of foreignness. As the economic theory of clubs (Buchanan, 1965), particularly when applied to alliances of nation states (Sandler, 1993) illustrates, such alliances enable nation states to achieve goals that are perhaps unattainable or too costly to achieve when acting independently. The development imperative of these economic–political alliances illustrates this principle. Thus, a firm's foreign expansion should be positively influenced by home country linkages with other alliance member countries.

Methodology

Data on foreign acquisitions by Indian firms were sourced from Thomson One Banker for the period January 2000 to December 2007. We selected the end of 2007 as a cutoff date to prevent the analysis being affected by the financial crisis which started shortly afterwards. Our data set reveals that Indian firms made 841 acquisitions of firms headquartered in 82 countries over the period. To perform the analysis at the country level we aggregated the acquisition data by country.

Our dependent variable is a firm's international expansion as measured by foreign acquisitions made by that firm. Since foreign acquisitions can be measured using both their number and their value, we used two dependent variables, each of which is explained by host country's membership of an international economic–political forum and the value of foreign trade between the home and the host country.

To test for the effects of country linkages on cross-border acquisitions we categorized country-level linkages into two categories: (i) trade linkages and (ii) non-trade linkages. Non-trade linkages are measured by a host country's membership of an international economic–political forum such as the G15, G20 and the Commonwealth. Non-trade linkages are further broken down into North–South linkages and South–South linkages. North–South linkages represent the connections between developed and developing economies and South–South linkages connections between developing countries only. For North–South linkages we considered the G20 and the Commonwealth, while South–South linkages were represented by membership of the G15. Trade linkages were measured by the home country's (i.e., India's) trade with other foreign countries (i.e., countries of the target firm).

We controlled for several (standard) host country-specific factors which encourage foreign expansion of a firm such as market size (MARKET) (measured by the GNIPC of the host economy), natural resource endowment (RESOURCE) (measured by the ratio of exports of ore and metals to merchandise exports), strategic assets and knowledge endowment of host economies (KNOWLEDGE) (measured by the number of patent applications), political risk (POLRISK) of the host county and openness of the host country (OPENNESS) (measured by the ratio of foreign trade to gross domestic product (GDP)). We further controlled for distance factors such as geographic distance between home and host country and cultural distance between home and host country. Distance factors are theoretically negatively related with the foreign expansion decision of a firm – the higher the distance the lower the level of FDI. Geographic distance (GEOGDIST) was measured by the distance between the capitals of the home and host countries. Cultural distance (CULTDIST) was measured using Kogut and Singh's (1988) cultural distance index between home and host countries. Political risk was measured using a weighted composite index made up of 12 different country-specific variables such as internal, external conflicts; religion, military in politics; socio-economic conditions; government stability; corruption, law and order; bureaucracy; and democratic accountability. The data for calculating political risk is collected from the International Country Risk Guide. The higher the index, the lower is the risk and vice versa.

Data for independent and control variables (GDP, GNIPC, ore and metal exports, patents and foreign trade) were sourced from the World Bank development indicators, while data for geographic distance were sourced from geobytes.com and data for cultural distance were obtained from geert-hofstede.com. Finally, our models can be expressed as follows:

(1) $\mathbf{Ln(MAValue_{it})} = \mathbf{a} + \mathbf{b}_1 \ (\mathbf{G15}) + \mathbf{b}_2 \ (\mathbf{G20}) + \mathbf{b}_3 \ (\mathbf{CW}) + \mathbf{b}_4 \ \mathbf{ln(FTRADE_{it})} + \mathbf{b}_5 \ \mathbf{ln(MARKET_{it})} + \mathbf{b}_6 \ \mathbf{ln(RESOURCE_{it})} + \mathbf{b}_7 \ \mathbf{ln(KNOWLEDGE_{it})} + \mathbf{b}_8 \ \mathbf{ln(OPENNESS_{it})} + \mathbf{b}_9 \ (\mathbf{POLRISK_{it}}) + \mathbf{b}_{10} \ (\mathbf{CULTDIST_{ij}}) + \mathbf{b}_{11} \ \mathbf{ln(GEOGDIST_{ij})}$

(2) $\mathbf{Ln(MANo_{it})} = \mathbf{a} + \mathbf{b}_1 \ (\mathbf{G15}) + \mathbf{b}_2 \ (\mathbf{G20}) + \mathbf{b}_3 \ (\mathbf{CW}) + \mathbf{b}_4 \ \mathbf{ln(FTRADE_{it})} + \mathbf{b}_5 \ \mathbf{ln(MARKET_{it})} + \mathbf{b}_6 \ \mathbf{ln(RESOURCE_{it})} + \mathbf{b}_7 \ \mathbf{ln(KNOWLEDGE_{it})} + \mathbf{b}_8 \ \mathbf{ln(OPENNESS_{it})} + \mathbf{b}_9 \ (\mathbf{POLRISK_{it}}) + \mathbf{b}_{10} \ (\mathbf{CULTDIST_{ij}}) + \mathbf{b}_{11} \ \mathbf{ln(GEOGDIST_{ij})}$

where i stands for host country; j for home country; and t for time. Thus, MAValue$_{it}$ refers to the value of an acquisition transaction in the ith country at time t, and MANo$_{it}$ refers to the number of acquisitions in the ith country at time t. MARKET$_{it}$ refers to market size of the ith country at time t. Similarly, RESOURCE$_{it}$ refers to natural resources in the ith country at time t, while CULTDIST$_{ij}$ refers to cultural distance between host and home country (India) and so on. We use a dummy variable for membership of the Commonwealth (equal to 1 if host country i is a member of the Commonwealth, 0 otherwise), G20 (equal to 1 for country i if country i is a member of the G20, 0 otherwise) and G15 (equal to 1 for country i if country i is member of the G15, 0 otherwise).

We matched the dependent variable (acquisitions in both numbers and value) by year by host countries to create a panel data set. As we expect a non-linear relationship among the variables, we transformed both the dependent and independent variables, excluding dummy variables, into natural logarithms and derived a log-log linear model. A log-log function enables the transformation of non-linear relationships between our dependent and independent variables into linear ones and measures FDI elasticity with respect to our set of explanatory variables (Crown, 1998).

We used Ordinary Least Squares (OLS) regression for estimations. Pooled estimation is preferred over panel data estimation since acquisitions do not take place every year. Our data set reveals that Indian firms have not made acquisitions each year in every host country. Thus, the panel data which accounts for both time series along different groups is not appropriate in our data settings. The alternative is OLS regression. Our results with OLS estimation were better than random effects with panel data estimation results.[4]

Findings and discussion

Our results, presented in Table 5.2 are robust and consistent across both number and value of foreign acquisitions, which includes tolerance and variance inflation factor (VIF) tests. VIF statistics above 10 and tolerance statistics below 0.10 indicate possible colinearity (Field, 2010). Statistics in Table 5.2 show that there is no colinearity problem. Descriptive statistics are included in Table 5.3. In the following section we discuss these results in detail.

Membership of the Commonwealth plays a significant role in attracting FDI by Indian MNEs and the same is true for the G20. Both the G20 and the Commonwealth are examples of North–South cooperation. On the other hand,

Table 5.2   Results

Variables	MANo.	MAVal.	VIF	1/VIF
South–South Country Alliance	0.657	0.262	1.75	0.571
(G15) (Alternative 1)	(0.766)	(0.838)		
North–South Country Alliance	1.281**	1.296*	1.14	0.874
(CW) (Alternative 2)	(0.619)	(0.677)		
North–South Country Alliance	1.879***	2.311***	1.39	0.716
(G20) (Alternative 3)	(0.622)	(0.681)		
Home–host Foreign Trade	0.149**	0.199***	1.68	0.593
(FTRADE)	(0.069)	(0.075)		
Host Market Size	0.11	0.13	1.52	0.659
(MARKET)	(0.096)	(0.105)		
Host Natural Resources	−0.002	−0.016	1.56	0.642
(RESOURCE)	(0.134)	(0.147)		
Host Knowledge Endowment	0.103**	0.108**	1.64	0.609
(KNOWLEDGE)	(0.042)	(0.046)		
Host Political Risk	0.756**	0.548	2.42	0.412
(POLRISK)	(0.307)	(0.336)		
Host Trade Openness	−0.307***	−0.32***	1.07	0.938
(OPEN)	(0.053)	(0.058)		
Cultural Distance	−0.86***	−0.787**	1.45	0.690
(CULTDIST)	(0.321)	(0.351)		
Geographic Distance	−0.821	−0.134	1.77	0.565
(GEOGDIST)	(0.531)	(0.581)		
Constant	−8.427***	−13.88***		
	(4.533)	(4.959)		
Observations	520	520		
R Square	20.84	20.4		
Root MSE	5.28	5.78		
F (11,508)	12.16***	11.83***		

Notes: *** Significant at 10 per cent; ** significant at 5 per cent; *significant at 1 per cent. Standard error in parentheses.

Table 5.3 Descriptive statistics

Variable	Mean	Std. dev.	Min	Max
MAValue	81.13838	709.7844	0	13,032.21
MANo	1.219649	4.441223	0	67
Host Market Size	16,098.05	12,845.36	520	53,320
Host Natural Resource	6.14055	12.02397	5.00E–03	84.7727
Host Knowledge Endowment	11,467.91	50,314.11	2	384,201
Host Political Risk	6.932125	1.181493	3.27	9.06
Host Trade Openness	77.83139	66.7175	19.35	462.46
Geographic Distance	4,129.1	2,382.777	422	10,526
Cultural Distance	1.567577	0.838708	0.33656	3.60789
South–South Country Alliance (G15)	0.1857143	0.389224	0	1
North–South Country Alliance (CW)	0.2142857	0.410693	0	1
North–South Country Alliance (G20)	0.2571429	0.43745	0	1
Home–host Foreign Trade	2.15E+09	4.22E+09	372503	3.90E+10

South–South linkages represented by the G15 are insignificant. Trade linkages were also significant – outward FDI by Indian companies follows trade.

The significance of the G20 and the Commonwealth shows that Indian MNEs' foreign expansion choices are strongly targeted towards these countries. FDI through acquisitions made by Indian MNEs can promote economic growth in these host economies. These results confirm the effectiveness of the G20 and the Commonwealth groupings in reducing trade and investment barriers and promoting private investment and cooperation with the aim of facilitating economic growth among member countries. Empirically it has been shown that FDI provides the much needed investment for growth of an economy (Balasubramanyam et al., 1999). However, it can be debated whether FDI through acquisition triggers the same developmental activity as that triggered by greenfield investment. We argue that acquisitions provide liquidity to the shareholders of the acquired firms which can be used to finance further expansion. In addition, changes in the management structure of the acquired firm can make the firm more efficient.

The Commonwealth has diverse goals including the resolution of conflict, the strengthening of democratic practices, achieving respect for human rights, while developing national capacity through economic growth, public-sector development, environmental and human development. The G20 seeks to coordinate economic policies and promote a sound economic environment for the growth of member states. All of these provide a better operating environment for MNEs and can indirectly promote foreign investment in member countries.

Since the G20 and Commonwealth are examples of North–South cooperation, many technological assets which are not found in developing member countries can be accessed from more advanced member countries, contributing to development. The significance of the control variable (Knowledge) supports the role of knowledge and importance of strategic assets which Indian MNEs seek to access through foreign acquisition.

While a number of G20 and Commonwealth countries (Canada, Australia and some African member countries) are well endowed in natural resources, our natural resource endowment control variable is insignificant. This insignificance might be explained by the characteristics of the Indian economy which is largely a service-based economy with services accounting for 55 per cent of GDP. Furthermore, merchandise exports account for only a small share (15 per cent) of total Indian exports (CIA, 2010).

South–South cooperation, represented here by the G15 grouping, offers surprising results. India was instrumental in the formation of the G15 and in the non-alignment movement which was the foundation of the G15. However, insignificance of the G15 variable suggests that structural changes within the Indian economy have led to a change in policy emphasis with greater weight being given to the services sector. To be competitive in the world economy Indian MNEs require knowledge and strategic assets and South–South cooperation no longer enables the acquisition of such assets to facilitate firms' foreign expansion. In essence, Indian MNEs are looking at developed countries to secure access to foreign technology, know-how and markets not available at home.

The concentration of acquisitions within the United Kingdom, Australia, Singapore and Canada indicates a bias towards developed countries, which could be due to the motivation behind such acquisitions – knowledge-, market- and natural-resources-seeking – a feature of India's FDI that has also been well documented in the literature (Balasubramanyam and Forsans, 2010; Pradhan, 2007). We also examined India's foreign trade linkages between home and host countries, and these were found to be significant. Exporting and importing are usually the initial steps in the internationalization process (Hatonen, 2009; Johanson and Wiedersheim, 1975; Johanson and Vahlne, 1977; Korhonen et al., 1996). Therefore countries with significant trade linkages may be seen as the first foreign destination for Indian firms that ventures overseas. This result is consistent with a desire both to reduce the liability of foreignness and to facilitate knowledge building for internationalization. It also confirms the trade-supporting nature of India's overseas investments.

Our control variable market size of the host country is insignificant. This suggests that generally Indian acquisitions are not market-seeking in nature. However, we expect that a further examination through split sample analysis, where countries with big market size are clustered separately, may reveal foreign acquisitions for market-seeking motives. This can be a guide for future research. Cultural distance between home and host countries is significant with negative sign. This is in line with theoretical explanations that culturally distant countries do not attract FDI. However, our other control variable, geographic distances between host and home countries, is not significant. Our explanation is that India is a special case. The South Asia region is economically least integrated in the world (Foreign and Commonwealth Office, 2007) and this makes the geographic distance insignificant in our study. Another control variable – political risk – is partially significant with positive sign. Higher political risk ranking (i.e., lower risk) positively affects FDI by Indian MNEs. This confirms the general perception that MNEs prefer to operate in low-risk environments (Harms, 2002).

Economic openness is significant with the negative sign. Economic openness was measured through trade openness. The negative sign suggests that the more trade openness of an economy, the less attractive it may be for an acquisition. A more open economy may be better served through exporting and may not require FDI (Asiedu, 2002).

Conclusion

This chapter has modelled the influences of membership of international forums on the FDI-based strategy of firms. Taking the case of foreign acquisitions by Indian firms (by number and value) over the period 2000 to 2007, it finds that conventional South–South linkages such as the G15 are not significant for Indian MNEs in their foreign expansion. However, North–South linkages represented by groups such as the G20 and the Commonwealth are significant.

The significance of the G20 and Commonwealth member countries in the foreign acquisition decisions of Indian MNEs demonstrates the appeal of such groupings for foreign investment. The attraction of the G20 and the Common-wealth occurs through efforts to reduce trade and investment barriers, develop national capacity through economic development and promote private invest-ments and cooperation among member countries. Efforts on other fronts within the Commonwealth such as resolving conflicts, strengthening democratic prac-tices and the rule of law, human rights, public-sector development, environment and human development are also noteworthy. Since these actions contribute to a better operating environment for MNEs, they can indirectly promote foreign investment between member countries. We have also identified a number of ways in which cross-national alliances impact on the risk and transactions costs of MNEs. Our results highlight that the attraction pool of resources (particularly knowledge-based assets), opportunities for learning and the ability to reduce the liability of foreignness through economic–political linkages between countries facilitates FDI by Indian investing firms.

Our results suggest that the key attraction for Indian MNEs acquiring overseas operations is the availability of knowledge and strategic assets. It is interest-ing to note that while there are many large and technologically advanced non-Commonwealth and non-G20 economies, the economic benefits of 'club membership' appear to be influencing the choice of specific target markets. As expected, given the structure of the Indian economy and the strengths of its MNEs, natural resources were not important in the international expansion of Indian firms.

The poor performance of the South–South linkages is explained by the shift in India's economic structure, preference for foreign partners and the necessity for Indian firms to pursue acquisitions in rich countries where the larger markets and the greatest concentration of intangible assets are to be found.

The openness of the host economy to trade also proved to be an important determinant of acquisition by Indian MNEs. Geographic distance variables do not perform with any degree of significance and do not seem to be factors in Indian MNE's foreign acquisition decisions. This may be due to the fact that South Asia is the least economically integrated area in the world economy (Foreign and Commonwealth Office, 2007) and it is also not a region that supplies technological assets needed by Indian MNEs through acquisitions.

The major contribution of the chapter lies in unveiling the concealed importance of the economic–political alliances of nations in the foreign expansion strategies of member country MNEs. In particular this chapter finds that country-specific linkages are important determinants of foreign investment behaviour. Linkage variables need to be used with discretion however. It is North–South links that are significant here; concentration on South–South links is not successful. Linkage variables require an understanding of the nature, structure and motives of FDI in order to be useful. This study is part of a larger project on the foreign expansion of Indian MNEs. Therefore the study did not look in detail at the intra-FDI flows among member states and their policies on FDI. This could be a research agenda for future work. Further research to test the robustness of these results would be useful. It would also be interesting to examine the determinants of outward investment by both developed and developing countries within such economic–political alliances and to explore in more detail the precise benefits that investors perceive when investing within such cross-national forums.

Notes

1. The G20 is a group of finance ministers and central bank governors for discussing key issues in the global economy and cooperating between the members from both industrialized and emerging economies for their growth and development. India and other emerging countries are given importance in the G20 because of their rising role in global development. The G20 holds high degree of influence and legitimacy in the global economy as it accounts for 90 per cent of global GNP and 80 per cent of world trade. It is important to note that the G20 wants to help member countries to cope with the reversal of the international capital flows, especially in the present global financial crisis. Although the observation of data suggests that Indian MNEs are making acquisitions in industrialized and emerging economies, the question is, is there any significant association of these acquisitions in the G20.
2. The G15 is actually a group of 17 developing countries from Asia, Africa and Latin America. The rationale for setting up the G15 was the feeling that there was considerable scope for cooperation among the developing countries for mutual commercial and economic benefits, especially over the medium and long term. Thus, the very nature of the group is 'South–South cooperation' with India as one of the leading member.
3. In this chapter country-specific linkages and economic–political alliances among county are used interchangeably.
4. Alternate results using panel data random effect are available upon request to authors.

References

E. Asiedu, 'On determinants of foreign direct investments to developing countries: Is Africa different?', *World Development*, 30(11) (2002) 107–19.

S. S. Athreye, 'The Indian software industry and its evolving service capability', *Industrial and Corporate Change*, 14(3) (2005) 393–418.

V. N. Balasubramanyam and N. Forsans, 'Internationalisation drivers of Indian multinational firms', *Asian Business & Management*, 9(3) (2010) 319–40.

V. N. Balasubramanyam, M. Salisu and D. Sapsford, 'Foreign direct investment as an engine of growth', *Journal of International Trade and Economic Development*, 8(1) (1999) 27–40.

J. Buchanan, 'An economic theory of clubs', *Economica*, 32(125) (1965) 1–14.

P. J. Buckley, 'The impact of the global factory on economic development', *Journal of World Business*, 44(2) (2009) 131–43.

P. J. Buckley and M. Casson, *The Future of the Multinational Enterprise*, (London: Macmillan, 1976).

P. J. Buckley and M. Casson, *The Economic Theory of the Multinational Enterprise*, (London: Macmillan, 1985).

P. J. Buckley and R. D. Pearce, 'Overseas production and exporting by the world's largest enterprises: a study in sourcing policy', *Journal of International Business Studies*, 10(1) (1979) 1–20.

P. J. Buckley, J. Clegg, N. Forsans and K. T. Reilly, 'Evolution of FDI in the United States in the context of trade liberalisation and regionalisation', *Journal of Business Research*, 56(10) (2003) 853–57.

B. Cameron, *The Case for Commonwealth Free Trade*, (London: Trafford, 2005).

S. Commander, R. Chanda, M. Kangasniemi and L. A. Winters, *Must Skilled Migration Be Brain Drain? Evidence from the Indian Software Industry*, (Institute for the Study of Labour, Discussion Paper IZA DP No. 1422, 2004), pp. 1–32.

CIA, *The World Fact Book*, (Washington, DC: Central Intelligence Agency, 2010).

W. H. Crown, *Statistical Models for the Social and Behavioural Sciences: Multiple Regression and Limited-Dependent Variable Models*, (Westport, CT: Praeger, 1998).

A. Desai Mihir, C. F. Foley and J. R. Hines, 'FDI and the domestic capital stock, international intrafirm production decisions', *American Economic Review*, 95(2) (2005) 33–8.

J. H. Dunning, 'Trade, Location of Economic Activity and the MNE: A Search for an Eclectic Approach', in B. Ohlin, P.-O. Hesselborn and P. Wijkman (eds), *The International Allocation of Economic Activity*, (London: Macmillan, 1977), pp. 395–418.

J. H. Dunning, 'Towards an eclectic theory of international production: some empirical tests', *Journal of International Business Studies*, 11(1) (1980) 9–31.

J. H. Dunning and G. Boyd (eds), *Alliance Capitalism and Corporate Management*, (Cheltenham and Northampton, MA: Edward Elgar, 2003).

B. Elango and C. Pattnaik, 'Building capabilities for international operations through networks: a study of Indian firms', *Journal of International Business Studies*, 38(4) (2007) 541–55.

P. Enderwick, 'Acquiring overseas market knowledge: a comparison of strategies of expatriate and immigrant employees', *Journal of Asia Business Studies*, 5(1) (2011) 77–97.

P. Enderwick, R. L. Tung and H. F. L. Chung, 'Immigrant effects and international business activity: an overview', *Journal of Asia Business Studies*, 5(1) (2011) 6–22.

A. Field, *Discovering Statistics Using SPSS*, (London: Sage Publications Ltd, 2010).

Foreign and Commonwealth Office, *Fourth Report of the Foreign Affairs Committee Session 2006–07: South Asia Response of the Secretary of State for Foreign and Commonwealth Affairs*, (UK, 2007).

T. Gao, 'Foreign direct investment and growth under economic integration', *Journal of International Economics*, 6(1) (2005) 157–74.

P. Harms, 'Do civil and political repression really boost foreign direct investments?', *Economic Inquiry*, 40(4) (2002) 651–63.

J. Hatonen, 'Making the locational choice: a case approach to the development of a theory of offshore outsourcing and internationalisation', *Journal of International Management*, 15(1) (2009) 61–76.

E. Helpman and P. Krugman, *Market Structure and Foreign Trade*, (Boston, MA: MIT Press, 1985).

J. Johanson and L.-G. Mattson, 'Internationalisation in Industrial Systems – Network Approach', in N. Hood and J. E. Vahlne (eds), *Strategies in Global Competition*, (London: Croom Helm, 1988), pp. 303–21.

J. Johanson and J. E. Vahlne, 'The internationalisation process of the firm – a model of knowledge development and increasing foreign market commitments', *Journal of International Business Studies*, 8(1) (1977) 23–32.

J. Johanson and P. F. Wiedersheim, 'The internationalisation of the firm – four Swedish cases', *Journal of Management Studies*, 12(3) (1975) 205–322.

B. Kogut and H. Singh, 'The effect of national culture on the choice of entry mode', *Journal of International Business Studies*, 19(3) (1988) 411–32.

H. Korhonen, R. Luostarinen and L. Welch, 'Internationalisation of SMEs: inward–outward patterns and government policy', *Management International Review*, 36(4) (1996) 315–29.

S. Lall, 'Vertical inter-firm linkages in LDCs: an empirical study', *Oxford Bulletin of Economics and Statistics*, 42(3) (1980) 203–06.

D. Medvedev, *Beyond Trade: the Impact of Preferential Trade Agreements on Foreign Direct Investment Inflows*, World Bank Working Paper, WPS 4065, (Washington, DC: The World Bank, 2006).

S. R. Miller and M. Richards, 'Liability of foreignness and membership in a regional economic group: an analysis of the European Union', *Journal of International Management*, 8(3) (2002) 323–37.

C. Milner, *Trading on Commonwealth Ties: A Review of the Structure of Commonwealth Trade and the Scope for Developing Linkages and Trade in the Commonwealth*, (London: Commonwealth Secretariat, 2008).

M. Motta and G. Norman, 'Does economic integration cause foreign direct investment?', *International Economic Review*, 37(4) (1996) 757–83.

T. P. Murtha and S. A. Lenway, 'Country capabilities and the strategic state: how national political institutions affect multinational corporations' strategies', *Strategic Management Journal*, 15(S2) (1994) 113–29.

M. Olsen and R. Zeckhauser, 'An economic theory of alliances', *Review of Economics and Statistics*, 48 (1966) 266–79.

B. Petersen and T. Pedersen, 'Coping with liability of foreignness: different learning engagements of entrant firms', *Journal of International Management*, 8(3) (2002) 339–50.

J. P. Pradhan, 'Trend and patterns of overseas acquisitions by Indian multinationals', *Institute for Studies in Industrial Development*, Working Paper 2007/10, (2007) 1–42.

H. Raff, 'Preferential trade agreements and tax competition for foreign direct investment', *Journal of Public Economics*, 88(12) (2004) 2745–63.

P. A. Samuelson, 'International trade and equalization of factor prices', *The Economics Journal*, 58(230) (1948) 163–84.

T. Sandler, 'The economic theory of alliances: a survey', *Journal of Conflict Resolution*, 37(3) (1993) 446–83.

Y. Shi and M. Gregory, 'International manufacturing networks – to develop global competitive capabilities', *Journal of Operations Management*, 16(2/3) (1998) 195–214.

UNCTC, *World Investment Report 2001: Promoting Linkages*, (New York and Geneva: United Nations, 2001).

S. Zaheer, 'Overcoming the liability of foreignness', *Academy of Management Journal*, 38(2) (1995) 341–63.

S. Zaheer and E. Mosakowski, 'The dynamics of the liability of foreignness: a global study of survival in financial services', *Strategic Management Journal*, 18(6) (1997) 439–64.

6

A Critical Review of Hidden Champions and Emerging Research Findings on Their International Strategies and Orientations

Alessa Witt and Chris Carr

Introduction

In contrast to the extensive reviews on global strategies particularly appropriate to large enterprises (Chng and Pangarkar, 2000; Peng and Pleggenkuhle-Miles, 2009), there is a dearth of literature that comprehensively reviews more niche-orientated global strategies appropriate to small and medium-sized enterprises (SMEs). Peng and Meyer (2011, p. 440) also agree that 'international business is often presented as primarily a matter of big MNEs competitive markets, especially in American textbooks'. They themselves respond to this and recognize further global strategy variants more appropriate for medium-sized companies based essentially on some form of focusing. They highlight in particular niche strategy variants such as 'globalfocusing' and 'Hidden Champions'. Reviews have mainly focused on niche players characterized by exceptional accelerated internationalization such as 'born globals',[1] (Knight and Cavusgil, 1996; Korot and Tovstiga, 1999; McKinsey and Co., 1993; Oviatt and McDougall, 1997; Rennie, 1993), and also 'born-again globals' (Bell et al., 2001).

Oviatt and McDougall (1997) argue for further research on firms exhibiting accelerated internationalization. This chapter therefore highlights, in line with Peng and Meyer (2011), Simon's (2009) niche-orientated global (or regional) players, referred to as 'Hidden Champions' (HCs). These companies achieve top three global market positions, or regional dominance, whilst staying remarkably focused and proactive, often in obscure niche sectors, such that their revenues remain below US$4 billion (Simon, 2009).

Despite their outstanding performance, there is still very little clarification on HCs' exact internationalization behaviour (Ernst and Young, 2004; Eschlbeck, 2005; Simon, 2009; Venohr and Meyer, 2007). For example, when do HCs pursue a born global internationalization, as compared to the traditional Uppsala Model?

This chapter is laid out as follows. It begins with a comprehensive literature review of traditional internationalization theory, born global firms and HCs. From this literature review, we propose our methodology and a more specific research proposition on the internationalization strategies of HCs. This is then followed by our exploratory findings. Finally, we propose an emerging research agenda on HCs, including a more institutionally based methodology, questioning the embeddedness of the HCs' theoretical performance model in the German context and culture.

Literature review

Simon (1996, 2007a, 2009) claims to have identified companies that have found a manner of going global that is particularly successful. Arguably, he has failed to completely address the full extent of our more recent knowledge of international entry modes and orientations in the literature in these areas. This section highlights the extent to which research needs to establish the exact link between strategy orientations and HCs. Before addressing the complex debates regarding the orientation of HCs, it is necessary that the reader be aware of the basic internationalization approaches.

Uppsala Model

The Uppsala Model describes an incremental internationalization process. Thereby, firms gradually internationalize in foreign markets through increasing market knowledge and market commitment (Johanson and Vahlne, 1977; Johanson and Wiedersheim-Paul, 1975). Well-established firms incrementally commit to greater resources, leading to entries into geographically further located markets (Leonidou and Katsikeas, 1996). Often referred to as the stage model, it argues that firms follow through four incremental stages of internationalization: regular exports, followed by exports through sales agents, eventually leading to a sales subsidiary and finally the establishment of an overseas production plant (Johanson and Vahlne, 1977).

Critics argue that the Uppsala Model is too deterministic and of limited value (Fina and Rugman, 1996), and simplifies the complex process of internationalization (Dichtl et al., 1984). It ignores any other forms of market entry modes such as acquisitions (Forsgren, 1990), strategic alliances and joint ventures, which 'are much more prevalent' (Madsen and Servais, 1997, p. 573).

Born globals

Traditional stage theory, despite technological, social and economic changes, is challenged by recent studies on the born global phenomenon (McDougall et al., 1994). In fact, Cavusgil (1994, p. 18) argues that 'gradual internationalization is dead'. Born globals are characterized by their accelerated internationalization behaviour at or near inception (Knight and Cavusgil, 1996; Madsen and Servais, 1997; McDougall et al., 1994b; Oviatt and McDougall, 1994, 1997; Rialp et al., 2005), whilst others argue born globals internationalize during the first three years of establishment (Knight et al., 2004). Although born globals are usually resource-constrained businesses, studies indicate that they are risk-averse, as they export soon after inception (Bell and McNaughton, 2000; Oviatt and

McDougall, 1994, 1997; Rennie, 1993). Amongst other reasons, they pursue a more accelerated internationalization as they rely on entrepreneurial skills and international networks (Gabrielsson et al., 2010; Knight, 2000).

Primarily, born globals rapidly internationalize to exploit first mover advantages (Bell and McNaughton, 2000) and to attain growth through international sales in niche markets (Knight and Cavusgil, 1996). They are independent firms and often high-technology start-ups (Jolly et al., 1992). Frequently, born globals are found in knowledge-intensive industries, offering innovative and specialized products with unique know-how and distinct features (Oviatt and McDougall, 1994, 1997). Their products often require additional and unique customer service, which encourages born globals to follow their customers into foreign markets (Gabrielsson et al., 2010).

Born globals rapid international expansion is more hybridized, as they simultaneously use multiple entry modes (Jolly et al., 1992; Madsen and Servais, 1997; McDougall et al., 1994; Oviatt and McDougall, 1997). This allows them to be far more flexible in their market entry choices, as compared to larger enterprises (Andersson and Wictor, 2003; Bell et al., 2001; Sharma and Blomstermo, 2003; Welch and Luostarinen, 1988). Common market entry modes include direct export, export via independent representatives, establishment of local sales subsidiaries and establishment of local manufacturing subsidiaries (Melén and Nordman, 2009).

Research on fast internationalizing firms seems to be far ahead of theoretical explanations (Rialp et al., 2005, p. 136; Weerawardena et al., 2007). More research should effectively focus on theoretical developments, time dimensions, continuous accelerated internationalization behaviour (Zahra, 2005) and their exact market entry modes.

Hidden champions

Simon (1992a, 1992b, 1996a, 1996b, 2007a, 2009) identified more globally orientated niche firms from Germany, which he terms 'Hidden Champions'. HCs are characterized as reaching at least global top three positions, or complete regional dominance, whilst keeping a low profile so that their revenues stay below US$4 billion (Simon, 2009).[2]

HCs are considered global niche players in their respective fields, targeting tightly defined niche markets and aiming for market leadership through continuous specialization (Meyer, 2009; Peng and Meyer, 2011). Unlike other niche players (Abell and Hammond, 1979; Buzzell and Gale, 1987; Leontiades, 1986), HCs aim for big market shares and view the entire world as their market (Simon, 2009).

These exceptionally successful midsize companies are often family-owned businesses, of which 32 per cent were established over 100 years ago (Simon, 2007a). In 2009 they had an export ratio of 61.5 per cent and on average export goods worth US$275 million (Simon, 2009). Thus, HCs are highly informed with 'an excellent intuitive understanding of their market – even in the absence of precise data' (Simon, 2009, p. 86). In fact, HCs reach quasi-monopolistic positions with global market shares between 70 and 100 per cent and 'relative market shares of

Table 6.1   Term 'Hidden Champions' combed in a systematic journal research

Author	HCs findings	Journal
Simon (1992a)	First study on German HCs	*Harvard Business Review*
Simon (1996a)	HCs identified in foreign countries	*Business Strategy Review*
Simon (1992b)	Service policies of German manufacturers (including HCs)	*European Management Journal*
Markides (2001)	Mentions Simon's (1996a) study as an example	*Business Strategy Review*
Meyer (2006)	'Globalfocusing', HCs theoretical model as an example for Danish firms	*Journal of Management Studies*
Eisenhardt (2008)	Mentions Simon's (1996a) study as an example	*Business Strategy Review*
Venohr and Meyer (2009)	Long-term study on HCs manufacturing companies	*Business Strategy Review*
Likiermann (2009)	Mentions Simon's (1996a) study as an example	*Business Strategy Review*
Meyer (2009)	'Globalfocusing' mentioning HCs as a successful global niche strategy variant	*Strategic Change*

2 to 4... in markets with a volume of US$1 billion to US$5 billion' (Kroeger et al., 2008, p. 9).

Our thorough systematic journal research scanned 14 key journals during 2004–2010[3] for the term 'Hidden Champions', including *Harvard Business Review, European Management Journal, Business Strategy Review, Strategic Change*, and the *Journal of Management Studies* (Table 6.1).

We further covered international literature, including German-speaking studies, which have paid enormous attention to the HCs phenomenon (Blackburn et al., 2001; Jungwirth, 2010; Kotler and Caslione, 2009; Kotler and Keller, 2006; Peng and Meyer, 2011; Voudouris et al., 2000; Yu and Chen, 2009). Results and research themes are presented in Table 6.2.

Numerous researchers referred to the significance of Simon's study, using HCs as an example of successful niche players (Behr and Semlinger, 2004; Friedrich, 2007; Gutmann and Kabst, 2000; Hooley et al., 2008; Mathews, 2006; Parker, 2005; Rasche, 2003), and as examples of the German Mittelstand[4] firms (Berghoff, 2006; Lawrence and Edwards, 2000).

The term 'niche strategy' forms the nearest term to HCs and has been systematically combed in academic journals.[5] We found 12 articles in the *Strategic Management Journal*, focusing on various topics, but only addressed the term 'niche strategies' in that context (see Appendix Table A.1). These articles have been published during 1983 until 2002, but there are no recent articles in these journals. This indicates that the subject on niche strategies and HCs have not been comprehensively addressed in the academic literature.

Table 6.2 Analysis of 14 major key independent studies reported on HCs

Selected study	Country	Main findings	Methodology
Simon (1996a)	Germany	Identified the first 457 HCs with own criteria. First development of the HCs model with nine key lessons (1) string leadership (2) ambitious goals (3) reliance on own strength (4) selected and motivated employees (5) continuous innovation (6) narrow market focus (7) competitive advantage (8) closeness to customer (9) global orientation.	Qualitative/ quantitative
Voudouris et al. (2000)	Greece	Identified 20 Greek HCs through own criteria. Suggested a new HCs model (1) intense specialization (2) commitment to customer service and quality (3) innovation (4) strong leadership and a healthy organizational climate.	Qualitative
Blackburn et al. (2000)	Canada	Identified three Canadian HCs through Simon's (1996a) definition. A new HCs model is suggested (1) customer (2) value propositions (3) strategic drivers (4) global visions.	Qualitative
Deng and Wan (2006)	China	Identify 80 firms that are classed as HCs. They summarize the main characteristics of Chinese HCs (1) clear goal (2) focus strategy (3) excellent entrepreneurs.	Not specified
Meyer (2006)	Denmark	Longitudinal study on two Danish firms transformed towards Simon's HCs model of global specialists.	Qualitative
Simon and Lippert (2007b)	Japan	Identified ten Japanese HCs. They suggests that the main difference of Japanese HCs is their strong focus on their home country and they have less turnover in foreign markets compared to German HCs.	Qualitative
Adenäuer (2007)	Germany	Tested the nine hypotheses derived from the HCs model on successful and less successful firms.	Quantitative
Simon (2009)	Germany, Austria, Switzerland	Identified German 1174 HCs (61 from Austria and 81 from Switzerland). Alterations of his HCs model to eight lessons (1) leadership with ambitious goals; (2) decentralization; (3) high-performance employees; (4) depth; (5) focus; (6) closeness to customer; (7) innovation; (8) globalization.	Qualitative/ quantitative

Table 6.2 (Continued)

Selected study	Country	Main findings	Methodology
Ding (2008)	Canada	Identifies two main determinants of Japanese HCs – (1) special disposition of entrepreneurs (2) – that moderate management accounting.	Not specified
Simon and Zatta (2008)	India	Identified five Indian HCs which fulfilled the 'five-pillar strategy' (a pre-requisite to become a HCs): (1) the will to excel; (2) clear and focused strategy; (3) globalization; (4) value orientation; (5) systematic value extraction.	Not specified
Venohr and Meyer (2009)	Germany	Longitudinal study of HCs. Figures on internationalization (foreign sales subsidiaries, manufacturing subsidiaries, internationals sales and distribution networks of German HCs)	Quantitative
Yu and Chen (2009)	China	Identified four Chinese HCs through Simon's (1996a) criteria. New HCs model suggesting six main success factors of Chinese HCs: (1) goal; (2) innovation; (3) entrepreneur; (4) focus; (5) globalization; (6) customer.	Qualitative
Witt (2010)	Germany	Internationalization strategy, market entry modes, and timing strategies of HCs. Comparison to internationalization theory.	Quantitative
Jungwirth (2010)	Austria	Studied 84 Austrian HCs and their marketing strategies identified using similar criteria to Simon.	Quantitative

Limited research has yet focused on the exact internationalization behaviour and associated entry modes of HCs (Table 6.3) and, arguably, Simon fails to fully address their internationalization in his studies and the extent of our knowledge in literature in these areas. Simon's (2009) findings merely suggest that the majority prefer entering markets via fully controlled subsidiaries and abnegate partnerships, especially for sales, service and manufacturing. Lawrence and Edwards (2000) argue that HCs use old-fashioned entry modes, but Simon (2009) suggests they increasingly make use of strategic alliances with companies targeting similar customers, and the concept of outsourcing to save costs and to maintain qualitative superiority, but only for non-core activities.

Research questions

The literature review allows a direct comparison of traditional internationalizers, born globals and HCs (Table 6.4), and presents several knowledge gaps, yet

Table 6.3 Analysis of five major key independent studies reported on the internationalization behaviour and entry modes of HCs

Selected study	Main finings	Methodology
Lawrence and Edwards (2000)	HCs are 'old fashioned'. They make no use of subcontracting, outsourcing, make or buy decisions, diversification, export agents, and strategic alliances.	Qualitative
Ernst and Young (2004)	HCs will include mergers and acquisitions as future strategy options.	Quantitative
Eschlbeck (2005)	HCs internationalize according to traditional stage theory.	Not specified
Venohr and Meyer (2007)	HCs have significant manufacturing presence in China and Eastern Europe. HCs prefer green-field sites as an entry mode.	Quantitative
Simon (2009)	74.4 per cent use exports. 77.1 per cent enter via fully owned and controlled subsidiary. On average HCs own 24 subsidiaries abroad. On average HCs own 8 manufacturing subsidiaries abroad. On average HCs own 16 sales and service organizations abroad. 16.8 per cent engage in joint ventures. HCs cooperate with existing firms targeting the same customer. HCs outsource non-core activities to save costs and to maintain qualitative superiority.	Qualitative

to be resolved. From this we propose two more specific questions on the HCs' internationalization behaviour and associated entry modes.

There is no empirical evidence on the HCs' internationalization process and therefore we argue in line with Eschlbeck's (2005) assumption that HCs follow traditional stage theory. We expect to find some HCs following a more incremental approach to internationalization, but differentiate from traditional internationalizers through their global or regional market leadership, thus leading to the following proposition.

Proposition 6.1 Some Hidden Champions might follow the Uppsala Model but differentiate from traditional internationalizers being Number 1, 2 or 3 globally or the European Number 1.

However, new literature is showing the very important role played by internationalization variants such as born globals (Madsen and Servais, 1997; McDougall et al., 1994; Oviatt and McDougall, 1994, 1997; Rennie, 1993), as to traditional stage theory (Johanson and Vahlne, 1977). Given HCs' niche strategy orientation, we predict to find some HCs pursuing accelerated internationalization, as

Table 6.4 Analysis and direct comparison of traditional internationalizers, born globals and HCs

	Traditional internationalizers	Born globals	Hidden champions
Triggers of internationalization	Experiential market knowledge, competitive advantage, economic conditions.	Small domestic market, network relationships, short product life cycle (PLC), competition, resources and capabilities, new more global strategic orientation.	Small domestic market, aim to reach new markets, high demand in foreign market, following the customer, expansion, competition, chance.
Learning to internationalize	At a pace governed by the ability to learn from (slowly) accumulated experience.	Learning occurs more rapidly because superior internationalization knowledge.	Limited evidence suggests more incremental internationalization, but learning occurs rapidly.
Market selection	Enter domestic market first, followed by incremental market entry into psychically close markets and gradually entering more distant markets.	Psychic distance irrelevant.	Enter both physically close and distant markets.
Extent of internationalization	International markets developed serially.	Many international markets developed at the same time.	Prefer mixture between simultaneous and incremental market entry.
Firm strategy	Not central to the firm's motivation to internationalize.	Realization of competitive advantage requires rapid, full internationalization; product market scope is focused niche.	Realization of competitive advantage requires rapid, full internationalization; product market scope is focused niche.
Home market	Domestic market developed first.	Domestic market largely irrelevant.	Domestic market largely irrelevant.
Entry modes	First entry with exports followed by entry modes with higher commitment (sales subsidiaries).	Direct export, licensing and franchising. Low commitment followed by foreign partnerships. Strategic alliances, joint ventures and subsidiaries.	Prefer export and wholly owned subsidiaries and abnegate partnerships such as joint ventures. Licensing, manufacturing and distribution companies.
Pace of internationalization	Slow and gradual internationalization	Rapid and accelerated internationalization soon after inception.	Limited evidence; but some use both gradual and rapid internationalization.
Time to internationalize	Not crucial to firms success; slow internationalize	Crucial for firm's success within a few years of inception.	Limited evidence; after inception but also at later point in time.

Source: Adapted from Chetty and Campbell-Hunt (2004).

numerous HCs internationalize soon after inception (Simon, 2009). Therefore we need clarification on when HCs pursue a born global internationalization strategy as compared to traditional internationalization.

Proposition 6.2   More recently established Hidden Champions might have a global orientation from the outset, and therefore might follow a more born global internationalization approach but differ being Number 1, 2 or 3 globally or the European Number 1.

If some HCs prove to be born globals, they are indeed very special cases. Unlike other born globals written about in literature, we know that HCs are characterized by remarkable competitive advantage and by performance in international markets in terms of actual achieved market shares.

Methodology

To fulfil the purpose of this study, and identify the exact internationalization behaviour and entry modes of German HCs, we used a methodology, consistent with other studies in this field (Crick and Spence, 2005; McDougall et al., 1994). In order to collect the data, a set of 12 specific questions was sent via email in 2008 to 143 HCs in Germany. The sample was drawn from Simon's (2009) study, of which the majority operates in the engineering industry. Of 143 HCs emailed we received 26 responses; given the sensitivity and confidentiality of this subject. Considering the rather small sample, this data should be considered as a preliminary investigation.

Our research included questions about company information and details.[6] This was followed by questions on HCs' internationalization behaviour and associated entry modes, allowing us to differentiate between traditional stage theory and born globals. Furthermore, more specific questions covered their market definition and perception of international expansion, set goals and ultimate outcomes.

Findings on hidden champions' internationalization strategies

In Table 6.5 we present our preliminary data on the internationalization process and associated entry modes of 26 HCs from Germany. HCs have been in business an average of 81 years, and employed 2,171 employees. The majority holds more than 41 foreign subsidiaries, which comes to an average of 31 subsidiaries generating 64 per cent of their turnover.

In line with Simon (2009), our findings suggest HCs prefer full controlled entry modes, such as wholly owned subsidiaries (81 per cent) and export (65 per cent) over less controlled entry modes, such as joint ventures (15 per cent). In previously conducted studies, licensing was not considered an entry mode option for HCs, but our data reveals that 19 per cent frequently make use of licensing. Our findings also demonstrate that distribution companies (50 per cent) as well as manufacturing companies (39 per cent) are commonly used among HCs. Roughly 35 per cent (marked 'unidentified' in Table 6.5) moved abroad using solely one entry mode, either exporting or wholly owned subsidiaries, thereby not following any internationalization pattern.

Table 6.5 Analysis of 26 hidden champions firms researched

Company	Year of establishment	Number of employees	Per cent of foreign turnover	Foreign subsidiaries	Export	Distribution company	Licensing	Joint venture	Manufacturing company	Wholly owned subsidiary	Results
1	–	8,200	81–90	>41	✓	✓	–	–	✓	✓	Traditional
2	1871	–	81–90	>41	✓	✓	–	✓	✓	✓	Traditional
3	–	–	71–80	>41	✓	✓	–	–	✓	✓	Traditional
4	1878	2,800	51–60	>41	✓	✓	–	–	✓	✓	Traditional
5	1930	400	6800	1–5	✓	–	–	–	–	–	Unidentified
6	1913	400	31–40	6–10	–	–	–	–	–	–	Unidentified
7	1876	6,800	–	31–35	–	–	–	–	–	✓	Unidentified
8	–	–	61–70	11–15	–	–	–	–	–	✓	Unidentified
9	–	–	41–50	16–20	–	–	–	–	–	✓	Unidentified
10	–	–	41–550	1–5	–	–	–	–	–	✓	Unidentified
11	–	–	61–70	>41	✓	–	–	–	–	–	Unidentified
12	–	–	61–70	11–15	✓	✓	–	–	–	✓	Unidentified
13	–	–	51–60	21–25	✓	✓	–	–	–	✓	Unidentified
14	1923	>1,000	41–50	>41	–	–	–	–	–	✓	Born global
15	1937	1,200	31–40	21–25	✓	–	–	–	–	✓	Born global**
16	1953	350	91–100	>41	✓	–	✓	–	✓	✓	Born global
17	1948	160	41–50	11–15	✓	✓	–	–	–	✓	Born global**
18	–	–	71–80	31–35	–	✓	✓	–	✓	–	Born global
19	1958	–	41–50	>41	✓	✓	–	–	–	✓	Born global
20	–	–	71–80	31–35	✓	✓	✓	✓	✓	✓	Born global
21	–	–	–	>41	✓	–	–	✓	–	✓	Born global
22	1985	642	91–100	>41	✓	✓	–	–	✓	✓	Born global
23	–	–	81–90	26–30	–	✓	✓	✓	–	✓	Born global
24	–	–	91–100	>41	✓	✓	–	–	✓	✓	Born global
25	–	–	91–100	>41	–	–	–	–	✓	✓	Born global
26	1948	160	31–40	11–15	✓	–	✓	–	–	✓	Born global
	1927	2,171	64 per cent	31*	65 per cent	50 per cent	19 per cent	15 per cent	39 per cent	81 per cent	

Notes: * Companies with more than 41 subsidiaries have been calculated using a maximum of 50 subsidiaries abroad, ** probably better defined as born-again globals.

The market entry was controlled by the demand from specific markets. The demand was generated from international trade fairs in Germany.

Executive from Company Five, operating in the engineering industry.

This statement indicates that HCs plan their market entry carefully. Frequently HCs follow their customers into foreign markets with an appropriate market entry option, which thereby triggers international expansion in no specific order.

Our preliminary data suggests 15 per cent of our sample follow the traditional stages of the Uppsala Model, and venture abroad using export, followed by export via sales agents, followed by wholly owned sales subsidiary abroad and finally the establishment of an overseas production plant. However, we argue that HCs differentiate form traditional internationalizers through their regional or global dominance, which therefore confirms our first proposition.

Half of our sample used a more accelerated internationalization and indeed leap-frogged stages of the Uppsala Model. This suggests a somewhat more born-global approach to internationalization. Company 14, founded in 1923, used export followed by a foreign subsidiary, indicating an accelerated internationalization. However, we have no empirical data on the year of their first international expansion, but according to Simon (2009) the majority of HCs internationalized soon after inception via either an export or wholly owned subsidiary.

> Different markets require different entry modes. Executive from Company Eight, operating in the machine building industry.

This statement indicates that HCs are more flexible in relation to their choice of entry choices mode. For example, an 85-year-old company, operating in the caster and wheels industry, entered markets using export followed directly by a wholly owned subsidiary abroad. Although, HCs show overlapping traits to born globals, we argue HCs differentiate by definition, as they are positioned either among the top three globally or as regional number one.

Furthermore, we found two companies (15 per cent) that could be reclassified as 'born-again globals'. Born-again globals begin by focusing on their domestic market and following traditional stage theory, but suddenly embark on a much more accelerated internationalization (Bell et al., 2001). Company 17 operating in the steel industry focused on their domestic market for nearly 30 years until they embarked a more accelerated internationalization into more than 50 countries. Also, Company 15 initially focused on Germany, but later rapidly internationalized into 60 countries through international agencies and also by holding eight wholly owned subsidiaries abroad.

In this sample, HCs have been in business for 81 years; thus we assume that most of these companies internationalized using a mixture of both stage theory and born globals internationalization, suggesting far more HCs to be classified as born-again globals.

Discussion and further research

Bearing in mind the research that we picked up in the literature, our findings confirm that some HCs follow the traditional Uppsala Model and some pursue a more born-globals internationalization. Clearly, HCs are not the same as born globals, but in fact they form a special case of born globals. HCs differ from born globals as they have a competitive advantage and appear to have achieved top positions in regional or top three global markets, which are not necessarily traits demonstrated by born globals. Therefore we suggest that HCs form an interesting new subcategory of the born globals phenomenon, which needs more critical research in the future.

More recent writers such as Bell et al. (2001) further raise a fascinating new question on 'born-again globals', which could be highly pertinent to our sample, as many HCs have been long established. Born-again globals are firms which solely focused on their domestic market and suddenly embarked on a more accelerated internationalization later in their development (ibid.). Although this was not the prime focus of our research, we revisited our data to address this issue, and indeed of our born globals (50 per cent), 15 per cent actually appear closer to a born-again global configuration compared to the pure notion of born globals. We still need to know more details on the HCs' internationalization such as their exact triggers of internationalization to fully distinguish HCs from born-again globals. Bell et al. (2001) suggests accelerated internationalization is triggered by a critical incident; for example, change in ownership and/or management buyout or following customers into new markets. Crucially, future research would be advised to include far more critical research on the exact internationalization process and strategy of HCs and all of these other internationalization variants.

Additionally, our findings indicate that globalization might not be the driving force for accelerated internationalization, as suggested by Oviatt and McDougall (1997). In this study, 25 per cent of HCs were established over 100 years ago but indeed they pursued a more accelerated internationalization strategy. For example, Company 16, established in 1953, entered a foreign market using export, distribution companies, followed by a manufacturing companies abroad. Additionally, we found HCs established between 1871 and 1985 pursued accelerated internationalization, so therefore accelerated internationalization might not be influenced by the establishment year of a firm.

Our survey also identified licensing as a market entry choice of HCs, which has yet not been identified by other writers. Future research should therefore clarify whether HCs pursue distinctive approaches to other entry modes such as mergers and acquisitions, international strategic alliances, offshoring, outsourcing, franchising and licensing, especially when entering emerging markets.

Simon (1996a, 2007a, 2009) fails to distinguish between HCs which are global market leaders and these which are regional leaders, as he uses the same term for both. Our findings share this same weakness in not distinguishing between these two types of HC. This calls for much more critical future research distinguishing the global HCs from merely regional players.

Rialp et al. (2005) propose the need for more theoretical explanations for these fast internationalizing firms. In case of HCs, we have a more elaborate theory relating to performance suggesting more specific key success factors. Simon's (2009, p. 365) 'Three Circles and Eight Lessons'[7] theoretical model highlights eight essential factors, which has received some endorsement (Peng and Meyer, 2011). Firms with traits similar to HCs can also be identified in the United States, Japan, India, China and New Zealand (Simon, 1996b; Simon and Lippert, 2007b; Simon and Zatta, 2008; Yu and Chen, 2009). Simon (2009) proposes the best-elaborated model to date in terms of global performance, highlighting eight key success factors of HCs, but fails to recognize adequately the embeddedness of the model in the German context and culture.

Simon (1996b) asserts a wider applicability of his success model to other institutional contexts, without testing his own model in these foreign countries. The latest literature pertaining to HCs in foreign markets have effectively demonstrated the necessity of further major institutional adaptations of this model (Blackburn et al., 2000; Voudouris et al., 2000; Yu and Chen, 2009). From a more institutionally based perspective, these studies and our own critical findings suggest that the model emerged as quite remarkably embedded in German Mittelstand characteristics defined by Muzyka et al. (1997) (Appendix Table A.2). This indicates limited transferability of the HCs' model into different institutional contexts as compared to Germany.

We therefore argue, in agreement with Peng (2010) and Khanna and Palepu (2010), that more ideal models, such as Simon's performance model, may or may not prove fully applicable in countries with dissimilar context and culture as compared to Germany, and will require some adaptations to reflect institutional contexts. Research should therefore take a more critical view of theoretical models of HCs, and take into account a wider range of contexts, also including new institutional contexts.

Future research needs to examine HCs against the more critical counterfactuals. We need to examine other global niche variants too, and propose the need for more comparative critical research on their evolutionary paths, and their ultimate impact in terms of global market share and commercial performance.

Conclusion

The purpose of this study was to identify the internationalization behaviour of German HCs. HCs are highly successful companies defined as being among the top three global industry players (or regional number one) operating in tightly defined niche markets (Simon, 2009). Whilst Simon (2009) elaborates very little about the different modes of internationalization, this chapter shows some useful preliminary data from 26 German HCs.

The exploratory data presented in this chapter shows some of the features and broad patterns of HCs' internationalization behaviour. It can be concluded that HCs do not all confirm with traditional stage theory. In fact half of our samples show internationalization approaches which substantially overlap with born globals, and frequently leap-frog stages of the Uppsala Model. Furthermore, we argue that two companies can be reclassified as born-again globals, as these solely focused on their domestic market and suddenly embarked on a more accelerated internationalization later in their development.

Thus, we suggest that globalization might not be the driving force behind HCs pursuing a more accelerated internationalization, as many were established over 100 years and embarked on a more rapid internationalization. Apart from export and wholly owned subsidiaries, we also identify the use of licensing as an entry mode used by HCs.

In summary, this chapter provides a comprehensive integrated literature review of HCs – the first in this field – together with our preliminary results, clarifying the importance of our proposed research agenda. Findings suggest that HCs might be a special case of other internationalization variants, as they differentiate through their global industry dominance or European leadership.

However, we still need to know more about the HCs' internationalization behaviour and associated entry modes in order to distinguish these firms from born globals and born-again globals. Our emerging research agenda proposes the need for a more critical investigation of the HCs' theoretical performance model, as it shows limited transferability and appears to be embedded in the German context and culture. Crucially, more research must focus on the evolutionary patterns and ultimate impact of global market share and commercial performance outcomes of these outstanding global niche players.

Appendix

Table A.1   Articles on 'niche strategy' in *Strategic Management Journal*

Author/s	Topic
Galbraith and Schendel (1983)	Empirical analysis of strategy types
Miller (1986)	Configurations of strategy and structure
Covin and Slevin (1989)	Small firms in hostile and benign environments
McDougall and Robinson (1990)	New venture strategies
Fiegenbaum and Karnani (1991)	Outlook flexibility
Simons (1991)	Strategic orientation and attention to control systems
McGrath et al. (1992)	Executive team actions, technology strategy and dominant designs
Teplensky et al. (1993)	Market entry and strategic adjustment
Carter et al. (1994)	New venture strategies
McDougall et al. (1994)	New ventures
Lasser and Kerr (1996)	Strategy in distribution relationships
Dean et al. (1998)	Difference in small and large firm responses
Robinson and McDougall (2001)	Entry barriers and new venture performance
Song et al. (2002)	Strategic choice decision

Table A.2 Comparison of HCs' model and Mittelstand characteristics

Hidden Champions (Simon, 2009)	Mittelstand (Muzyka et al., 1997)
Leadership with ambitious goals	Yes
	New managerial direction and behaviour/defining clear company objectives/growth targets
Decentralization	Not specified
High-performance employees	Yes
	Personnel retrained/employment of competent staff
Depth	Yes
	Products sold based on the companies' expertise
Focus	Yes
	Concentrating on niche markets/exploitation of successive niche opportunities
Closeness to customer	Yes
	Constant rapport with customers/adapt operations to customers' need
Innovation	Yes
	Innovation as a value-based process/technological innovation
Globalization	Not specified

Notes

1. The concept of born-global firms has been expressed using different terms that have been used interchangeably by various academics, describing the same phenomenon of early and fast internationalizing firms (Sharma and Blomstermo, 2003); global start-ups (Jolly et al. 1992) and born globals (Rennie, 1993).
2. Simon (1996a) identified 457 low-profile, under US$1 billion revenue, firms, often medium-sized businesses from Germany, achieving regional dominance or top two global market shares. Simon's (2009) study loosened his earlier definition of HCs, without any explanation, through inclusion of all top three global market positions and German, Austrian and Swiss firms up to US$4 billion revenues, and taking his number of identified firms up to 1,174.
3. *Journal of International Business, Strategic Management Journal, International Journal of Management Reviews, Harvard Business Review, Management International Review, Journal of Management Studies, Journal of World Business, Sloan Management Review, California Management Review, International Journal of Management Reviews, Business Strategy Review, Strategic Change*, and the *European Management Journal*.
4. Mittelstand firms are small and medium-sized businesses in Germany, which are often family-owned firms employing up to 5,000 people and are characterized by their distinctive contribution to the German economy (Berghoff, 2006).
5. *Journal of International Business Studies, Strategic Management Journal, International Journal of Management Reviews, Harvard Business Review, Management International Review, Journal of Management Studies, Journal of World Business, Sloan Management Review*, and *California Management Review*.
6. Company details included name, address, homepage, number of employees, year of establishment, industry sector.

7. The model is depicted in 'three nested circles': an 'outer circle' identifying their unique approach to external opportunities, the 'inner circle' identifying the internal competencies and the business core summarizing the firm's core competencies. The core: (1) leadership with ambitious goals. The inner circle: (2) decentralization (3) high-performance employees (4) depth. The outer circle: (5) focus (6) closeness to customers (7) innovation (8) globalization (Simon, 2009, p. 365).

References

D. F. Abell and J.S. Hammond, *Strategic Market Planning: Problems and Market Planning*, (Englewood Cliffs, NJ: Prentice-Hall, 1979).

C. Adenäuer, 'Erfolgsunternehmen in der Industrie-Analyse von Einflussfaktoren auf Grundlage des BDI-Mittelstandspanels', in I. F. M. Bonn (ed.), *Jahrbuch zur Mittelstandsforschung 1/2007*, (Bonn, Germany: Deutscher Universitäts-Verlag, 2007), pp. 15–48.

S. Andersson and I. Wictor, 'Innovative internationalisation in new firms: born-globals – the Swedish case', *Journal of International Entrepreneurship*, 1(3) (2003) 249–75.

M. V. Behr and K. Semlinger, *Internationalisierung kleiner und mittlerer Unternehmen*, (Munich: ISF München, 2004).

J. Bell and R. McNaughton, 'Born Global Firms: A Challenge to Public Policy in Support of Internationalization', in J. Pels and D. W. Stewart (eds), *Marketing in a Global Economy*, (Buenos Aires: American Marketing Association, 2000), pp. 176–85.

J. Bell, R. McNaughton and S. Young, 'Born-again global firms. An extension to the 'born global' phenomenon', *Journal of International Marketing*, 7(3) (2001) 173–89.

H. Berghoff, 'The end of family business? The Mittelstand and German Capitalism in transition, 1949–2000', *Business History Review*, 80(2) (2006) 263–95.

J. Blackburn, B. Merrilees, J. Tiessen and M. Lindman, *Hidden (SME) Champions: The Role of Innovation and Strategy*, (New Zealand: College of Business, Massey University, 2000).

R. D. Buzzell and B. T. Gale, *The PIMS Principle*, (New York: Free Press, 1987).

N. M. Carter, T. M. Stearns, P. D. Reynolds and B. A. Miller, 'New venture strategies: theory development with an empirical base', *Strategic Management Journal*, 15 (1994) 21–41.

S. T. Cavusgil, 'From the Editor in Chief', *Journal of International Marketing*, 2(3) (1994) 4–6.

S. Chetty and C. Campbell-Hunt, 'A strategic approach to internationalization: a traditional versus a 'born global' approach', *Journal of International Marketing*, 12(1) (2004) 57–81.

P.-L. Chng and N. Pangarkar, 'Research on global strategy', *International Journal of Management Reviews*, 2(1) (2000) 91–110.

J. G. Covin and D. P. Slevin, 'Strategic management of small firms in hostile and benign environments', *Strategic Management Journal*, 10 (1989) 75–87.

D. Crick and M. Spence, 'The internationalization of 'high performing' UK high-tech SMEs: a study of planned and unplanned strategies', *International Business Review*, 14(2) (2005) 167–85.

T. J. Dean, R. L. Brown and C. E. Bamford, 'Differences in large and small firm responses to environmental context: strategic implications from a comparative analysis of business formations', *Strategic Management Journal*, 19 (1998) 709–28.

D. Deng and Z. Wan, *Focus On: Understanding of Chinese Hidden Champions*, (Hangzhou, China: Zhekiang University Press, 2006).

E. Dichtl, M. Liebold, H. G. Köglmayr and S. Müller, 'The export decision of small and medium-sized firms: a review', *Management International Review*, 24(2) (1984) 49–60.

K. Ding, 'How to become successful Hidden Champions: case study of Japanese SMEs', *Business Frontier*, 27 (2008).

K. Eisenhardt, 'Strategic decisions and all that jazz', *Business Strategy Review*, 8(3) (2008) 1–3.

Ernst and Young, *Zukunft gestalten-verantwortlich handeln, Siegerstrategien Im deutschen Mittelstand*, (2004). Accessed September 2010.

D. Eschlbeck, 'Hidden Champions und Born Global Firms', in H.-D. Haas and S.-M. Neumair (eds), *Internationale Wirtschaft Rahmenbedingungen, Akteure, räumliche Prozesse*, (München: Oldenbourg Wissenschaftverlag, 2005), p. 709.

A. Fiegenbaum and A. Karnani, 'Outlook flexibility – a competitive advantage for small firms', *Strategic Management Journal*, 12 (1991) 101–14.

E. Fina and A. Rugman, 'A test of internalization theory and internationalization theory: the Upjohn Company', *Management International Review*, 36(3) (1996) 199–213.

M. Forsgren, 'Managing the international multi-center firm: case studies from Sweden', *European Management Journal*, 8(2) (1990) 261–67.

K. Friedrich, *Erfolgreich durch Spezialisierung* (München: Redline Verlag, 2007).

M. Gabrielsson, T. Seppälä and P. Gabrielsson, *Hybrid Competitive Strategies for Achieving Superior Performance During Global Expansion: Empirical Evidence of ICT Firms from Small and Open Economies*, (Competitive paper at the Academy of International Business (AIB) Annual Meeting, Rio de Janeiro, Brazil), 26–29 June 2010.

C. Galbraith and D. Schendel, 'An empirical analysis of strategy types', *Strategic Management Journal*, 4 (1983) 153–73.

J. Gutmann and R. Kabst, *Internationalisierung im Mittelstand: Chancen Risiken – Erfolgsfaktoren*, (Lengerich, Germany: Gabler Verlag, 2000).

G. Hooley, N. F. Piercy and B. Nicoulaud, *Marketing Strategy and Competitive Positioning*, (England: Prentice Hall, 2008).

J. Johanson and J.-E. Vahlne, 'The internationalization process of the firm: a model of knowledge development and increasing foreign commitments', *Journal of International Business Studies*, 8(1) (1977) 23–32.

J. Johanson and F. Wiedersheim-Paul, 'The internationalization of the firm: four Swedish cases', *Journal of Management Studies*, 12(3) (1975) 305–22.

V. K. Jolly, M. Alahuta and J. Jean-Pierre, 'Challenging the incumbents: how high technology start-ups compete globally', *Journal of Strategic Change*, 1(2) (1992) 71–82.

G. Jungwirth, 'Die Marketing-Strategien der mittelständischen österreichischen Weltmarkt-führer', in J.-A. Meyer (ed.), *Strategien von kleinen und mittleren Unternehmen*, (Cologne: Josef EUL Verlag, 2010), pp. 179–99.

T. Khanna and K. G. Palepu, *Winning in Emerging Markets: A Road Map for Strategy and Execution*, (Boston, MA: Harvard Business Press, 2010).

G. A. Knight, 'Entrepreneurship and marketing strategy: the SME under globalization', *Journal of International Marketing*, 8(2) (2000) 12–32.

G. A. Knight and S. T. Cavusgil, 'The born global firm: a challenge to traditional internationalization theory', *Advances in International Marketing*, 8 (1996) 11–26.

G. A. Knight, T. K. Madsen and P. Servais, 'An enquiry into born global firms in Europe and the USA', *International Marketing Review*, 21 (2004) 645–65.

L. Korot and G. Tovstiga, 'Profiling the Twenty-First-Century Knowledge Enterprise', in A. Rugman (ed.), *Research in Global Strategic Management*, Volume 7, (Emerald Group Publishing Limited, 1999), pp. 157–72.

P. Kotler and J. Caslione, *Chaotics – The Business of Managing and Marketing in the Age of Turbulence*, (New York: Amacom, 2009).

P. Kotler and K. L. Keller, *Marketing Management 12e*, (New Jersey: Pearson, Prentice Hall, 2006).

F. Kroeger, A. Vizjak and M. Moriarty, *Beating the Global Consolidation Endgame*, (New York: McGraw Hill, 2008).

W. M. Lassar and J. L. Kerr, 'Strategy and control in supplier-distributor relationships: an agency perspective', *Strategic Management Journal*, 17 (1996) 613–32.

P. A. Lawrence and V. Edwards, *Management in Western Europe*, (London: Macmillan Press, 2000).

L. C. Leonidou and C. S. Katskikeas, 'The export development process: an integrative review of empirical models', *Journal of International Business Studies*, 27(3) (1996) 517–51.

J. Leontiades, 'Going global–global strategy vs. national strategies', *Long Range Planning*, 19(6) (1986) 96–104.

A. Likierman, 'Successful leadership – how would you know?', *Business Strategy Review*, 20(1) (2009) 44–9.

T. K. Madsen and P. Servais, 'The internationalization of born globals: an evolutionary process?', *International Business Review*, 6(6) (1997) 561–83.

C. Markides, 'Strategy as balance: from either–or to and', *Business Strategy Review*, 12(3) (2001) 1–10.

J. A. Mathews, 'Dragon multinationals: new players in 21st century globalization', *Asia Pacific J Manage*, 23(1) (2006) 5–27.

P. McDougall, J. G. Covin, R. B. Robinson and L. Herron, 'The effects of industry growth and strategy breadth on new venture performance and strategy content', *Strategic Management Journal*, 15(7) (1994) 537–54.

P. McDougall and R. B. Robinson Jr., 'New venture strategies: an empirical identification of eight "archetypes" of competitive strategies for entry', *Strategic Management Journal*, 11 (1990) 447–67.

P. McDougall, S. Shane and B. M. Oviatt, 'Explaining the formation of international new ventures: the limits of theories from international business research', *Journal of Business Venturing*, 9(6) (1994a) 469–87.

C. G. McGrath, I. C. MacMillan and M. L. Tushman, 'The role of executive team actions in shaping dominant designs: towards the strategic shaping of technological progress', *Strategic Management Journal*, 13 (1992) 137–61.

McKinsey and Co., *Emerging Exporters. Australia's High Value-Added Manufacturing Exporters*, (Melbourne: McKinsey & Company and the Australian Manufacturing Council, 1993).

S. Melén and E. Nordman, 'The internationalization modes of born globals: a longitudinal study', *European Management Journal*, 27(4) (2009) 243–54.

K. E. Meyer, 'Globalfocusing: from domestic conglomerates to global specialists', *Journal of Management Studies*, 43(5) (2006) 1109–44.

K. E. Meyer 'Globalfocusing: corporate strategies under pressure', *Strategic Change*, 18(5/6) (2009) 195–207.

D. Miller, 'Configurations of strategy and structure: towards a synthesis', *Strategic Management Journal*, 7 (1986) 233–49.

D. Muzyka, H. Breuninger and D. G. Rossell, 'The secret of new growth in old German 'Mittelstand' companies', *European Management Journal*, 15(2) (1997) 147–57.

B. Oviatt and P. McDougall, 'Toward a theory of international new ventures', *Journal of International Business Studies*, 25(1) (1994) 45–64.

B. Oviatt and P. McDougall, 'Challenges for internationalization process theory: the case of international new ventures', *Management International Review*, 37 (1997) 85–99.

B. Parker, *Introduction to globalization and business*, (Maidstone, Kent: SAGE Publications, 2005).

M. Peng and E. G. Pleggenkuhle-Miles, 'Current debates in global strategy', *International Journal of Management Reviews*, 11(1) (2009) 51–68.

M. Peng, *Global Business*, (Mason, OH: Cengage Learning, 2010).

M. Peng and K. E. Meyer, *International Business*, (London: Cengage Learning, 2011).

C. Rasche, 'Was zeichnet die "Hidden Champions" aus?', in K. H. Stahl and H. H. Hinterhuber (eds), *Erfolgreich im Schatten der Großen*, (Berlin: Erich Schmidt Verlag, 2003), pp. 217–37.

M. Rennie, 'Born global', *McKinsey Quarterly*, 4 (1993) 45–52.

A. Rialp, J. Rialp, D. Urbano and Y. Vaillant, 'The born-global phenomenon: a comparative case study research', *Journal of International Entrepreneurship*, 3(2) (2005) 133–71.

K. C. Robinson and P. McDougall, 'Entry barriers and new venture performance: a comparison of universal and contingency approaches', *Strategic Management Journal*, 22 (2001) 659–85.

D. D. Sharma and A. Blomstermo, 'The internationalization process of born globals: a network view', *International Business Review*, 12(6) (2003) 739–53.

H. Simon, 'Lessons from Germany's Midsize Giants', *Harvard Business Review*, 70(2) (1992a) 115–23.

H. Simon, 'Service policies of German manufacturers: critical factors in international competition', *European Management Journal*, 10(4) (1992b) 404–11.

H. Simon, *Hidden Champions – Lessons from 500 of the World's Best Unknown Companies*, (Boston, MA: Harvard Business School Press, 1996a).

H. Simon, 'You don't have to be German to be a Hidden Champion', *Business Strategy Review*, 7(2) (1996b) 1–13.

H. Simon, *Hidden Champions des 21. Jahrhunderts*, (Frankfurt am Main: Campus Verlag, 2007).

H. Simon, *Hidden Champions of the 21st Century*, (London and New York: Springer Verlag, 2009).

H. Simon and S. Lippert, 'Hidden Champions des 21. Jahrhunderts Deutschland und Japan im Vergleich', *Japanmarkt*, (2007) 10–15.

H. Simon and D. Zatta, 'Growth strategies from the Hidden Champions: lessons from Indian and international companies', in P. Da-Cruz and S. Cappallo (eds), *Growth of Hidden Champions*, (Gesundheitsmarkt Indien. Wiesbaden: Gabler GWV Fachverlage, 2008), pp. 187–205.

R. Simons, 'Strategic orientation and top management attention to control systems', *Strategic Management Journal*, 11 (1991) 49–62.

M. Song, R. J. Calantone and C. A. Di Benedetto, 'Competitive forces and strategic choice decisions: an experimental investigation in the United States and Japan', *Strategic Management Journal*, 23 (2002) 969–78.

J. D. Teplensky, J. R. Kimberly, Alan L. Hillman and J. S. Schwatz, 'Scope, timing and strategic adjustment in emerging markets: manufacturer strategies and the case of MRI', *Strategic Management Journal*, 14 (1993) 505–27.

B. Venohr and K. E. Meyer, 'Uncommon common sense', *Business Strategy Review*, 20 (2009) 38–43.

B. Venohr and K. E. Meyer, *The German Miracle Keeps Running*, (Fachhochschule für Wirtschaft in Berlin, 2007), pp. 1–35.

I. Voudouris, S. Lioukas, S. Makridakis and Y. Spanos, 'Greek Hidden Champions: lessons from small, little-known firms in Greece', *European Management Journal*, 18(6) (2000) 663–74.

J. Weerawardena, G. S. Mort, P. W. Liesch and G. Knight, 'Conceptualizing accelerated internationalization in the born global firm: a dynamic capabilities perspective', *Journal of World Business*, 42(3) (2007) 294–306.

L. S. Welch and R. K. Luostarinen, 'Internationalization: evolution of a concept', *Journal of General Management*, 14(2) (1988) 34–55.

A. Witt, *Internationalization Strategies of Hidden Champions*, (Hamburg: Management Laboratory Press, 2010).

H. Yu and Y. Chen, *Factors underlying Hidden Champions in China: Case Study*, (Halmstad, Sweden: School of Business and Engineering, University of Halmstadt, 2009).

S. A. Zahra, 'Entrepreneurial risk taking in family firms', *Family Business Review*, 18(1) (2005) 23–40.

7
The Role of Language on Affiliates' Competence Creation: Evidence from the MNE Linkage Across 45 Countries

Yong Yang and Caleb C. Y. Kwong

Introduction

Does a 'common language' matter when it comes to knowledge and competence creation of affiliates by multinational enterprises (MNEs)? While there are signs that knowledge and competencies are diffusing and equilibrating throughout the world (Ernst and Kim, 2002), the development of innovation pockets suggests that the diffusion process has remained far from equal. This chapter aims to examine the reasons behind such unequal geographical dispersion of innovation by focusing on a specific contextual factor, namely, the role of a common language in the process of diffusion. Specifically, this chapter focuses on how a common language between a parent and its affiliates facilitates or hinders the development of knowledge and competencies within the latter. Whilst a number of host country factors have been thoroughly explored in the literature (Yamawaki, 2004), there has been little attempt thus far to link the effect of multinational parents' home country to the knowledge and competence development of affiliates. Arguably, with the exception of several qualitative papers (Buckley et al., 2005; Marschan et al., 1997; Welch et al., 2005), the role of common language on innovation development of affiliates has not been adequately explored within the international business (IB) literature. In particular, no study that we are aware of examines such a linkage using quantitative analysis.

The first hypothesis examines the extent to which the parent's knowledge or technological capability actually enhances the competence development of their overseas affiliates. Although it is an increasingly important research topic in IB literature, to our knowledge this is the first study to explore this issue utilizing a large cross-country firm-level data set with links between parent and affiliates to explore the linkage. Once this hypothesis is established, the main analysis of the chapter is on the role of common language in the location choice made by knowledge-orientated MNEs for developing competencies and knowledge via overseas subsidiaries. Utilizing a firm-level panel of more than 1,514 multinationals and more than 3,712 of their overseas affiliates, covering 45 home and host countries in the period 1997–2007, we found evidence that the knowledge and technological capability of the parent enhances the creation of competencies within its affiliates – a finding that is robust to a large set of different specifications. Moreover, for knowledge-orientated MNEs, we found that competence creation for affiliates is higher when both parent and affiliate share the same language. Further research focusing on why culture and language matter would advance our understanding of the location choice of competence-creating affiliates.

The rest of the chapter is structured as follows. The first section discusses theories and proposes our hypotheses, followed by the description of data used in our analysis. We then present the main results and finally conclude.

Language and the location choice of overseas knowledge and competency development by MNEs

As global competition based on knowledge has intensified, the ability to tap into knowledge and competencies across the world is becoming increasingly essential (Kogut, 1989). Traditionally a field dominated by the developed world, the rise of non-traditional clusters and centres in developing nations has resulted in the wider dispersion of MNE knowledge activities and the increased recognition of the innovation potential of affiliates (Dunning, 1993; Meyer et al., 2011; Singh, 2007). Many now believe that foreign affiliates are better at developing support-orientated innovation that is most suitable to local customers and that supports production for the local market (Birkinshaw and Hood, 2001; Gerybadze and Reger, 1999; Ito and Wakasugi, 2007). By developing links with local scientific and technical communities, it is also believed that MNEs were able to develop knowledge-sourcing innovation within their foreign affiliates (Almeida, 1996; Driffield et al., 2010; Florida, 1997; Singh, 2008). The fact that these affiliates are geographically away from the core of the MNE means that they are often better able to implement innovative practices without the hindrance of bureaucratic procedures (Johnson and Medcof, 2007), but, with adequate communication and intellectual property protection, still remained under the strategic control of the parent (Birkinshaw et al., 2000; Gassmann and von Zedtwitz, 1999). Therefore, despite the high costs involved in having multiple innovation centres, there has been an increased emphasis on 'innovation at the edge' that may allow MNEs to fully utilize their aggregate innovation potential (Birkinshaw and Hood, 2001; Meyer et al., 2011).

Creating a knowledge-intensive environment in a socially embedded organization is a dynamic capability (Meyer et al., 2011) that requires MNEs not only to effectively utilize the resources, manpower and technologies available in the vast number of host countries, but also to connect and coordinate between different affiliates that are embedded in very diverse local, cultural and institutional contexts (Figueiredo, 2011; Lam, 2003; Meyer et al., 2011; Morgan, 2001; Narula and Dunning, 2010; Song et al., 2011; Whitley, 1999, 2001; Zanfei, 2000). At the organizational level, the knowledge orientation of the parent undoubtedly has an effect on an MNE's intention to invest in knowledge and competency of its affiliates. Searching and investing in the development of knowledge and competency in affiliates is being increasingly seen as an integral part of the strategic positioning of MNE's wider global operations (Dierickx and Cool, 1989). A strong knowledge orientation of the parent enables a culture of knowledge and competency creation to flourish and allows the MNE to disseminate such a culture to its affiliates (Ito and Wakasugi, 2007; Penner-Hahn and Shaver, 2005; Zejan, 1990). Therefore, we come to the following groundwork hypothesis, which, although, as discussed previously, is not a novel hypothesis, nevertheless, provides the necessary groundwork for the subsequent hypotheses:

Hypothesis 7.1 An MNE is more likely to invest in knowledge and competency development in an affiliate if the parent itself is knowledge orientated.

Clearly, home and host country factors that are external to the organization also play significant roles in the process. An extensive literature drawing from the institutional perspective (Zanfei, 2000) the national innovation system perspective (Cantwell and Santangelo, 2000) as well as the subsidiary foci perspective (Hogenbirk and van Kranenburg, 2006) has pinpointed a number of contextual and technological factors that may affect an MNE's decision to invest in knowledge and competency development in a particular host country (Doh et al., 2005). These include the technological state of the host country (Ito and Wakasugi; 2007; Zejan, 1990), the presence of a strong research infrastructure including higher institutions and laboratories (Doh et al., 2005), availability of an educated workforce (Kumar, 2001), the cost of manpower (Athukorala and Kohpaiboon, 2010) as well as institutional and other contextual factors of the host country such as intellectual property rights protection (Ito and Wakasugi, 2007), information and communication technologies (ICT) development (Kedia and Mukherjee, 2009), economic development (Doh et al., 2005), market size and market condition (Athukorala and Kohpaiboon, 2010; Zejan, 1990).

The cultural-embeddedness perspective points to the importance of cultural interaction in the facilitation of the affiliates' development, and, as mentioned in the introduction, this chapter focuses on the role of common language in facilitating the competency development of affiliates within an MNE. Previous literature indeed indicates that language and broader cultural influence are interrelated (Welch et al., 2005). Language forms an integral element of the cultural (Kogut and Singh, 1988) and psychic distance (Johanson and Wiedersheim-Paul, 1975) constructs, and has long been seen as an important cultural differentiator (Usunier, 1998) and foundation of one's social identity (Hill, 2002) – arguably even more so than ethnicity (Giles and Johnson, 1981) and nationalism (Oakes, 2001).

From an organization's point of view, language affects its ability to function in the international arena (Feely and Harzing, 2003; Harzing and Feely, 2008; Marschan et al., 1997). A common language facilitates communication and interaction, which is particularly essential for the sharing of knowledge and information. Studies have found a shared language to be a major facilitator of successful knowledge articulation, with a common language being more important the more intensive the knowledge transfer process is (Buckley et al., 2005). Whilst technical or procedural competencies can be more easily transferred between units, as explicit knowledge can be more easily codified via the use of documents, manuals, rulebooks and so on, the more abstract and tacit creative management ideas are less easily transferred due to the barrier of mutual understanding between knowledge holders (Kogut and Zander, 1993). In these cases, language competency is particularly important for the articulation and assimilation of un-codified and complex knowledge, as well as visions, norms and identity that are difficult to translate (Buckley et al., 2005). For the more complex forms of knowledge, social understanding is equally important in enabling the recipients to understand, learn and implement transferred technologies and management skills (Sohn, 1994). Therefore there is a need to go beyond working language competency but also social knowledge for the articulation of knowledge to work. A shared language certainly facilitates such social sharing and therefore is likely to be seen as a highly desirable factor when an MNE is deciding upon the location of knowledge and competency development. On the other hand, poor communication across units could be a stumbling block in an MNE's quest for global integration (Marschan et al., 1997). Language difference increases uncertainty, which can lead to lower trust and interaction avoidance, which in turn results in lower commitment to each other in the long run (Gudykunst, 1995). This would make the transfer of information and competency difficult from both sides (Buckley et al., 2005).

In practice, firms would adopt a number of mechanisms to combat the language difference. Translation is one of the most common practices. Firms may translate all the important documents into the native language. Alternatively, they may employ translators when appropriate, or use expatriates or locals who are fluent in the parent language as their conduit and connector to communicate between a parent and its affiliates (Anderson and Rasmussen, 2004; Harzing and Feely, 2008). However, the use of translation services would increase the costs of operating the affiliate considerably. Firms often resort to translating only key documents, resulting in the majority of information not being translated and creating room for manoeuvre for local managers to suit their agendas (Marschan et al., 1997). Moreover, as mentioned previously, translation may be less appropriate the more implicit and un-codified the knowledge is (Kogut and Zander, 1993). This is particularly problematic for firms intending to engage in knowledge-intensive activities (Buckley et al., 2005). Evidence also suggests that translators often adjust the original message into a more open-ended one, which can sometimes be more culturally appropriate but, nevertheless, not what was originally intended (Fai and Marschan-Piekkari, 2003). These translation errors, whether intentional or unintentional, make knowledge transfer less efficient and more costly. Finally, for the purpose of assimilation, language needs to be spoken not only at the top level but also at production and shop levels (Buckley et al., 2005), without which power fell to a small number of employees who act as the language node between the parent and the affiliate. Whilst expatriate modes are often isolated from the local majority (Selmer, 2006), fluent locals may distort rules to suit their local needs, rather than contributing to the development of the MNE as a whole (Marschan et al., 1997; Marschan-Piekkari et al., 1999a, 1999b; Welch et al., 2005). Such self-serving behaviour often develops into mutual resentment, with both sides reluctant to pass on important information, and can result in a lack of information flow between parent and affiliates (Welch et al., 2005). These factors directly and indirectly increase the costs of communication and reduce the attractiveness for parents of investing in the competency development of affiliates.

The reliance on a few language nodes often also results in a centralized hierarchical structure for MNEs entering into a country with a different language. Studies have found that language differences increase the implementation of control and coordination by the parent on the affiliate (Björkman and Piekkari, 2009). They have also found that the extent of formalization also increases. This is because language differences often result in lower person-to-person contact, making the use of control by socialization more difficult (Barner-Rasmussen and Björkman, 2007). As a result the use of formal rules and regulations becomes even more important. However, such a centralized and formalized structure is arguably more suitable for production purposes, but less appropriate in other pursuits such as research and development, as knowledge and information are often un-codified and complex.

On the other hand, some argue that language differences can assist decentralization of power (Marschan et al., 1997), which can be favourable to knowledge development. However, this is often the case where, rather than centralization and formalization, MNEs resort to a complete hands-off strategy, as they believe that investing in the affiliate may not be productive (Barner-Rasmussen, 2003). Such neglect often results in little competency and knowledge being passed on to the affiliate. Based on the literature highlighted above, we come to the following hypothesis:

Hypothesis 7.2   A Knowledge-orientated MNE is more likely to invest in knowledge and competency development in an affiliate if they share a common language.

Data

Our analysis draws on Orbis, a data set including detailed accounting and financial information for the largest firms across the world. The data is collected and made available by Bureau van Dijk, an international consultancy firm. See Ribeiro et al. (2010) for more information on the Orbis data set and Bhaumik et al. (2010), which uses the same data set. The records of each company include information on whether the company has ownership stakes in its affiliates and each affiliate's location. These affiliates are identified by company name and country. We are therefore able to find matches between multinational parents and their matched foreign affiliates.

We consider firms that have information available on sales, capital, intermediate inputs, number of employees and firm age. Firms without at least one of these variables are excluded from our sample. Given access restrictions due to the fact that the data are relatively expensive, and the data issues shown above, information was not available for all affiliates of all multinationals. However, a large linkage data set could still be created, covering a total of 1,514 multinational parents and 3,712 of their foreign affiliates from 45 countries during the period from 1997 to 2007. A total of 1,921 out of 3,712 affiliates are located in continents different to their parents.

Descriptive statistics

Having described our data sources above, our next step is to present the descriptive statistics of data set. Table 7.1 presents the summary statistics from our data regarding 1,514 multinational parents and 3,712 of their overseas affiliates, which relate to 19,373 observations.

Monetary values were converted into euro using exchange rates retrieved from the International Monetary Fund (IMF). As one would expect, in Table 7.1 we

Table 7.1 Descriptive statistics (all firms)

Variable	Mean	Std. Dev.	Obs
Multinational parent			
Total factor productivity, parent	9.600	0.638	19,373
Turnover, parent	14,135.9	25,336.5	19,373
Capital, parent	16,461.3	27,461.0	19,373
Intermediate, parent	9,118.2	19,095.2	19,373
Number of employees, parent	55,534.5	71,377.4	19,373
Firm age, parent	66.8	48.2	18,451
Sector, parent	36.0	18.6	17,703
Affiliate			
Total factor productivity, affiliate	8.364	0.601	19,373
Turnover, affiliate	539.3	2,733.7	19,373
Capital, affiliate	538.8	2,846.3	19,373
Intermediate, affiliate	383.4	2,156.7	19,373
Number of employees, affiliate	1,907.4	6,278.9	19,373
Firm age, affiliate	28.3	27.6	19,373
Sector, affiliate	42.1	19.6	18,261
Same language	0.258	0.438	19,343
Same continent	0.517	0.500	19,373
Survey year	2,002.4	2.6	19,373

Notes: All monetary variables are in millions of euros. 'TFP, parents (affiliates)' is total factor productivity of multinational parents (affiliates). 'Turnover, parents (affiliates)' is annual sales of the multinational parents (affiliates). 'Capital, parents (affiliates)' is capital of the multinational parents (affiliates). 'Intermediate input, parents (affiliates)' is intermediate inputs of multinational parents (affiliates). 'Employment, parents (affiliates)' is number of employees of multinational parents (affiliates). 'Firm age, parent (affiliate)' is the number of years since the establishment of the multinational parent (affiliate). 'Sector, parent (affiliate)' is sector of multinational parents (affiliate). 'Same language' is a dummy equal to one if home and host countries share the same language. 'Same continent' is a dummy equal to one if home and host countries are in the same continent (Asia, Africa, South America, North America, Europe and Oceania). 'Survey year' is the year of survey.

found that affiliates have lower total factor productivity (8.364 vs. 9.600), much smaller sales (€539 vs. €14,135 million), capital (€539 vs. €16,461 million), intermediate inputs (€383 vs. €9,118 million) and number of employees (1,907 vs. 55,535 employees). On average, affiliates are much younger (28.3 vs. 66.8 years) than their parents. Table 7.1 shows that on average 25.8 per cent of home and host countries share the same language and 51.7 per cent of home and host countries are located in same continent.

As we are interested in highlighting the role of culture, Table 7.2 splits the sample into a same language group and a different language group. The left panel of Table 7.2 presents summary statistics for the same language group when home and host countries share the same language, while the right panel presents descriptive statistics for the different language group when home and host countries do not share the same language.

In order to provide a further feel of the data, we divide firm samples into the same continent and different continent groups. 1,921 out of 3,712 affiliates are located in continents different to their parents. The left panel of Table 7.3 presents summary statistics of the same continent group, where home and host countries are in the same continent, while the right panel presents the descriptive statistics of the different continent group, where home and host countries are not in the same continent. We did not find a considerable difference between the two groups, apart from parent capital, number of employees of affiliate and age of affiliate. It also shows that 8.8 per cent of home–host country pairs share the same language when they are in the same continent, while 44 per cent of pairs share the same language when they are in different continents.

This chapter uses total factor productivity (TFP) as a proxy for the level of knowledge and technological capability of a particular organizational unit. TFP is one of the most common measurements of productivity, although it is one that is difficult to compute given its data requirements (Martins and Yang, 2009). The rationale for our approach is that TFP captures the ability of the firm to combine a given set of inputs in order to generate outputs. Holding intermediate inputs, capital and labour inputs constant, TFP is explained merely in terms of knowledge and technology (Levinsohn and Petrin, 2003; Olley and Park, 1996). We calculate the total factor productivity using the STATA official command 'levpet'. Equally, if the quality of either input increases, this will increase the returns to that input, and in turn increase TFP. Technology is therefore seen to be embedded in TFP. From an efficiency-seeking perspective, MNEs may choose to concentrate on certain types of activities in overseas countries using affiliates with sophisticated technological advancements, and then internalize technological achievements within the organization, leading to an overall productivity improvement (Dunning and Lundan, 2008).

We present a scatter plot of both the total factor productivity of parents (TFP_{it}^P) and their overseas affiliates (TFP_{it}^A) in Figure 7.1. We also draw a linear fit to this scatter plot. Here we find a clear positive correlation between TFP_{it}^P and TFP_{it}^A, suggesting that technological capability and knowledge of affiliates are higher when their parents are knowledge oriented.

Table 7.2 Descriptive statistics (same language vs. different language)

Variable	Mean	Std. Dev.	Obs	Mean	Std. Dev.	Obs
	Same language			Different language		
Multinational parent						
Total factor productivity, parent	9.391	0.565	4,995	9.673	0.646	14,348
Sales, parent	8,968.8	24,033.0	4,995	15,960.2	25,549.8	14,348
Capital, parent	9,436.7	19,867.7	4,995	18,930.2	29,277.2	14,348
Intermediate, parent	6,178.4	18,404.8	4,995	10,159.7	19,240.0	14,348
Number of employees, parent	35,435.7	48,443.5	4,995	62,608.0	76,606.4	14,348
Firm age, parent	58.0	46.1	4,596	69.7	48.5	13,825
Sector, parent	39.8	21.2	4,657	34.7	17.4	13,016
Affiliate						
Total factor productivity, affiliate	8.409	0.506	4,995	8.349	0.630	14,348
Sales, affiliate	462.7	1,220.6	4,995	567.0	3,093.4	14,348
Capital, affiliate	530.2	1,814.5	4,995	542.8	3,129.3	14,348
Intermediate, affiliate	310.9	754.6	4,995	409.4	2,465.7	14,348
Number of employees, affiliate	2,214.3	6,073.5	4,995	1,803.7	6,351.8	14,348
Firm age, affiliate	28.3	29.5	4,995	28.3	26.9	14,348
Sector, affiliate	45.6	21.8	4,908	40.8	18.6	13,323
Same continent	0.176	0.381	4,995	0.634	0.482	14,348
Survey year	2,002.2	2.6	4,995	2,002.4	2.6	14,348

Notes: All monetary variables are in millions of euros. 'Same language' – home and host countries share the same language. 'Different language' – home and host countries do not share the same language. 'TFP, parents (affiliates)' is total factor productivity of multinational parents (affiliates). 'Turnover, parents (affiliates)' is annual sales of the multinational parents (affiliates). 'Capital, parents (affiliates)' is capital of the multinational parents (affiliates). 'Intermediate input, parents (affiliates)' is intermediate inputs of multinational parents (affiliates). 'Employment, parents (affiliates)' is the number of employees of multinational parents (affiliates). 'Firm age, parent (affiliate)' is the number of years since the establishment of multinational parent (affiliate). 'Sector, parent (affiliate)' is sector of multinational parents (affiliate). 'Same continent' is a dummy equal to one if home and host countries are in the same continent (Asia, Africa, South America, North America, Europe and Oceania). 'Survey year' is the year of survey. Table 7.2 shows that on average parents have higher total factor productivity (9.673 vs. 9.391) when a parent and its affiliate do not locate in countries that share a common language, relative to those who do. Multinational parents who locate in a country that does not share the same language as their affiliate countries have larger sales (€15,960 vs. €8,969 million), capital (€18,930 vs. €9,437 million), intermediate inputs (€10,160 vs. €6,178 million), and that they are older (70 vs. 58 years) than parents who locate subsidiaries in a country that shares the same language. It also shows that 17.6 per cent of home–host country pairs are in the same continent when they share the same language, while 63.4 per cent pairs are in the same continent but do not share the same language.

Results

Our Hypothesis 7.1 is to examine the role of technological capability of multinational parents on their overseas affiliate's knowledge and competencies. Theories suggest that such technology flows are likely to be technological capability and

Table 7.3 Descriptive statistics (same continent vs. different continent)

Variable	Mean	Std. Dev.	Obs	Mean	Std. Dev.	Obs
	Same continent			Different continent		
Multinational parent						
Total factor productivity, parent	9.595	0.679	10,014	9.604	0.591	9,359
Sales, parent	13,902.4	23,487.7	10,014	14,385.6	27,174.9	9,359
Capital, parent	17,474.3	29,131.0	10,014	15,377.4	25,510.6	9,359
Intermediate, parent	8,490.5	17,206.3	10,014	9,789.8	20,908.5	9,359
Number of employees, parent	55,019.9	74,936.3	10,014	56,085.2	67,361.1	9,359
Firm age, parent	65.8	51.5	9,715	68.0	44.2	8,736
Sector, parent	36.894	19.081	8,946	35.094	18.066	8,757
Affiliate						
Total factor productivity, affiliate	8.312	0.644	10,014	8.420	0.545	9,359
Sales, affiliate	520.8	3,248.1	10,014	559.1	2,044.7	9,359
Capital, affiliate	541.8	3,201.0	10,014	535.5	2,409.8	9,359
Intermediate, affiliate	363.3	2,627.9	10,014	404.9	1,496.3	9,359
Number of employees, affiliate	1,725.7	5,377.9	10,014	2,101.9	7,112.9	9,359
Firm age, affiliate	30.1	29.9	10,014	26.4	24.7	9,359
Sector, affiliate	41.6	18.9	9,564	42.7	20.4	8,697
Same language	0.088	0.284	9,984	0.440	0.496	9,359
Survey year	2,002.3	2.6	10,014	2,002.4	2.6	9,359

Notes: All monetary variables are in millions of euros. 'Same continent' – home and host countries are in the same continent. 'Different continent' – home and host countries are in different continents. 'TFP, parents (affiliates)' is total factor productivity of multinational parents (affiliates). 'Turnover, parents (affiliates)' is annual sales of the multinational parents (affiliates). 'Capital, parents (affiliates)' is capital of the multinational parents (affiliates). 'Intermediate input, parents (affiliates)' is intermediate inputs of multinational parents (affiliates). 'Employment, parents (affiliates)' is the number of employees of multinational parents (affiliates). 'Firm age, parent (affiliate)' is the number of years since the establishment of multinational parent (affiliate). 'Sector, parent (affiliate)' is sector of multinational parents (affiliate). 'Same language' is a dummy equal to one if home and host countries share the same language. 'Same continent' is a dummy equal to one if home and host countries are in the same continent (Asia, Africa, South America, North America, Europe and Oceania). 'Survey year' is the year of survey.

productivity enhancing, as their effects are to transfer some of the knowledge capability within MNEs. A relatively standard approach from the literature was employed, linking technological capability and knowledge of parents to the productivity of the affiliates in order to capture technology flows (Dunning and Lundan, 2008) using the following equation:

$$TFP_{it}^A = \beta_1 TFP_{it}^P + \beta_2 X_{it} + \alpha_i + \gamma_t + e_{it}. \tag{7.1}$$

The key variables are TFP_{it}^A, the total factor productivity of the multinational affiliate i at year t, and TFP_{it}^P the total factor productivity of the multinational parent of the same affiliate i in the same year t. Equation (7.1) also includes other

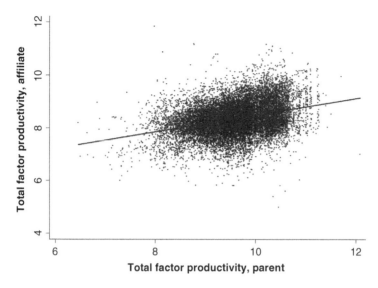

Figure 7.1   Scatter plot of TFP of parent and TFP of affiliate, and linear fit to the scatter plot
Notes: The horizontal axis presents the total factor productivity of multinational parents. The vertical axis presents the total factor productivity of multinational affiliates.

control variables (X_{it}), including capital per worker, firm age of the affiliate (both measured in logs) and different combinations of fixed effects, including industries (58) and countries (45), and year effects (γ_t). Finally, the most detailed specifications also controlled for firm fixed effects (α_i). The key parameter is β_1, which shows the elasticity of parent productivity with respect to the knowledge and productivity of the affiliate. Hypothesis 7.1 focuses the attention on β_1 in the baseline model, to determine the average impact of parent's total factor productivity on affiliate's technological capability and competency development.

Table 7.4 reports our estimate of (7.1). Column 1 does not control for any fixed effect, while Column 2 controls for country, sector and year fixed effects. Column 3 controls for country–year interaction fixed effects. Column 4 controls for sector–year interaction fixed effects. Column 5 controls for country–sector interaction fixed effects. Column 6 controls for firm fixed effects and business cycle effects. Across Columns 1–6, we found that affiliate capital per worker and firm age have their predicted positive effects upon knowledge and competency development of the affiliate, and all of them are significant at 1 per cent. The most detailed specification in Column 6 controls for firm and year fixed effects suggests that 1 per cent increase in capital is associated with 0.045 per cent increases in technological capability and knowledge competence of affiliates.

Turning to our key variable, we found in Column 1 that the productivity of the parents has a positive and significant effect upon the affiliate's technological capability and knowledge competence. The elasticity is 0.224 and is precisely estimated at significance level of 1 per cent, suggesting that 1 per cent increase in parents' productivity leads to 0.224 per cent increase in affiliates' knowledge competence.

Table 7.4 Competence generation – main results

	(1)	(2)	(3)	(4)	(5)	(6)
TFP, parent	0.224***	0.203***	0.225***	0.208***	0.204***	0.124***
	(0.006)	(0.006)	(0.006)	(0.006)	(0.006)	(0.013)
Capital, affiliate	0.229***	0.142***	0.137***	0.233***	0.148***	0.045***
	(0.004)	(0.004)	(0.004)	(0.005)	(0.005)	(0.009)
Firm age, affiliate	0.104***	0.073***	0.057***	0.126***	0.072***	0.220***
	(0.004)	(0.004)	(0.004)	(0.004)	(0.004)	(0.016)
Constant	3.120***	4.570***	4.369***	3.160***	4.377***	6.073***
	(0.069)	(0.094)	(0.068)	(0.078)	(0.079)	(0.174)
Country FE		X				
Year FE		X				
Sector FE		X				
Country*Year FE			X			
Sector*year FE				X		
Country*Sector FE					X	
Firm FE						X
R-squared	0.29	0.50	0.48	0.36	0.59	0.94
No. of observation	19,373	18,261	19,373	18,261	18,261	19,373
F statistics	2,178.473	274.7603	1,142.338	1,745.786	887.8328	293.7488

Notes: Dependent variable is total factor productivity of a multinational affiliate. All explanatory variables are in logarithms. Values in parentheses are robust standard errors. 'TFP, parent' is total factor productivity of the multinational parent. 'Capital, affiliate' is capital per worker of the multinational affiliate. 'Firm age, affiliate' is the number of years since the establishment of the multinational affiliate. Column 1 does not control for any fixed effects. Column 2 controls for country, sector and year fixed effects. Column 3 controls for country-year interaction fixed effects. Column 4 controls for sector–year interaction fixed effects. Column 5 controls for country-sector interaction fixed effects. Column 6 controls for firm fixed effects and year fixed effects. Significance levels: *, 0.10; **, 0.05; ***, 0.01.

The first column is just a simple ordinary least square estimator without controlling for any fixed effects. One may argue that, since our analysis draws on a large set of firms containing 1,514 multinational parents and 3,712 overseas affiliates, covering 58 industries and 45 countries during the period from 1997 to 2007, estimates in Column 1 are biased without controlling for country, sector and year heterogeneity. In order to address this issue, Columns 2–5 control for different combination of country, sector and year effects, and we find the productivity of the parents plays a positive role on affiliates' knowledge competence, ranging from 20.3 per cent to 22.5 per cent, significant in each model. Finally, in Column 6, we add the most detailed specification, controlling for firm fixed effects and business cycle effects, and with them the result still shows a positive effect of parents' productivity on affiliates' knowledge competence. The estimate shows that a 1 per cent increase in the parent's TFP is associated with a 0.124 per cent increase in the affiliate's knowledge competence.

One may still argue that better-performing overseas affiliates will transfer knowledge to their multinational parents, in particular considering the literature on reverse knowledge transfer (compare Driffield et al., 2010; Griffith et al., 2006; Iwasa and Odagiri, 2004; Singh, 2007) examining knowledge flows running from affiliates to their parent companies. In order to solve or at least alleviate this issue, we draw on a generalized method of moment (GMM) estimator that instruments for current-period parent total factor productivity using multinational parents' capital and number of employees. We also found that, after controlling for the affiliate and year fixed effects, parents' TFP continues to plays a positive role in the knowledge competence of affiliates. Furthermore, the Sargan tests of over-identification and weak identification and under-identification indicate that the instruments employed in the instrumental variable estimator are valid.[1]

Hypothesis 7.2 then examines the importance of a common language, using the following specifications:

$$TFP_{it}^A = \beta_3 TFP_{it}^P * SameLanguage_{it} + \beta_4 TFP_{it}^P + \beta_5 X_{it} + \alpha_i + \gamma_t + e_{it}. \qquad (7.2)$$

In this specification all variables have the same interpretation as in (7.1), while $SameLanguage_{it}$ in (7.2) is a dummy equal to one if home and host countries share the same language, and $TFP_{it}^P * SameLanguage_{it}$ is the interaction term of interest and β_3 in terms of Hypothesis 7.2.

Using (7.2), our main interest is the interaction term between parent's total factor productivity and a dummy variable (*SameLanguage*) equal to one if multinational parent and affiliate are located in countries sharing the same language. Table 7.5 reports our results, following a similar structure to Table 7.4. The results across all columns in Table 7.5 show that the total factor productivity of parents continues to play a positive and significant role in affiliates' knowledge and competence generation, ranging from 0.108 to 0.239 (all columns are at significance levels). Next we turn to our main interest, which is the interaction term between the total factor productivity of parent and the same language dummy. The coefficients on this variable are all positive and at the significance level of

Table 7.5 Location choice and competence generation

	(1)	(2)	(3)	(4)	(5)	(6)
TFP, parent * Same language	0.014***	0.005***	0.005***	0.013***	0.006***	0.066**
	(0.001)	(0.001)	(0.001)	(0.001)	(0.001)	(0.027)
TFP, parent	0.239***	0.206***	0.228***	0.221***	0.207***	0.108***
	(0.006)	(0.006)	(0.006)	(0.006)	(0.006)	(0.015)
Capital, affiliate	0.226***	0.142***	0.137***	0.229***	0.149***	0.045***
	(0.004)	(0.004)	(0.004)	(0.005)	(0.005)	(0.009)
Firm age, affiliate	0.105***	0.073***	0.057***	0.124***	0.072***	0.220***
	(0.004)	(0.004)	(0.004)	(0.004)	(0.004)	(0.016)
Constant	2.973***	4.755***	4.334***	3.047***	4.328***	6.065***
	(0.069)	(0.099)	(0.069)	(0.078)	(0.080)	(0.172)
Country FE		X				
Year FE		X				
Sector FE		X				
Country*Year FE			X			
Sector*year FE				X		
Country*Sector FE					X	
Firm FE						X
R-squared	0.30	0.50	0.48	0.37	0.59	0.94
No. of observation	19,343	18,231	19,343	18,231	18,231	19,343
F statistics	1,699.778	266.1112	858.7542	1,364.823	671.435	275.2871

Notes: Dependent variable is total factor productivity of a multinational affiliate. All explanatory variables are in logarithms. Values in parentheses are robust standard errors. 'Same language' is a dummy equal to one if home and host countries are in the same language. 'TFP, parent' is total factor productivity of the multinational parent. 'Capital, affiliate' is capital per worker of the multinational affiliate. 'Firm age, affiliate' is the number of years since the establishment of the multinational affiliate. Column 1 does not control for any fixed effects. Column 2 controls for country, sector and year fixed effects. Column 3 controls for country–year interaction fixed effects. Column 4 controls for sector–year interaction fixed effects. Column 5 controls for country–sector interaction fixed effects. Column 6 controls for firm fixed effects and year fixed effects. Significance levels: *, 0.10; **, 0.05; ***, 0.01.

at least 5 per cent, indicating that the impact of parent's productivity on affiliate technological capability and knowledge competence is higher when a parent and its overseas affiliate are located in countries sharing same language. The role of the same language on affiliate's knowledge and competence generation ranges between 0.005 and 0.066.

In order to test the robustness of the results in Table 7.5 regarding the influence of location of knowledge generation of affiliates, we check different specifications. Table 7.1 shows that 25.8 per cent of parent–affiliate–year observations equal one for the same language variable, a dummy equal to one when home and host countries share the same language; thus a reasonable question to ask is whether the role of parent productivity in affiliate technological capability is different when we split samples in terms of different location of multinational affiliates. We re-estimate (7.1) using the same language group, where home and host countries share the same language, and report the results in Table 7.6. Column 6 suggests that the influence of parent productivity on affiliate knowledge competence is positive, with a coefficient of 0.229, suggesting that a 1 per cent increase in parent TFP is associated with 0.229 per cent increase in affiliate's knowledge competence. Next, we re-estimate (7.1) using the different group, where home and host countries do not share the same language, and report the results in Table 7.7. We again find the role of parent productivity in affiliate technological capability and competence generation is positive and significant in Column 6, and the size of the effect is 0.097 and at a significance level of 1 per cent. Comparing Tables 7.6 and 7.7, we find that the role of parents' total factor productivity on affiliates' competence generation is higher (0.229 in Table 7.6 vs. 0.097 in Table 7.7) when home and host countries share the same language, relative to pairs when they are located in countries using a different language, and thus this is consistent with the findings in Table 7.5 when we introduce the interaction term of total factor productivity and the same language dummy.

Conclusion

Consistent with previous studies (Cohen and Levinthal, 1990; Zejan, 1990), this chapter found that the knowledge orientation of a subsidiary is related to the knowledge orientation of the parent. With this groundwork hypothesis confirmed, this chapter further examines the effect of common language on the knowledge and competency development of subsidiaries. The cultural embeddedness perspective predicts that efficiency-driven MNEs would search for host locations that provide them with the most easily accessed knowledge and competencies, due to high costs and uncertainties. The perspective predicts that cultural similarity is particularly crucial for the successful transfer of knowledge, particularly in the high-tech sector where knowledge and competencies are more complex and often un-codified. This chapter confirms the long-held view that a common language is an important consideration for multinational parents when considering the location of subsidiaries mandated with knowledge and competency development. We found that the impact from parent's productivity on affiliate's knowledge and

Table 7.6 Competence generation (home and host countries share the same language)

	(1)	(2)	(3)	(4)	(5)	(6)
TFP, parent	0.321***	0.306***	0.317***	0.307***	0.308***	0.229***
	(0.013)	(0.012)	(0.013)	(0.013)	(0.013)	(0.028)
Capital, affiliate	0.149***	0.117***	0.109***	0.139***	0.117***	0.039***
	(0.007)	(0.008)	(0.007)	(0.008)	(0.008)	(0.013)
Firm age, affiliate	0.054***	0.045***	0.039***	0.053***	0.044***	0.198***
	(0.006)	(0.007)	(0.006)	(0.007)	(0.007)	(0.025)
Constant	3.423***	3.597***	3.989***	3.667***	3.962***	5.319***
	(0.140)	(0.208)	(0.147)	(0.146)	(0.142)	(0.305)
Country FE		X				
Year FE		X				
Sector FE		X				
Country*Year FE			X			
Sector*year FE				X		
Country*Sector FE					X	
Firm FE						X
R-squared	0.28	0.41	0.37	0.40	0.49	0.91
No. of observation	4,995	4,908	4,995	4,908	4,908	4,995
F statistics	438.0818	76.40597	301.1189	357.9636	331.1101	82.33395

Notes: Dependent variable is total factor productivity of the multinational affiliate. All explanatory variables are in logarithms. Values in parentheses are robust standard errors. TFP, parent' is total factor productivity of the multinational parent. 'Capital, affiliate' is capital per worker of the multinational affiliate. 'Firm age, affiliate' is the number of years since the establishment of the multinational affiliate. Column 1 does not control for any fixed effects. Column 2 controls for country, sector and year fixed effects. Column 3 controls for country–year interaction fixed effects. Column 4 controls for sector–year interaction fixed effects. Column 5 controls for country–sector interaction fixed effects. Column 6 controls for firm fixed effects and year fixed effects. Significance levels: *, 0.10; **, 0.05; ***, 0.01.

Table 7.7 Competence generation – (home and host countries do not share same language)

	(1)	(2)	(3)	(4)	(5)	(6)
TFP, parent	0.218***	0.180***	0.202***	0.200***	0.184***	0.097***
	(0.007)	(0.007)	(0.006)	(0.008)	(0.007)	(0.015)
Capital, affiliate	0.252***	0.150***	0.146***	0.256***	0.164***	0.047***
	(0.005)	(0.005)	(0.005)	(0.005)	(0.006)	(0.011)
Firm age, affiliate	0.124***	0.082***	0.063***	0.147***	0.082***	0.232***
	(0.005)	(0.005)	(0.005)	(0.005)	(0.005)	(0.020)
Constant	2.814***	4.710***	4.434***	2.849***	4.318***	6.247***
	(0.080)	(0.159)	(0.079)	(0.093)	(0.101)	(0.207)
Country FE		X				
Year FE		X				
Sector FE		X				
Country*Year FE			X			
Sector*year FE				X		
Country*Sector FE					X	
Firm FE						X
R-squared	0.32	0.53	0.51	0.39	0.63	0.94
No. of observation	14,348	13,323	14,348	13,323	13,323	14,348
F statistics	1,844.666	247.4396	816.2746	1,452.416	581.3905	218.9769

Notes: Dependent variable is total factor productivity of the multinational affiliate. All explanatory variables are in logarithms. Values in parentheses are robust standard errors. 'TFP, parent' is total factor productivity of the multinational parent. 'Capital, affiliate' is capital per worker of the multinational affiliate. 'Firm age, affiliate' is the number of years since the establishment of the multinational affiliate. Column 1 does not control for any fixed effects. Column 2 controls for country, sector and year fixed effects. Column 3 controls for country–year interaction fixed effects. Column 4 controls for sector–year interaction fixed effects. Column 5 controls for country–sector interaction fixed effects. Column 6 controls for firm fixed effects and year fixed effects. Significance levels: *, 0.10; **, 0.05; ***, 0.01.

competency development is higher when a parent and its overseas affiliate are located in countries that share a common language – a finding that remains robust after controlling for firm characteristics and various fixed effects.

The finding seems to suggest that, as the nature of knowledge is often complex and un-codified, when it comes to the development of competencies and knowledge, MNEs are more inclined to support subsidiaries that share a common language with the parent, rather than investing in a country requiring adaptation to a different language. Whilst previous studies have suggested that the use of translation services and designated translators within organizations can facilitate the transfer of knowledge within MNEs (Janssen et al., 2004), our finding appears to suggest that translation alone cannot resolve the knowledge transfer barriers between parent and subsidiaries. The high cost of translation as well as the extensiveness of translation required for knowledge-intensive activities means that the attractiveness of investing in the competence of subsidiaries that do not share a common language with the parent is substantially reduced. Moreover, the use of translation, either through an external service or internally through a designated employee, can lead to distortion of the message, resulting in the original message from the parent not being fully conveyed. Such reliance on a small number of individuals can also result in a centralized hierarchical structure that is unfavourable to the development of innovation and technologies.

Nevertheless, the reliance of subsidiaries that share a common language with the parent may significantly limit the talent pool for the MNE, which may hinder their technological and innovative development. The increasingly popular notion of 'innovation from the edge' suggests that MNEs may lose out if they do not attempt to capture the innovation potential of these new technological frontiers (Birkinshaw and Hood, 2001). Whilst MNEs are beginning to tap into these new supplies, language, and to a certain extent, culture, remain a considerable obstacle, as this chapter concludes. Nevertheless, whilst the overall trend shows that investing in the knowledge and competencies of non-native subsidiaries remains unpopular, there are, nevertheless, successful examples. Technological clusters such as the Silicon Valley are filled with companies from all across the world attempting to benefit from the external externalities created within such a diverse environment (Lee et al., 2000). Further examination of the role of language in these technological clusters may enhance our understanding of the role of language in the transfer of knowledge, both from parent to subsidiaries and vice versa. Certainty the use of English as a common language appears to be useful in the above context and studies have found that many technologically orientated MNEs have overcame the language barrier using this approach (Welch and Welch, 2008).

However, our finding also has important internal, organizational ramifications. In order to capture innovation from all parts of the world, MNEs need to consider different ways to enter countries where they do not share a common language. Human resources can certainly play an important role in increasing the language standard of both parent and host country nationals, to facilitate communications between units (Feely and Harzing, 2003; Harzing and Feely, 2008). A rigorous and systematic internal language training programme may improve the overall language standard within an MNE, resulting in a reduced reliance on a small number of language nodes, which may have negative consequences. Alternatively, human resources can impose strict recruitment criteria in terms of language competencies (Feely and Harzing, 2003). For instance, Nestlé's recruitment policy is largely language driven (Lester, 1994). Such language requirements can then be embedded into the career development of employees, for example, the electronics company Siemens requests their workers to be fluent in at least two official languages of the company in order to progress within it (Marschan-Piekkari et al., 1999b). Finally, to develop and transfer knowledge and competencies often require structural transformation within a MNE. As a centralized structure is found to hinder innovation (Kim, 1980; Zmud, 1982), firms may need to consider the implementation of a polycentric structure to allow these affiliates to be more autonomous. Many Japanese and Korean MNEs are renowned for developing R&D clusters in other non-native-speaking developed economies by creating a decentralized structure within these affiliates that is more favourable to the development of innovation and technologies, despite the fact that an ethnocentric approach may be adopted for the rest of the organizational hierarchy (Pearce, 1999).

From the government's point of view, the chapter implies that education beyond technical knowledge is required in order to attract foreign knowledge investments successfully or for local companies to invest in knowledge and competencies abroad. Whilst many countries such as Korea and Japan have successfully developed a highly knowledge-orientated workforce, foreign language training has traditionally not been an emphasis of their education curriculum. This, together with other cultural differences, has resulted in massive cultural adjustments that their expatriates will have to make when moving aboard. Government therefore needs to encourage technical students to engage in language training throughout their education. Singapore, the Netherlands and Scandinavian countries are all successful examples of how such a multilingual policy is being adopted (McRae, 1997; Pakir, 2003; Phillipson, 2003) and therefore further study on their educational curriculum would provide more information as to how such a knowledge facilitation strategy can be implemented.

Finally, whilst a shared language is undoubtedly an important facilitator of the transfer of knowledge and competencies, communication of knowledge does not depend only on the language they speak, but also the internal cognitive capabilities that translate the articulate message into the intended message. Such articulation of knowledge requires social knowledge to be adequately developed (Buckley et al., 2005) and therefore employees from different operations need to be able to understand and be sensitive to each other.

Acknowledgement

We appreciate comments from Gary Cook and Vania Sena. We also thank the participants at the Academy of International Business 2012 conference in Liverpool and the Chinese Economic Association 2012 conference in the School of Oriental and African Studies, University of London, for helpful comments. The authors gratefully acknowledge the financial support from the University of Essex under internal grant DH00760.

Note

1. GMM-IV estimates and tests of over-identification and weak identification and under-identification are available upon request.

References

P. Almeida, 'Knowledge sourcing by foreign multinationals: patent citation analysis in the U.S. semiconductor industry', *Strategic Management Journal*, 17(Winter Special Issue) (1996) 155–65.

H. Andersen and E. Rasmussen, 'The role of language skills in corporate communication', *Corporate Communications: An International Journal*, 9(3) (2004) 231–42.

P. Athukorala and A. Kohpaiboon, 'Globalisation of R&D by US-based multinational enterprises', *Research Policy*, 39(10) (2010) 1335–47.

W. Barner-Rasmussen, 'Knowledge Sharing in Multinational Corporations. A Social Capital Perspective', Doctoral Dissertation, Hanken School of Economics, Helsinki, 2003.

W. Barner-Rasmussen and I. Björkman, 'Language fluency, socialization and inter-unit relationships in Chinese and Finnish subsidiaries', *Management and Organization Review*, 3(1) (2007) 105–28.

S. Bhaumik, N. Driffield and S. Pal, 'Does ownership structure of emerging-market firms affect their outward FDI & quest: the case of the Indian automotive and pharmaceutical sectors?', *Journal of International Business Studies*, 41 (2010) 437–50.

J. Birkinshaw, U. Holm, P. Thilenius and N. Arvidsson, 'Consequences of perception gaps in the headquarters-subsidiary relationship', *International Business Review* 9 (2000) 321–44.

J. Birkinshaw and N. Hood, 'Unleash innovation in foreign subsidiaries', *Harvard Business Review*, 79(3) (2001) 131–37.

A. Björkman and R. Piekkari, 'Language and foreign subsidiary control: an empirical test', *Journal of International Management*, 15(1) (2009) 105–17.

P. Buckley, M. Carter, J. Clegg and H. Tan, 'Language and social knowledge in foreign knowledge transfer to China', *International Studies of Management and Organisation*, 35(1) (2005) 47–56.

J. Cantwell and G. Santangelo, 'Capitalism, profits and innovation in the new techno-economic paradigm', *Journal of Evolutionary Economics*, 10(1) (2000) 131–57.

W. Cohen and D. Levinthal, 'Absorptive capacity: a new perspective on learning and innovation', *Administrative Science Quarterly*, 35(1) (1990) 128–52.

I. Dierickx and K. Cool, 'Asset stock accumulation and sustainability of competitive advantage', *Management Science*, 35(12) (1989) 1504–11.

J. Doh, G. Jones, R. Mudambi and H. Teegen, 'foreign research and development and host country environment: an empirical examination of U.S. International R&D', *Management International Review*, 45(2) (2005) 121–54.

N. Driffield, J. Love and S. Menghinello, 'The multinational enterprise as a source of international knowledge flows: direct evidence from Italy', *Journal of International Business Studies*, 41(2) (2010) 350–59.

J. H. Dunning, *Multinational Enterprises and the Global Economy*, (Wokingham: Addison Wesley, 1993).

J. H. Dunning and M. Lundan, *Multinational Enterprises and the Global Economy*, (Cheltenham: Edward Elgar, 2008).

D. Ernst and L. Kim, 'Global production networks, knowledge diffusion, and local capability formation', *Research Policy*, 31(8–9) (2002) 1417–29.

F. Fai and R. Marschan-Piekkari, 'Language issues in cross-border strategic alliances: an investigation of technological knowledge transfers', Annual Meeting of the European International Business Academy, Copenhagen, 10–13 December 2003.

A. Feely and A. Harzing, 'Language management in multinational companies', *Cross Cultural Management: An International Journal*, 10(2) (2003) 37–52.

P. Figueiredo, 'The role of dual embeddedness in the innovative performance of MNE subsidiaries: evidence from Brazil', *Journal of Management Studies*, 48(2) (2011) 417–40.

R. Florida, 'The globalisation of R&D: results survey of foreign-affiliated R&D laboratories in the USA', *Research Policy*, 26(1) (1997) 85–103.

O. Gassmann and M. von Zedtwitz, 'New concepts and trends in international R&D organization', *Research Policy*, 28(1) (1999) 231–50.

A. Gerybadze and G. Reger, 'Globalization of R&D: recent changes in the management of innovation in transnational corporations', *Research Policy*, 28(2–3) (1999) 251–74.

H. Giles and P. Johnson, 'The role of language in ethnic group relations', in J. Turner and H. Giles (eds), *Intergroup Behavior*, (Oxford: Blackwell, 1981), pp. 199–243.

R. Griffith, R. Harrison and J. Reenen, 'How special is the special relationship? Using the impact of U.S. R&D spillovers on U.K. firms as a test of technology sourcing', *The American Economic Review*, 96(5) (2006) 1859–75.

W. Gudykunst, 'Anxiety/Uncertainty Management (AUM) Theory: Current Status', in R. Wiseman (ed.), *Intercultural Communication Theory*, (Thousand Oaks, CA: Sage, 1995), pp. 8–58.

A. Harzing and A. Feely, 'The language barrier and its implications for HQ–subsidiary relationships', *Cross Cultural Management: An International Journal*, 15(1) (2008) 49–61.

P. Hill, 'Language and National Identity', in A. Liddicoat and K. Muller (eds), *Perspectives on Europe: Language Issues and Language Planning in Europe*, (Melbourne: Language Australia, 2002), pp. 11–20.

A. Hogenbirk and H. van Kranenburg, 'Roles of foreign owned subsidiaries in a small economy', *International Business Review*, 15(1) (2006) 53–67.

B. Ito and R. Wakasugi, 'What factors determine the mode of overseas R&D by multinationals?', *Research Policy*, 36(8) (2007) 1275–87.

T. Iwasa and H. Odagiri, 'Overseas R&D, knowledge sourcing, and patenting: an empirical studies of Japanese R&D investment in the US', *Research Policy*, 33(5) (2004) 807–28.

M. Janssens, J. Lambert and C. Steyaert, 'Developing language strategies for international companies: the contribution of translation studies', *Journal of World Business*, 39(4) (2004) 414–30.

J. Johanson and F. Wiedersheim-Paul, 'The internationalization of the firm – four Swedish cases', *Journal of Management Studies*, 12(3) (1975) 305–23.

W. Johnson and J. Medcof, 'Motivating proactive subsidiary innovation: agent-based theory and socialization models in global R&D', *Journal of International Management*, 13(4) (2007) 472–84.

B. Kedia and D. Mukherjeeb, 'Understanding offshoring: a research framework based on disintegration, location and externalization advantages', *Journal of World Business*, 44(3) (2009) 250–61.

L. Kim, 'Organizational innovation and structure', *Journal of Business Research*, 8(2) (1980) 225–45.

B. Kogut, 'A note on global strategies', *Strategic Management Journal*, 10 (4) (1989) 383–89.

B. Kogut and H. Singh, 'The effect of national culture on the choice of entry mode', *Journal of International Business Studies*, 19(3) (1988) 411–32.

D. Kogut and U. Zander, 'Knowledge of the firm and the evolutionary theory of the multinational corporation', *Journal of International Business Studies*, 24(4) (1993) 625–45.

N. Kumar, 'Determinants of location of overseas R&D activity of multinational enterprises: the case of US and Japanese corporations', *Research Policy*, 30(1) (2001) 179–93.

A. Lam, 'Organizational learning in multinationals: R&D networks of Japanese and US MNEs in the UK', *Journal of Management Studies*, 40(3) (2003) 673–703.

C. Lee, W. Miller, M. Hancock and H. Rowen, *The Silicon Valley Edge: A Habitat for Innovation and Entrepreneurship*, (Stanford, CA: Stanford University Press, 2000).

T. Lester, 'Pulling down the language barrier', *International Management*, 49(6) (1994) 42–4.

J. Levinsohn and A. Petrin, 'Estimating production functions using inputs to control for unobservables', *Review of Economic Studies*, 70(2) (2003) 317–41.

R. Marschan, D. Welch and L. Welch, 'Language: the forgotten factor in multinational management', *European Management Journal*, 15(5) (1997) 591–98.

R. Marschan-Piekkari, D. E. Welch and L. S. Welch, 'In the shadow: the impact of language on structure, power and communication in the multinational', *International Business Review*, 8(4) (1999a) 421–40.

R. Marschan-Piekkari, D. Welch and L. Welch, 'Adopting a common corporate language: IHRM implications', *The International Journal of Human Resource Management*, 10(3) (1999b) 377–90.

P. Martins and Y. Yang, 'The impact of exporting on firm productivity: a meta-analysis of the learning-by-exporting hypothesis', *Review of World Economics*, 145(3) (2009) 431–45.

K. McRae, *Conflict and Compromise in Multilingual Societies: Finland*, (Waterloo, ON: Wilfrid Laurier University Press, 1997).

K. Meyer, R. Mudambi and R. Narula, 'Multinational enterprises and local contexts: The opportunities and challenges of multiple embeddedness', *Journal of Management Studies*, 48(2) (2011) 235–52.

G. Morgan, 'The Multinational Firm: Organizing Across Institutional and National Divides', in G. Morgan, P. H. Kristensen and R. Whitley (eds), *The Multinational Firm: Organizing Across Institutional and National Divides*, (Oxford: Oxford University Press, 2001), pp. 1–26.

R. Narula and J. Dunning, 'Multinational enterprises, development and globalisation: some clarifications and a research agenda', *Oxford Development Studies*, 38(3) (2010) 263–87.

L. Oakes, *Language and National Identity: Comparing France and Sweden*, (Philadelphia, PA: Benjamins Publishing, 2001).

G. Olley and A. Pakes, 'The dynamics of productivity in the telecommunications equipment industry', *Econometrica*, 64(6) (1996) 1263–97.

A. Pakir, 'Medium-of-Instruction Policy in Singapore', in J. Tollefson and A. Tsui (eds), *Medium of Instruction Policies: Which Agenda? Whose Agenda?*, (Mahwah, NJ: Lawrence Erlbaum Publishers, 2003), pp. 117–33.

R. Pearce, 'Decentralised R&D and strategic competitiveness: globalised approaches to generation and use of technology in multinational enterprises (MNEs)', *Research Policy*, 28(2/3) (1999) 157–78.

J. Penner-Hahn and M. Shaver, 'Does international research and development increase patent output? An analysis of Japanese pharmaceutical firms', *Strategic Management Journal*, 26(2) (2005) 121–40.

R. Phillipson, *English-only Europe? Challenging Language Policy*, (London: Routledge, 2003).

S. P. Ribeiro, S. Menghinello and K. D. Backer, 'The OECD ORBIS database: responding to the need for firm-level micro-data in the OECD', *OECD Statistics Working Papers* (2010/11).

J. Selmer, 'Language ability and adjustment: Western expatriates in China', *Thunderbird International Business Review*, 48(3) (2006) 347–68.

J. Singh, 'Asymmetry of knowledge spillovers between MNCs and host country firms', *Journal of International Business Studies*, 38(5) (2007) 764–86.

J. Singh, 'Distributed R&D, cross-regional knowledge integration and quality of innovative output', *Research Policy* 37 (1) (2008) 77–96.

J. H. Sohn, 'Social knowledge as a control system: a proposition and evidence from the Japanese FDI behavior', *Journal of International Business Studies*, 25(2) (1994) 295–324.

J. Song, K. Asakawa and Y. Chu, 'What determines knowledge sourcing from host locations of overseas R&D operations? A study of global R&D activities of Japanese multinationals', *Research Policy*, 40(3) (2011) 380–90.

J-C. Usunier, *International and Cross-Cultural Management Research*, (London: Sage, 1998).

D. Welch and L. Welch, 'The importance of language in international knowledge transfer', *Management International Review*, 48(3) (2008) 339–60.

D. Welch, L. Welch and R. Piekkari, 'Speaking in tongues – the importance of language in international management process', *International Studies of Management and Organisation*, 35(1) (2005) 10–27.

R. Whitley, *Divergent Capitalisms*, (Oxford: Oxford University Press, 1999).

R. Whitley, 'How and Why Are International Firms Different? The Consequences of Crossborder Managerial Coordination for Firm Characteristics and Behaviour', in G. Morgan, P. H. Kristensen and R. Whitley (eds), *The Multinational Firm: Organizing Across Institutional and National Divides*, (Oxford: Oxford University Press, 2001), pp. 27–68.

H. Yamawaki, 'Who survives in Japan? An empirical analysis of European and U.S. multinational firms in Japanese manufacturing industries', *Journal of Industry, Competition and Trade*, 4(2) (2004) 135–53.

A. Zanfei, 'Transnational firms and the changing organization of innovation activities', *Cambridge Journal of Economics*, 24(5) (2000) 515–42.

M. C. Zejan, 'R&D activities in affiliates of Swedish multinational enterprises', *Scandinavian Journal of Economics*, 92(3) (1990) 487–500.

R. Zmud, 'Diffusion of modern software practices: influence of centralization and formalization', *Management Science*, 28(12) (1982) 1421–31.

8
Reconceptualizing Cross-Border Knowledge Acquisition: An Empirical Investigation into Antecedents

Mia Hsiao-Wen Ho

Introduction

The growing importance of cross-border knowledge acquisition is recognition that competitive advantage can no longer be solely ascribed to national idiosyncrasies, but rather depends on resources and capabilities exchanged or acquired from international networks (Mathews, 2003; Squire et al., 2009). As the global competition continues to intensify, the acquisition of new organizational knowledge from external sources has become a managerial priority in that it provides the basis for organizational renewal and sustainable competitive advantage (Inkpen, 1998). Research on knowledge acquisition has been burgeoning since the 1990s; yet exploration of such issues within international contexts is a relatively recent phenomenon (Bresman et al., 1999). Indeed, international scholars have acknowledged that the role of management knowledge is a crucial and under-researched phenomenon of globalization (Buckley and Ghauri, 2004).

Nonetheless, substantial studies have proposed and examined a variety of determinants of successful knowledge acquisition both within and across organizational boundaries (e.g., Cui et al., 2006; Gupta and Govindarajan, 2000; Kachra and White, 2008). These determinants, compiled and categorized by van Wijk, Jansen and Lyles (2008), include knowledge, organizational and dyad- or network-level characteristics. With few exceptions (e.g., Lyles and Salk, 1996; Perez-Nordtvedt et al., 2008), however, most researchers have failed to examine these determinants simultaneously. The ignorance of possible relationships among these determinants could render a biased assumption that knowledge acquisition, either within or across organizations, is influenced by a set of irrelevant factors.

The understandings of how knowledge is created, retained, retrieved and applied, and how the interplay of the different factors affects cooperative outcomes in international strategic alliances, remained largely unexplored (Meier, 2011). As the nature of international strategic alliances involves firms with heterogeneous contexts, rare research has incorporated the contextual concern with cross-border knowledge acquisition. In an attempt to redress these imbalances in the existing literature, this research aims to reconceptualize the antecedents of cross-border knowledge acquisition by empirically investigating the role played by contextual factors in relation to knowledge, organizational and relational determinants of knowledge acquisition within international strategic alliances.

In order to achieve the research objective, this research first of all identifies the key antecedents of knowledge acquisition within international strategic alliances and categorizes them into four dimensions – knowledge, organizational, relational and contextual characteristics. This research examines the influence of each factor on cross-border knowledge acquisition and then tests the dynamic linkages among these factors, either complement or substitutive relationships. By doing so, this research is able to fill the gaps in the existing literature on cross-border knowledge acquisition and contributes to a further integration of the alliance theories and understanding of the better management of cross-border collaborations.

Literature review

Research on knowledge acquisition is not a new fad. The strategic importance and implications for competitiveness of the firm have been the major concern of knowledge acquisition by the knowledge-based theorists (e.g., Kogut and Zander, 1992; Wiklund and Shepherd, 2003). Inkpen (1998, 2000) proposed that acquisition of new knowledge through strategic alliances is the lifeblood of experimentation, innovation and change for firms and thus through cooperation firms could gain access to their partners' broad knowledge-based resources and capabilities. This view of alliances as a knowledge channel is critical, but it overlooks the potential threats, resulting from the geographically dispersed locations between alliance partners to cross-border knowledge acquisition. Although some researchers have acknowledged that knowledge acquisition is a difficult, frustrating and often misunderstood process (e.g., Inkpen, 1998, 2000; Park et al., 2008; Szulanski, 1996), they have not specified the conditions in which acquisition of the new knowledge would be impeded and what alliance partners could do to mitigate such complication. Accordingly, this research starts from a novel angle to identify the key impediments of cross-border knowledge acquisition, in addition to the existing understanding of the facilitators proposed in prior literature.

The key antecedents of cross-border knowledge acquisition

Various antecedents of cross-border knowledge acquisition have been discussed in prior studies. Lyles and Salk (1996) pioneered the association of contextual factors with cross-border knowledge acquisition research and suggested that the relation between knowledge acquisition and organizational characteristics, such as absorptive capacity and partner involvement, is positively moderated by structural mechanisms (ownership) but negatively moderated by contextual factors, such as cultural conflicts and misunderstanding between partner firms. Inkpen (1998) argued that knowledge acquisition through international strategic alliances is influenced by the value and accessibility of the knowledge, effectiveness of learning and managerial and cultural alignment between firms. Additionally, Park et al. (2008) examined the impact of cultural distance on knowledge acquisition through international joint ventures and found a negative association between cultural distance and success of knowledge acquisition.

These studies generally recognized the importance of cultural differences between alliance partners on knowledge acquisition. However, as noted by Meier (2011), there has been limited research examining how and why different cultural dimensions influence cross-border knowledge acquisition, and not to mention that even limited research has associated other dimensions of contextual differences, such as institutional or technological distances, with the issue of knowledge acquisition through international strategic alliances. To enrich this theoretical gap in prior literature, this research applies a more encompassing concept of institutional distance to investigate the contextual impacts on cross-border knowledge acquisition. Building upon the emergent institution-based view (Peng, Wang and Jiang, 2008), which emphasizes that institutions matter and suggests the need to treat them as crucial exogenous variables, this research advances the existing literature by incorporating institutional factors with cross-border knowledge acquisition because they 'directly determine what arrows a firm has in its quiver as it struggles to formulate and implement strategy' (Ingram and Silverman, 2002, p. 20).

Akin to the theoretical development of cultural distance, institutional distance defined as the extent of different regulatory, normative and cognitive institutional frameworks between the two countries (Kostova, 1996) has been widely applied to examine various phenomena in international business contexts (e.g., Gaur and Lu, 2007; Xu and Shenkar, 2002). Yet unlike cultural distance, which focuses on a single dimension of analysis, institutional distance broadens the analytical framework into regulatory, normative, and cognitive layers and provides holistic lenses based on institutional theory to explain the dynamics of cross-border collaborations. In line with the existing literature on institutional distance (e.g., Gaur and Lu, 2007; Kostova, 1996; Xu and Shenkar, 2002), this research epitomizes institutional distance as the major contextual antecedent of knowledge acquisition within international strategic alliances and hypothesizes its negative effect on cross-border knowledge acquisition.

Hypothesis 8.1   Institutional distance between countries from where partner firms originate negatively affects knowledge acquisition within international strategic alliances.

Besides the noxious impact of institutional distance, the feature of cross-border knowledge, however, also stands for the critical impediment of knowledge acquisition. Resource and knowledge-based theorists (Barney et al., 2011; Grant, 1991) have widely advocated that the rationales of international strategic alliance formation are the needs to assess, acquire and control competitive resources, knowledge and capabilities from foreign partners. However, as noted by Inkpen and Beamish (1997), such international partnerships would become less stable if one partner firm accumulates key resources from the other. Consequently, the transferor firm might face a 'boundary paradox' (Quintas et al., 1997, p. 389) – in which the firm must protect its knowledge from imitation by the other but keep open to knowledge transfer at the same time with respect to accomplishing the coopera-tive objective. To resolve such paradox during the knowledge transfer process, the transferor firm might take certain action(s) to protect its knowledge with respect to slowing the diffusion of superior practices and technologies and to stimulating the recipient firm to forego imitation (King and Zeithaml, 2001; McEvily et al., 2000). Accordingly, the feature of the transferred knowledge across national boundaries, perceived by the recipient/acquire firm, is depicted as knowledge protectiveness, which would pose negative impact on knowledge acquisition.

Hypothesis 8.2 Knowledge protectiveness negatively affects knowledge acquisition within international strategic alliances.

Following the process-oriented assumption of knowledge acquisition in prior liter-ature (Kwan and Cheung, 2006), it is suggested that knowledge must be accessible before it can be acquired; but even if there is a high level of accessibility of the knowledge, resulting from the transferor's transparency towards knowledge trans-fer, it does not guarantee a successful acquisition by the recipient. This is because some firms may lack the capacity to learn. Thus the extent to which a firm is able to 'recognise the value of new external knowledge, assimilate it, and apply it to commercial ends' (Cohen and Levinthal, 1990, p. 138) is dependent on its absorptive capacity. Within the domain of organizational learning research, increasingly scholars have delved into the development of the construct and recognized it as a critical contributor to a firm's long-term survival and success because it can reinforce, complement, and refocus the firm's knowledge base (e.g., Lane et al., 2006; Lyles and Salk, 1996). Hence, this research proposes absorptive capacity as an important organizational factor facilitating knowledge acquisition across national boundaries.

Hypothesis 8.3 Absorptive capacity positively affects knowledge acquisition within international strategic alliances.

In addition to the firm's ability to acquire new knowledge, properties of inter-firm relationships have also been substantially discussed and recognized as focal facilitators of knowledge acquisition in prior literature (e.g., Easterby-Smith et al., 2008; Squire et al., 2009). As these properties are relevant to social resources embedded in partnerships, they encompass multi-facets of social contexts, such as social ties, trusting relationships and value systems (van Wijk et al., 2008). Despite the various dimensions of inter-organizational factors, previous research has generally agreed upon the positive role played by them in terms of facili-tating resource and knowledge exchange between firms. For instance, drawing upon technology transfer research, Johnson (1999) considered relational capi-tal, a firm's ability to interact positively with business community members, as a stimulator in technology management for wealth creation. Liu et al. (2010) in a recent empirical study on alliance learning also found that relational capital, a relational rent generated in an exchange relationship that cannot be generated by either firm in isolation, has a positive influence on knowledge acquisition. Accordingly, this research suggests that relational capital as a focal relational factor positively influences the amount of knowledge acquired by the alliance partner.

Hypothesis 8.4   Relational capital positively affects knowledge acquisition within international strategic alliances.

Unlike most prior research focusing on compiling antecedents of knowledge transfer and learning into knowledge, organizational and network/relational characteristics (e.g., Martinkenaite, 2011; van Wijk et al., 2008), this research incorporates contextual concern with the existing antecedents of cross-border knowledge acquisition. This not only highlights the potential impediments of knowledge acquisition, resulting from the heterogeneous contexts of partner firms and their defence, protective behaviour and perception towards knowledge transfer, but also identifies the critical facilitators, which could be accumulated from harmonious relationships between firms along with collaborations and manifested by their abilities to absorb the transferred knowledge. Recognizing these important antecedents and their direct impacts on cross-border knowledge acquisition, however, it is still not clear how the interplay among these factors affects knowledge acquisition within international strategic alliances. In response to this question, a further review of the literature is crucial to reconceptualize the underlying relationships among knowledge, organizational, relational and contextual antecedents of cross-border knowledge acquisition.

The process-dependent nature of knowledge acquisition

As a popular phenomenon studied in the organizational learning literature, knowledge acquisition is defined as the activities and process by which a firm identifies, learns and uses new knowledge (Friesl, 2011). Knowledge acquisition centres more on the choices and actions related solely to the recipient firms, which in this research distinguishes from knowledge transfer, which primarily concerns the two-way processes through which 'one unit is affected by the experience of another' (Argote and Ingram, 2000, p. 151). In this research, cross-border knowledge acquisition is characterized as the manifestation of the results of knowledge transfer between partner firms across national boundaries. Knowledge transfer and acquisition are perceived as two sides of a coin in which they are distinctive in the activities and contexts involved but well-attached to elucidate the underlying mechanisms of alliance operations between firms. Indeed, Andersen (2008) explicated that learning itself is guided by preexisting knowledge. The feature of cross-border knowledge – protectiveness – would thereby impede the recipient firm's absorptive capacity to acquire new knowledge through an international strategic alliance. Building upon the process-dependent assumption of knowledge transfer and learning, absorptive capacity as a focal mediator of knowledge protectiveness on cross-border knowledge acquisition is hypothesized in this research.

Hypothesis 8.5   Knowledge protectiveness negatively affects absorptive capacity.

Although resource- and knowledge-based theories (e.g., Barney et al., 2011; Grant, 1991) have considered intrinsic competition between firms over valuable resources, knowledge and capabilities as the results of knowledge protection during cooperation, they have not explained the possible reasons causing such 'boundary paradox' (Quintas et al., 1997, p. 389) and how can it be alleviated to increase the amount of knowledge acquired.

In order for knowledge to be transmitted and assimilated effectively and efficiently, Guzman and Wilson (2005) maintained that it must be congruent with the existing social context. However, it does not happen easily in conditions in which knowledge transfer is taking place between firms, let alone in cases of international collaborations. In fact, increasing research has noted that knowledge transfer across national boundaries is particularly challenging from an organizational perspective given differences in time, and spatial and cultural distances posing significant barriers to such transfer (e.g., Javidan et al., 2005; Perez-Nordtvedt et al., 2008; Salk and Lyles, 2007). For example, Cummings and Teng (2003) discovered that knowledge and norm distances are negatively associated with knowledge transfer in the case of international R&D collaborations. Though lacking empirical foundation, Bresman et al. (1999) attributed the problems engaged in knowledge transfer to the emergence of geographic and cultural distances between alliance partners. Paralleling these prior studies, this research proposes institutional distance as the main rationale of the firm's protective behaviour and perception towards knowledge transfer, which would increase the noxious impact of knowledge protectiveness whilst at the same time decrease the amount of knowledge acquisition within an alliance.

Hypothesis 8.6   Institutional distance between countries from where partner firms originate positively affects knowledge protectiveness.

Albeit knowledge acquisition arises from the direct experience of the organization and its members (Lyles, 1994), prior research has neglected to examine the underlying mechanisms of such experience between firms. Particularly, even if there are harmonious relationships between firms, a high level of knowledge acquisition might not be necessarily guaranteed in that the recipient firm might experience difficulties in absorbing the knowledge. A more detailed analysis of how relational underpinnings of the alliance operations facilitate the knowledge acquired by the recipient firm is therefore noted in this research. In addition to linking a direct path between relational factor and knowledge acquisition based on prior literature (e.g., Kale et al., 2000; Liu et al., 2010; Park et al., 2008), this research argues that the association between the two could be mediated by the feature of cross-border knowledge. In an empirical research on investigating the antecedents of knowledge transfer, Simonin (1999) discovered that the experience of a firm with its alliance partner's knowledge is negatively associated with the corresponding level of protectiveness in the transfer process. With more experience accumulated from frequent communications, interactions and reciprocities between alliance partners, the less difficulties and misunderstandings would occur while absorbing the transferred knowledge. In this regard, knowledge acquisition through international strategic alliances is directly hampered by the protective knowledge, yet such negative influence of knowledge protectiveness could be mitigated by the quality of the partnerships.

Hypothesis 8.7   Relational capital negatively affects knowledge protectiveness.

Research settings

Research context

Over the past few decades, the greatest change in the way business is being conducted has been the intensifying importance of relationships based on partnerships instead of on ownership (Buckley and Ghauri, 2004). The phenomenon is especially evident in the information and communication technology (ICT) industries where the business environments are fast moving and highly competitive, with complexity and uncertainty. Thanks to the thriving growth of ICT industries, Taiwan has played a crucial role in the global ICT supply chain, involving frequent international collaborations with partners from other economies, in particular China, Japan and the United States. As such, it has become a necessity to establish international strategic alliances by Taiwanese ICT firms, whose primary rationale is to enhance the global competitiveness and visibility by learning certain knowledge and skills from their foreign partners. Owing to their exceptional performance, research on Taiwanese ICT industries has been increasingly addressed. Most prior research has centred on economic perspectives, elucidating the linkages between the output of the ICT industries and the economic development in Taiwan (e.g., Dahl and Lopez-Claros, 2006); but relatively little has been done into the investigation of knowledge-related issues, given the knowledge-intensive nature of the industries. In this void, the empirical examination of antecedents of knowledge acquisition through international strategic alliances is focused on Taiwanese ICT industries in this research.

Data sources

Unlike much prior research using small-scale surveys (e.g., Ko et al., 2005; Yang et al., 2008), this research employs large-scale and cross-sectional survey research on a sample of 598 international strategic alliances in Taiwanese ICT industries for the primary data collection. This research also collects some secondary data from The Global Information Technology Report 2010–2011 (Dutta and Mia, 2011), published annually by the Geneva-based World Economic Forum, to constitute the institutional distance measures. Institutional distance between alliance partners can thus be examined by the comparison between their country-of-origin rankings in a set of indicators in both secondary data sources. Notably, as multiple data sources are used in this research, common method variance regarding the condition that both dependent and independent variables are perceptual measures derived from the same respondents in the questionnaire design (Podsakoff and Organ, 1986) is therefore not a problem in this research.

Population and sampling procedure

The target population of this research is Taiwan-based ICT manufacturers, which have acquired knowledge from other partner(s) through international strategic alliance experience. Firstly, a total of 5,422 ICT firms, including both foreign- and local-based ICT firms, were identified through the Ministry of Economic Affairs (MOEA) platform, an official economic statistics database regularly updated by the Taiwanese government. The definition of ICT industries, based on the most recent Core ICT Indicators published by the Geneva-based International Telecommunication Union (2010, p. 53), is those that 'use electronic processing to detect, measure and/or record physical phenomena or to control a physical process', and the coverage of the industries is divided into manufacturing and service categories. This research targeted ICT manufacturing industries as the primary focus so as to avoid any insignificant result which may be derived from a large number of small-scale providers of ICT service industries in Taiwan (e.g., the one-person company). By definition, ICT manufacturing products include laptops, personal computers, flat panel displays, modems, motherboards and other electronic components and products (Dahl and Lopez-Claros, 2006). Hence, 3,976 foreign and local-based ICT manufacturers were recognized by the same database, which provides a user-friendly interface containing industry classifications, company ID, main product/service, number of employees, address, website, telephone and fax numbers.

Because one of the research objectives is to address the possible effect of institutional distance between alliance partners on cross-border knowledge acquisition, it is important to frame the samples involved in this research as purely local-based. By browsing the electronic resource of National Chengchi University Library (i.e., Dun and Bradstreet/D&B Foreign Enterprises in Taiwan), 3,313 Taiwan-based ICT manufacturers were authenticated in the third phase. Owing to easy access to the secondary data, an initial sample of 724 Taiwan-based ICT manufacturers with international strategic alliance experience were screened by a combination of various public/private resources, including the official Market Observation Post System (MOPS) and the databases of the Industry and Technology Intelligence Service (ITIS) and China Credit Information Service (CCIS) in Taiwan. Grounding on Tsang's (1999) research, this research defines international strategic alliances as international cooperative arrangements involving at least one foreign and one domestic firm in the form of R&D coalition, coproduction agreement, franchising, licensing or joint venture. To screen the sample with experience in cross-border knowledge acquisition, a mixed checking approach was applied, comprising investigating companies' websites, emailing or phoning contact, and a suitable sample set of 598 Taiwan-based ICT manufacturers was finalized.

Respondent profile

This research collected both mail- and web-based questionnaires to reach respondents during June and September 2012 with follow-ups every couple of weeks.

The target respondents in the sampling firms were top management, R&D and alliance managers because they are most knowledgeable about the issue of cross-border knowledge acquisition investigated in this research. Due to the personal and industrial connections of my family business, this research achieved 34.6 per cent (207/598) as the valid response rate, which is much higher than the general response rate of 15–25 per cent obtained in the prior research on Taiwanese ICT industries (e.g., Jean et al. 2010; Liu et al., 2010).

Measures

Apart from the indicators of institutional distance, other measures of the theoretical constructs are developed to constitute the items/questions in the questionnaire and assessed by the five-point Likert scale, ranging from '1 = strongly disagree/very low' to '5 = strongly agree/very high' to allow for consistency in the response pattern. For the purpose of research reliability and validity, all measures developed in this section are adapted from prior conceptual or empirical studies. First of all, this research measures the major dependent variable – knowledge acquisition – using a five-item Likert-type scale captured from Tsang, Nguyen and Erramilli's (2004) research concerning the levels of new technological, product development, manufacturing, marketing and managerial expertise acquired by the alliance partner. Next, this research follows Nielsen and Nielsen's (2009) and Szulanski's (1996) studies to operationalize knowledge protectiveness as two-item Likert-type scale measures, including the extent to which the alliance partner has restricted access to its knowledge base and experienced difficulty in absorbing the transferred knowledge. Synthesizing Zahra and George's (2002) conceptual research with Zhao and Anand's (2009) empirical study, this research adapts absorptive capacity as a firm's ability to assimilate and acquire the transferred knowledge within the alliance context and assesses the construct by three-item Likert-type scale measures in the questionnaire, including the extent to which the firm is able to assimilate and acquire the transferred knowledge as well as the extent to which its cooperative structure is open and flexible and knowledge infrastructure is effective. In line with the prior empirical research (e.g., Kale et al., 2000; Liu et al., 2010), moreover, this research defines relational capital as a multidimensional construct manifested by partner interactions, mutual trust and reciprocal commitment, and measures it by the six-item Likert type scale.

Building on the similar institutional distance measures developed in the prior research (e.g., Chao and Kumar, 2010; Gaur and Lu, 2007), which were mainly taken from secondary sources (i.e., The Global Competitiveness Report, World Competitiveness Yearbook), this research initially adopted a seven-item scale measure from The Global Information Technology Report (Dutta and Mia, 2011) to reflect the institutional differences between partner firms. The selection of the appropriate measures is based on the relevance to the research scope of ICT industries in Taiwan. Due to the composite scales of the collected data, the calculation of the values for institutional distance measures is adjusted by the variance explained of each measure and the formula presented below:

$$ID_{tf} = \sum_{i=1}^{n} [(I_t - I_f)^2 / V_I]/n,$$

where ID_{tf} refer to the institutional distance between Taiwan (t) and the foreign country (f); I_t refers to the institutional distance indicator for Taiwan; I_f refers to the institutional distance indicator for the foreign country; V_I is the variance of indicator I; and n is the number of indicators.

The formula originates from Kogut and Singh's (1988) research on cultural distance, in which the authors corrected the variance to impose certain weights on the indicators in the composite index of Hofstede's cultural dimensions; this formula has been popularly applied by the subsequent research on the examination of cultural or institutional differences in international contexts (e.g., Chao and Kumar, 2010; Gaur and Lu, 2007). Finally, some dimensions such as alliance duration (Simonin, 2004), country of origin of the alliance partner (Liu et al., 2010), equity structures (Das, 2005) have been acknowledged as the key variables influencing alliance performance. To examine if knowledge acquisition is affected by the aforementioned variables, this research ran a preliminary analysis of variance (ANOVA) via SPSS 18 (SPSS) and found no significant differences. These as control variables were discounted in this research.

Data analysis

To investigate the causal relationships among the theoretic constructs, this research applies structural equation modelling (SEM) techniques via the LISREL 8.5 statistical programme (Joreskog and Sorbom, 1996). Due to its flexible interplay between theory and data, SEM has been a useful and popular tool used by researchers to bridge theoretical and empirical knowledge for better understanding of the various phenomena in the real world (Fornell and Bookstein, 1982). Such an approach provides a unique analysis that simultaneously considers questions of both measurement and prediction (Kelloway, 1998), allowing for modelling based on both latent and manifest variables – a critical feature in the investigation of the conceptual model with theoretic constructs as the abstractions of unobservable phenomena (Simonin, 2004). In the following sections, this research analyses the data via a sequence of statistical assessments towards hypotheses testing, starting from the confirmatory factor analysis on measure reliability and validity, descriptive statistics on sample characteristics, to path analysis on structural model evaluation and comparison.

Research findings

Measurement model assessment

While the premise of confirmatory factor analysis is to assess the variance of an observed variables with others within the context of a latent construct, it makes sense to evaluate the construct with paired measures; hence, excluding knowledge protectiveness, other constructs with multiple measures – institutional distance, knowledge acquisition, absorptive capacity and relational capital – are qualified to undergo analysis in this section. To confirm the theoretical conception of measurement models, first of all, factor analysis is applied. Two measures with low factor loadings (<0.4) were withdrawn based on Hulland's (1999) recommendation, namely, effectiveness of law-making bodies (ID1) and judicial independence (ID3). The analysis results yield robust composite reliability and convergent validity for the rest of the measures as all possess significant factor loadings (λ) related to their underlying constructs (t-values > 1.96), Dillon–Goldstein's rho values range from 0.72 to 0.93 ($\rho_c > 0.7$), and average variance extracted (AVE) values are higher than the threshold value of 0.5 after the elimination of the disregarded measures (Table 8.1).

Table 8.1 Confirmatory factor analysis on the measurement model

Construct/measures	λ	t-Value	α	ρ_c	AVE
Institutional Distance (ID) –			0.75	0.81	0.59
adapted from Chao and Kumar (2010),	0.65	5.17			
Gaur and Lu (2007)	0.84	5.56			
ID2: Laws relating to ICT	0.69	5.79			
ID4: Intellectual property	0.92	5.67			
protection	0.80	5.26			
ID5: Property rights					
ID6: Efficiency of legal framework in setting disputes					
ID7: Efficiency of legal framework in challenging regulations					
Relational Capital (RC) – adapted			0.84	0.93	0.66
from Kale et al. (2000), Liu et al. (2010)	0.62	2.23			
RC1: The extent to which the	0.95	3.74			
alliance is characterized by friendly					
and respectful interactions between	0.90	2.08			
the partners	0.95	3.75			
RC2: The extent to which the alliance	0.97	4.22			
is involved in frequent face-to-face	0.71	2.98			
communications and onsite					
visits between the partners					
RC3: All alliance partners never cheat or mislead each other during cooperation					
RC4: All alliance partners offer fair deals to each other during cooperation					
RC5: All alliance partners make decisions based on mutual benefits					
RC6: All alliance partners are highly committed to work with each other to solve problems					
Absorptive Capacity (AC) –			0.67	0.72	0.66
adapted from Zahra and George					
(2002), Zhao and Anand (2009)	0.91	14.23			
AC1: The extent to which your firm					
has the ability to assimilate and acquire	0.88	13.64			
the transferred knowledge	0.70	7.09			

AC2: Your firm has an open and
flexible structure in receiving the
transferred knowledge
AC3: Your firm has effective
knowledge infrastructure in
receiving the transferred
knowledge

Knowledge Acquisition (KA) –			0.88	0.93	0.94
adapted from Tsang et al. (2004)					
To what extent does your firm					
acquire the following knowledge	0.95	35.88			
from the alliance partner?	0.87	32.81			
KA1: New technological expertise	0.75	26.16			
KA2: New product development	0.78	24.43			
expertise	0.92	34.70			
KA3: New manufacturing expertise					
KA4: New marketing expertise					
KA5: New managerial expertise					

Notes: λ = factor loading; α = Cronbach's alpha; ρ_c = Dillon–Goldstein's rho; AVE = average variance extracted.

However, not only should each latent construct be strongly reflected by the assigned measures, but it should not have a stronger correlation with any other constructs in the theoretic model; otherwise, it would imply that the construct might not be conceptually distinct from others by sharing the same types of measures. To evaluate such discriminant validity of each latent construct, an advocated approach of comparison between the square root of AVE and construct correlations is applied (Chin, 2010). A common criterion for assessing discriminant validity is that the shared variance between the latent constructs and the assigned measures should be greater than the variance shared with other constructs (Gotz, Liehr-Gobbers and Krafft, 2010). The statistical results compiled in Table 8.2 suggest that all constructs possess discriminant validity because their

Table 8.2 Descriptive statistics, latent construct correlations and discriminant validity

Construct	Mean	S.D.	ID	RC	KP	AC	KA
Institutional Distance (ID) §	1.65	1.02	**0.77**				
Relational Capital (RC)	4.02	0.69	0.02	**0.81**			
Knowledge Protectiveness (KP)	2.25	0.66	0.23	0.05	**0.77**		
Absorptive Capacity (AC)	3.96	0.60	0.29	0.04	0.68	**0.81**	
Knowledge Acquisition (KA)	3.72	0.56	0.17	0.06	0.62	0.69	**0.97**

Notes: § = different scales are used from survey items; Diagonal terms (in bold) are square root of the average variance extracted. Off-diagonal terms are the correlation of latent constructs.

correlations with others do not present greater values than the square root of their own AVEs.

Structural model assessment

Tables 8.3 and 8.4 report the parameter estimates and goodness-of-fit indices of the original and modified structural models, respectively. Due to its sensitivity to sample size (Bagozzi and Yi, 1988), the chi-square statistic of both structural models are significant (p-value < 0.00). Yet compared with the original model, the modified model excluding the insignificant direct paths from institutional distance and relational capital to knowledge acquisition presents the sufficiently small ratio of chi-square to degree of freedom ($2.33 < 3$), which is indicative of a satisfactory fit (Kline, 2010). Additionally, other fit indices such as comparative fit index (CFI $= 0.93$), normed fit index (NFI $= 0.87$), non-normed fit index (NNFI $= 0.90$), the standardized root mean square residual (RMR $= 0.05$) and the root mean squared error of approximation (RMSEA $= 0.083$) indicate an adequate fit for the modified structural model, as all statistics present within acceptable ranges suggested by Bagozzi and Yi (1988). However, this research finds that these fit indices for the original model do not provide better solutions to explain the proposed phenomena in the research (CFI $= 0.11$, NFI $= 0.15$, NNFI $= 0.17$; RMR $= 0.37$; RMSEA $= 0.30$). The modified model is therefore accepted as a plausible representation of the collected data in this research. As multi-level structural paths are hypothesized in the model, the mediating effect of the key endogenous variable should be examined. This research tests the alternative model by withdrawing knowledge protectiveness and finds that the chi-square statistic of the model is significantly higher than that of the hypothesized one ($\chi^2 = 118.04$, d.f. $= 1$).

Table 8.3   The original structural parameter estimates and model fit indices ($N = 207$)

Path	Hypothesis	Standardized coefficient	t-Value
Institutional Distance → Knowledge Acquisition	H1(−)	0.03	1.05
Knowledge Protectiveness → Knowledge Acquisition	H2(−)	−0.15	2.51*
Absorptive Capacity → Knowledge Acquisition	H3(+)	0.41	6.01**
Relational Capital → Knowledge Acquisition	H4(+)	0.06	1.17**
Knowledge Protectiveness → Absorptive Capacity	H5(−)	−0.35	4.48*
Institutional Distance → Knowledge Protectiveness	H6(+)	0.14	2.53**
Relational Capital → Knowledge Protectiveness	H7(−)	−0.19	2.58

Notes: Model Fit Indices: χ^2 (88 d.f.) $= 355.61$, p-value < 0.00; CFI $= 0.11$, NFI $= 0.15$, NNFI $= 0.17$; RMR $= 0.37$; RMSEA $= 0.30$; * = path coefficient is significant at 0.95 level; ** = path coefficient is significant at 0.99 level.

Table 8.4 The modified structural parameter estimates and model fit indices ($N = 207$)

Path	Hypothesis	Standardized coefficient	*t*-Value
Knowledge Protectiveness → Knowledge Acquisition	H2(–)	−0.16	2.79**
Absorptive Capacity → Knowledge Acquisition	H3(+)	0.50	7.44**
Knowledge Protectiveness → Absorptive Capacity	H5(–)	−0.35	4.41**
Institutional Distance → Knowledge Protectiveness	H6(+)	0.16	2.69**
Relational Capital → Knowledge Protectiveness	H7(–)	−0.21	3.24**

Notes: Model Fit Indices: χ^2 (88 d.f.) = 205.26, *p*-value < 0.00; CFI = 0.93; NFI = 0.87; NNFI = 0.90; RMR = 0.05; RMSEA = 0.083; * = path coefficient is significant at 0.95 level; ** = path coefficient is significant at 0.99 level.

The modified mediating effect of knowledge protectiveness is therefore supported by the empirical evidence. Apart from the full mediating role played by knowledge protectiveness of institutional distance and relational capital, we find that absorptive capacity is a partial mediator of knowledge protectiveness on knowledge acquisition because of the significant path coefficients among the constructs (Table 8.4).

Focusing on the individual effects of the structural paths in the model, this research further finds that institutional distance is strongly related to knowledge protectiveness (H6), which in turn, significantly decreases the amount of knowledge acquired by the partner firm (H2). Other than the negative effect of institutional distance, this research discovers a significantly positive impact of relational capital on knowledge protectiveness (H7), suggesting that a high level of relationship quality within an alliance can mitigate the inherent institutional differences between the foreign and domestic partners and thus reduce the protectiveness perception and behaviour towards the transferred knowledge. Moreover, despite the negative impact of knowledge protectiveness on knowledge acquisition (H2), this research finds that the partner firm's absorptive capacity is positively associated with knowledge acquisition at the significance level of 0.99 (H3). However, even if the firm has strong absorptive capacity towards the transferred knowledge, the amount of knowledge acquired cannot be secured at a satisfactory level because of the negative influence from the protective knowledge (H5). In short, the research findings support that the distinctive feature of cross-border knowledge – protectiveness – is a critical mediator of contextual and relational factors on organizational learning and knowledge acquisition through international strategic alliances. The antecedents of cross-border knowledge acquisition – knowledge, organizational, contextual and relational characteristics – are therefore found to be interdependently attached to influence the consequences of knowledge acquisition within international strategic alliances.

Discussion and conclusion

Given the increasing attention that has been paid to knowledge acquisition through strategic alliances in the last 25 years, the field has been highly complex, fragmented, incoherent and heterogeneous in terms of the theoretical approaches applied (Meier, 2011).This research thus aims to reconceptualize the antecedents of cross-border knowledge acquisition and empirically investigate the interplay among these antecedents and their impacts on knowledge acquisition within international strategic alliances. This research identifies critical features of cross-border knowledge as protectiveness and attributes such behaviour and perception towards knowledge transfer as the result of inherent institutional differences between the countries from where alliance partners originate. The findings indeed support the mediating role played by knowledge protectiveness in the linkage between institutional distance and cross-border knowledge acquisition, which implies the potential synthesis of the knowledge- and institution-based views in the literature.

To alleviate such negative impacts of inherent contextual differences between alliance partners, this research suggests that firms can build up their relationship with other members in international strategic alliances. The empirical findings validate the argument and specify relational capital as the key facilitator of cross-border knowledge acquisition. Unlike some prior studies (e.g., Liu et al., 2010; Park et al., 2008), this research indicates that relational capital does not pose a direct impact on knowledge acquisition but rather has an indirect influence by mitigating the firm's protectiveness behaviour and perception during knowledge transfer, thus increasing the knowledge acquired. Also, this research highlights the process-dependent nature of knowledge acquisition by distinguishing it from the knowledge transfer process. Particularly, this research reconsiders both knowledge transfer and acquisition as two sides of a coin in which they are distinctive in the activities and contexts involved but well-attached to elucidate the underlying mechanisms of alliance operations between firms. Consequently, the feature that knowledge acquisition is *cross-border* would have a direct impact on the firm's ability to acquire the transferred knowledge. The findings support such a process-dependent assumption and reveal a direct negative relationship between knowledge protectiveness and absorptive capacity.

By establishing international strategic alliances, firms nowadays can possess unique opportunities to leverage their strengths with the help of foreign partners and thus gain competitive advantage in the global markets. Although alliances create potential for learning, unfortunately they cannot ensure that the learning potential can be realized by the partner firms. This is because only few firms systematically manage the process of knowledge acquisition (Inkpen, 1998). Understanding cross-border knowledge acquisition is thus important because it is often a frustrating and complicated process. The findings of this research therefore provide explanations and solutions for better management of knowledge acquisition through international strategic alliances. In conclusion, this research contributes to the existing literature by initiating possible integration of the theories – the knowledge- and institution-based, relational views, and organizational learning theory – to explicate both impediments and facilitators of cross-border knowledge acquisition and to systematically examine the underlying relationships among these antecedents of cross-border knowledge acquisition.

References

E. S. Andersen, *Rethinking Project Management: An Organisational Learning Perspective*, (Essex: Pearson Education Limited, 2008).

L. Argote and P. Ingram, 'Knowledge transfer: a basis for competitive advantage in firms', *Organisational Behaviour and Human Decision Processes*, 82(1) (2000) 150–69.

R. P. Bagozzi and Y. Yi, 'On the evaluation of structural equation models', *Journal of the Academy of Marketing Science*, 16(1) (1988) 74–94.

J. Barney, Jr. D. J. Ketchen and M. Wright, 'The future of resource-based theory: revitalisation or decline?', *Journal of Management*, 37(5) (2011) 1299–315.

H. Bresman, J. Birkinshaw and R. Nobel, 'Knowledge transfer in international acquisitions', *Journal of International Business Studies*, 30(3) (1999) 439–62.

P. J. Buckley and P. N. Ghauri, 'Globalisation, economic geography and the strategy of multinational enterprises', *Journal of International Business Studies*, 35(2) (2004) 81–98.

M. C.-H. Chao and V. Kumar, 'The impact of institutional distance on the international diversity–performance relationship', *Journal of World Business*, 45(1) (2010) 93–103.

W. W. Chin, 'How to Write up and Report PLS Analyses', in V. Esposito Vinzi, W. W. Chin, J. Henseler and H. Wang (eds), *Handbook of Partial Least Squares: Concepts, Methods and Applications*, (Germany: Springer, 2010), pp. 655–90.

W. M. Cohen and D. A. Levinthal, 'Absorptive capacity: a new perspective on learning and innovation', *Administrative Science Quarterly*, 35(1) (1990) 128–52.

A. S. Cui, D. A. Griffith, S. Cavusgil and M. Dabic, 'The influence of market and cultural environmental factors on technology transfer between foreign MNCs and local subsidiaries: a Croatian illustration', *Journal of World Business*, 41(2) (2006) 100–11.

J. L. Cummings and B.-S. Teng, 'Transferring R&D knowledge: the key factors affecting knowledge transfer success', *Journal of Engineering Technology Management*, 20(1/2) (2003) 39–68.

A. Dahl and A. Lopez-Claros, 'The Impact of Information and Communication Technologies on the Economic Competitiveness and Social Development of Taiwan', in S. Dutta, A. Lopez-Claros and I. Mia (eds), *The Global Information Technology Report 2005–2006: Leveraging ICT for Development*, (Basingstoke: Palgrave Macmillan, 2006), pp. 107–18.

T. K. Das, 'Deceitful behaviours of alliance partners; potential and prevention', *Management Decision*, 43(5) (2005) 706–19.

S. Dutta and I. Mia (eds), *Global Information Technology Report 2010–2011: Transformations 2.0*, (Basingstoke: Palgrave Macmillan, 2011).

M. Easterby-Smith, M. A. Lyles and E. W. K. Tsang, 'Inter-organisational knowledge transfer: current themes and future prospects', *Journal of Management Studies*, 45(4) (2008) 677–90.

C. Fornell and F. L. Bookstein 'Two structural equation models: LISREL and PLS applied to consumer exit-voice theory', *Journal of Marketing Research*, 19(4) (1982) 440–52.

M. Friesl, 'Knowledge acquisition strategies and company performance in young high technology companies', *British Journal of Management*, published online 15 March 2011.

A. S. Gaur and J. W. Lu, 'Ownership strategies and survival of foreign subsidiaries: impacts of international distance and experience', *Journal of Management*, 33(1) (2007) 84–110.

O. Gotz, K. Liehr-Gobbers and M. Krafft 'Evaluation of Structural Equation Models Using the Partial Least Squares Approach', in V. Esposito Vinzi, W. W. Chin, J. Henseler and H. Wang (eds), *Handbook of Partial Least Squares: Concepts, Methods and Applications*, (Germany: Springer, 2010), pp. 691–711.

R. M. Grant, 'The resource-based theory of competitive advantage: implications for strategy formulation', *California Management Review*, 33 (Spring) (1991) 114–35.

A. Gupta and V. Govindarajan, 'Knowledge flows within multinational corporations', *Strategic Management Journal*, 21(4) (2000) 473–96.

G. A. C. Guzman and J. Wilson, 'The "soft" dimension of organisational knowledge transfer', *Journal of Knowledge Management*, 9(2) (2005) 59–74.

J. Hulland, 'Use of partial least squares in strategic management research: a review of four recent studies', *Strategic Management Journal*, 20(2) (1999) 195–204.

P. Ingram and B. S. Silverman, *The New Institutionalism in Strategic Management: Advances in Strategic Management*, (Greenwich: JAI Press, 2002).

A. C. Inkpen, 'Learning and knowledge acquisition through international strategic alliances', *Academy of Management Executive*, 12(4) (1998) 69–80.

A. C. Inkpen, 'Learning through joint ventures: a framework of knowledge acquisition', *Journal of Management Studies*, 37(7) (2000) 1019–43.

A. C. Inkpen and P. W. Beamish, 'Knowledge, bargaining power, and the instability of international joint ventures', *The Academy of Management Review*, 22(1) (1997) 177–202.

International Telecommunication Union, *Core ICT Indicators*, (Geneva, Switzerland: Place des Nations, 2010).

M. Javidan, G. K. Stahl, F. Brodbeck and C. P. M. Wilderom, 'Cross-border transfer of knowledge: cultural lessons from project GLOBE', *The Academy of Management Executive*, 19(2) (2005) 59–76.

R.-J (Bryan) Jean, R. R. Sinkovics and S. T. Cavusgil, 'Enhancing international customer–supplier relationships through IT resources: a study of Taiwanese electronics suppliers', *Journal of International Business Studies*, 41 (2010) 1218–39.

W. H. A. Johnson, 'An integrative taxonomy of intellectual capital: measuring the stock and flow of intellectual capital components in the firm', *International Journal of Technology Management*, 18(5/6) (1999) 562–75.

K. Joreskog and D. Sorbom, *LISREL 8: User's Reference Guide*, (Skokie, IL: Scientific Software International, 1996)

A. Kachra and R. E. White, 'Know-how transfer: the role of social, economic/competitive, and firm boundary factors', *Strategic Management Journal*, 29(4) (2008) 425–45.

P. Kale, H. Singh and H. Perlmutter, 'Learning and protection of proprietary assets in strategic alliances: building relational capital', *Strategic Management Journal*, 21(3) (2000) 217–37.

E. K. Kelloway, *Using LISREL for Structural Equation Modelling: A Researcher's Guide*, (London: Sage, 1998).

A. W. King and C. P. Zeithaml, 'Competencies and firm performance: examining the causal ambiguity paradox', *Strategic Management Journal*, 22(1) (2001) 75–99.

R. B. Kline, *Principles and Practice of Structural Equation Modelling*, (London: The Guilford Press, 2010).

D-.G. Ko, L. J. Kirsch and W. R. King, 'Antecedents of knowledge transfer from consultants to clients in enterprise system implementations', *MIS Quarterly*, 29(1) (2005) 59–85.

B. Kogut and H. Singh, 'The effect of national culture on the choice of entry mode', *Journal of International Business Studies*, 19(3) (1988) 411–32.

B. Kogut and U. Zander, 'Knowledge of the firm, combinative capabilities, and the replication of technology', *Organisation Science*, 3(3) (1992) 383–97.

T. Kostova, *Success of the Transnational Transfer of Organisational Practices within Multinational Companies*. Unpublished Ph.D. Thesis, (University of Minnesota: Minneapolis, 1996).

M. M. Kwan and P.-K. Cheung, 'The knowledge transfer process: from field studies to technology development', *Journal of Database Management*, 17(1) (2006) 16–32.

P. J. Lane, B. R. Koka and S. Pathak, 'The reification of absorptive capacity: a critical review and rejuvenation of the construct', *Academy of Management Review*, 31(4) (2006) 833–63.

C.-L. (Eunice) Liu, P. N. Ghauri and R. R. Sinkovics, 'Understanding the impact of relational capital and organisational learning on alliance outcomes', *Journal of World Business*, 45(3) (2010) 237–49.

M. A. Lyles, 'The impact of organisational learning on joint venture formations', *International Business Review*, 3(4) (1994) 459–67.

M. A. Lyles and J. E. Salk, 'Knowledge acquisition from foreign parents in international joint ventures', *Journal of International Business Studies*, 27(5) (1996) 905–27.

I. Martinkenaite, 'Antecedents and consequences of inter-organisational knowledge transfer: emerging themes and openings for further research', *Baltic Journal of Management*, 6(1) (2011) 53–70.

J. A. Mathews, 'Competitive dynamics and economic learning: an extended resource-based view', *Industrial and Corporate Change*, 12(1) (2003) 115–45.

S. K. McEvily, S. Das and K. McCabe, 'Avoiding competence substitution through knowledge sharing', *The Academy of Management Review*, 25(2) (2000) 294–311.

M. Meier, 'Knowledge management in strategic alliances: a review of empirical evidence', *International Journal of Management Review*, 13(1) (2011) 1–23.

B. B. Nielsen and S. Nielsen, 'Learning and innovation in international strategic alliances: an empirical test of the role of trust and tacitness', *Journal of Management Studies*, 46(6) (2009) 1031–56.

B. I. Park, A. Giroud, H. Mirza and J. Whitelock, 'Knowledge acquisition and performance: the role of foreign partners in Korean IJVs', *Asian Business and Management*, 7(2) (2008) 11–32.

M. W. Peng, D. Y. L. Wang and Y. Jiang, 'An institution-based view of international business strategy: a focus on emerging economies', *Journal of International Business Studies*, 39(5) (2008) 920–36.

L. Perez-Nordtvedt, B. L. Kedia, D. K. Datta and A. A. Rasheed, 'Effectiveness and efficiency of cross-border knowledge transfer: an empirical examination', *Journal of Management Studies*, 45(4) (2008) 714–44.

P. M. Podsakoff and D.W. Organ, 'Self-reports in organisational research: problems and prospects', *Journal of Management*, 12(4) (1986) 531–44.

P. Quintas, P. Lefrere and G. Jones, 'Knowledge management: a strategic agenda', *Long Range Planning*, 30(3) (1997) 385–91.

J. Salk and M. A. Lyles, 'Gratitude, nostalgia and what now? Knowledge acquisition and learning a decade later', *Journal of International Business Studies*, 38(1) (2007) 19–26.

B. L. Simonin, 'Transfer of marketing know-how in international strategic alliances: an empirical investigation of the role and antecedents of knowledge ambiguity', *Journal of International Business Studies*, 30(3) (1999) 463–90.

B. L. Simonin, 'An empirical investigation of the process of knowledge transfer in international strategic alliances', *Journal of International Business Studies*, 35(5) (2004) 401–27.

B. Squire, P. D. Cousins and S. Brown, 'Cooperation and knowledge transfer within buyer–supplier relationships: the moderating properties of trust, relationship duration and supplier performance', *British Journal of Management*, 20(4) (2009) 461–77.

G. Szulanski, 'Exploring internal stickiness: impediments to the transfer of best practices within the firm', *Strategic Management Journal*, 17 (1996) 27–43.

E. W. K. Tsang, 'A preliminary typology of learning in international strategic alliances', *Journal of World Business*, 34(3) (1999) 211–29.

E. W. K. Tsang, D. T. Nguyen and M. K. Erramilli, 'Knowledge acquisition and performance of international joint ventures in the transition economy of Vietnam', *Journal of International Marketing*, 12(2) (2004) 82–103.

R. Van Wijk, J. J. P. Jansen and M. A. Lyles, 'Inter- and intra-organisational knowledge transfer: a meta-analytic review and assessment of its antecedents and consequences', *Journal of Management Studies*, 45(4) (2008) 830–53.

J. Wiklund and D. Shepherd, 'Knowledge-based resources, entrepreneurial orientation, and the performance of small and medium-sized businesses', *Strategic Management Journal*, 24(13) (2003) 1037–314.

D. Xu and O. Shenkar, 'Institutional distance and the multinational enterprise', *Academy of Management Review*, 27(4) (2002) 608–18.

Q. Yang, R. Mudambi and K. E. Meyer, 'Conventional and reverse knowledge flows in multinational corporations', *Journal of Management*, 34(5) (2008) 882–902.

S. A. Zahra and G. George, 'Absorptive capacity: a review, reconceptualization, and extension', *The Academy of Management Review*, 27(2) (2002) 185–203.

Z. J. Zhao and J. Anand, 'A multilevel perspective on knowledge transfer: evidence from the Chinese automotive industry', *Strategic Management Journal*, 30(9) (2009) 959–83.

Part III

Placing Multinational Enterprise Activities

9
Service Sector Clustering and Multinational Enterprise: Evidence from UK Film and Television

Gary Cook and Naresh R. Pandit

Introduction

Geographical clustering is a major characteristic of industrial growth and has recently become the subject of intense interest in academic (Fujita et al., 1999; Porter, 1998; Saxenian, 1994; Swann et al., 1998), business practitioner (*The Economist*, 1999; Owen, 1999) and government policy (DTI White Paper, 1998) circles. Porter (1990, 2000), in common with much of the literature in economic geography, has identified two key trends which are powerfully shaping the context for corporate strategy in the twenty-first century: on the one hand the manifest rise in the importance of *local* concentrations of economic activity and excellence; and on the other a fast-paced increase in the globalization of business. Within the academic literature, there has been a burgeoning of literature within the field of economic geography which has centred on the nature of local concentrations of economic activity, with particular interest in those which are most dynamic. The intense interest among geographers, including relevance for corporate strategy (Clark et al., 2000; Scott, 2000), stands in contrast to the relatively more muted impact within the management and specifically the strategy and international business fields (Buckley and Ghauri, 2004). What makes this particularly odd are, firstly, that the intense interest of policymakers has been stimulated by the seminal work of strategy scholar Michael Porter (1990), and, secondly, Porter has repeatedly emphasized the benefits of membership of strong clusters for enhanced international competitiveness.

Research on the foreign direct investment (FDI) activities of multinational enterprises (MNEs) has a long and rich tradition (Dunning, 2003). Research on the advantages, disadvantages and processes that arise in geographical business clusters has a similar tradition (Marshall, 1890; Porter, 1998). Whilst it is clear that there is a considerable amount of MNE FDI in clusters (Kozul-Wright and Rowthorn, 1998), and that this activity is increasing (Nachum, 2003), the body of research on the interface of these two topics is small (Birkinshaw and Solvell, 2000). However, it is growing fast in the face of increased globalization, deregulation and advances in information and communication technology all of

157

which have begun to prompt a re-evaluation of the spatial organization of MNE activity. This study, asks three related questions:

1. What theoretical reasons have been advanced that might explain the level of MNE activity in the central London media cluster?
2. How and why are the advantages, disadvantages and processes that arise in the central London media cluster similar and different for MNEs and non-MNEs?
3. What, if anything, distinguishes the perceived advantages and disadvantages of domestic and overseas MNEs?

The chapter is structured as follows. The first section reviews the literature on the MNE FDI/clusters interface, followed by a concise description of the central London media cluster, with emphasis on film and television. The third section details the methodology of the study before a section presenting the findings and discusses these in relation to the literature on the MNE FDI/clusters interface. A final section concludes and offers business policy recommendations.

Literature on the MNE FDI/clusters interface

From the perspective of the MNE, a better understanding of geographical clustering is desirable because performance may improve if certain activities are located in clusters where higher levels of productivity (Henderson, 1986; Porter, 1998) and innovation (Baptista and Swann, 1998; Porter, 1998) may be achievable. Moreover, since clusters are usually expensive and congested locations (Swann et al., 1998), unless an activity needs to be located in a cluster, it will pay the MNE to move it elsewhere. These reasons, coupled with the trends of increased globalization, deregulation and advances in information and communication technologies, mean that MNEs are increasingly employing cluster-based thinking to inform their investment and location decisions (Enright, 1998).

There is a small but rapidly growing body of more specific evidence that shows that MNEs are disproportionately attracted to clusters (Gong, 1995; Head et al., 1995, 1999; Wheeler and Moody, 1992) and that MNE FDI in clusters is increasing (Nachum, 2003). This evidence suggests that 'liability of foreignness' (Zaheer, 1995) – disadvantages faced by firms in foreign locations due to unfamiliarity and inferior access to local assets – is being more than compensated by the advantages of cluster location. Conceptually, these advantages may be categorized as those that are available to all firms at a location ('general cluster advantages') and those that are of particular benefit to MNEs ('MNE cluster advantages'). In this regard, it is important to acknowledge that there are (at least) two distinct groups of MNEs. Firstly, there are domestic firms for whom location in the cluster may provide part of the springboard to international expansion. Secondly, there are overseas MNEs that may be attracted into the cluster to capitalize on advantages which, whilst they may overlap with those from which domestic firms benefit, may, nevertheless, be distinct from them. Beyond so-called 'fixed effects' (Swann et al., 1998) – advantages that exist at a location that are *not* a function of the co-presence of related firms and institutions (e.g., climate, time zone and cultural capital) – there are advantages that are directly related to the co-presence that exists within a cluster which are sometimes referred to as 'economies of agglomeration' (Pandit and Cook, 2005).

The majority of the literature acknowledges and builds on the classic insights of Marshall (1890) into the sources of superior performance in clusters (industrial districts in Marshall's terms): labour market pooling; the emergence of specialized input suppliers and technological spillovers. Cultural industries are highly concentrated in urban locations (Hall, 2000; Power, 2002). Scott and Storper (2003) suggest that the superior economic dynamism of cities rests on the coexistence of four key factors: economies of scale in capital-intensive infrastructure; dynamic forward and backward linkages among firms, which promote information flows regarding business opportunities, resource availability and labour market conditions, among other things; dense local labour markets; and localized relational assets or social capital promoting learning and innovation. Scott and Storper's list is not exhaustive. The volume and sophistication of demand within the city may be critical (Kitson et al., 2004; Porter, 1990). In Porter's conception, sophisticated, demanding customers will drive quality standards and innovation (von Hippel, 1988). In design-led industries, an important capacity of a regional production/innovation system is the ability to adapt quickly and effectively to changing demand (Rantisi, 2002). The existence of concentrated demand for specialized services also provides an incentive for workers to invest in specialized skills and competencies (Scott and Storper, 2003), which is another dynamic of cumulative causation. Jacobs' (1972, 1985) analysis lays considerable importance on the nature of external linkages a city has, a point also emphasized by Hall (2000) as a powerful contributor to periods of creative flourishing in cities. The importance of external connectivity for remaining at the forefront of innovation has been more widely acknowledged in the literature (Boggs and Rantisi, 2003; Cumbers and McKinnon, 2004; Pred, 1977). These advantages are important in terms of the clusters providing a platform for indigenous firms to succeed in international business, Porter's (1990) chief thesis, but also provide the attraction of a location for inward direct investment.

There is a well-developed literature that attempts to generally explain MNE FDI in terms of the benefits that certain locations provide for investing MNEs. Dunning (1993) presents an FDI typology differentiating between investments that are 'natural-resource seeking', 'market-seeking', 'efficiency-seeking' and 'strategic asset-seeking'. More recently, he has drawn from economic geography (Dunning, 1998) to elaborate the location element of his 'OLI' framework by incorporating clusters thinking. On the subject of MNE location in *clusters*, Birkinshaw and Hood (2000) find such activity to be rational as subsidiaries located in clusters make greater strategic contributions to parent companies than subsidiaries that are not located in clusters. Enright (1998) elaborates a typology of such contributions. 'Listening posts' aim to absorb knowledge from the cluster and then disseminate it within the wider enterprise (Dupuy and Gilly, 1999). Nachum and Keeble (2003) state that the ability to tap into cluster-specific knowledge is particularly important when important knowledge is tacit. 'Stand-alone corporate portfolio investments' serve as centres for particular business activities perhaps benefiting from the reputation spillover of a particular location. Nachum (2000) supports this line of thinking by identifying the increased importance and autonomy of foreign subsidiaries.

Another type is the subsidiary that 'supplies products and activities' for the MNE's other activities and finally there is the subsidiary which absorbs 'skills and capabilities' from the cluster and then transfers these to the wider enterprise. Beaverstock's (1994) study of multinational banks elaborates this type of MNE FDI by finding that such firms benefit from the ability to transfer skills and capabilities between subsidiaries in their worldwide operations through international personnel movements. This may be particularly the case when an industry has more than one prominent location and so the MNE may benefit from locating in all prominent locations in order to pick up skills and capabilities in one to pass on to the others. An additional motivation for MNEs locating in clusters is provided by Harrison (1994). He argues that a cluster location may enable MNEs to concentrate on their core competences and outsource non-core activities to specialist suppliers that are geographically proximate. Similarly, Nachum and Keeble (2003) argue that MNEs will locate in clusters to benefit from the highly specialized, non-standard inputs that are available there.

Although this typology encourages us to think of MNEs 'taking' from clusters, we should guard against such a conclusion. Studies by Head et al. (1995), Nachum (2000) and Wheeler and Moody (1992) show that MNEs can play a major role in cluster development and evolution. Indeed, Birkinshaw and Hood's (2000) analysis of the characteristics of 229 foreign-owned subsidiaries located in clusters finds that such subsidiaries are more embedded and more internationally oriented than subsidiaries that are not located in clusters. In a seminal article Amin and Thrift (1992) argue persuasively that the emphasis on local production complexes is overdone as it does not recognize the importance of emerging global corporate networks and interconnected global city regions (Scott, 2001). Bathelt et al. (2004) suggest that multinationals provide important 'pipelines' within which tacit knowledge (among other types) can flow in a way which would be less easy between third parties at equivalent distance.

Some understanding is needed of how small and medium-sized enterprises (SMEs) capitalize on firm and cluster strengths by internationalizing, not least to inform policymaking, but also because several dynamic SMEs in media have manifested internationalization as an important element of their growth strategies. One important piece of received wisdom in the literature is that small firms are at a relative disadvantage to large firms in terms of any form of internationalization, but above all FDI (Buckley, 1997; Hollenstein, 2005). Nevertheless, there is evidence that the amount of FDI attributable to small firms has been growing rapidly in recent years, albeit from a small base, such that the share of small firms in FDI has been rising (Acs and Preston, 1997). Buckley, drawing on Dunning's (1993) OLI framework, suggests reasons why the extent of small firm FDI might be industry-specific. In some industries efficient scale is large relative to market size and in such cases small firms will struggle to survive unless they can find a defensible niche. By contrast, he argues that small firms will be better placed where scale is less important and local skills and rapid information processing are more to the fore. Indeed, Hollenstein (2005) finds that full ownership of an affiliate is optimal where a firm has highly specific knowledge and is a leading player in a market niche.

The central London media cluster

Media industries are very highly agglomerated in central London. Table 9.1 provides a set of standard location quotients, which shows the share of media employment to total employment in the region divided by the share of media employment to total employment at the national level. A value above 1 indicates a region has a disproportionate amount of media employment. This underscores the dominance of London, which is especially marked in film distribution, cable and satellite broadcasting, post production and special effects and commercials production.

Economies of scale in programme production are not pronounced (Cave, 1989). Economies of scale are significant in what may somewhat loosely be called

Table 9.1 Location quotients in the audio visual industries by sector and selected region, 2005

	Wales	Scotland	London	South East	South West	West Midlands	North West
Broadcast TV	1.3	0.7	3.4	0.4	0.6	0.5	0.7
Cable and satellite television	0.0	0.0	6.0	0.5	0.0	0.0	0.0
Independent production (television)	1.9	0.4	3.6	0.7	0.6	0.2	0.7
Broadcast radio	0.7	0.8	2.9	1.0	0.6	0.6	0.5
Animation	1.5	0.4	3.0	0.5	1.5	0.7	1.2
Post production	0.4	0.2	5.1	0.6	0.2	0.2	0.3
Digital special effects	0.0	0.0	5.6	1.0	0.0	0.0	0.0
Facilities (studio/ equipment hire)	0.5	0.8	3.0	1.2	0.8	0.2	0.4
Commercials production	0.0	0.0	5.6	0.2	0.0	0.0	0.6
Corporate production	1.8	0.4	2.7	2.3	0.9	0.0	0.3
Film distribution	0.0	0.0	6.5	0.0	0.0	0.0	0.0
Processing laboratories	0.0	0.0	4.4	2.3	0.0	0.0	0.0
Other	0.0	0.0	3.4	0.7	0.6	0.6	0.5

Source: Skillset.

'distribution', which relates to the acquisition of broadcasting rights and bundling them into packages, typically in the form of a channel offering. Large distributors are able to absorb a large number of programmes which may be barely commercial and recoup on the relatively small numbers of hits, making major media companies important agents organizing financing, deal making and distribution. The existence of these large economies of scale and scope is of first rank importance. Firstly, the fact that broadcasters (and studios in the case of Hollywood) are large will create a natural physical agglomeration (Ellison and Glaeser, 1997). Secondly, the large scale of broadcasters relative to (most) independent production companies and final consumers brings elements of both monopsony and monopoly power, a feature given high prominence in Aksoy and Robins' (1992) account of Hollywood. Economies of scope are also an important reason why major media multinationals have become an increasingly important feature of the industry (Gibson and Kong, 2005).

West London is dominated by the headquarters of the BBC. This dominance is reinforced by similar dominance in allied industries such as publishing, music and entertainment (Turok, 2003). As Bathelt (2005) suggests, hub firms play a number of important roles within a particular agglomeration. They establish basic ground rules for programme formats. They attract new businesses as they are important customers. Hub firms are important for other reasons too. Traditionally, the BBC and to a lesser extent the ITV companies have been important trainers of labour. Both the BBC and ITV companies have also since 1990 provided sometimes considerable assistance to fledgling independent companies, without which some might have been short-lived.

Globalization has been an important influence on both film and television. Escalating production costs have also led to a significant rise in the number of mergers, alliances, international co-productions and other types of international production and marketing arrangements as broadcasters seek to recover costs across the widest market (Moran, 1998; Shew, 1992).

London is an important location for media conglomerates. Some of them, of course, are UK firms such as ITV. All the major media conglomerates have a substantial presence in London, Metro-Goldwyn-Mayer, Paramount Pictures, Sony Picture Entertainment (Columbia Tristar), Twentieth Century Fox, Universal, Walt Disney and Warner Brothers. London is important as a global node for a variety of reasons. It is a primary cultural metropolis which makes it attractive to creative individuals as well as being a melting pot of ideas (the two are interrelated). It can provide firms not only with ideas but also production capability sophisticated enough to meet any demand. The United Kingdom in particular, and Europe, are highly important markets for US exports, and the United Kingdom is a useful beachhead for penetrating Europe. Being able to interact with others in the process of trying to discover commercial ideas helps lower risk and is a key attraction of urban settings (Banks et al., 2000). The characteristics of London as a broadcasting and, more broadly, a media centre has strong similarities with Scott's (2004) account of Hollywood as a 'bifurcated' production system where large media companies with substantial in-house production capability are interwoven with a highly (flexibly) specialized array of independent companies, which they rely on to spread risk, diversify their product offerings and to sound out emerging market opportunities. Like Hollywood, London has strong narratives which support its status as a major international centre in television broadcasting, advertising and filmmaking.

Methodology

The findings reported below are based on a questionnaire survey conducted between January and April 2004. This questionnaire survey built on a previous interview-based comparative study, which involved 24 London-based firms and 7 other expert respondents from the policy and industry analysis fields. The questionnaire sought to both provide quantitative evidence of the importance of different types of cluster process claimed to be important in the literature and deepen understanding of the nature of the London cluster, by far the dominant media cluster in the United Kingdom. The questions were derived in part from analysis of the extant literature and in part based on the findings of the previous study. The questionnaire used was subject to extensive pretesting and was mailed to a stratified random sample of 1,500 companies drawn from a bespoke database built up from the FAME financial database and the Broadcast Production Guide, the leading industry trade directory. The previous interview survey has helped in interpreting some of the econometric results. In all 204 usable questionnaires were returned, an apparent response rate of 13.6 per cent. There were 187 usable replies from companies, of which 150 were non-MNEs and 37 were MNEs. The MNE cohort comprised 20 of UK origin, 10 of US origin, 2 of European origin and 5 from other regions. Companies were asked to rate factors using a five-point Lickert scale ranging from 1 = not important to 5 = very important. Comparing responses with the distribution of firms mailed to revealed that apart from a lower than proportional response from advertising firms, which are not the central focus of analysis here, there was no obvious evidence of non-response bias.

Results

The key advantages and disadvantages from the questionnaire, 45 items in all, were used as the basis for a factor analysis with the objective of reducing the data to key underlying constructs and also to compute factor scores to use as a basis for comparing MNEs and non-MNEs. Factor extraction was by principal axis factoring. The principal method used to determine the number of factors to use was the scree plot (Cattell, 1966), which indicated seven factors at the point of inflection. Each of these seven factors has some reasonable interpretation. According to Stevens (2002) the scree plot method is reliable provided there are over 200 observations and the sample size here of 187 is very close to that threshold. The scree plot is preferred to Kaiser's criterion of retaining all factors with an eigenvalue greater than one, as neither of the rules of thumb for Kaiser's criterion being accurate are satisfied. The average communality value after extraction, 0.543, is less than 0.6 and there are less than 300 observations.

The method of rotation used was Varimax, which has the benefit of producing more interpretable clusters of variables on each factor, important because the factors themselves are of independent interest in this analysis (Field, 2005). In principle, there is some case for oblique rotation as there are reasonable theoretical grounds for suspecting the factors to be correlated with one another. Oblimin rotation was used as a robustness check. The substantive interpretation of the factors extracted was the same, and no pair of factors had a particularly high simple correlation, the maximum being 0.4. For this reason the results using Varimax rotation are reported. Nothing crucial hinges on this choice. Stevens (2002) suggests that with 187 observations any variable which has a loading of 0.384 or more on a factor is important. Based on this rule of thumb, factor loadings after rotation in excess of 0.384 only are reported in Table 9.2 for ease of interpretation and clarity. Table 9.3 presents the rotation sum of square loadings for seven factors.

As regards the validity of the factor analysis, the Kaiser–Meyer–Olkin measure of sampling adequacy is very good at 0.843, indicating reliable factors will be extracted. The correlations in the anti-image matrix all lie between 0.618 and 0.932, indicating good sampling adequacy. Cronbach's α is generally satisfactory, as reported in Table 9.4, with all values lying above the 0.7 threshold and the value of a in each case was not sensitive to deletion of items in each subscale.

These factors have a ready interpretation in the light of the extant literature on positive and negative externalities in clusters. The first group of variables loading highly onto Factor 1 all represent what might broadly be termed social capital. Considerable importance has been placed on building up trust and personal relationships which encourage mutual support. This leads in turn to a higher degree of information sharing and cooperation which may enhance not only innovation but greater productive efficiency. The loading of face-to-face contact is evidence of a classic advantage of proximity, which allows not only trust to be built and maintained but also complex, tacit information to be exchanged. The loading of customer and peer firm help with innovation onto this factor provides support for the mainstream perspective in the literature that social capital and 'untraded interdependencies' are important in supporting the cooperation and knowledge transfer which are essential underpinnings of superior performance in innovation in dynamic clusters. Furthermore, there is clear evidence of a link between the formation of social capital and the ability to realize key benefits of labour market pooling. The ability to form multi-disciplinary teams quickly is essential in project-based industries like film, television and commercials production. The ability to form project teams which will gel quickly rests on important social institutions which socialize workers into norms of the industry, allowing them to collaborate with others possessing different but complementary skills. Moreover, there exist rich circuits of information regarding the competence and reliability and individuals which are essential in allowing teams which will perform at a high level to be drawn together quickly.

Table 9.2 Rotated factor matrix

Variable	Factor 1	Factor 2	Factor 3	Factor 4	Factor 5	Factor 6	Factor 7
Proximity promotes trust	0.808						
Proximity aids easy communication	0.799						
Proximity makes it easier to build and maintain personal contacts	0.745						
Proximity makes it easier to assemble multi-disciplinary teams	0.386						
Proximity makes it easier to have face to face contact	0.646						
We generally have complementary expertise to firms in close proximity	0.695						
Our address is important to being conceived as credible		0.583					
Our location makes it easier to take market share		0.824					
We benefit from proximity to market leading customers		0.600					
Our location makes it easier for customers external to London to interact with us		0.472					
Our location has the advantage of access to real-time information about market trends		0.449		0.464			
We benefit from being near leading competitors		0.682					

Table 9.2 (Continued)

Variable	Factor 1	Factor 2	Factor 3	Factor 4	Factor 5	Factor 6	Factor 7
Local rivalry among competitors is a powerful spur		0.647					
We are able to benchmark against competitors		0.638		0.433			
We benefit from support from local government				0.610			
We benefit from access to venture capital due to our location				0.484			
The cost of premises is a disadvantage					0.635		
Poor infrastructure is a disadvantage					0.506		
The cost of housing is a disadvantage					0.665		
Government regulation is a problem					0.404		
Poor transportation in central London is a disadvantage					0.609		
Poor national transportation links are a disadvantage							0.755
Poor international transport links are a disadvantage							0.844
A pool of talented labour with innovative skills helps innovate			0.421			0.385	
Labour mobility helps spread knowledge and good practice	0.407		0.641				

A fluid labour market helps attract good staff			0.750
A fluid labour market helps us quickly tailor our staffing levels to our needs			0.788
It is generally easy to recruit good people at short notice			0.805
Local customers help us innovate	0.458		
Local firms in the same line of activity help us innovate	0.400		
Local academic institutions help us innovate		0.661	
Local industry associations help us innovate		0.535	
Local government helps us innovate		0.612	
We benefit from access to a strong, skilled labour supply			0.697
We benefit from being able to find firms who will supply bespoke services			0.678
We benefit from proximity to professional bodies			0.508

Table 9.3   Sum of square loadings

Factor	Rotation sum of square loadings		
	Total	Per cent of variance	Cumulative per cent
Social capital (factor 1)	4.103	11.397	11.397
Market competition (factor 2)	3.829	10.635	22.032
Labour market pooling (factor 3)	3.060	8.501	30.533
Innovation (factor 4)	2.899	8.052	38.586
Congestion (factor 5)	2.104	5.843	44.429
Specialized supply (factor 6)	1.936	5.376	49.807
Connectivity (factor 7)	1.620	4.501	54.308

Table 9.4   Cronbach's α measure of scale reliability

Factor	Cronbach's α
Factor 1. Social capital	0.884
Factor 2. Market competition	0.875
Factor 3. Labour market pooling	0.870
Factor 4. Innovation	0.799
Factor 5. Congestion	0.732
Factor 6. Specialized supply	0.737
Factor 7. Connectivity	0.818

The second group relates to benefits of being close to leading competitors. It is notable that the spur of rivalry and the ability to benchmark load heavily onto this factor, supporting one of Porter's (1990, 1998) leading contentions. The ability to access real-time information is also highly important. Clearly, the emphasis is on market competition, with the ability to take market share from rivals being the variable loading most heavily onto this factor, which is redolent of Hotelling models of competition (Hotelling, 1929). The importance of the ability of customers external to London to interact with firms located in the cluster indicates the status of London as a focus for national and international demand, the significance of which is generally overlooked in the literature.

There is an emerging recognition in the literature that access to labour is a prime attraction to firms and central to the dynamics of clustering, reflected in Factor 3. A pool of talented labour attracts firms, and also the most successful firms, and these firms in turn attract yet more labour. As the labour pool deepens, so workers have the incentive to invest in higher levels of and more specialized human capital. This is a critical resource and as the labour pool itself, as opposed to individual workers, is highly place-specific, a source of abiding regional advantage to firms located in the cluster. Labour market mobility is a classic means through which knowledge diffuses in a cluster.

Factor 4 is somewhat more difficult to interpret; however, it generally indicates the importance of local institutions supporting innovation, particularly as has been suggested in the *innovative milieu* literature (Camagni, 1991). Real-time information on market trends is important given the nature of innovation in media which is in part based on appealing to shifting customer tastes and, more subtly, keeping abreast of what commissioning editors believe to be the state of preferences among consumers. All sections of media are constantly seeking novelty in order to gain what is likely to be a short-lived advantage over rivals. In terms of benchmarking against competitors, rapid imitation is a very important feature of innovation and non-price competition in media. The ability to source venture capital is consistent with local institutions supporting innovation.

The fifth group of variables loading onto Factor 5 represent classic congestion costs, which have been widely suggested as presenting forces which may slow cluster growth or even lead to cluster decline. Cost of premises and cost of housing are fundamental indicators of congestion, being driven by competition for a fixed supply of land in prime locations. The poor state of transportation in central London reflects another dimension of competition for space and 'overheating'. Perhaps the odd one out among these factors is government regulation which is not so obviously related to congestion and competition in factor markets. It is, nevertheless, a friction on doing business.

The sixth factor indicates the classic Marshallian advantage of the emergence in an industrial district of a specialized supply infrastructure. The ability to find firms able to supply bespoke services and a strong, skilled labour pool are classic Marshallian externalities. As the cluster deepens, so a greater array of specialized suppliers emerges. This has manifestly been the case in film and television in London over the last 25 years. This sophisticated supplier base is a foundation for innovation and efficiency. Professional bodies, such as the British Academy of Film and Television Arts, the Film Council, the Royal Television Society, the Producers' Alliance for Cinema and Television and the Moving Image Society also provide a range of important services which support both productive efficiency and innovation.

Factor 7 relates to connectivity as proxied by national and international transport links, which are seen by many respondents as representing a material disadvantage of London. This may also be construed as another manifestation of congestion, with the ability to get into and around central London, particularly from Heathrow, being time-consuming and unpleasant. This factor is somewhat weak, given that only two elements load onto it; however, this particular factor is stable in that it emerges despite changes in included variables, extraction or rotation method. It also has a justification in terms of theory, given the increasing importance being placed on external connectivity as an essential component of cluster strength within the economic geography literature.

Distinguishing MNEs and non-MNEs.

The factor scores derived from the factor analysis were entered into a logit analysis to identify factors which discriminate between MNEs and non-MNEs. The factor scores based on the regression method were used and inspection of the correlation matrix revealed no serious correlation between scores on the seven factors. A number of control variables were added to the model. A set of dummy variables for the principal line of activity were added, representing the three main categories of broadcast programme production, film production and post production (e.g., editing, special effects and sound work). A dummy variable was added to indicate whether or not the firm was located in W1 (broadly corresponding to Soho), which is the heart of the media cluster in central London. Six variables were included which identified how important a London location was in helping firms innovate through developing, respectively, new products, new services, better ways of delivering products or services, developing new markets, improving organizational structure and reorienting the company strategically. A set of dummies was included which indicated whether or not the firm had received important or very important benefits from interaction with personnel in another local company in each of the following ways: meeting at local business events; contact by telephone for short-term problem solving; contact by telephone for information; mixing with industry colleagues in social settings; chance meetings where interesting information had been heard. A set of dummies was included to capture the extent of reliance on the South East as a source of labour and another set for the proportion of work derived from contact with other firms in London. Three variables were included to investigate how important informal channels of recruitment were for hiring senior management, senior staff (e.g., senior editors) and specialist staff. This reflects the hypothesized importance of personal contacts and reputation networks in recruitment of highly skilled knowledge workers.

The results of the logit analysis appear in Table 9.5. The results are mainly in line with expectation. The negative and significant coefficient on social capital is consistent with the view that multinationals will tend to be less embedded in the cluster due to the fact they are less reliant on external agents in the cluster for resources and competences, as they will be relatively well endowed with these in-house. The positive and significant coefficient on labour market pooling indicates a strategic asset-seeking motive. This makes sense in creative industries where talented labour is of immense importance in terms of developing superior content. That support for innovation from local institutions and availability of specialized supply should be negative and insignificant is also consistent with the fact that MNEs possess resource strength, which means they will be apt to be less reliant than non-MNEs on such factors. It is important to bear in mind that MNEs do give the underlying variables on these factors generally high rating, just not as high as the non-MNEs.

Coefficients on the other included variables are all intuitively reasonable. MNEs are significantly more likely to be located in the very centre of the cluster in W1. This makes sense. On the one hand, as has been demonstrated in the literature review, MNEs will be drawn to clusters by the ability to tap into strategic assets, including information. This places a premium on selecting a particularly favourable location. Moreover, MNEs may be supposed to possess high levels of competence, which may render them better able to exploit the externalities

Table 9.5 Logit analysis results discriminating MNEs from non-MNEs

Variable	Full model		Restricted model	
	Coefficient	Z	Coefficient	Z
Constant	−2.431	−2.36**	−2.551	−2.55**
Firm is in broadcast television production	−2.765	−2.48**	−2.385	−2.23**
Firm is in film production	−2.025	−2.16**	−1.759	−2.43**
Firm is in post production	0.105	0.14	0.185	0.28
Firm is located in W1	0.987	1.67*	1.105	1.81*
Social capital	−0.904	−2.37**	−0.788	−2.55**
Market competition	0.049	0.11	0.018	0.06
Labour market pooling	1.302	3.04***	1.208	3.34***
Innovation	−0.090	−0.25	−0.197	−0.53
Congestion	−0.544	−1.53	−0.530	−1.23
Specialized supply infrastructure	−0.237	−0.65	−0.145	−0.44
Connectivity	−0.021	−0.06	−0.161	−0.45
21–40 per cent of work from local firms	0.991	1.21	1.122	1.91*
41–60 per cent of work from local firms	−0.609	−0.59		
61–80 per cent of work from local firms	−0.163	−0.20		
81–100 per cent of work from local firms	−1.863	−1.70*	−1.699	−2.53**
21–40 per cent of staff recruited from South East	2.362	2.49**	2.164	3.91***
41–60 per cent of staff recruited from South East	1.155	1.46	0.880	1.30
61–80 per cent of staff recruited from South East	−1.263	−1.59	−1.472	−1.82*
81–100 per cent of staff recruited from South East	−1.977	−2.79***	−2.042	−3.38***
London location helps innovate by developing new products	0.183	0.20		
London location helps innovate by developing new services	−0.348	−0.35		
London location helps innovate by developing new methods of delivery	−0.711	−1.07	−0.876	−1.40
London location helps innovate by developing new markets	1.687	2.38**	1.262	1.70*
London location helps innovate by developing new organizational structures	−0.724	−0.68		
London location helps innovate by re-orienting the company strategically	−0.571	−0.69		
Firm benefits from mixing with industry colleagues at business events	0.197	0.32		
Firm benefits from telephone contact with industry colleagues for problem solving	−0.755	−1.04	−0.627	−0.94

Table 9.5 (Continued)

Variable	Full model		Restricted model	
	Coefficient	Z	Coefficient	Z
Firm benefits from telephone contact with industry colleagues for information seeking	1.313	1.73*	1.269	1.71*
Firm benefits from mixing socially with industry colleagues	0.825	1.13	0.762	1.14
Firm benefits from chance meetings with industry colleagues where interesting information is heard	1.159	1.54	1.018	1.53
Informal channels are important for recruiting senior management	1.237	1.92*	1.050	1.95*
Informal channels are important for recruiting senior staff	−0.897	−1.34	−0.918	−1.50
Informal channels are important for recruiting specialist staff	−0.355	−0.54		
Log-likelihood	−59.451		−61.309	
χ^2	67.13***		56.85***	

Notes: ***significant at 1 per cent, **significant at 5 per cent, *significant at 10 per cent.

available in the cluster. Therefore they will be prepared to outbid others for access to the most favourable locations. A separate analysis reveals that firms located in W1 are significantly *less* likely to complain about the cost of premises, even though these costs are *highest* in that location. One interpretation is that they feel those high prices are worth paying and that firms that are unable to compete for those locations are the ones that feel most disadvantaged. In terms of the types of innovation which presence in the cluster supports, it is revealing that it is the ability to develop new markets which is the only type to be significantly and positively associated with MNEs. This clearly indicates a market-seeking motive behind location. Other types of innovation do not particularly distinguish MNEs from non-MNEs; however, the ability to innovate by developing new ways to deliver goods or services to customers is negative and close to significance at the 10 per cent level. Yet again, one interpretation is that this particular competence is likely to be well developed within MNEs.

MNEs are significantly more likely to value contact with other firms in the cluster for gaining information, but less likely (though not significantly so) to value such contact for problem solving. This indicates that MNEs value the ability to gain 'intelligence', whereas they are apt to have considerable resources in-house to call upon when it comes to solving problems. This speaks of a 'listening post' function. The coefficients on gaining benefits from mixing with industry colleagues in social settings and chance meetings in the street where interesting information is heard are both positive, the latter falling just outside significance. Again, separate analysis reveals that firms which stress informal channels of communication are significantly more likely to be located in W1. This reinforces the impression that access to intelligence is critical for MNEs and it is consistent about the need for heads of major companies to engage with each other in key global nodes in order to make sense of developments in their industry (Amin and Thrift, 1992).

Finally, in terms of the ability to use informal channels to recruit staff, it is the ability to recruit senior mangers which is significantly and positively associated with MNEs. Assessing the ability of those who might fill senior management positions is both important and fraught with difficulty. Here the rich circuits of information which exist within major clusters are apt to prove an advantage and one which bears crucially on the strategic capability of MNEs.

Domestic versus foreign MNEs

The basic insights of the simple logit model were built on by conducting a multinomial logit model which attempted to use the same set of variables to 'explain' in a more fine-grained way the distribution of firms over the following categories: non-MNEs (all domestic firms by definition); domestic MNEs; overseas MNEs. Since there were very few observations in the latter two categories, only the restricted model reported in the previous section could be estimated and considerable scepticism should accompany consideration of the results.

There are some interesting points of both similarity and contrast between the domestic and overseas MNEs (see Table 9.6). Regarding industry effects, being in programme production or film production is negative and significant in both cases, whereas being in post production is positive and significant for the overseas multinationals. As will be argued in greater detail in the next section, there are clear industry-specific factors which explain this contrast, coupled with the fact that London is the world's pre-eminent centre for post production, therefore exerts an unusually strong attraction on overseas multinationals. The coefficient on social capital becomes negative and significant in the case of the overseas multinationals, which is entirely as would be expected given their 'liability of foreignness', which makes it more difficult for them to embed themselves in local networks. What is more, they may have less need to do so if it is true that they are already endowed with superior competencies and resources. This conclusion is underscored by the fact that the coefficient on support for innovation from local institutions is also negative and significant for the overseas multinationals only. Moreover, the existence of a specialized supply infrastructure is negative and significant for the overseas MNEs, again indicating frictions which prevent them becoming as deeply embedded into local business networks, less need to draw on the local supply infrastructure or some combination of the two.

Overseas MNEs are significantly less likely to rely on work coming via other local companies than are UK MNEs. This is eminently reasonable, since overseas MNEs will have their home markets elsewhere. That UK MNEs should be significantly less likely to rely on location in London as a factor to support innovation in the form of developing new ways of delivering goods and services is not so easy to explain. Overseas MNEs rate the benefit of hearing information in chance

Table 9.6 Multinomial logit analysis discriminating non-MNEs, domestic and foreign MNEs

Variable	UK MNEs		Overseas MNEs	
	Coefficient	Z	Coefficient	Z
Constant	−2.825	−2.20**	−5.886	−2.68***
Firm is in broadcast television production	−2.528	−1.86*	−4.124	−3.04***
Firm is in film production	−1.811	−2.30**	−3.684	−2.09**
Firm is in post production	−0.335	−0.37	1.383	1.66*
Firm is located in W1	1.175	1.71*	1.084	1.21
Social capital	−0.481	−1.39	−1.746	−1.76*
Market competition	0.379	0.96	−0.687	−1.33
Labour market pooling	0.583	1.52	2.468	2.12**
Innovation	0.288	0.63	−1.232	−2.85***
Congestion	−0.606	−1.16	−0.602	−1.05
Specialized supply infrastructure	0.161	0.31	−0.669	−2.05**
Connectivity	−0.093	−0.21	−0.560	−0.90
21–40 per cent of work from local firms	0.928	1.31	2.002	2.33**
41–60 per cent of work from local firms				
61–80 per cent of work from local firms				
81–100 per cent of work from local firms	−1.108	−1.29	−2.581	−2.55**
21–40 per cent of staff recruited from South East	1.746	2.75***	0.556	0.44
41–60 per cent of staff recruited from South East	1.077	1.51	0.617	0.53
61–80 per cent of staff recruited from South East	−0.371	−0.46	−5.016	−1.45
81–100 per cent of staff recruited from South East	−1.969	−2.61***	−3.561	−2.00**
London location helps innovate by developing new products				
London location helps innovate by developing new services				
London location helps innovate by developing new methods of delivery	−1.730	−2.14**	−0.713	−0.65
London location helps innovate by developing new markets	1.173	1.31	3.026	1.62

London location helps innovate by developing new organizational structures				
London location helps innovate by re-orienting the company strategically				
Firm benefits from mixing with industry colleagues at business events				
Firm benefits from telephone contact with industry colleagues for problem solving	−0.753	−1.05	0.041	0.04
Firm benefits from telephone contact with industry colleagues for information seeking	1.432	1.79*	0.937	1.21
Firm benefits from mixing socially with industry colleagues	0.962	1.11	0.564	0.86
Firm benefits from chance meetings with industry colleagues where interesting information is heard	0.212	0.25	3.065	2.29**
Informal channels are important for recruiting senior management	0.468	0.84	2.663	2.14**
Informal channels are important for recruiting senior staff	−0.224	−0.34	−2.370	−2.48**
Informal channels are important for recruiting specialist staff				
Log-likelihood	−70.182			
χ^2	112.32***			

Notes: ***significant at 1 per cent, **significant at 5 per cent, *significant at 10 per cent.

meetings significantly more highly. This reinforces the impression that tapping into intelligence is an important advantage of locating in a major global node. In respect of the labour market, overseas MNEs rate the ability to recruit senior *managers* through informal channels significantly more highly than indigenous firms, but the ability to recruit senior *staff* significantly less highly. Once more this indicates that the peculiar advantage of a global node is that it is a focus for strategic decision-making, as Amin and Thrift (1992) suggest, and that global nodes attract the highest-quality labour.

Industry-specific effects on internationalization strategies

Why is post production positively associated with MNE status, and programme and film production negatively related? The experience of internationalization in post production bears out some, but not all, of Buckley's hypotheses. Post production does exhibit the technological characteristics which are identified by Buckley as being favourable to FDI by small firms. Although quite capital-intensive, and more capital-intensive than programme production, technology is small-scale in post production compared to typical manufacturing industries. An average-sized post production house would require a capital investment of a few million pounds, rather than hundreds of millions of pounds. Labour is a key resource and access to the right type of labour is critical. Finally, it is a highly knowledge-intensive business where creativity, ability to use advanced technology and the ability to interpret the clients' creative vision and requirements is all.

Programme production does not lend itself as easily to FDI and also has a range of means of exploiting its intellectual property, which mean that overseas location is not as important. These factors can be related to Dunning's OLI framework. Post production is a service which is typically advantageous to deliver in close proximity to the customer to ensure the end product meets the creative vision. In terms of exploiting intellectual property overseas in programme production, then such a market-seeking advantage for overseas location is less important. The product is easy to export. Transport costs are negligible in the case of direct programme sales and very low for videos and DVDs, the production of which can in any event be easily subcontracted. Format sales, where the basic programme 'recipe' is sold to be worked into a local version by an overseas company, are now a reasonably well-established and successful contractual mode of exploiting the intellectual property in programme ideas and there are no internalization advantages which warrant overseas production. The key tacit knowledge required to make a programme acceptable to an overseas audience resides in local firms and the intellectual property in the idea itself is reasonably easily transferred under the licensing agreement.

Conclusion

The factor analysis reported in the chapter has revealed that some classic sources of cluster advantage and disadvantage are manifest in the London media cluster, one of the most prominent and successful of UK clusters. Social capital and institutions, deep, fluid labour markets, specialized supply, strong local demand and customers and a balance of competition and cooperation are all important sources of advantage. Nevertheless, success is clearly bringing associated problems in terms of congestion and rising land prices. Moreover, London suffers from strains on its national and international transport linkages.

Most of the sources of advantage and disadvantage bear roughly equally upon MNEs and non-MNEs; however, there are some important influences which distinguish the two groups of firms. Moreover, these differences make sense in terms of both the conventional theory of MNE and the more recent literature which has sought to meld this theory with a clusters perspective. Social capital and the specialized supply infrastructure, whilst important in an absolute sense to MNEs, are significantly less important to them than to non-MNEs. This makes sense given that MNEs have internal resource strengths which make them relatively less reliant on externalities. Moreover, overseas MNEs may suffer from a 'liability of foreignness' which makes it more difficult for them to become embedded in the cluster. MNEs are also significantly less reliant on London as a source of work or labour. MNEs tend to be located in the geographic centre of the cluster, which provides the most attractive location in terms of realizing positive externalities and, in the case of domestic MNEs, may be part of the source of their international competitiveness. In terms of the strategic motivations for being in London, three emerge as significantly associated with MNEs: access to a strong, skilled labour supply, particularly senior management; the ability to develop new markets; and the ability to garner intelligence. These are consonant with the strategic asset- and market-seeking motives and the 'listening post' motivations which have been articulated in the extant literature.

Some important differences were identified between the advantages accruing to domestic versus foreign MNEs, although again it is important to note that they share much in common. Overseas MNEs appear to be less embedded in the cluster, deriving significantly smaller advantage from social capital and the specialized supply infrastructure. This could plausibly be due to a greater liability of foreignness, greater internal resource strength or some combination of the two. They are also less reliant on local firms for business; understandable given their home market is elsewhere. The fact that overseas multinationals also perceive a significantly greater advantage in terms of being able to recruit senior managers speaks both of a strategic asset-seeking motive for inward direct investment and of the status of London as a major strategic node in the industry.

References

Z. J. Acs and L. Preston, 'Small and medium-sized enterprises, technology and globalization: Introduction to a special issue on small and medium-sized enterprises in the global economy', *Small Business Economics*, 9(1) (1997) 1–6.

A. Aksoy and K. Robins, 'Hollywood for the 21st century: global competition for critical mass in image markets', *Cambridge Journal of Economics*, 16(1) (1992) 1–22.

A. Amin and N. Thrift, 'Neo-Marshallian nodes in global networks', *International Journal of Urban and Regional Research*, 16(4) (1992) 571–87.

M. Banks, A. Lovatt, J. O'Connor and C. Raffo, 'Risk and trust in the cultural industries', *Geoforum*, 31(4) (2000) 453–64.

R. M. L. N. Baptista and G. M. P. Swann, 'Do firms in clusters innovate more?' *Research Policy*, 27(5) (1998) 527–42.

H. Bathelt, 'Cluster relations in the media industry: exploring the "distanced neighbour" paradox in Leipzig', *Regional Studies*, 39(1) (2005) 105–27.

H. Bathelt, A. Malmberg and P. Maskell, 'Clusters and knowledge: local buzz, global pipelines and the process of knowledge creation', *Progress in Human Geography*, 28(1) (2004) 31–56.

J. V. Beaverstock, 'Re-thinking skilled international labour migration: world cities and banking organisations', *Geoforum*, 25(3) (1994) 323–38.

J. M. Birkinshaw and N. Hood, 'Characteristics of foreign subsidiaries in industry clusters', *Journal of International Business Studies*, 31(1) (2000) 141–54.

J. M. Birkinshaw and O. Solvell, 'Preface', *International Studies of Management and Organization*, 30(2) (2000) 3–9.

J. S. Boggs and N. M. Rantisi, 'The "relational turn" in economic geography', *Journal of Economic Geography*, 3(2) (2003) 109–16.

P. J. Buckley, 'International technology transfer by small and medium-sized enterprises', *Small Business Economics*, 9(1) (1997) 67–78.

P. J. Buckley and P. N. Ghauri, 'Globalisation, economic geography and the strategy of multinational enterprises', *Journal of International Business Studies*, 35(2) (2004) 81–98.

R. Camagni, 'Local 'Milieu', Uncertainty and Innovation Networks: Towards a New Dynamic Theory of Economic Space', in R. Camagni (ed), *Innovation Networks: Spatial Perspective*, (London: Belhaven, 1991), pp. 121–42.

R. B. Cattell, 'The Meaning and Strategic Use of Factor Analysis', in R. B. Cattell (ed), *Handbook of Multivariate Experimental Psychology*, (Chicago: Rand McNally, 1966).

M. Cave, 'An Introduction to Television Economics', in G. Hughes and D. Vines (eds), *Deregulation and the Future of Commercial Television*, (Aberdeen: University of Aberdeen, 1989), pp. 9–37.

G. L. Clark, M. P. Feldman and M. S. Gertler (eds), *The Oxford Handbook of Economic Geography*, (Oxford: Oxford University Press, 2000).

A. Cumbers and D. MacKinnon, 'Introduction: clusters in urban and regional development', *Urban Studies*, 41(5/6) (2004) 959–69.

DTI, *Our Competitive Future: Building the Knowledge Driven Economy*, Cmnd. 4176, (London: HMSO, 1998).

J. H. Dunning, *Multinational Enterprises and the Global Economy*, (Reading, MA: Addison-Wesley, 1993).

J. H. Dunning, 'Location and the multinational enterprise: a neglected factor?' *Journal of International Business Studies*, 29(1) (1998) 45–66.

J. H. Dunning, 'The Key Literature on IB Activities: 1960–2000', in A. M. Rugman and T. L. Brewer (eds), *The Oxford Handbook of International Business*, (Oxford: Oxford University Press, 2003).

C. Dupuy and J. P. Gilly, 'Industrial groups and territories: the case of Matra-Marconi-Space in toulouse', *Cambridge Journal of Economics*, 23(2) (1999) 207–25.

Economist (The), 'The Big Bang legacy', October 19th 2006.

G. Ellison and E. L. Glaeser, 'Geographic concentration in US manufacturing industries: a dartboard approach', *Journal of Political Economy*, 105(5) (1997) 889–927.

M. J. Enright, 'Regional Clusters and Firm Strategy', in A. D. Chandler, O. Solvell and P. Hagstrom (eds), *The Dynamic Firm: The Role of Technology, Strategy, and Regions*, (Oxford: Oxford University Press, 1998), pp. 315–42.

A. P. Field, *Discovering Statistics Using SPSS for Windows*, (London: Sage, 2005).

M. Fujita, P. Krugman and A. J. Venables, *The Spatial Economy*, (Cambridge, MA: The MIT Press, 1999).

C. Gibson and L. Kong, 'Cultural economy: a critical review', *Progress in Human Geography*, 29(5) (2005) 541–61.

H. Gong, 'Spatial patterns of foreign investment in China's cities, 1980–1989', *Urban Geography*, 16(3) (1995) 198–209.

P. Hall, 'Creative cities and economic development', *Urban Studies*, 37(4) (2000) 639–49.

B. Harrison, *Lean and Mean: The Changing Landscape of Corporate Power in the Age of Flexibility*, (London: The Guilford Press, 1994).

K. Head, J. C. Ries and D. L. Swenson, 'Agglomeration benefits and location choices: evidence from Japanese manufacturing investments in the United States', *Journal of International Economics*, 38(3/4) (1995) 223–47.

K. Head, J. C. Ries and D. L. Swenson, 'Attracting foreign manufacturing: investment promotion and agglomeration', *Regional Science and Urban Economics*, 29(2) (1999) 197–218.

J. V. Henderson, 'Efficiency of resource usage and city size', *Journal of Urban Economics*, 19(1) (1986) 47–70.

H. Hollenstein, 'Determinants of international activities: are SMEs different?', *Small Business Economics*, 24(5) (2005) 431–50.

H. Hotelling, 'Stability in competition', *Economic Journal*, 39(153) (1929) 41–57.

J. Jacobs, *The Economy of Cities*, (Harmondsworth: Penguin, 1972).

J. Jacobs, *Cities and the Wealth of Nations. Principles of Economic Life,* (Harmondsworth: Penguin, 1985).

M. Kitson, R. Martin and P. Tyler, 'Regional competitiveness: an elusive yet key concept?', *Regional Studies*, 38(9) (2004) 991–99.

R. Kozul-Wright and R. Rowthorn, 'Spoilt for choice? Multinational corporations and the geography of international production', *Oxford Review of Economic Policy*, 14(2) (1998) 74–92.

A. Marshall, *Principles of Economics*, (London: Macmillan, 1890).

A. Moran, *Copycat TV. Globalisation, Program Formats and Cultural Identity,* (Luton: University of Luton Press, 1998).

L. Nachum, 'Economic geography and the location of TNCs: financial and professional service FDI to the USA', *Journal of International Business Studies*, 31(3) (2000) 367–85.

L. Nachum, 'Liability of foreignness in global competition? Financial service affiliates in the City of London', *Strategic Management Journal*, 24(12) (2003) 1187–208.

L. Nachum and D. Keeble, 'Neo-Marshallian clusters and global networks: the linkages of media firms in central London', *Long Range Planning*, 36(5) (2003) 459–80.

D. Owen, 'Economic geography rewritten', *The Business Economist*, 30(1) (1999) 23–38.

N. R. Pandit and G. A. S. Cook, 'The Clustering of the British Financial Services Industry', in C. Karlsson, B. Johansson and R. Stough (eds), *Industrial Clusters and Inter-Firm Networks*, (Cheltenham: Edward Elgar, 2005), pp. 173–99.

M. E. Porter, *The Competitive Advantage of Nations*, (London: Macmillan, 1990).

M. E. Porter, 'Clusters and Competition: New Agendas for Companies, Governments, and Institutions', in M.E. Porter, *On Competition*, (Cambridge, MA: HBS Press, 1998), pp. 197–287.

M. E. Porter, 'Locations, Clusters and Company Strategy', in G. L. Clark, M. P. Feldmann and M. S. Gertler (eds), *The Oxford Handbook of Economic Geography*, (Oxford: Oxford University Press, 2000), pp. 253–74.

D. Power, ' "Cultural industries" in Sweden: an assessment of their place in the Swedish economy', *Economic Geography*, 78(2) (2002) 103–27.

A. Pred, *City-Systems in Advanced Economies. Past Growth, Present Processes and Future Development Options*, (London: Hutchinson, 1977).

N. Rantisi, 'The competitive foundations of localised learning and innovation: the case of women's garment production in New York City', *Economic Geography*, 78(4) (2002) 441–62.

A. Saxenian, *Regional Advantage: Culture and Competition in Silicon Valley and Route 128*, (Cambridge, MA: Harvard University Press, 1994).

A. J. Scott, 'Economic Geography: The Great Half Century', in G. L. Clark, M. P. Feldmann and M. S. Gertler (eds), *The Oxford Handbook of Economic Geography,* (Oxford: Oxford University Press, 2000), pp. 18–47.

A. J. Scott (ed.), *Global City-Regions*, (Oxford: Oxford University Press, 2001).

A. J. Scott, 'A new map of Hollywood: the production and distribution of American motion pictures', *Regional Studies*, 36(9) (2004) 957–75.

A. J. Scott and M. Storper, 'Regions, globalization, development', *Regional Studies*, 37(6/7) (2003) 379–593.

W. B. Shew, 'Trends in the Organization of Programme Production', in T. Congdon (ed.), *Paying for Broadcasting*, (London: Routledge, 1992).

J. P. Stevens, *Applied Multivariate Statistics for the Social Sciences*, 4th Edition, (Mahwah, NJ: Lawrence Erlbaum Associates, 2002).

G. M. P. Swann, M. Prevezer and D. Stout (eds), *The Dynamics of Industrial Clustering: International Comparisons in Computing and Biotechnology*, (Oxford: Oxford University Press, 1998).

I. Turok, 'Cities, clusters and creative industries: the case of film and television in Scotland', *European Planning Studies*, 11(5) (2003) 549–65.

E. von Hippel, *The Sources of Innovation*, (Oxford: Oxford University Press, 1988).

D. Wheeler and A. Moody, 'International investment location decisions', *Journal of International Economics*, 33(1/2) (1992) 57–76.

S. Zaheer, 'Overcoming the liability of foreignness', *Academy of Management Journal*, 38(2) (1995) 341–63.

10
Redundancies in External Relationships of Multinational Corporations – A Firm-Level Conceptual Model

Phillip C. Nell, Ulf Andersson and Björn Ambos

Introduction

The conceptualization of the multinational corporation (MNC) as a differentiated network suggests that the subsidiaries' level of embeddedness in their local environment is crucial, as it is the basis for subsidiary-specific advantages and entrepreneurship (Andersson et al., 2002; Frost, 2001). In addition to possessing important resources, the subsidiaries of a differentiated MNC are conceptualized as being relatively autonomous and powerful, striving at least in part for their own goals (Birkinshaw, 1997; Hedlund, 1986; Nohria and Ghoshal, 1997; Rugman and Verbeke, 2001). The headquarters' (HQ's) role is to design differentiated coordination and control mechanisms to ensure that the MNC acts as a differentiated but integrated network of units (Nohria and Ghoshal, 1997). However, this HQ role is very difficult to fulfil if not contradictory. Especially critical is the underlying assumption that HQs have *knowledge* about a large variety of subsidiary contexts, and that they are able to and possess the power to orchestrate and manage the differentiated network (Björkman and Forsgren, 2000; Holm et al., 1995).

Against this background, recent research has reported the interesting phenomenon that HQs also build direct relationships to their subsidiaries' local networks. We call this 'network redundancy', that is, a situation in which both the subsidiaries and the corresponding HQs are embedded into the same local external network, that is, to the same external network actors. Network redundancy is a common phenomenon, for example, Forsgren et al. (2005) report that for approximately 10 per cent of all subsidiaries in their sample, the corresponding HQs have as well strongly embedded themselves into the local subsidiary network; and for 40 per cent of all subsidiaries, HQs have at least some degree of embeddedness. While there is initial research on this issue, it is unclear why and under which circumstances network redundancy develops. On the one hand, it seems to contradict the 'division of labour' assumption of bureaucratic organizations and the traditional logic of resource allocation (Williamson, 1975). Developing and maintaining embedded relationships to the environment is very costly and consumes managerial resources (Boehe, 2007; Luo, 2003; Mizruchi and Galaskiewicz, 1994; Narula and Zanfei, 2004). In addition, from a network perspective, HQ relationships to the subsidiary network seem to break the rule of efficiency and effectiveness (Burt, 1992). The efficiency and effectiveness rule says that investment in a new relationship should not be done if the contact can be reached through existing relationships and that resources should rather be committed to existing relationships. On the other hand, some scholars have claimed that redundancy and duplication of activities is a necessary feature of modern organizations that operate in turbulent environments (Birkinshaw and Lingblad, 2005; Hedlund, 1980). Initial empirical work has also shown that MNCs operating with overlapping relationships to external actors profit from subsidiary embeddedness while maintaining the HQ's capacity to fulfil its role in the differentiated MNC (Andersson et al., 2007; Holm et al., 1995; Nell et al., 2011; Yamin and Forsgren, 2006). Yet, most of this work focuses on the subsidiary level. A firm-level theoretical framework and discussion is so far missing.

We shed light on this puzzle. Our contribution is two-fold. First, our chapter advances a firm-level theoretical framework that explains the phenomenon of network redundancy in MNCs, which we claim is an important pillar to an increased understanding of the MNC as a differentiated network organization. We attempt to explain the extent to which contingencies influence if benefits or costs of network redundancy overweigh. We also add to the MNC embeddedness literature by integrating a more complex and hence realistic picture of MNC external embeddedness and by showing that our more holistic approach is fruitful for further research. Second, we make a modest empirical contribution by analysing data from a recent study on this topic. We find some preliminary support for the relationship between our environmental contingencies and network redundancy which complements previous results on the subsidiary level (Nell et al., 2011).

Literature background

Subsidiaries are suggested to be embedded in differing local environments exposing the MNC to a wide range of resources and capabilities (Ghoshal and Nohria, 1989). The relationships to the environment are a basis for differentiation (Pearce and Papanastassiou, 1997) and a very important source of knowledge (Foss and Pedersen, 2002). It is important to distinguish between relational and structural embeddedness. Relational embeddedness refers to a dyadic perspective, that is, to specific relationships between two actors (Granovetter, 1985; Gulati, 1998). The relationship is defined as being strongly embedded when it is very close and intense with mutual interdependence (Andersson et al., 2002; Frost, 2001). Structural embeddedness refers to the fact that firms are embedded in sets of connected relationships (Cook and Emerson, 1978). Here, the perspective moves from the dyadic relationship (e.g., firm to customer) towards the integral network including, for example, customers' customers or customers' suppliers. In this structural perspective, emphasis is put on the overall network and its characteristics, such as the overall network density or the number of existing structural holes (Brass and Burkhardt, 1993; Brass et al., 1998). In this chapter we are focusing on the relational embeddedness dimension.[1]

The definition of the network to which individuals, units, or firms can develop embedded relationships has varied with the level of analysis (Dacin et al., 1999). For example, the network has been defined as a 'business network' with business relationships between the actors that involve buying and selling processes (Andersson et al., 2002; Tsai and Ghoshal, 1998). This is based on the idea that 'all firms work in cooperation with others in offering their products and services to the market' (Chen et al., 2004, p. 321). Others have emphasized the importance of social relationships and hence social networks in contrast to the business network approach (Tsai, 2000). However, the definition of business relationships seems to include information and social relationships as well.[2] In the following, our focus will be set on the organizational unit level and we will refer mainly to business relationships (buying and selling exchange relationships), information relationships and, occasionally, social ties on the individual level on which business relationships are based (Chen et al., 2004; Hansen, 1999).

Previous research on subsidiary embeddedness

The existing work on *MNC embeddedness* has primarily focused on the subsidiary-level relational embeddedness in a local network (e.g., Andersson, 1996; Andersson et al., 2002; Asakawa, 1996; Boehe, 2007; Holm et al., 2005; Mu et al., 2007; Schmid and Schurig, 2003). The subsidiary is often seen as a local 'quasi-firm' (Forsgren, 2004) which is the 'local market interface' (Mu et al., 2007). It is assumed that subsidiaries develop and foster their external relationships in order to respond to environmental challenges (Holm et al., 2005; Luo, 2002, 2003). In addition, a necessary condition seems to be that they have enough resources and liberty to do so (Andersson et al., 2005). In fact, it is acknowledged that MNCs use methods of coordinating and controlling international activities to influence the behaviour of subsidiaries (Baliga and Jaeger, 1984; Martinez and Jarillo, 1989) and some of these mechanisms have been shown to hinder the development of subsidiary embeddedness (Andersson et al., 2005).

Suppressing the development of subsidiary embeddedness has disadvantages. Embedded subsidiaries are able to create new knowledge and be innovative since their strong relationships allow for trustful collaboration and fine-grained information and knowledge exchange (e.g., Andersson et al., 2002; Holm et al., 2005; Nobel and Birkinshaw, 1998). Hence, subsidiary embeddedness is a necessary feature of the differentiated MNC to take advantage of its multinationality and to profit from different knowledge sources in their various host markets (Kogut and Zander, 1992).

Beside the knowledge aspects, it has also been shown that embedded subsidiaries can exploit substantial influence on their own status and their responsibilities within the MNC (Andersson et al., 2002, 2007; Forsgren, 2004). Very intensive interaction of the subsidiary with its external network can come at the expense of the subsidiary's interaction with their own MNC or own HQ (Andersson and Björkman, 2005). This decreases the level of HQ knowledge and understanding of the local context (Forsgren, 2004; Holm et al., 1995). Recent findings also indicate that knowledge of embedded subsidiaries does not automatically lead to knowledge transfer back to the MNC (Hakanson and Nobel, 2001; Holmström, 2010; Mu et al., 2007). This shows that MNCs have difficulties in integrating embedded subsidiaries back into the organization (compare Asakawa, 2001). Hence, subsidiary embeddedness might lead to a control and coordination problem for the HQ (Holm et al., 1995) since it gives rise to a situation in which subsidiaries are powerful (Andersson et al., 2007) and autonomous (Andersson and Forsgren, 1996).

Development of the concept of network redundancy

From the above, we conclude that MNCs might want to foster the embeddedness of subsidiaries for learning and knowledge purposes while they need to find tools to manage the control gap that is likely to emerge simultaneously during the embedding process. One phenomenon mentioned in recent research which might help the MNC to achieve a situation of embedded but controlled subsidiaries is 'network redundancy' of the MNC in the same network.

In general, scholars have acknowledged that the conceptualization of the MNC as a multi-centre organization also includes that relationships to the external network exist on many different levels of the organization (Halinen and Törnroos, 1998). HQs can develop their own set of direct relationships independent of the subsidiary network, that is, networks to which subsidiaries do not have direct linkages. Dacin et al. (1999) suggest that the opportunity for relationships on higher levels of the organization (such as HQs) has increased with the trend towards globalization as the latter can be interpreted 'as a dis-embedding process that strips individuals and firms from their local structures and allows for restructuring at a more global level' (p. 341). An example is a HQ's own communication and social relationships with specific actors to which the subsidiaries are not connected (e.g., the corporate HQ of P&G). In this situation, there is no redundancy.

Researchers have also begun to investigate the role of HQ external relationships to the local subsidiary's network (Andersson et al., 2007; Nell et al., 2011), hereafter called *HQ local embeddedness*. Andersson et al. (2002, p. 992) note that 'the HQ must take part and develop its own relationships with important customers and suppliers in the subsidiary's network'.

Nell et al. (2011, p. 498) give the following examples:

At Boehringer Ingelheim, a German pharmaceutical company, the marketing staff of the Eastern European regional HQ maintains direct linkages to important customers and health care organizations in the Eastern European countries in order to understand developments in the highly turbulent pharmaceutical markets. These linkages help the regional HQ staff to exercise control over the 28 country operations, to defend strategies of standardization and harmonization of marketing approaches, and to perceive business opportunities which are often not perceived by the subsidiaries themselves.

At Dental, a Swiss medical technology firm with 25 subsidiaries worldwide, the headquarters maintains relatively strong linkages to the local subsidiaries' key network partners such as universities, industry associations and research institutes, in order to complement knowledge acquisition and processing capacity of the subsidiaries.

Note that our concept of HQ local embeddedness does not mean that the HQ only develops relationships to actors at the HQ location (i.e., the country where the HQ unit is located) but to several local networks of their geographically dispersed subsidiaries. Our concept of network redundancy is based on both subsidiary local embeddedness and HQ local embeddedness. It is defined as a situation in which both the subsidiary and the HQ has developed a strong relationship to the same local network (Figure 10.1). However, contrary to the work of Nell et al. (2011), we conceptualize network redundancy on the firm level and not on the level of the individual subsidiary.

Theoretical framework and development of propositions

In general, we would not expect many cases to be in a situation of network redundancy. We expect most cases to be in the lower right corner of Figure 10.1. In this situation the subsidiaries are relatively strongly embedded with strong relationships to local actors. The HQ only maintains a few and rather weak relationships to these actors and hence network redundancy is low. This should be a standard way of operating since this configuration is lean and efficient.

Furthermore, we would also expect that relationships of established subsidiaries can reach very high levels of embeddedness while the HQ's local relationships are probably mainly communication and social relationships without direct buying/selling exchange activities involved. Again, this reflects an efficient way of distributing work in the dispersed MNC: HQs might selectively link up to the subsidiary network, but the strongest level of relational embeddedness remains

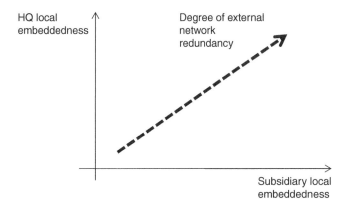

Figure 10.1 The concept of network redundancy to external local networks

between the subsidiary and the local partners – otherwise, there would be no need for the subsidiary in the first place. These are our first two propositions:

Proposition 10.1   In a random sample of MNC subsidiaries, the majority of cases will not operate with network redundancy.

Proposition 10.2   On average, HQ local embeddedness is lower than subsidiary local embeddedness.

Besides these overall propositions, we develop a model which predicts the degree of network redundancy on the firm level. Our model consists of environmental factors as well as firm-specific factors (see Figure 10.2). Contrary to Nell et al. (2011), which investigated antecedents of HQ linkages to the local subsidiary network, our model is limited to factors that influence *both* subsidiary and HQ local embeddedness as we argue that both these factors influence the balance between costs and benefits of network redundancy on the firm level.

Environmental context

It is well-accepted that firms enter relationships to external actors in response to challenges and opportunities posed by the environment (Pfeffer and Salancik, 1978; Thompson, 1967). We integrate 'environmental uncertainty' in our model. It is an important characteristic of the environment and frequently used in research on inter-organizational relationships (e.g., Beckman et al., 2004; Koka et al., 2006). In addition, we use the intensity of competition as a second variable. Both variables have been captured previously as antecedents of HQ linkages to local subsidiary networks (Nell et al., 2011).

Uncertainty is created through turbulence in the environment. Turbulence can be defined as the rate of change in technology associated with the development of products (Menon et al., 1997) or the rate of change in the composition of customers and their preferences (Jaworski and Kohli, 1993). It is reflective of the overall industry and not specifically the state of that industry in a particular market (Hewett et al., 2003). Under turbulence, product needs and preferences of customers and consumers change substantially and industry opportunities and challenges emerge simultaneously (Rawski, 1994). Therefore, firms need

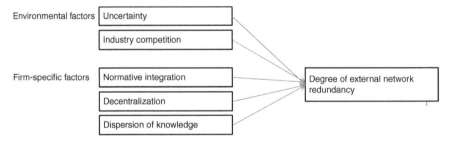

Figure 10.2   Research model: antecedents of the degree of network redundancy to local networks

to maximize chances to fully identify opportunities and risks (Birkinshaw and Lingblad, 2005). This can be achieved through strong market orientation (Boyd and Fulk, 1996) and high-quality information gathering via strong relationships to other actors in the market. To this end, turbulence is a driver of subsidiary embeddedness.

Furthermore, in such environments, a single dominant source of information and logic of interpretation should be avoided (Birkinshaw and Lingblad, 2005; Prahalad and Bettis, 1995). Hedlund (1980) has claimed that firms need to be very creative and need to involve several hierarchical levels to respond appropriately to turbulent environments. Hence, environmental uncertainty is prone to drive a situation in which not only subsidiaries strive for deepened external relationships but HQs also create their own relationships to the external actors (compare Nell et al., 2011).

Proposition 10.3   The degree of environmental uncertainty is positively associated with the degree of MNC network redundancy in a given MNC.

Intensity of competition is defined as a situation in which an industry's competitors are very prone to fighting and retaliation, which creates market instability (Porter, 1980). Customers may have many alternative options to satisfy their needs and wants (Jaworski and Kohli, 1993). Hence, competitive pressures challenge the position of players in the market and make them more dependent on other firms (Caves and Porter, 1978). Therefore, authors have argued that intense competition makes it necessary to neutralize this pressure through external relations (Holm et al., 2005; Luo, 2003).

However, in contrast to the level of environmental uncertainty, the level of competition is also a sign of a mature industry in which there is substantial cost pressure (Birkinshaw and Lingblad, 2005). Prices tend to decrease when competition is very intense and firms will therefore eliminate overlapping activities where possible and strive for efficiency in their operations. Hence, while embeddedness is a very important countermeasure to increased competition, firms will still try to streamline their organizations and avoid the duplication of relationships to the external networks. HQ local embeddedness in addition to strong subsidiary local embeddedness is not very likely (Nell et al., 2011).

Proposition 10.4   The intensity of industry competition is negatively associated with the degree of network redundancy in a given MNC.

Organizational context

We consider two control variables: decentralization of decision-making and normative integration as key indicators of the HQ–subsidiary control relationship (Nohria and Ghoshal, 1994). Another variable which shifts the balance between costs and benefits of network redundancy is the dispersion of MNC knowledge.

Decentralization of decision-making

Decentralization of decision-making puts the locus of authority in the hands of the subsidiary managers (Pugh et al., 1968). If additional control mechanisms are lacking that might help to constrain subsidiary behaviour, autonomous subsidiaries can be expected to act predominantly in the interests of their own organizational unit. By definition, a high degree of embeddedness means that there are other specific actors than HQs in the subsidiary's environment that the subsidiary considers as being important (Andersson et al., 2007). Hence, activities of autonomous subsidiaries will be directed to the more immediate and important actors in their environment and less to firm-internal partners. Therefore, a high level of subsidiary embeddedness has been empirically linked to high levels of autonomy (Andersson and Forsgren, 1996; Asakawa, 2001).

However, the emphasis of autonomous subsidiaries on the local optimum creates a control gap for the HQ (Ghoshal and Bartlett, 1990). In such a situation, HQ relations to local networks are becoming more relevant since they improve the HQ's first-hand knowledge of the local context and break subsidiary influence (Andersson, 2007). HQ's own local relationships are an additional information channel. Birkinshaw et al. (2001) argue that multiple external relationships on several levels of the MNC enhance internal information processing capacity of the MNC. Hence, we argue that especially in case of autonomous subsidiaries, HQ local embeddedness can serve as a mechanism to maintain control and power over the subsidiary (Andersson et al., 2007; Nell et al., 2011; Yamin and Forsgren, 2006).

Proposition 10.5   The degree of decentralization of decision-making is positively associated with the degree of network redundancy in a given MNC.

Normative integration

Subsidiaries are normatively integrated if the parent company manages to establish shared values (Edström and Galbraith, 1977; Ouchi and Maguire, 1975). Normative integration is achieved through extensive usage of job rotations, international teams and task forces, international training and development programs and a strong focus on the corporate culture. For the HQ, normative integration is an alternative control mode (Ghoshal and Nohria, 1989; Hedlund, 1986). Dispersed units which are normatively integrated show greater commitment to the organization, identify more with the firm, and are more loyal and willing to cooperate. Thus, normatively integrated subsidiaries are more likely to behave in the interest of the whole corporation and there is, therefore, less pressure for HQs to build relationships to the subsidiary network and to reduce the control gap. Furthermore, the development of embeddedness requires a lot of investments from the subsidiary. Subsidiaries need to understand the counterparts' capabilities and importance and the relational linkages must be nurtured and deepened, which consumes managers' time and attention (Andersson et al., 2005). The subsidiary's relationships with its environment run the risk of being limited by HQs that use too much control. Normative integration requires subsidiary managers to travel extensively to HQs or corporate meetings, participate in trainings, and work in international teams and project groups. This would mean that subsidiary managers commit more time to an MNC's internal issues and less to the local environment. In sum, as HQs might not face severe control problems and subsidiaries might not be inclined to develop external embeddedness, we propose the following:

Proposition 10.6   The degree of normative integration is negatively associated with the degree of network redundancy in a given MNC.

Dispersion of MNC knowledge

An MNC's knowledge base is strongly dispersed if the knowledge reservoirs are to a large extent located in geographically dispersed subsidiaries. In the context of inter-organizational relations, the competencies of a firm or a unit are a driver of its attractiveness as perceived by potential external partners (e.g., Powell et al., 1996). R&D subsidiaries which are evaluated as being very knowledgeable have been found to be more embedded into their environment (Hakansson and Nobel, 2001). As the level of embeddedness is itself conducive to creating new knowledge, it becomes a self-enforcing process in which a competent subsidiary is able to strongly embed to competent partner firms, which in turn enables the subsidiary to develop new knowledge.

Regarding the HQ level, it is obvious that the degree of dispersion of MNC knowledge is a challenge to the integration and transfer of the knowledge within the MNC. First, valuable knowledge developed in external relationships is arguably tacit in nature (compare Lane and Lubatkin, 1998), which means that no single unit within the MNC including the HQ has exact and full knowledge of where important competencies are located (Forsgren et al., 2005). HQ's own relationships to the external partners help them to be aware of where and to what extent valuable knowledge is available in specific subsidiaries (Andersson et al., 2007; Forsgren et al., 2005; Nell et al., 2011). Second, the control problem is more severe when the subsidiary is very knowledgeable, as this translates into a situation in which the subsidiaries are powerful (Mudambi and Navarra, 2004). In case these subsidiaries are less willing to transfer knowledge to other units of the MNCs, the HQ's ability to force subsidiaries to share their knowledge is crucial (Forsgren et al., 2005). HQ's own relationships to the subsidiary network can break subsidiary power (Andersson et al., 2007) and might help realize reverse knowledge transfers from the subsidiary to the rest of the MNC (Forsgren et al., 2005). In sum, dispersed knowledge seems to be linked to subsidiary embeddedness, which creates both a control problem and an incentive to the HQ to engage in knowledge detection and transfer activities. There is also first-hand evidence that resource-strong and high-performing subsidiaries attract HQ attention (Nell et al., 2011). Therefore:

Proposition 10.7   The degree of dispersion of MNC knowledge is positively associated with the degree of network redundancy in a given MNC.

Network redundancy and MNC performance

One important issue that we did not develop further in the above text is the effect of network redundancy on MNC performance. We have focused on the conditions under which network redundancy is likely to occur but that does not mean that network redundancy is, per se, a driver of performance when it occurs. We argue that network redundancy is a relevant aspect of the MNC's organizational design. Therefore, we suggest that the performance benefits of network redundancy are contingent on environmental and organizational context. We suggest a configurational approach of fit between network redundancy and the environmental and organizational contingencies. MNCs which use network redundancy following the above-mentioned propositions should, ceteris paribus, be performing better than MNCs which deviate from this profile (compare Doty et al., 1993; Drazin and Van de Ven, 1985). High redundancy in relatively stable environments in which the firm operates in a centralized fashion and where key resources such as knowledge are located on the HQ level should therefore be negatively related to performance. Similarly, a lack of redundancy in very turbulent environments in which the MNC operates with a stronger network-like organization (decentralized, only normatively integrated, and with strong dispersion of knowledge) should be negatively related to performance.

Proposition 10.8   The greater the level of fit between an organization's actual profile of environmental and organizational factors and its level of network redundancy, the higher its performance.

Data analysis and discussion

We do not intend to formally test all our propositions because we do not have data on the firm level. We collected 193 responses from European subsidiaries of MNCs (compare Nell et al., 2011, for a more detailed description of the data) – that is, we have information on network redundancy only on the level of the individual subsidiary and cannot infer directly to the level of the whole MNC. We only attempt to provide additional evidence to support the idea of a link between environmental contingencies and network redundancy that complements Nell et al. (2011).

To measure relational embeddedness we asked the subsidiaries to indicate the extent to which they have developed strong relationships with local competitors, customers, suppliers, governments and industry associations (six-point scale). We summed the values for these indicators to derive a proxy for the local embeddedness of the subsidiary. We repeated this procedure for the corresponding values of the HQ with regard to the same network actors to which the subsidiaries have indicated their relationship strength values. Based on the two embeddedness variables we constructed the dichotomous variable 'External Network Redundancy' through median split. We assigned a '1' to those subsidiaries for which their embeddedness value, as well as their HQ's value, was above the median of subsidiary embeddedness and HQ embeddedness, respectively (the upper right corner in Figure 10.1), thus indicating redundancy. Note that this operationalization differs from previous work (Nell et al., 2011) and it therefore helps in assessing the robustness of previous results.

We collected secondary data on the industry and host country level (the country of the subsidiary). Our goal was to develop proxies for our environmental contingency variables and to add to previous literature that has integrated perceptional measures of uncertainty and competition (Nell et al., 2011). From the IMD world competitiveness reports we selected the following indicators:

To proxy *environmental uncertainty*:

- Strong economy resilience to economic cycles (IMD question: 'Resilience of the economy to economic cycles is strong'.)

To proxy *intensity of competition*:

- Ease of doing business (IMD question: 'Ease of doing business is supported by regulations'.)
- Competition (IMD question: 'The legal and regulatory framework encourages the competitiveness of enterprises'.)

From EUROSTAT we compiled data on foreign direct investment (FDI) and economic output to proxy *environmental uncertainty*:

- Coefficient of variation (Std. Dev. divided by mean) between 2003 and 2006 for FDI inflows into the subsidiary country. High variation means strong turbulence in the participation of foreign firms in the market. *Source*: EUROSTAT.
- Coefficient of variation of European production output between 2003 and 2007 for the focal firm's industry. *Source*: EUROSTAT: 'Statistics on the production of manufactured goods Value' (Prodcomm database). This variable is larger the more an industry within Europe undergoes large variation in terms of industry output (in value terms). It hence captures environmental turbulence.
- Coefficient of variation of total production output between 2003 and 2007 for the subsidiary's country across all industries. *Source*: EUROSTAT: 'Statistics on the production of manufactured goods Value' (Prodcomm database). This variable proxies overall country-level turbulence.

To analyse the data we conducted a series of statistical tests. First, we calculated the overall responses to the variable HQ local embeddedness (Figure 10.3). We found evidence that HQs strongly embed only on rare occasions. Roughly 12 per cent of our sample's subsidiaries indicate that the HQs are very strongly embedded to their local network. In addition, only 23 per cent of all subsidiaries belong to the group of subsidiaries operating with network redundancy. This lends preliminary support to our Proposition 10.1.

Furthermore, according to our expectations, a one-sample *t*-test shows that the relationship strength of the subsidiary to their network is larger than the HQ's relationships to the same network (compare Table 10.1). This is preliminary support for Proposition 10.2.

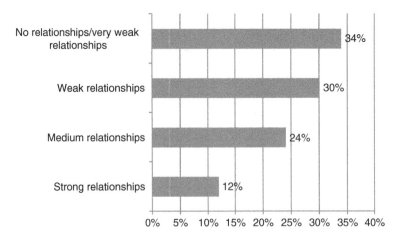

Figure 10.3 Descriptives: HQ local embeddedness

Table 10.1 Differences between subsidiary and HQ local embeddedness[a]

	N	**Mean**	**Std. dev.**	**One-sample *t*-test**
Subsidiary local embeddedness	189	25.3	6.6	$t = -23.28$; Sig. $p < 0.000$
HQ local embeddedness	188	11.8	7.9	

[a]One-sample *t*-test with reference value 25.3 (mean of subsidiary local embeddedness); 2-tailed.

Regarding the association with environmental contingency variables (Propositions 10.3–10.4) we conducted a series of *t*-tests to compare the redundancy group with the non-redundancy group (Table 10.2). There is some limited support for our propositions. No significant difference has been found for the variables 'ease of doing business', 'competition' and 'production output variation at the country level'. We found support for a link between an economy's resilience to cycles and network redundancy. However, contrary to our proposition, this variable signifies stability in the economic conditions. Yet, this variable shows higher values for subsidiaries of high network redundancy than for subsidiaries with low redundancy.

On the other hand, there is support for our proposition that environmental turbulence is positively linked to network redundancy regarding the coefficients of variation for *FDI inflows* and *production output* of the firm's industry in Europe. The first variable captures the extent to which international MNC activity in the host country varies over the years. This happens when there is strong volatility, for example, due to changing FDI regulations, recessions or strong but relatively steady growth or decline. The second variable captures if total production output in the industry is varying substantially within Europe. This can occur due to economic cycles or increased competition by extra-European economies. Both

Table 10.2 Analysis of environmental factors[a]

	Mean value in situation of low external network redundancy	Mean value in situation of high external network redundancy	Significance
Country-specific indicators:			
• Strong economy resilience to economic cycles[b]	4.9	5.1	**
• Ease of doing business[c]	5.0	5.2	
• Competition[d]	4.1	4.3	
• Variation in FDI inflows for subsidiary country[e]	0.59	0.69	*
• Variation of production output for subsidiary country[f]	0.21	0.19	
Industry-specific indicators:			
• Variation of production output for firm industry in Europe[g]	0.49	0.55	**

[a]Two independent samples *t*-tests; 2-tailed. *** $p < 0.01$; ** $p < 0.05$; * $p < 0.10$.
[b]IMD question on a 10-point scale: 'Resilience of the economy to economic cycles is strong'.
[c]IMD question on a 10-point scale: 'Ease of doing business is supported by regulations'.
[d]IMD question on a 10-point scale: 'The legal and regulatory framework encourages the competitiveness of enterprises'.
[e]Coefficient of variation (Std. dev. divided by mean) between 2003 and 2006 for FDI inflows into subsidiary country. *Source*: EUROSTAT.
[f]Coefficient of variation of total production output 2003–2007 for the subsidiary's country across all industries. *Source*: EUROSTAT: 'Statistics on the production of manufactured goods Value' (Prodcomm database).
[g]Coefficient of variation of production output 2003–2007 for the focal firm's industry in Europe. *Source*: EUROSTAT: 'Statistics on the production of manufactured goods Value' (Prodcomm database).

variables show that the subsidiaries that operate with high network redundancy are situated in the more turbulent environment.

Discussion

Our chapter has advanced the understanding of the phenomenon of network redundancy in MNCs by showing how it is shaped by a set of environmental and organizational variables. Our contribution is two-fold.

First, we make a theoretical contribution and add to several strands of literature. In contrast to previous work (especially Nell et al., 2011), this chapter advances a firm-level model. To this end, our chapter is an extension of the embeddedness literature and the work on the differentiated MNC (compare Nohria and Ghoshal, 1997). The concept of network redundancy offers important insights into the benefits of redundant networks benefits (in terms of offering

a way for HQs to be able to fill its role as an orchestrator of the differentiated MNC) as well as substantial costs (in terms of duplication of activities and
redundancies). We directly add to the literature claiming that efficiency and
effectiveness in organizations is very important. Our study shows that, indeed,
firms do break the rule of efficiency and effectiveness (Burt, 1992) (i.e., of avoiding redundancies) but only in rare occasions. We suggest that this is due to
the high costs that come with such redundancies (Boehe, 2007; Luo, 2003;
Mizruchi and Galaskiewicz, 1994). This means that there are important contingencies that play a role in determining when firms and MNCs deviate from the
goals of an efficient and effective setup. We link this argument to the general
contingency literature and argue that there are two sets of contingency factors:
firm-internal factors (organizational factors) and environmental factors. This is
novel since often research focuses only on environmental contingencies, neglect-
ing other organizational design characteristics which simultaneously influence.
We posit that internal factors are very important in shaping external network
redundancies because they characterize the control gap between HQs and subsidiaries and they have a direct impact on how the subsidiary level adapts to the
local environment. This is an issue elaborated on only very limitedly in previous research (for a notable exception see Andersson and Björkman, 2005). Our
framework extends previous work on the subsidiary level. We argue that redundancy is created by variables that influence both the level of subsidiary and HQ
embeddedness.

In more general terms and in line with Nell et al. (2011), our work highlights that future research can profit from a more holistic and complex concept
of MNC–external actor interaction. Our idea of network redundancy spans two
levels of the organization: the HQ level and the subsidiary level. External relationships of the MNC exist on every level, especially in a multi-centre differentiated organization, with the possibility of creating redundancies. The strong
previous focus on corporate-level networks (e.g., alliance networks), or subsidiary-
level business networks (classic subsidiary relational embeddedness literature)
is, in our view, simplistic and misses out learning from the links between the
two. We have shed first light on such multi-level investigation by emphasizing redundancies. Future research could investigate further the extent to which
higher-level alliances (and their management) impact subsidiary-level operational
relationships.

Second, we make a very modest empirical contribution. We confirm that HQs
are less strongly related to local networks than the respective local subsidiaries.
This is to a large extent due to the fact that roughly one-third of all subsidiary networks were left without HQ attention. We also show preliminary support for our
propositions that firms operate with more or less external network redundancies
depending on environmental characteristics. There is some support for our proposition that turbulence in the external environment is more likely to lead to
situations of redundancies. A strong variation in FDI inflows into a country and
strong variation in terms of industrial output is connected to more external network redundancy. Note that we measured our indicators on a time span of three

to four years before data collection, that is, three to four years before the subsidiaries informed us about the redundancies. This differentiates our research
from dominating cross-sectional studies. It is an indicator that the link between
environmental contingencies and external network redundancy is indeed causal.
Our work also supports previous results that have used perceptional measures
of uncertainty (Nell et al., 2011). We do not find any association between environmental competition and redundancy. Hence, both perceptionally and in this
study, featured objective measures of competition seem to be related to network
redundancies.

However, we did not find significant results for our other variables. Moreover,
strong resilience of an economy to shocks and crises are positively related to
external network redundancy. This was unexpected. This could be because our
variable might also capture the overall prosperity and availability of high-quality
knowledge in an economy. Knowledge-intensive economies might be less prone
to industry cycles than economies that largely rely on basic goods and commodi-
ties. Under situations of high knowledge intensity within the economy, both
subsidiaries and HQs might be interested in strong local relationships and hence
redundancy to maximize the learning.

Of course, there are limitations with regard to our secondary data proxies in the way they are capturing our concepts of uncertainty and competition. While both dimensions are conceptually distinct, it seems hard to distinguish them empirically. Furthermore, the level of analysis is an issue that
needs to be resolved before an empirical testing of our propositions. Our variables cover country-level indicators and industry indicators. It is obvious that
subsidiaries are nested in countries, country-level industries and regional or
global industries. However, it is not clear which level is more important to
the issue of network redundancy. This might be an important area for future
research.

There are several other interesting research avenues. First of all, our emphasis
in this chapter is on the conceptual part; it lacks empirical investigation. Second,
future research should also investigate more in detail the actual or perceived costs
of network redundancy from a HQ perspective but probably also from a subsidiary
perspective. In our model, we take into consideration that network redundancy
can have positive as well as negative performance effects but we do not develop
the discussion of the costs in case of negative performance effects. For example,
in addition to obvious costs that occur on the HQ level such as additional staff
needed for the resource-consuming relationships to various local contexts, costs
could occur on the subsidiary level, for example, through transfer prices. Third,
while in our view it has some important advantages to propose a model on the
firm level, research on network redundancy in particular markets could be very
helpful to understand the phenomenon more holistically. Some of the propositions might be transferable to the market level but there might be additional
variables that play an important role. For example, the general importance of a
subsidiary and its market could play a decisive role in attracting HQs to develop
their own relationships to the local environment (Bouquet and Birkinshaw, 2008).

Similarly, the specific subsidiary's knowledge base would be important (Andersson et al., 2007).

Notes

1. Note that we do not imply that structural embeddedness is not important. However, for the sake of simplicity, we focus on subsidiary's and HQ's relational embeddedness only.
2. Forsgren et al. (2005, p. 17) note that an 'important aspect of the exchange is the exchange of information. In a business relationship, managers in the two firms develop and maintain extensive contacts with each other.'

References

U. Andersson, I. Björkman and M. Forsgren, 'Managing subsidiary knowledge creation: the effect of control mechanisms on subsidiary local embeddedness', *International Business Review*, 14(5) (2005) 521.

U. Andersson and M. Forsgren, 'Subsidiary embeddedness and control in the multinational corporation', *International Business Review*, 5(5) (1996) 487–508.

U. Andersson, M. Forsgren and U. Holm, 'The strategic impact of external networks: subsidiary performance and competence development in the multinational corporation', *Strategic Management Journal*, 23(11) (2002) 979.

U. Andersson, M. Forsgren and U. Holm, 'Balancing subsidiary influence in the federative MNC: a business network view', *Journal of International Business Studies*, 38(5) (2007) 802–19.

K. Asakawa, 'The Multinational Tension in R&D Internationalization: Strategic Linkage Mechanisms of Distant Contextual Knowledge in Japanese Multinational Companies', *INSEAD*. Fontainebleau, INSEAD (1996).

K. Asakawa, 'Organizational tension in international R&D management: the case of Japanese firms', *Research Policy*, 30(5) (2001) 735.

B. R. Baliga and A. M. Jaeger, 'Multinational corporations: control systems and delegation issues', *Journal of International Business Studies*, 15(2) (1984) 25.

C. M. Beckman, P. R. Haunschild and D. J. Phillips, 'Friends or strangers? Firm-specific uncertainty, market uncertainty, and network partner selection', *Organization Science*, 15(3) (2004) 259–75.

J. Birkinshaw, 'Entrepreneurship in multinational corporations: the characteristics of subsidiary initiatives', *Strategic Management Journal*, 18(3) (1997) 207.

J. Birkinshaw and M. Lingblad, 'Intrafirm competition and charter evolution in the multibusiness firm', *Organization Science*, 16(6) (2005) 674.

J. Birkinshaw, O. Toulan and D. Arnold, 'Global account management in multinational corporations: theory and evidence', *Journal of International Business Studies*, 32(2) (2001) 231.

I. Björkman and M. Forsgren, 'Nordic international business research', *International Studies of Management & Organization*, 30(1) (2000) 6.

D. M. Boehe, 'Product development in MNC subsidiaries: local linkages and global interdependencies', *Journal of International Management*, 13(4) (2007) 488–512.

C. Bouquet and J. Birkinshaw, 'Weight versus voice: how foreign subsidiaries gain attention from corporate headquarters', *Academy of Management Journal*, 51 (3) (2008) 577–601.

B. K. Boyd and J. Fulk, 'Executive scanning and perceived uncertainty: a multidimensional model', *Journal of Management*, 22(1) (1996) 1.

D. J. Brass and M. E. Burkhardt, 'Potential power and power use: an investigation of structure and behavior', *Academy of Management Journal*, 36(3) (1993) 441.

D. J. Brass, K. D. Butterfield and B. C. Skaggs, 'Relationships and unethical behavior: a social network perspective', *Academy of Management Review*, 23(1) (1998) 14.

R. S. Burt, *Structural Holes: The Social Structure of Competition*, (Cambridge, MA: Harvard University Press, 1992).

R. E. Caves and M. E. Porter, 'Market structure, oligopoly, and stability of market shares', *The Journal of Industrial Economics*, 29(1) (1978) 1.

T.-J. Chen, H. Chen and Y.-H. Ku, 'Foreign direct investment and local linkages', *Journal of International Business Studies*, 35(4) (2004) 320–33.

K. S. Cook and R. M. Emerson, 'Power, equity and commitment in exchange networks', *American Sociological Review*, 43(5) (1978) 712–39.

M. T. Dacin, M. J. Ventresca and B. D. Beal, 'The embeddedness of organizations: dialogue & directions', *Journal of Management*, 25(3) (1999) 317.

D. H. Doty, W. H. Glick and G. P. Huber, 'Fit, equifinality, and organizational effectiveness: a test', *Academy of Management Journal*, 36(6) (1993) 1196.

R. Drazin and A. H. Van de Ven, 'Alternative forms of fit in contingency theory', *Administrative Science Quarterly*, 30(4) (1985) 514.

A. Edström and J. R. Galbraith, 'Transfer of managers as a coordination and control strategy in multinational organizations', *Administrative Science Quarterly*, 22(2) (1977) 248.

M. Forsgren, 'The Use of Network Theory in MNC Research', in V. Mahnke and T. Pedersen (eds), *Knowledge Flows, Governance and the Multinational Enterprise – Frontiers in International Management Research*, (Basingstoke: Macmillan, 2004), pp. 18–37.

M. Forsgren, U. Holm and J. Johanson, *The Embedded Multinational – A Business Network View*, (Cheltenham: Edward Elgar, 2005).

N. J. Foss and T. Pedersen, 'Transferring knowledge in MNCs: the role of sources of subsidiary knowledge and organizational context', *Journal of International Management*, 8(1) (2002) 49.

T. S. Frost, 'The geographic sources of foreign subsidiaries' innovations', *Strategic Management Journal*, 22(2) (2001) 101.

S. Ghoshal and C. Bartlett, 'The multinational corporation as an interorganizational network', *Academy of Management Review*, 15 (4) (1990) 603–25.

S. Ghoshal and N. Nohria, 'Internal differentiation within multinational corporations', *Strategic Management Journal*, 10(4) (1989) 323–37.

M. Granovetter, 'Economic action and social structure: the problem of embeddedness', *American Journal of Sociology*, 91(3) (1985) 481–510.

R. Gulati, 'Alliances and networks', *Strategic Management Journal*, 19(4) (1998) 293.

L. Hakansson and R. Nobel, 'Organizational characteristics and reverse technology transfer', *Management International Review*, 41(4) (2001) 395–420.

A. Halinen and J.-A. Törnroos, 'The role of embeddedness in the evolution of business networks', *Scandinavian Journal of Management*, 14(3) (1998) 187–205.

M. T. Hansen, 'The search-transfer problem: the role of weak ties in sharing knowledge across organization subunits', *Administrative Science Quarterly*, 44(1) (1999) 82.

G. Hedlund, 'The role of foreign subsidiaries in strategic decision-making in Swedish multinational corporations', *Strategic Management Journal*, 1(1) (1980) 23.

G. Hedlund, 'The hypermodern MNC – a heterarchy?', *Human Resource Management*, 25(1) (1986) 9–36.

K. Hewett, M. S. Roth and K. Roth, 'Conditions influencing headquarters and foreign subsidiary roles in marketing activities and their effects on performance', *Journal of International Business Studies*, 34(6) (2003) 567.

U. Holm, C. Holmström and D. Sharma, 'Competence development through business relationships or competitive environment? – subsidiary impact on MNC competitive advantage', *Management International Review (MIR)*, 45(2) (2005) 197.

U. Holm, J. Johanson and P. Thilenius, 'Headquarters' knowledge of subsidiary network contexts in the multinational corporation', *International Studies of Management & Organization*, 25(12) (1995) 97–120.

C. L. Holmström, 'Managing the Transfer of Externally Embedded Subsidiary Knowledge: The Role of Headquarters Control Mechanisms', in U. Andersson and U. Holm (eds), *Managing the Contemporary Multinational: The Role of Headquarters,* (Cheltenham: Edward Elgar, 2010), pp. 231–53.

B. J. Jaworski and A. K. Kohli, 'Market orientation: antecedents and consequences', *Journal of Marketing,* 57(3) (1993) 53–71.

B. R. Koka, R. Madhavan and J. E. Prescott, 'The evolution of interfirm networks: environmental effects on patterns of network change', *The Academy of Management Review,* 31(3) (2006) 721.

P. J. Lane and M. Lubatkin, 'Relative absorptive capacity and interorganizational learning', *Strategic Management Journal,* 19(5) (1998) 461–77.

Y. Luo, 'Organizational dynamics and global integration: a perspective from subsidiary managers', *Journal of International Management,* 8(2) (2002) 189.

Y. Luo, 'Industrial dynamics and managerial networking in an emerging market: the case of China', *Strategic Management Journal,* 24(13) (2003) 1315.

J. I. Martinez and J. C. Jarillo, 'The evolution of research on coordination mechanisms in multinational corporations', *Journal of International Business Studies,* 20(3) (1989) 489.

A. Menon, B. J. Jaworski and A. K. Kohli, 'Product quality: impact of interdepartmental interactions', *Academy of Marketing Science Journal,* 25(3) (1997) 187.

M. S. Mizruchi and J. Galaskiewicz, 'Networks of Interorganizational Relations', in S. Wasserman and J. Galaskiewicz (eds), *Advances in Social Network Analysis: Research in the Social and Behavioral Sciences,* (Thousand Oaks, CA: Sage, 1994), pp. 230–53.

S. C. Mu, D. R. Gnyawali and D. E. Hatfield, 'Foreign subsidiaries' learning from local environments: an empirical test', *Management International Review (MIR),* 47(1) (2007) 79.

R. Mudambi and P. Navarra, 'Is knowledge power? Knowledge flows, subsidiary power and rent-seeking within MNCs', *Journal of International Business Studies,* 35(5) (2004) 385–406.

R. Narula and A. Zanfei, 'Globalisation of Innovation: The Role of Multinational Enterprises', in J. Fagerberg, D. Mowery and R. Nelson (eds), *The Oxford Handbook of Innovation,* (Oxford: Oxford University Press, 2004), pp. 318–45.

R. Nobel and J. Birkinshaw, 'Innovation in multinational corporations: control and communication patterns in international R&D operations', *Strategic Management Journal,* 19(5) (1998) 479.

N. Nohria and S. Ghoshal, 'Differentiated fit and shared values: alternatives for managing headquarters–subsidiary relations', *Strategic Management Journal,* 15(6) (1994) 491.

P. C. Nell, B. Ambos and B.B. Schlegelmilch, 'The MNC as an externally embedded organization: An investigation of embeddedness overlap in local subsidiary networks', *Journal of World Business,* 46(4) (2011) 497–505.

N. Nohria and S. Ghoshal, *The Differentiated Network. Organizing Multinationals for Value Creation,* (San Francisco, CA: Jossey-Bass, 1997).

W. G. Ouchi and M. A. Maguire, 'Organizational control – two functions', *Administrative Science Quarterly,* 20(4) (1975) 559–69.

R. Pearce and M. Papanastassiou, 'Global-Innovation Strategies of MNEs and European Integration: The Role of Regional R&D Facilities', in R. Pearce (Ed.), *Global Competition and Technology,* (New York: St. Martin's Press, 1997), pp. 123–52.

J. Pfeffer and G. R. Salancik, *The External Control of Organizations: A Resource Dependence Perspective,* (New York: Harper & Row, 1978).

M. E. Porter, *Competitive Strategy,* (New York: The Free Press, 1980).

W. W. Powell, K. W. Koput and L. Smith-Doerr, 'Interorganizational collaboration and the locus of innovation: networks of learning in biotechnology', *Administrative Science Quarterly,* 41(1) (1996) 116.

C. K. Prahalad and R. Bettis, 'The dominant logic: retrospective and extension', *Strategic Management Journal,* 16(1) (1995) 5.

D. S. Pugh, D. J. Hickson, C. R. Hinings and C. Turner, 'Dimensions of organization structure', *Administrative Science Quarterly,* 13(1) (1968) 65–105.

T. G. Rawski, 'Chinese industrial reform: accomplishments, prospects and implications', *American Economic Review*, 84(2) (1994) 271–75.

A. M. Rugman and A. Verbeke, 'Subsidiary-specific advantages in multinational enterprises', *Strategic Management Journal*, 22(3) (2001) 237–50.

S. Schmid and A. Schurig, 'The development of critical capabilities in foreign subsidiaries: disentangling the role of the subsidiary's business network', *International Business Review*, 12(6) (2003) 755.

J. D. Thompson, *Organizations in Action*, (New York: McGraw-Hill, 1967).

W. Tsai, 'Social capital, strategic relatedness and the formation of intraorganizational linkages', *Strategic Management Journal*, 21(9) (2000) 925–39.

W. Tsai and S. Ghoshal, 'Social capital and value creation: the role of intrafirm networks', *Academy of Management Journal*, 41(4) (1998) 464.

O. E. Williamson, *Markets and Hierarchies – Analysis and Antitrust Implications: A Study in the Economics of Internal Organization*, (New York: The Free Press, 1975).

M. Yamin and M. Forsgren, 'Hymer's analysis of the multinational organization: power retention and the demise of the federative MNE', *International Business Review*, 15(2) (2006) 166.

11
Examining Strategy Diversity and Interdependence in the MNC's Subsidiaries and Their Functional Activities

Paz Estrella Tolentino, Odile E. M. Janne and Pi-Chi Chen

Introduction

The increasing evolution of multinational corporations (MNCs) into differentiated networks of value-adding activities has presented enormous challenges to the analysis of strategic orientations at various organizational levels of the MNC. As MNCs have adopted less hierarchical and more interdependent strategies and structures, there is doubt about their strategic evolution over time towards a normative (optimal) transnational (Bartlett and Ghoshal, 1989), heterarchical (Hedlund, 1986) or multifocal form (Berggren, 1996; Prahalad and Doz, 1987; Zander, 2002). The continuing relevance of the (national) foreign subsidiary has also been questioned. Furthermore, there is confusion over what constitutes a MNC's foreign subsidiary, especially since a separate functional value-adding activity may define the subsidiary itself (Birkinshaw and Pedersen, 2009).

We outline these ongoing debates in the next section, and then propose to address the controversies in the context of a resource-based theoretical approach to international strategy that is embedded within a systemic interpretation of the integration–responsiveness (IR) framework in strategic management. The third section contains our propositions concerning the differentiation, interdependence and (co-)evolution towards increasing complexity of the strategy choices of foreign subsidiaries and their functional activities. The study's empirical context is American MNCs in Taiwan's IT industry. The fourth section explains the data and methodology, while the fifth section discusses the empirical results. The concluding section looks at the study's conceptual and empirical implications, limitations as well as avenues for further research.

Debate and theory

MNCs' subsidiary and functional subunits: the debate

The strategy roles and evolution towards increasing strategic complexity have been defined at different levels of the MNC, but there is little conclusive attempt at linking the corporate to the subsidiary or the subsidiary to the functional activities (Harzing, 2000; Jindra, 2005; Jarillo and Martinez, 1990; Taggart 1997a, 1998). Moreover, the literature focusing on the strategy of distinct functional activities has often developed independently from the broader international strategy literature.

On the one hand, specific MNC value-adding activities have become the primary unit of analysis in some studies and the national subsidiary has become irrelevant, especially in developed countries (Birkinshaw and Pedersen, 2009). The argument is that broad subsidiary typologies seem unable to capture the MNC's increasingly fine-sliced specialized network of value chain activities, each with their discrete strategy challenges (Rugman and Verbeke, 2001; Rugman et al., 2011). The challenges of managing innovation are claimed to 'apply to specific businesses, functions and product lines only, and not to all activities of the subsidiary' (Bartlett and Ghoshal, 1990, p. 245). The project level of analysis is sometimes identified as the most relevant focus for study (Andersson et al., 2011; Whitley, 2006).

On the other hand, there are studies that have aggregated at different levels the distinctive effect on, and unique response of, functional activities to global integration (I) and local responsiveness (R) pressures. Prahalad and Doz (1987) imply that such differences among functional activities (or other subunits) can be merged meaningfully at the relevant business unit. Similarly, Ghoshal and Bartlett (1988) combine the responses of all functional/departmental managers to focus on (national) subsidiary-level analysis. The heterogeneity of subsidiaries is often undermined in some other studies that impose conditions on functional activity characteristics in their sample selection, such as manufacturing subsidiaries (Lin and Hsieh, 2010; Taggart, 1997a, 1997b, 1998) or R&D laboratories (Papanastassiou, 1999).

In emphasizing the importance of understanding strategic orientations at various organizational levels of the MNC, we challenge the analytical anachronism of the national subsidiary, defined to include all activities of a MNC in a single country, against the sub-subsidiary unit which is defined as any distinct value-adding activity in that country. The theme of interdependence, rather than autonomy, of strategic orientations is a recurrent one in the subsidiary (Young and Tavares, 2004) and innovation literature, although the relationships between headquarters and subsidiaries, and among subsidiaries, have been rather more emphasized.

Differentiation and local interdependence: a resource-based approach

At the heart of the resource-based explanation of the heterogeneous strategy roles of subsidiaries and their functional activities is the representation of the firm as a repository of capabilities that cannot be easily communicated and transferred. The complex role of subsidiaries, and their areas of expertise, has been investigated in the literature on subsidiary-specific competencies (Rugman and Verbeke, 2001), centres of excellence (Frost et al., 2002), internationally integrated laboratories (Pearce, 1999), subsidiary R&D units (Kuemmerle, 1999; Nobel and Birkinshaw, 1998) and (broader) product mandates (Pearce, 1999). Foreign subsidiaries may perform one or several different specialist roles when MNCs attempt to benefit from both location advantages and (internal) network integration (Andersson and Forsgren, 2000; Dunning, 1998; Rugman and Verbeke, 2001). Since strategic roles and competencies can appear in any functional activity, national subsidiary roles may differ from their more specialist competence. The subsidiary may remain part of a tightly integrated relationship with headquarters while having a key area of responsibility for a particular function or product (Roth and Morrison, 1992). Furthermore, a change specific to a functional activity does not necessarily lead to a corresponding change in the subsidiary role (Rugman et al., 2011).

As national subsidiary management focuses on creating value beyond that created collectively by their different functional activities, the quest for strategic integration (Burgelman and Doz, 2001) becomes a form of dynamic capability (Teece et al., 1997). Core technological competencies (Prahalad and Doz, 1987; Prahalad and Hamel, 1990) and organizational capabilities (Bartlett and Ghoshal, 1989; Ghoshal and Bartlett, 1990) define resource-based rationales for strategy interdependence in the multiple organizational levels of the firm. More generally, strategy interdependence in an MNC occurs when the strategy choices at each organizational level influences, and is in turn influenced by, the strategy choices at other organizational levels. While international strategy interdependence within the MNC network has been the subject of much study (Ghoshal and Nohria, 1989; O'Donnell, 2000; Roth, 1995; Subramanian and Watson, 2006), the national (local) strategy interdependence between the MNC's subsidiaries and their functional activities is far less understood.

There are two ways to discuss strategy interdependence between these MNC subunits. First, the type, strategy role and associated subsidiary characteristics influence the functional activities supported locally by a subsidiary (Roth and Morrison, 1992). Subsidiary roles influence differentiated functional capabilities, procedural justice and performance (Lin and Hsieh, 2010). Most functional activities in locally responsive subsidiaries are independent, and there are also few highly integrated functional activities in global subsidiaries, while many value chain functions in multifocal subsidiaries are coordinated with the parent company and other subsidiaries (Jarillo and Martinez, 1990; Taggart, 1997a). Subsidiary organizational competencies require national managers to reconcile corporate and local concerns (Bartlett and Ghoshal, 1989). Devinney et al. (2000) extended the IR framework to show the diverse organizational forms and strategic choices open to managers for their value chain activities in each international strategic orientation.

Second, the strategy role and associated characteristics of functional activities may influence, or even determine, the role (and evolution) of subsidiaries. Increasing R&D competencies affect the production role of subsidiaries (Papanastassiou, 1999), and the combined R&D, marketing and production functions the emergence of world product mandate subsidiaries (Rugman and Douglas, 1986). The way the I and R pressures affect functional activities has implications for the ways MNCs organize themselves (Devinney et al., 2000), and therefore the role of foreign subsidiaries. Enright and Subramaniam (2007) proposed a subsidiary role typology based on subsidiary capabilities and scope, which can complement and enrich, rather than compete with, existing typologies based on the IR framework.

Multi-level strategic choices: the IR framework

While the resource-based theoretical approach to strategy and competitive advantage recognizes the context specificity in the creation, accumulation and transfer of valuable resources, it is less precise in stipulating the contingencies that make some resources valuable in some context and not in others, particularly when explaining international strategy (Regnér and Zander, 2011). Subunit strategy contexts are likely to vary substantially within the MNC, given diverse environments and managerial perceptions which depend on the kind of activity being performed.

The IR framework, influential in strategic management, identifies the two I and R contextual demands which define strategic choice among the strategy alternatives (Prahalad and Doz, 1987).[1] These include globally integrated (G) (high I–low R), locally responsive (L) (low I–high R), multifocal (M) (high I–high R) and quiescent (Q) (low I–low R) (Taggart, 1998).[2] The framework has been applied separately at the level of the firm (Bartlett and Ghoshal, 1989), subsidiaries (Bartlett and Ghoshal, 1989; Harzing, 2000; Jarillo and Martinez, 1990; Leong and Tan, 1993; Taggart, 1997a, 1998; Lin and Hsieh, 2010), specific value chain activities (Ghoshal, 1987; Hannon et al., 1995; Jindra, 2005; Solberg, 2000; Tai and Wong, 1998) and businesses (Prahalad and Doz, 1987; Roth and Morrison, 1990).

However, network-based organizations embody complex sets of global and local interactions and strategies well beyond what the simple dichotomy may imply (Buckley and Ghauri, 2004; Iammarino et al., 2009). There are diverse possible associated organizational forms within the modern MNC's integrated network, and there is likely to be differentiation, interdependence and (co-)evolution towards increasing complexity of the strategy choices open to managers in the various organizational levels. The IR framework has limited capacity to deal with this, especially when considering how the configuration and interdependencies of the firm's value chain determine the strategies of the firm and dominant industry characteristics (Devinney et al., 2000; Enright and Subramanian, 2007).

Figure 11.1 provides a systemic interpretation of the IR framework showing the possible heterogeneous strategic choices of the MNC's subsidiary and their functional activities. A subsidiary's strategic choice may embody diverse strategic choices in each constituent value chain activity.

Contrary to the environmental contingency perspective, our framework does not offer a deterministic model of the optimum strategy in each context. In embedding a resource-based approach into such a systemic framework we can better understand the non-deterministic differentiation, interdependence and (co-)evolution towards increasing complexity of the strategy choices of foreign subsidiaries and their functional activities.

Strategic choice of value chain activities of foreign subsidiaries	R&D	G	M	G	M	G	M	G	M
		Q	L	Q	L	Q	L	Q	L
	Production	G	M	G	M	G	M	G	M
		Q	L	Q	L	Q	L	Q	L
	Marketing	G	M	G	M	G	M	G	M
		Q	L	Q	L	Q	L	Q	L
	Sales	G	M	G	M	G	M	G	M
		Q	L	Q	L	Q	L	Q	L
	Services	G	M	G	M	G	M	G	M
		Q	L	Q	L	Q	L	Q	L
		Quiescent (Q)		Locally responsive (L)		Globally integrated (G)		Multifocal (M)	
	Subsidiary strategic choice								

Figure 11.1 Systemic roles of subsidiary and functional units

Propositions

Interdependence

Some functional activities (typically R&D and Production) may generally be more globally integrated and less locally responsive than others (such as Marketing, Sales and Service), although a mixed system can be adopted within each functional activity (e.g., the R and D in R&D, design and promotion in Marketing) where specific activities can be more globally integrated or locally responsive depending on the location as well as subsidiary strategy type. To analyse interdependence of strategy choices between subsidiaries and functional activities, it may therefore be necessary to define the strategy orientation of functional activities more subtly in terms of their relative emphasis on each I and R dimension separately rather than on their strategy types as shown in Figure 11.1 (Grøgaard, 2012), and we have proceeded on this basis. The analysis of strategy types of subsidiaries remains relevant in this context, although more complex and differentiated in their realization at the sub-subsidiary/functional level. We propose that the functional activities' relative response to, and influence on, each I and R pressure will vary according to their subsidiary strategy type.

Proposition 11.1a   There are significant differences in the extent of global integration and local responsiveness of functional activities in accordance with their subsidiary strategy type.

Subsidiaries' competencies are often found highest in the Marketing, Sales and Production functions (Foss and Pedersen, 2004). IT firms, in particular, emphasize downstream activities to foster closer customer relationships and identify market opportunities more effectively (Chen and Tsou, 2012). Foreign subsidiaries in a small economy are also likely to expand sales beyond the domestic market (Hogenbirk and van Kranenburg, 2006). Taiwan's rapidly growing economy and its role as a bridge to mainland China and Southeast Asia have propelled MNCs to respond to the diverse needs of these markets (Fang et al., 2002). Accordingly, the downstream functional activities of IT MNCs in Taiwan may focus on acquiring local market knowledge as a means to expand into other foreign markets. We therefore propose that the relative response of downstream functional activities of IT MNCs in Taiwan to, and influence on, each I and R pressure will vary depending on their subsidiary's strategy role.

Proposition 11.1b   In particular, there are significant differences in the extent of global integration and local responsiveness of downstream functional activities (i.e., Marketing, Sales and Services) in accordance with their subsidiary strategy type.

Evolution

The attainment of strategic complexity may not be consistent with the evolution of the MNC towards a 'new model'. Rather, the MNC and their differentiated subunits pursue increasingly complex distinctive combinations of strategic choices which, in the context of the IR framework, are captured less in terms of changing strategy roles but more in terms of increasing levels of the strategy dimensions of I and/or R. Similar to Proposition 11.1a, we therefore propose that functional activities evolve in strategy complexity using differentiated paths which proceed at varying pace, and which will be encouraged, defended and constrained by their subsidiary's role and characteristics, and vice versa.

Proposition 11.2   There is a significant difference in the evolution of the strategy orientation of any functional activity towards higher global integration and/or higher local responsiveness in accordance with their subsidiary strategy type.

In particular, the accumulation, creation and transfer of resources associated with the learning of local responsiveness and further integration, a unique systemic benefit of MNC, would in turn imply further strategy interdependence between subsidiaries and their functional activities (Subramanian and Watson, 2006), reinforcing over time the validity of Proposition 11.1a.

Data and method

American MNCs in Taiwan's IT industry provide this study's empirical context. The industry receives the most approved private foreign investment in Taiwan and American companies have been the largest foreign investors in recent years (Investment Commission, 2008). Taiwan has become the world's largest supplier of IT-related products and services, and Taiwanese firms have become preferred OEM and ODM[3] suppliers for global IT industry leaders (Ernst, 2010).

Data collection

The primary sources of data and information were gathered through semi-structured and questionnaire interviews. The sample consisted of 16 American MNCs operating in Taiwan, which are major global players in the IT industry: Agilent Technologies, Advanced Micro Devices (AMD), Avocent, Cisco Systems, Dell, Electronic Data Systems (EDS), Garmin, General Electric (GE), Google, Hewlett-Packard (HP), International Business Machines (IBM), Intel, Microsoft, Motorola, National Instruments (NI) and Sun Microsystems. Each of these MNCs operated a wholly owned foreign subsidiary in Taiwan at the time of the study, performing a broad range of value chain activities. We interviewed all subsidiary managing directors and 100 of their functional unit managers between 2007 and 2008 (see Appendix Table A.1). Each interview lasted between 60 and 90 minutes. The functional unit managers played leading roles in one of five functional activities in the head offices in Taipei, including R&D, Production, Marketing, Sales and Service.

Measures

We based the formative I and R constructs partly on Jarillo and Martinez (1990), Taggart (1998) and others, and partly on indicators developed specifically to reflect the peculiar features of Taiwan's IT industry (see Table 11.1). We adapted those indicators for functional activities. All items were measured by a seven-point scale ranging from 1 = extremely low to 7 = extremely high. We developed indices based on the median level of I and R dimensions reported by the respondents. Moreover, we asked all respondents to provide answers relevant to 10 years earlier (in 1997) using their past knowledge of operations.[4]

We adopted several strategies to enhance data validity and reliability. We described the interview questions and scales carefully, and provided examples during the interviews to ensure uniform responses. We adopted a common data collection procedure in every interview. We scrupulously selected and analysed the case study companies with relevant theories and replication logic in a comparative case study. We anchored each construct measure on prior research to minimize errors and biases. We piloted and pre-tested questionnaires to ensure the reliability of prospective answers. We also requested respondents to provide answers based on their recollection of the actual situation ten years ago (Jarillo and Martinez, 1990; Taggart, 1998), rather than personal estimates. Finally, in order to minimize any potential common method variance (CMV) bias (Chang et al., 2010; Malhotra et al., 2006), we collected data from different organizational levels (subsidiary and functional units) and at different points in time (in 2007 and 2008). Harman's single-factor test results also indicate that no single factor explains the majority of the variances in the IR variables at the subsidiary and functional activity levels in 2007 and 1997.

Data analysis

We used formative I and R constructs to determine the subsidiary strategy types (Venaik et al., 2004). For each subsidiary, we first calculated a mean of each strategy

Table 11.1 Measurement of IR dimensions at the subsidiary level

Integration (I)	Responsiveness (R)
1. Products specified or developed for parent's market (Prahalad and Doz, 1987; Taggart, 1998)	1. Products developed or substantially adapted to the local environment (Prahalad and Doz, 1987; Taggart, 1998)
2. Integration of R&D with parent/regional HQ (Jarillo and Martinez, 1990)	2. Local market area served (Prahalad and Doz, 1987; Taggart, 1998; Yu, 2000)
3. Integration of production with parent/regional HQ (Jarillo and Martinez, 1990)	3. Percentage of inputs that come from subsidiary (Jarillo and Martinez, 1990)
4. Integration of marketing, sales and service with parent/regional HQ (Jarillo and Martinez, 1990)	4. Percentage of locally produced goods over total sales (Jarillo and Martinez, 1990)
5. Dependency on linkages within the internal network (Prahalad and Doz, 1987; Taggart, 1998)	5. Proportion of local staff who hold high positions (Yu, 2000)
6. Sharing of knowledge within the internal network (technical knowledge is shared by all subsidiaries and HQ) (Prahalad and Doz, 1987; Taggart, 1998; Yu, 2000)	6. Networking with local research institutions and suppliers/distributors (Jarillo and Martinez, 1990)
7. Scope of service which a subsidiary provides for MNC worldwide market areas (subsidiaries sell/serve or help to sell/serve output to the customers of other subsidiaries of the MNC) (Hood and Young, 1987; Prahalad and Doz, 1987; Taggart, 1998; Yu, 2000)	

dimension of I and R. We then applied cluster analysis (Jarillo and Martinez, 1990; Roth and Morrison, 1990; Taggart, 1998), using both hierarchical (Ward) and non-hierarchical (K-means) methods to identify subsidiary strategy type. The Kruskal–Wallis and Mann–Whitney tests determined the existence of significant differences in the strategy dimensions among subsidiaries of different strategy types, and among functional activities belonging to different subsidiary strategy types in 1997 and 2007. We also used qualitative information from interviewees to verify the apparent differentiation, interdependence and evolution towards complexity in the strategic orientations of subsidiaries and functional activities among and within subsidiary strategy types.

Results and discussion

The cluster analysis identified the existence of a three-cluster solution consisting of seven M, four G and five L subsidiaries for the sample. Table 11.2 shows some characteristics of our subsidiary strategy types.

G subsidiaries are the youngest and have the highest shared managerial philosophy among their functional activities, which are as tightly coordinated as M subsidiaries. Such coordination is least in L subsidiaries, and the extent of shared

Table 11.2 Membership and characteristics of subsidiary strategy types, 2007

Characteristics	Subsidiary strategy types (Members)		
	Globally integrated (Dell, Garmin, Google, Microsoft)	Locally responsive (Avocent, Cisco, EDS, NI, Sun Microsystems)	Multifocal (Agilent, AMD, GE, HP, IBM, Intel, Motorola)
Average age of company (years)	23	28	74
Average age of subsidiary (years)	15	17	35
Average corporate employment (employee numbers)	50,254	49,228	174,051
Average number of locations in Taiwan (kind/s of functional activities)	3 (across R&D, Production, Sales, Service)	2.7 (more dispersed Sales and Service only)	3.7 (across R&D, Production, Sales, Service)
Coordination among functional activities (median)	4.00	3.38	4.00
Managerial philosophy shared within subsidiary (median)	4.17	4.00	4.00

Note: Values are calculated from the responses obtained.

managerial philosophy among functional activities of L and M subsidiaries is not as high. The M subsidiaries tend to be part of larger-sized MNCs and considerably older. Their functional activities are most geographically dispersed in Taiwan.

Unit of analysis: differentiation and interdependence

Table 11.3 provides evidence of any systematic differences in the strategy dimensions among subsidiaries of different strategy types, and among functional activities belonging to different subsidiary strategy types in 1997 and 2007. The subsidiary strategy types can be differentiated by the extent of I in 1997, and by the extent of both I and R in 2007. Over the period, M subsidiaries have significantly either a high or highest degree of I. In 2007, M subsidiaries also have the significantly highest degree of R, followed by L and then G subsidiaries.

The findings at the functional level provide some support for Proposition 11.1a. Functional activities have different combinations of I that mirror their subsidiary strategy type; and such differences, similar to findings at the subsidiary level, are more sharply defined and statistically significant in 2007 than in 1997. The three subsidiary strategy types could be distinguished in 1997 by the extent of I of Service. Their increasing differentiation by 2007 is evident in the growing extent of

Table 11.3 Comparison of median of overall degrees of integration and responsiveness of subsidiaries and functional activities *among* different subsidiary strategy types, 1997 and 2007

Functional activities	Subsidiary strategy types (2007)			Kruskal–Wallis test among types	Subsidiary strategy types (1997)			Kruskal–Wallis test among types
	Globally integrated	Locally responsive	Multifocal		Globally integrated	Locally responsive	Multifocal	
(1) Degree of integration, 2007					**(1) Degree of integration, 1997**			
Subsidiary level:	5.00	4.00	5.00	0.002**	4.00	4.00	5.00	0.047*
Functional level:								
R&D (n = 21)	6.00 (n = 7)	6.00 (n = 4)	6.00 (n = 10)	–[5]	5.00 (n = 5)	5.00 (n = 4)	6.00 (n = 10)	0.122
Production (n = 14)	6.00 (n = 3)	5.00 (n = 1)	6.00 (n = 10)	0.002**	5.00 (n = 3)	5.00 (n = 1)	5.00 (n = 10)	–
Marketing (n = 18)	6.00 (n = 5)	5.00 (n = 5)	6.00 (n = 8)	0.014*	5.00 (n = 3)	5.00 (n = 5)	5.00 (n = 8)	0.655
Sales (n = 21)	5.00 (n = 4)	5.00 (n = 6)	6.00 (n = 11)	0.009**	4.00 (n = 3)	4.00 (n = 6)	4.00 (n = 11)	0.664
Service (n = 26)	4.50 (n = 6)	4.00 (n = 8)	5.00 (n = 12)	0.005**	3.00 (n = 5)	4.00 (n = 8)	4.00 (n = 12)	0.054+
(2) Degree of local responsiveness, 2007					**(2) Degree of local responsiveness, 1997**			
Subsidiary level:	5.00	5.80	5.86	0.007**	3.50	4.00	4.50	0.139
Functional level:								
R&D	4.00	4.00	4.00	0.029*	4.00	4.00	4.00	0.361
Production	4.00	4.00	4.00	0.819	4.00	4.00	4.00	0.819
Marketing	4.00	4.00	4.00	0.273	4.00	4.00	4.25	0.511
Sales	5.00	5.00	5.00	0.690	4.50	5.00	5.00	0.153
Service	5.00	5.00	5.00	0.678	5.00	5.00	5.00	0.323

Notes: The IR values indicated are average score values calculated from the set of respondents.
Significance: $+p < 0.1$, $*p < 0.05$, $**p < 0.01$, $*** p < 0.001$.
Excluding Google in 1997.

Level		IR dimensions	Subsidiary strategic types		
	R&D	I	–	–	–
		R			
Functional activities	Production	I			
		R	–	–	–
	Marketing	I			
		R	–	–	–
	Sales	I			
		R	–	–	–
	Services	I			
		R	–	–	–
Subsidiary		I			
		R			
			Locally responsive (R)	Globally integrated (I)	Multifocal (M)

Figure 11.2 Systemic strategic dimensions of subsidiaries and functional activities, 2007

Notes: No significant difference; black : same significant value; dark grey : highest score, light grey : intermediate/second highest score, no colour: lowest score.
Source: Table 11.3.

I of their downstream activities (Marketing, Sales and Service) and Production, and the degree of R of R&D. The findings accord with Proposition 11.1b which avers that the strategy dimensions of downstream functional activities will particularly distinguish among subsidiary strategy types, although more particularly in their degree of I.

Figure 11.2 summarizes the significant IR strategy dimensions of functional activities according to subsidiary strategy type in a way that is comparable to our proposed model in Figure 11.1. It shows for our sample that, overall, the strategic choices in terms of IR dimensions in each constituent value chain activity (and particularly the I dimension) vary with their subsidiary strategy type.

To complement the analysis based on aggregated constructs of I and R, Table 11.4 shows how each subsidiary strategy type relates uniquely to their functional activities in terms of disaggregated indicators of I and R. We can significantly distinguish different subsidiary strategy types and their constituent functional activities in terms of almost all indicators of I, and two indicators of R ('percentage of locally produced goods over total sales' and 'local networking').

Like M subsidiaries, the relative emphasis of G subsidiaries on parent global products and production is evident in their high extent of 'products specified for their parent's market', 'integration of subsidiary production' and 'dependency on linkages within internal network' (I variables 1, 3 and 5). Their R&D activities are

Table 11.4 Comparison of median of various indicators of IR dimensions of subsidiaries and functional activities *among* different subsidiary strategy types, 2007

IR indicators		Subsidiary strategy types			Kruskal–Wallis test among types	Mann–Whitney test between pairs[6]
		Globally integrated	Locally responsive	Multifocal		
Degree of integration (I dimension)						
1. Products specified for parent's market (subsidiary level)		5.00	3.00	5.00	0.003**	(G,L)(L,M)
Functional level:	R&D	6.00	6.00	5.50	0.915	
	Production	7.00	7.00	5.50	0.122	
	Marketing	5.00	5.00	5.50	0.727	
	Sales	5.00	5.00	6.00	0.087+	(G,M)
	Service	4.50	5.00	5.00	0.545	
2. Integration of subsidiary R&D with parent/regional HQ (subsidiary level)		5.00	4.00	6.00	0.003**	(G,M)(L,M)
Integration of your functional activities with parent/regional HQ:	R&D	6.00	6.00	6.00	0.146	
	Production	6.00	6.00	6.00	–	
	Marketing	6.00	6.00	6.00	0.143	
	Sales	5.00	5.00	5.00	–	
	Service	4.50	5.00	5.00	0.040*	(G,L)
3. Integration of subsidiary production (subsidiary level)		5.00	4.00	5.00	0.004**	(G,L)(L,M)
4. Integration of subsidiary marketing, sales and service functions (subsidiary level)		4.50	4.00	4.00	0.784	

Table 11.4 (Continued)

IR indicators	Subsidiary strategy types			Kruskal–Wallis test among types	Mann–Whitney test between pairs[6]
	Globally integrated	Locally responsive	Multifocal		
5. Dependency on linkages within internal network (subsidiary level)	6.00	5.00	6.00	0.092+	(L,M)
Functional level:					
R&D	6.00	6.00	6.00	0.174	
Production	6.00	5.00	6.00	0.028*	(G,L)(L,M)
Marketing	5.00	6.00	6.00	0.045*	(G,M)(L,M)
Sales	5.00	5.00	6.00	0.001**	(G,M)(L,M)
Service	4.00	4.00	5.00	0.001**	(G,M)(L,M)
6. Sharing of knowledge within the internal network (subsidiary level)	5.00	5.00	6.00	0.015*	(G,M)(L,M)
Functional level:					
R&D	6.00	6.00	6.00	0.286	
Production	5.00	5.00	6.00	0.026*	(G,M)(L,M)
Marketing	6.00	4.00	6.00	0.003**	(G,L)(L,M)
Sales	5.50	5.00	6.00	0.005**	(G,L)(L,M)
Service	5.00	4.00	5.00	0.000***	(G,L)(L,M)
7. Scope of service which a subsidiary serves for MNC worldwide market areas (subsidiary level)	4.50	4.00	5.00	0.090+	(G,L)(L,M)
Functional level:					
R&D	6.00	6.00	6.00	0.094+	
Production	5.00	5.00	6.00	0.019*	(G,M)(L,M)
Marketing	6.00	4.00	6.00	0.008**	(G,L)(L,M)
Sales	5.00	5.00	6.00	0.001**	(G,M)(L,M)
Service	5.00	4.00	5.00	0.000***	(G,L)(L,M)

Degree of local responsiveness (R dimension)

1. Products are developed or substantially adapted to the local environment (subsidiary level)		5.00	6.00	6.00	0.162
Functional activities are developed or adapted to the local environment:					
	R&D	5.00	5.00	5.00	0.611
	Production	5.00	6.00	5.00	0.113
	Marketing	5.00	5.00	5.00	0.477
	Sales	5.00	5.00	5.00	0.690
	Service	5.50	5.00	5.00	–
2. Local market area served (subsidiary level)		4.50	5.00	5.00	0.141
Functional level:	R&D	5.00	5.00	5.00	0.937
	Production	5.00	6.00	6.00	0.504
	Marketing	5.00	5.00	5.50	0.595
	Sales	5.00	5.00	5.00	0.751
	Service	5.50	5.00	5.00	0.796
3. Percentage of inputs that come from the local (subsidiary level)		5.00	6.00	6.00	0.824
Functional level:	R&D	3.00	4.00	3.50	0.344
	Production	4.00	4.00	3.50	0.236
	Marketing	3.00	3.60	4.00	0.214
	Sales	4.50	5.00	5.00	0.192
	Service	5.00	5.00	5.00	0.123
4. Percentage of locally produced goods over total sales (subsidiary level)		4.50	5.00	**6.00**	0.049*	(G,M)(L,M)
Functional level:	R&D	3.00	4.00	4.00	0.104
	Production	3.00	4.00	4.00	0.113
	Marketing	4.00	4.00	4.00	0.063+
	Sales	5.00	**4.50**	5.00	0.003**	(G,L)(L,M)
	Service	5.00	5.00	5.00	–

Table 11.4 (Continued)

IR indicators	Subsidiary strategy types			Kruskal–Wallis test among types	Mann–Whitney test between pairs[6]
	Globally integrated	Locally responsive	Multifocal		
5. Proportion of local staff who hold high positions (subsidiary level)	5.50	6.00	6.00	0.424	
Functional level:					
R&D	3.00	4.00	3.50	0.229	
Production	3.00	4.00	4.00	0.261	
Marketing	**3.00**	4.00	4.00	0.012*	(G,L)(G,M)
Sales	4.50	5.00	5.00	0.478	
Service	5.00	5.00	5.00	0.316	
6. Local networking (subsidiary level)	5.50	6.00	6.00	0.052+	(G,L)(G,M)
Functional level:					
R&D	4.00	4.00	4.00	–	
Production	4.00	4.00	4.00	–	
Marketing	4.00	4.00	4.00	–	
Sales	5.00	5.50	**6.00**	0.001**	(G,M)(L,M)
Service	**5.00**	6.00	6.00	0.000***	(G,L)(G,M)

Notes: The IR values indicated are average score values calculated from the set of respondents.
Significance: $+p < 0.1$, $*p < 0.05$, $**p < 0.01$, $***p < 0.001$
Subsidiaries: G = globally integrated, L = locally responsive, M = multifocal
Bold: most differentiated between pairs.

relatively centralized (I variable 2) with most subsidiaries operating R&D centres to improve their access to Taiwan's ODMs and OEMs. Marketing, Sales and Service are not their core activities and these depend less on internal network linkages than Production (I variable 5), but, nevertheless, share some knowledge (I variable 6) to support their parent company. These have the lowest level of R in terms of the 'percentage of locally produced goods over total sales' (subsidiary level), 'proportion of local staff who hold high positions' (for Marketing) and extent of 'local networking' (for Sales and Service).

The L subsidiaries, established to serve Taiwan's market, score the lowest in all significant indicators of I, except in 'sharing of knowledge within the internal network' where they, along with the G subsidiaries, score lower than M subsidiaries. They are most differentiated of all subsidiary strategy types in having the lowest median on 'products specified for parent's market', 'integration of subsidiary production', 'dependency on linkages within internal network' and 'scope of service for MNC worldwide market areas' (I variables 1, 3, 5 and 7). Their functional activities, predominantly downstream activities, share the least knowledge and provide the least scope of service for worldwide market areas within the MNC (I variables 6 and 7). The extent of local networking for their Sales and Service is high (R variable 6).

Geared to serve corporate global production as well as Taiwan's market, M subsidiaries and their functional activities tend to have a hybrid mix of strong I and R characteristics. Similar to G subsidiaries, M subsidiaries have strong integration of products, production and internal linkages (I variables 1, 3 and 5). Similar to L subsidiaries, M subsidiaries have strong local networking (R variable 6). At the functional level, their upstream activities are responsible for global production, and therefore work very closely with their worldwide R&D and production centres. Subsidiary R&D is most differentiated of all subsidiary strategy types in having the highest extent of integration with parent/regional HQ (I variable 2). Their Production and Sales seem relatively more focused on global markets than their equivalent in G and L subsidiaries (I variable 7), and Production is also most differentiated in having the highest extent of knowledge sharing within the internal network (I variable 6). Their Marketing, Sales and Service uniquely combine significantly high dependence on linkages with high knowledge sharing within the MNC network. Their Marketing and Service also provide a broad scope of services to serve the MNC worldwide market area, comparable to equivalent functions in G subsidiaries (I variables 5, 6 and 7). Their Sales are differentiated in their highest focus on global products (I variable 1), and local networking (R variable 6).

Evolution: differentiation and (co-)evolution

Table 11.5 provides evidence of any evolution towards strategic complexity by significant increases in the strategy dimensions of I and/or R among subsidiaries of different strategy types, and among functional activities belonging to different subsidiary strategy types, between 1997 and 2007. The evidence shows that M subsidiaries have evolved the most in complexity with significant increases in both strategy dimensions. All their functional activities also exhibited significantly

Table 11.5 Comparison of median of overall degrees of integration and responsiveness of subsidiaries and functional activity *within* different subsidiary strategy types, 1997 and 2007

	Subsidiary strategy types								
	Globally integrated			Locally responsive			Multifocal		
	2007	1997	Mann–Whitney U test between 1997 and 2007	2007	1997	Mann–Whitney test between 1997 and 2007	2007	1997	Mann–Whitney test between 1997 and 2007
(1) Degree of integration									
Subsidiary level:	5.00	4.00	–[7]	4.00	4.00	–	5.00	5.00	0.030*
Functional level:									
R&D	6.00	5.40	0.00**	6.00	5.40	0.013*	6.00	5.60	0.000***
Production	6.00	5.40	0.034*	5.00	4.00	0.317	6.00	5.00	0.000***
Marketing	6.00	5.00	0.112	5.00	5.00	1.000	6.00	5.00	0.003**
Sales	5.00	4.00	0.014*	5.00	4.00	0.005**	6.00	4.00	0.000***
Service	4.50	3.00	0.019*	4.00	4.00	0.143	5.00	4.00	0.000
(2) Degree of local responsiveness									
Subsidiary level:	5.00	3.50	–	6.00	4.00	–	6.00	4.50	0.001**
Functional level:									
R&D	4.00	4.00	0.336	4.00	4.00	0.850	4.00	4.00	0.026*
Production	4.00	4.00	0.025*	4.00	4.00	0.317	4.00	4.00	0.942
Marketing	4.00	4.00	0.172	4.00	4.00	0.317	4.00	4.25	0.027*
Sales	5.00	4.50	0.014*	5.00	5.00	0.093+	5.00	5.00	0.088+
Service	5.00	5.00	–	5.00	5.00	0.317	5.00	5.00	0.015**

Notes: The integration–responsiveness values indicated are average score values calculated from the set of respondents.
Significance: $+p < 0.1$, $*p < 0.05$, $**p < 0.01$, $***p < 0.001$.
Excluding Google in 1997.

higher I between 1997 and 2007, and R&D, Sales and Service remain significantly strong in R. There has also been significantly higher I for most functional activities of G subsidiaries, as well as higher R for their Production and Sales. Functional activities of L subsidiaries show the least change towards strategic complexity, with only increased I for R&D and increased I and R for Sales. The data therefore provide some confirmation for Proposition 11.2 that the evolution towards increasing complexity in the strategy of functional activities varies significantly with their subsidiary strategy type.

Conclusion

We conceptually and empirically explored the non-deterministic differentiation, interdependence and (co-)evolution towards increasing complexity of the strategy choices of foreign subsidiaries of MNCs and their functional activities. We developed a conceptual framework which embedded a resource-based, dynamic capabilities, perspective within a systemic interpretation of the IR framework. In the context of American MNCs in Taiwan's IT industry, we empirically showed significant differentiation of strategic choices of functional activities, particularly downstream, according to their subsidiary strategy type. Moreover, such differences, similar to findings at the subsidiary level, are more sharply defined and statistically significant in 2007 than in 1997. The evolution towards increasing strategy complexity between 1997 and 2007 have proceeded the farthest in subsidiaries and functional activities of the multifocal type, followed by those of the globally integrated and locally responsive types. The evolution towards strategic complexity suggests further strategy interdependence between subsidiaries and functional activities, and the emergence of MNCs with increasingly differentiated networks of value-adding activities rather than the 'normative' transnational, heterarchical or multifocal MNCs.

Given our finding of interdependence and (co-)evolution of strategic choices of national subsidiary and their functional activities, we challenge the view of the national subsidiary as an endangered analytical species. A subsidiary's strategic type, however, embodies different strategy dimensions rather than strategy types in each constituent functional activity. Multifocal subsidiaries combine the highest levels of R&D integration, Marketing, Sales and Services dependence on internal network linkages, Production knowledge sharing and Production and Sales provision of a broad scope of services within the MNC with the highest local networking extent of Sales. Services of globally integrated subsidiaries are the least integrated with their parent companies and their Sales less focused on the parent's market; at the same time, their Marketing and Service functions are the least locally responsive in terms of the share of local staff holding senior positions and local networking, respectively. The downstream functional activities of locally responsive subsidiaries, although integrated to some extent, share the least knowledge and provide the narrowest scope of service for worldwide market areas within the MNC. The investigation of such complexity in multi-level strategy choices in the MNC is a promising area for further study.

We recognize some limitations of our study. The relatively small sample size prevented a more thorough testing of the conceptual framework. Other than response bias, there is relative lack of 'more objective' primary and secondary data due to the particular context of Taiwan. A reflective methodological approach may be considered in future studies, along with other multivariate multilevel analytical methods. A knowledge-based interpretation of the IR framework may also be explored to explain how the systemic MNC reconciles the I and R pressures through learning and innovation. Future research may also seek to examine the relationship in the strategy choices of foreign subsidiaries and functional activities in other contexts.

Appendix

Table A.1 Number of interviews conducted with functional unit managers of foreign subsidiaries of American MNCs in Taiwan's IT industry

	Subsidiary/ Function	R&D	Production	Marketing	Sales	Service	Total
1.	Agilent Technologies	1	1	1	1	2	6
2.	AMD	1	1	1	1	1	5
3.	Avocent	X	X	1	2	2	5
4.	Cisco Systems	1	1	1	1	2	6
5.	Dell	2	2	1	1	1	7
6.	Electronic Data Systems	1	X	1	1	2	5
7.	Garmin	1	1	1	1	2	6
8.	GE	1	2	1	2	1	7
9.	Google	2	X	2	1	1	6
10.	HP	2	2	1	2	2	9
11.	IBM	2	2	2	2	3	11
12.	Intel	2	1	1	2	1	7
13.	Microsoft	2	X	1	1	2	6
14.	Motorola	1	1	1	1	2	6
15.	NI	1	X	1	1	1	4
16.	Sun Microsystems	1	X	1	1	1	4
	Total	21	14	18	21	26	100

Note: X means that no such operations exist in the subsidiaries.

Notes

1. We use the terms 'strategy role' and 'strategy type' interchangeably in this chapter to denote their same meaning.
2. Bartlett (1986) similarly outlined global, multinational and transnational strategies and Bartlett and Ghoshal (1989) included the international strategy.
3. OEM: original equipment manufacturer; ODM: original design manufacturer.
4. All respondents were also asked to reflect on what their answer would have been five years earlier (2002) and the data was consistently similar, but less dramatically different from the 1997 data.

5. No sufficient difference.
6. Results at $p < 0.1$.
7. No sufficient difference.

References

U. Andersson and M. Forsgren, 'In search of centre of excellence: network embeddedness and subsidiary roles in multinational corporations', *Management International Review*, 40(4) (2000) 329–50.

U. Andersson, R. Mudambi and M. Persson, *Unpacking Lateral Knowledge Transfer in Multinational Corporations*. International Business Conference. Reading, UK, 11–12 April 2011.

C. A. Bartlett, 'Building and Managing the Transnational: The New Organizational Challenge', in M. E. Porter (ed), *Competition in Global Industries*, (Boston, MA: Harvard Business School Press, 1986), pp. 367–404.

C. A. Bartlett and S. Ghoshal, *Managing Across Borders: The Transnational Solution*, (Boston, MA: Harvard Business School Press, 1989).

C. A. Bartlett and S. Ghoshal, 'Managing Innovation in Transnational Corporations' in C. A. Bartlett, Y. Doz and G. Hedlund (eds), *Managing the Global Firm*, (London: Routledge, 1990), pp. 215–55.

C. Berggren, 'Building a truly global organization? ABB and the problems of Integrating a multidomestic enterprise', *Scandinavian Journal of Management*, 12(2) (1996) 123–37.

J. Birkinshaw and T. Pedersen, 'Strategy and Management in MNE Subsidiaries', in A. M. Rugman (ed.) *Oxford Handbook of International Business*, 2nd Edition, (Oxford: Oxford University Press, 2009), pp. 367–88.

P. J. Buckley and P. N. Ghauri, 'Globalisation, economic geography and the strategy of multinational enterprises', *Journal of International Business Studies*, 35(2) (2004) 81–98.

R. A. Burgelman and Y. L. Doz, 'The power of strategic integration', *MIT Sloan Management Review*, 42 (2001) 28–38.

S-J. Chang, A. van Witteloostuijn and L. Eden, 'From the editors: common method variance in international business research', *Journal of International Business Studies*, 41(2) (2010) 178–84.

J-S. Chen and H-T. Tsou, 'Performance effects of IT capability, service process innovation, and the mediating role of customer service', *Journal of Engineering and Technology Management*, 29(1) (2012) 71–94.

T. M. Devinney, D. F. Midgley and S. Venaik, 'The optimal performance of the global firm: formalizing and extending the integration–responsiveness framework', *Organization Science*, 11(6) (2000) 674–95.

J. H. Dunning, 'Location and the multinational enterprise: a neglected factor?', *Journal of International Business Studies*, 29(1) (1998) 45–66.

M. J. Enright and V. Subramanian, 'An organizing framework for MNC subsidiary typologies', *Management International Review*, 47(6) (2007) 895–924.

D. Ernst, 'Upgrading through innovation in a small network economy: insights from Taiwan's IT industry', *Economics of Innovation and New Technology*, 19(4) (2010) 295–324.

S-C. Fang, J. L. Lin, L. Y. C. Hsiao, C-M. Huang and S-R. Fang, 'The relationship of foreign R&D units in Taiwan and the Taiwanese knowledge-flow system', *Technovation*, 22(6) (2002) 371–83.

N. J. Foss and T. Pedersen, 'Organizing knowledge processes in the multinational corporation: an introduction', *Journal of International Business Studies*, 35(5) (2004) 340–49.

T. S. Frost, J. M. Birkinshaw and P. C. Ensign, 'Centers of excellence in multinational corporations', *Strategic Management Journal*, 23(11) (2002) 997–1018.

S. Ghoshal, 'Global strategy: an organizing framework', *Strategic Management Journal*, 8(5) (1987) 425–40.

S. Ghoshal and C. A. Bartlett, 'Creation, adoption, and diffusion of innovations by subsidiaries of multinational corporations', *Journal of International Business Studies*, 19(3) (1988) 365–88.

S. Ghoshal and C. A. Bartlett, 'The multinational corporation as an interorganizational network', Academy *of Management Review,* 15(4) (1990) 603–25.

S. Ghoshal and N. Nohria, 'Internal differentiation within multinational corporations', *Strategic Management Journal,* 10(4) (1989) 323–37.

B. Grøgaard, 'Alignment of strategy and structure in international firms: an empirical examination', *International Business Review,* 21(3) (2012) 397–407.

J. M. Hannon, I.-C. Huang and B.-S. Jaw, 'International human resource strategy and its determinants: the case of subsidiaries in Taiwan', *Journal of International Business Studies,* 26(3) (1995) 531–54.

A. Harzing, 'An empirical analysis and extension of the Bartlett and Ghoshal typology of multinational companies', *Journal of International Business Studies,* 31(1) (2000) 101–20.

G. Hedlund, 'The hypermodern MNC – a heterarchy?', *Human Resource Management,* 25(1) (1986) 9–25.

A. E. Hogenbirk and H. L. van Kranenburg, 'Roles of foreign owned subsidiaries in a small economy', *International Business Review,* 15(1) (2006) 53–67.

N. Hood and S. Young, 'Inward investment and the EC: UK evidence on corporate integration strategies', *Journal of Common Market Studies,* 26(2) (1987) 193–206.

S. Iammarino, O. E. M. Janne and P. McCann, 'Multinational Firms and Technological Innovation: The "Global versus Local" Challenge', in M. Farshchi, O. E. M. Janne and P. McCann (eds), *Technological Change and Mature Industrial Regions: Firms, Knowledge and Policy,* (Cheltenham: Edward Elgar, 2009), pp. 29–43.

Investment Commission, *Statistics on Approved Foreign Investment by Country,* (Taiwan: Ministry of Economic Affairs, 2008).

J. C. Jarillo and J. L. Martinez, 'Different roles for subsidiaries: the case of multinational corporations in Spain', *Strategic Management Journal,* 11(7) (1990) 501–12.

B. Jindra, 'A strategy view on knowledge in the MNE – integrating subsidiary roles and knowledge flows', *East–West Journal of Economics and Business,* 8(1/2) (2005) 43–72.

W. Kuemmerle, 'The drivers of foreign direct investment into research and development – an empirical investigation', *Journal of International Business Studies,* 30(1) (1999) 1–24.

S. M. Leong and C. T. Tan, 'Managing across borders: an empirical test of the Bartlett and Ghoshal [1989] organizational typology', *Journal of International Business Studies,* 24(3) (1993) 449–64.

S-L. Lin and A-T. Hsieh, 'International strategy implementation: roles of subsidiaries, operational capabilities, and procedural justice', *Journal of Business Research,* 63(1) (2010) 52–9.

N. Malhotra, S. Kim Sung and A. Patil, 'Common method variance in IS research: a comparison of alternative approaches and a reanalysis of past research', *Management Science,* 52(12) (2006) 1865–83.

R. Nobel and J. M. Birkinshaw, 'Patterns of control and communication in international research and development units', *Strategic Management Journal,* 19(5) (1998) 479–98.

S. W. O'Donnell, 'Managing foreign subsidiaries: agents of headquarters, or an interdependent network?', *Strategic Management Journal,* 21(5) (2000) 525–48.

M. Papanastassiou, 'Technology and production strategies of multinational enterprise (MNE) subsidiaries in Europe', *International Business Review,* 8(2) (1999) 213–32.

R. Pearce, 'The evolution of technology in multinational enterprises: the role of creative subsidiaries', *International Business Review,* 8(2) (1999) 125–48.

C. K. Prahalad and Y. L. Doz, *The Multinational Mission: Balancing Local Demands and Global Vision,* (New York: The Free Press, 1987).

C. K. Prahalad and G. Hamel, 'The core competence of the corporation', *Harvard Business Review,* 68(3) (1990) 79–91.

P. Regnér and U. Zander, 'Knowledge and strategy creation in multinational companies. Social-identity frames and temporary tension in knowledge combination', *Management International Review,* 51(6) (2011) 821–50.

K. Roth, 'Managing international interdependence: CEO characteristics in a resource-based framework', *The Academy of Management Journal*, 38(1) (1995) 200–31.

K. Roth and A. J. Morrison, 'An empirical analysis of the integration–responsiveness framework in global industries', *Journal of International Business Studies*, 41(4) (1990) 541–64.

K. Roth and A. J. Morrison, 'Implementing global strategy: characteristics of global subsidiary mandates', *Journal of International Business Strategy*, 23(4) (1992) 715–35.

A. Rugman and S. Douglas, 'The strategic management of multinationals and world product mandating', *Canadian Public Policy – Analyse de Politique*, 7(2) (1986) 320–28.

A. Rugman and A. Verbeke, 'Subsidiary-specific advantages in multinational enterprises', *Strategic Management Journal*, 22(3) (2001) 237–50.

A. Rugman, A. Verbeke and W. Yan, 'Re-conceptualizing Bartlett and Ghoshal's classification of national subsidiary roles in the multinational enterprise', *Journal of Management Studies*, 48(2) (2011) 253–77.

C. A. Solberg, 'Educator insights. standardisation or adaptation on the international marketing mix: the role of the local subsidiary/representative', *Journal of International Marketing*, 8(1) (2000) 78–9.

M. Subramanian and S. Watson, 'How interdependence affects subsidiary performance', *Journal of Business Research*, 59(8) (2006) 916–24.

J. H. Taggart, 'An evaluation of the integration–responsiveness framework: MNC manufacturing subsidiaries in the UK', *Management International Review*, 37(4) (1997a) 295–318.

J. H. Taggart, 'R&D complexity in UK subsidiaries of manufacturing multinational corporations', *Technovation*, 17(2) (1997b) 73–82.

J. H. Taggart, 'Strategy shifts in MNC subsidiaries', *Strategic Management Journal*, 19(7) (1998) 663–81.

S. H. C. Tai and Y. H. Wong, 'Advertising decision making in Asia: "glocal" versus "regcal" approach', *Journal of Managerial Issues*, 10(3) (1998) 318–39.

D. J. Teece, G. Pisano and A. Shuen, 'Dynamic capabilities and strategic management', *Strategic Management Journal*, 18(7) (1997) 509–33.

S. Venaik, D. F. Midgley and T. M. Devinney, 'A new perspective on the integration–responsiveness pressures confronting multinational firms', *Management International Review*, 44(1) (2004) 15–48.

R. Whitley, 'Project-based firms: new organizational form or variations on a theme?', *Industrial and Corporate Change*, 15(1) (2006) 77–99.

S. Young and A. T. Tavares, 'Centralization and autonomy: back to the future', *International Business Review*, 13(2) (2004) 215–37.

M-C. Yu, *A Study of Organizational Configuration, Strategy, and Control in Multinational Corporations*, Ph.D. thesis (Taiwan: National Cheng Kung University, 2000).

I. Zander, 'The formation of international innovation networks in the multinational corporation: an evolutionary perspective', *Industrial and Corporate Change*, 11(2) (2002) 327–53.

12
Exploring Foreign Direct Investment and Technology and Knowledge Transfer Issues in Africa

Ellis Osabutey

Introduction

This chapter explores why foreign direct investment (FDI) inflow is not improving technology and knowledge (T&K) transfer in Africa. In doing so it examines theoretical and empirical literature to explore the potential conduits as well as possible obstacles that may explain this phenomenon. It is expected that this chapter will set the pace for a more detailed exploration of the key factors that policymakers and host countries in Africa need to explore in order to improve T&K transfer from FDI.

In developing countries FDI represents one of the most dynamic international resource inflows (UNCTAD, 1999). In Lim's (2001) view, FDI is a conduit for transferring advanced technology to host countries. FDI spillovers occur when T&K possessed by multinational corporations (MNCs) are transferred to local firms and workers (Blomström et al., 2000). The benefits of acquiring new T&K and other externalities from MNC affiliates have encouraged many developing nations to develop FDI-based development strategies which use favourable policies to attract foreign investments (Javorcik, 2008). Many developing countries, however, continue to lag behind the technology frontier (Isaksson et al., 2005; Pack and Saggi, 1997) and clearly Africa is no exception. Pack and Saggi (1997) suggest that in order for a developing country to be able to fully absorb and implement new technology (and knowledge), considerable effort towards assimilation is required because such inflows and domestic abilities to utilize them interact in complex ways.

The International T&K transfer literature has spanned various decades. Over the last decade the discussion of technology transfer or knowledge transfer (KT) within the literature has failed to capture the effect of FDI dynamics and other factors on effective T&K transfer in Africa. There is an almost total exclusion of sub-Saharan Africa (SSA) in particular in the literature. Many developing countries, including SSA countries, in the 1960s and 1970s discouraged foreign investment and pursued import substitution industrialization policies (Dupasquier and Osakwe, 2006). Many of these countries restricted technology inflow through FDI. This contributed to their firms having poor capabilities and being uncompetitive because they were technically inefficient and lagged behind technologically (Lall and Pietrobelli, 2002). On the contrary, over the same period, East Asian countries embraced FDI with remarkable success (Lall, 2003; Saggi, 2002; Stiglitz, 1996). Developing countries such as Singapore developed large and competitive industrial sectors by employing an all-encompassing industrial policy supported by institutional frameworks that used FDI as a conduit for technology transfer and skill development (Lall and Pietrobelli, 2002).

There is abundant evidence that countries in Africa have made significant progress towards improving their business environment and have now opened up their economies to attract FDI because of these expected benefits (Asiedu, 2006; Nwankwo, 2012). African economies have proved resilient in the midst of the global financial crises and have posted high economic growth rates and very high returns on investment (Ernst and Young, 2011). Because of Africa's promising growth potential, global businesses can no longer ignore the continent (Boston Consulting Group, 2010) and UNCTAD (2012) expects FDI growth (inflow) in Africa to continue to increase. There is also an observed shift from predominantly resource-seeking to some market-seeking FDI in Africa (Cleeve, 2007; Nwankwo, 2012) because of a growing middle class.

There is extensive theoretical and empirical literature that emphasizes that FDI increases the productivity and economic growth of host countries. Although some research findings show a positive relationship between FDI and technology diffusions (Elmawazini et al., 2008), most empirical studies on Africa, with specific focus on SSA, have not succeeded in finding unequivocal positive spillovers (Zhang, 2001). Most African countries do not appear to be reaping spillovers such as T&K transfer from evident growing FDI inflow. There is a lingering question as to whether the bulk of FDI that the continent is attracting is quality or quantity FDI. The term 'quality FDI' often refers to high value-added FDI and/or FDI with positive linkages and spillover effects for the domestic economy (Borensztein et al., 1998). It is argued that the effect of FDI and its quality depend significantly on domestic policies, especially measures to develop human capital and social, physical and institutional infrastructures (Cleeve, 2012). Most countries in SSA are making considerable policy changes such as political and institutional reforms to improve their business climate in order to attract FDI which is expected to create employment, enhance economic growth and also facilitate T&K transfer (Ayadi et al., 2010). Osabutey and Debrah (2012) observe that the majority of the FDI policies and initiatives focus on FDI attraction to the detriment of spillover effects such as T&K transfers. In much the same way most FDI studies on Africa focus on evaluating the factors that can enhance the attraction of FDI and not the spillovers from FDI (Asiedu, 2004, 2006; Cleeve, 2012; Mmieh and Owusu-Frimpong, 2004).

SSA's representation in both the theoretical and empirical literature is woefully inadequate. Much of the recent literature has failed to explain why T&K transfer has been poor in some developing countries in spite of evident participation of foreign firms in various sectors of their economies. The existing but scarce SSA literature in this regard fails to examine, in-depth, the factors as well as the institutional framework that can facilitate potential T&K transfer. Studies regarding policy towards enhancing spillover effects in Africa are scarce. This study attempts to fill this gap. It is important to improve the understanding of governments, policymakers and researchers, among others, of FDI and related T&K transfer issues in SSA. It is necessary to review the theory and practice on the subject, identify the potential opportunities, current challenges and obstacles and discuss what needs to be done as well as suggest an agenda for future research. Essentially, this study explores the factors that can facilitate effective T&K transfer through foreign firms in SSA countries and specifically:

- Examine factors that would influence effective T&K transfer in Africa.
- Evaluate the institutional and policy framework that would facilitate T&K transfer in Africa.

The exploratory nature of the chapter is in line with the analytical research approach. The rest of the chapter is organized as follows: First, the relevant theoretical perspectives are evaluated and discussed. Second the relevant empirical literature is reviewed. Third, key factors that can facilitate T&K transfer in Africa are explored. Fourth, a conceptual framework and set of propositions for Africa are developed. Finally, the conclusions, implications and agenda for future research are discussed.

Theoretical perspectives

The expectation of spillovers from foreign firms is based on the belief that MNCs engaged in FDI have specific sets of advantages such as superior technology, management practices, marketing strategies, among others, over local firms (Dunning, 1993; Hymer, 1976). The FDI theories provide some explanations on how FDIs can facilitate inter- and intra-firm T&K transfer. When the MNC is unable to internalize these advantages and local firms and workers are able to learn and benefit from them then spillovers occur (Crespo and Fontoura, 2007).

Technology transfer and knowledge transfer

Technology transfer has been a subject of considerable interest to groups such as governments, policymakers, international funding agencies and business executives, because of its links to economic growth (Li-Hua, 2004; Lim, 2001; World Economic Forum, 2011). Technology transfer involves more than the capability to acquire new knowledge, or generate improved production processes (Miles, 1995). Sahal (1982) refers to technology as 'configuration' and observes that technology must rely on specifiable, subjectively determined products and processes. He argues that the study of technology transfer needs to pay attention to the knowledge relevant for its use and applications as well. Technology transfer and KT therefore go hand in hand (Li-Hua, 2004; Osabutey and Debrah, 2011). Technology transfer and KT are therefore viewed as an integral T&K transfer process because technology transfer cannot be evaluated without the accompanying knowledge, and KT cannot be evaluated without employing a knowledge management (KM) system that relies on information and communications technology (ICT) to enhance effectiveness (Osabutey and Debrah, 2011).

Institutions and technology and knowledge transfer

Institutional theory has been influenced by North (1990) and Scott (1995), who view strategic choices of firms as the outcome of the interactions between institutions and organizations. North (1994) defined institutions as 'humanly devised constraints that structure human interaction'. Scott (1995) on the other hand defined institutions as the regulative, normative and cognitive activities and structures that bring stability and meaning to social behaviour. Institutional theory suggests that formal constraints (laws, constitutions, contracts, rules and so on), informal constraints (conventions, self-imposed codes of conduct, norms of behaviour and so on) and their enforcement characteristics regulate economic activities (North, 1990; Scott, 1995). Institutions preside over societal transactions in politics (e.g., corruption), law (e.g., economic and regulatory infrastructure) and society's ethical norms (Peng et al., 2008).

The relationship between institutions, organizations and governments is essential for development. Studies have shown that developed economies tend to be more integrated in terms of institutional rules, market transactions, infrastructure and enforcement mechanisms, whilst less developed economies are less so (Khanna and Palepu, 1999; Makino et al., 2004). Emerging or developing economies are generally characterized by 'institutional voids' which can be defined as the lack of institutional facilities, norms and regulations needed for a well-functioning economy. Developing economies are generally characterized by weak contract enforcement regimes, inadequate disclosure and weak governance regimes (Khanna and Palepu, 1999, 2006; North, 1990). There is an increasing recognition of the influence of formal and informal institutions in the performance and responses to changes in the business environment (Peng et al., 2008). A country's economic growth rate is affected by the quality of its institutions (Adams, 2009; Makki and Somwaru, 2004). Lim (2001) argues that FDI's major contribution to economic growth is derived from 'its role as a conduit for transferring advanced technology' (Lim, 2001, p. 3). Institutional theory is a suitable framework for evaluating T&K transfer in response to a nation's pressures to conform to shared norms of its institutional environment (DiMaggio and Powell, 1983; Roberts and Greenwood, 1997).

Corruption's relationship with FDI flow and T&K transfer

Following Macrae (1982), Kwok and Tadesse (2006) defined corruption as an arrangement that involves an exchange between two parties (the 'demander' and the 'supplier') which has an influence on the allocation of resources either immediately or in the future; and involves the use or abuse of public or collective responsibility for private ends. As an element of institutional framework, corruption is an important factor in international business but this has not been adequately researched (Anokhin and Schulze, 2009; Jain, 2002). When rules are disregarded by public officials for personal gain then corruption occurs (Jain, 2002). This tends to generally undermine the basis upon which trust in business relationships is built, thus leading to an increase in business risks (Anokhin and Schulze, 2009). Increasing business risks invariably increases business costs and would inevitably increase costs to end users as well as reduce profits that accrue to both domestic and foreign firms. As a result corruption reduces FDI flow (Lambsdorff, 2003; Mauro, 1995; Wei, 2000) because it discourages some foreign firms from investing in certain locations. Jain (2002) highlight three elements which determine corruption: (1) power and authority to design and administer regulations; (2) associated economic rents with this power; and (3) a judicial system that does not provide an adequately high probability of exposure or penalty.

Kwok and Tadesse (2006) in reviewing MNCs as agents of institutional change in host nations examined FDI and corruption. They observed that corruption distorts efficient allocation of resources and rewards unproductive behaviour by channelling unmerited and sometimes unjustified contracts and rights to firms at the expense of efficient and innovative firms in exchange for bribes. More importantly, because it introduces additional costs it adversely affects total factor productivity (Lambsdorff, 2003; Rivera-Batiz, 2002), a proxy for T&K transfer. Firms may arguably not be encouraged to introduce new and improved T&K or innovation to increase their productivity, if there are opportunities to gain unfair advantage through corruptive practices. Mauro (1995) earlier found that corruption and other institutional factors reduce FDI and consequently economic growth. Corruption can, arguably, therefore adversely affect T&K transfer if FDI's contribution to growth is derived from T&K transfer. Corruption also influences the source of investment because corrupt nations generally tend to attract FDI from other corrupt nations (Hellman and Kaufmann, 2004). Therefore, it is also argued that corrupt nations are less likely to benefit from investment by high-quality companies that employ sophisticated technologies (Anokhin and Schulze, 2009). Mongay and Filipescu (2012) observe a correlation between corruption and the ease of doing business and conclude that corruption reduces the quantity and type of technical knowledge that FDI might bring to the host country. In respect of firm-level human resource development (HRD), Debrah and Ofori (2006) argue that corruption is inimical to HRD in some developing countries because there were no incentives to excel in order to gain competitive advantage as quality standards were not enforced under corrupt regimes.

Human resource development, knowledge management and T&K transfer

HRD draws on a wide range of disciplines and is related to human resource management (HRM) and leadership (Stewart, 2005). HRD definitions principally reveal that it involves the use of organizational learning (OL) interventions and organizational development (OD) principles with the specific focus on improving skills, knowledge and understanding with consequent enhancement in individual and organizational performance and effectiveness (Swanson, 2001; Sydhagen and Cunningham, 2007). Recent literature suggests that HRD is connected with the concept of OL, KM and OD (Raiden and Dainty, 2006; Stewart, 2005). Stewart (2005) argues that the KM concept has overtaken the learning organizational concept. These concepts, however, clearly constitute learning and could be viewed as constructs with the same meaning (Osabutey et al., 2012). It is important to note that, within the HRD literature, HRD is viewed as a key to sustainable economic development (Li and Nimon, 2008; Paprock, 2006). Particularly for developing countries the literature appears to support state intervention in skill development (Debrah and Ofori, 2001; Finlay and Niven, 1996). In this regard it is argued that where local firms, in particular, are unable to adequately meet the skill development targets, state intervention is required to supply needed quality, quantity and variety of human resource. Osabutey et al. (2012) suggests that in the globalized business environment there was the need for governments in developing countries to actively improve the competitiveness of their local firms by improving their capacities and capabilities. They suggest that in developing countries, state intervention and local firm HRD incentive systems should be integrated. In this regard governments need to put incentives in place that would also encourage local firms to invest in HRD systems and programmes. In this regard a good combination of government and local firm responsibilities are required but local firms need to be encouraged to do so. In addition, local firms should also be encouraged through similar incentives to utilize new T&K and to develop KM/OL systems and programmes to enhance their competitiveness.

Wahab et al. (2009) discussed the traditional models of T&K transfer, appropriability, dissemination, knowledge utilization and communications and indicated that in the 1970s the economic international trade T&K transfer model was dominant in the literature (Bessant and Francis, 2005). A decade later, the emphasis shifted towards effectiveness of technology for economic development and in the 1990s the significance of learning at the organizational level (through OL/KM systems) as key elements in facilitating T&K transfer (Figuereido, 2001) also gained eminence. This means that T&K transfer issues should discuss not only how government policies enable foreign participation in the local economy, but how the process takes place with a conscious effort aimed at developing local firms. In addition, local firms at the organizational level need to take some responsibility for their learning. Other researchers have developed T&K transfer models based on the knowledge-based view (KBV) and OL (Daghfous, 2004). Further synthesis of the KT literature and the review of the KM concept indicate that KT is arguably a subset of KM or a subset of social relations/HR. This is because the impact of external T&K on performance would only be felt if firms make a conscious effort to create, acquire, disseminate and share knowledge. Without efforts at the firm level not much transfer can take place. Therefore KM/OL at the firm level can also influence T&K transfer and Egbu (2000) argues that KM is 10 per cent technology and 90 per cent people issues and therefore the HRM/HRD literature cannot be ignored. As invisible assets are embodied in people, HRM policies and practices are crucial for OL/KM. OL/KM results from a combination of hard and soft organizational practices anchored in specific HR activities (Pucik, 1988).

Absorptive capacity and education, technical training and R&D

In order to build technological capabilities and capacities, most developed and developing countries introduce various selective policies to attract R&D-related FDI (Fu et al., 2011). Romer (1986) and Lucas (1988) argue that R&D contributes to the long-run growth of local economies. Fu et al. (2011) emphasize that international T&K transfer can be enhanced if the absorptive capacity of local firms and organizations are adequate. In other words local firms and organizations need to develop the ability to identify, assimilate and exploit knowledge from foreign firms (Girma, 2005). So in other words, in addition to human capital, R&D expenditure is also very important (Fu et al., 2011). A key element of absorptive capacity is therefore derived from R&D activities by local firms because such firms create knowledge and promote learning (Griffith et al., 2004). This agrees with the argument earlier that there is a relationship between KM and T&K transfer. Local firms therefore have the added responsibility of internal R&D. Fu et al. (2011) go ahead to argue that R&D activities of local universities and research institutions within the host country contribute to absorptive capacity. In a sense developing absorptive capacity depends on local education and training, local firms HRD, KM, R&D as well as local universities and research institutions R&D.

Empirical literature on FDI and growth, productivity and T&K transfer in Africa

The limited empirical literature on SSA employs statistical and econometric methods to evaluate the effect of FDI on economic growth and productivity. Adams (2009) analyses the impact of FDI and domestic investment on economic growth using a panel data set for 42 SSA from 1990 to 2003. The results demonstrate that domestic investment significantly correlated positively with economic growth in both OLS and fixed estimation, but FDI is significantly correlated positively in only the OLS estimation. In addition, his findings revealed that FDI had an initial negative effect on local investment and subsequent positive effects in later periods. Adams argued that the absorptive capacity in most of the countries in the region was not at the threshold that would allow FDI to develop local skills and transfer T&K. Adams (2009) also noted that the institutional variable is positive and significantly correlated with economic growth; consistent with other studies that show that the economic growth rate is affected by the quality of institutions (Makki and Somwaru, 2004). He argued that SSA policymakers needed a targeted approach which focuses on promoting and attracting some types of FDI and regulating others with additional aims of increasing absorptive capacity of local firms through corporation of foreign firms to encourage mutual benefit.

Lumbila (2005) used panel data from 47 African countries between 1980 and 2000 and found a positive significant effect of FDI on economic growth. He noted that the impact of FDI on growth was, however, smaller than the impact from domestic and foreign aid. This implies that FDI's contribution to growth is below expected levels. He also notes that the impact of FDI is hindered by absorptive capacity in terms of poor human capital and infrastructure, as well as institutional deficiencies and poor macroeconomic performance. Ayanwale (2007) used data from 1970 to 2002 and found that the effect of FDI on growth of the Nigerian economy was not significant, which was consistent with findings by Akinlo (2004). Managi and Bwalya (2010) used panel data for Kenya, Tanzania and Zimbabwe and argued that their results show that intra- and inter-industry productivity spillovers existed for Kenya and Zimbabwe only. Although these results are mixed, the majority of the findings indicate that FDI did not significantly impact on economic growth as expected.

Ayanwale (2007) argues that the low level of education contributes to insignificant impact of FDI on growth in Nigeria. Osabutey and Debrah (2012) also note that although Ghana has improved its democratic credentials and business environment with consequent increase in FDI inflow, technology transfer and technology development remain low because of the level of technical knowledge in particular; reflected in the generally poor science and technology education in most of Africa. The World Economic Forum (2011), Africa Competitiveness Report, notes that the stock of human capital with higher education in Africa continues to lag behind. African higher education institutions are not producing adequate students in science, engineering and technology compared to rapidly growing economies such as China and Korea. Africa needs to take a cue from Korea and other East Asian economies to invest heavily in technical skills education and training to support economic growth. In addition, tertiary education and pedagogy and curriculums needs revision (Osabutey and Debrah, 2012; World Economic Forum, 2011). According to Cloete et al. (2011) of the Centre of Higher Education Policy (CHET), countries in SSA have woefully failed to adequately appreciate the link, in particular, between university education planning and economic development planning. Whilst general education is expected to support the human capital development policy, a demand-driven tertiary educational system is necessary for increasing absorptive capacity and T&K development and transfer.

Elmawazini and Nwanko (2012) used panel data from five SSA countries and found that FDI rather increases the technology gap between SSA and OECD countries. They argue that low absorptive capacity of local firms contributes to this worrying trend. Osabutey and Debrah (2012) attributed the poor or weak FDI-linked T&K transfer to policy lacunae in most of SSA and suggested an urgent need to review economic and development policies to foster relevant links between FDI policy, education and human capital development policy, trade and industrial policy, technology development and technology transfer policy as well as private-sector and local firm development policy.

A review of the measures of corruption/transparency indicates that, with the exception of four, SSA countries are in the lower half of the 2011 Corruption Perception Index (Transparency International, 2012). This means that the majority of SSA countries are perceived as corrupt. It is no wonder that corruption is thought to be a key factor that has hindered the development of Africa. There are few studies that analyse the effect of corruption on investment growth. Asiedu and Freeman (2009) show that it varies from region to region and that although in general corruption has a negative and significant effect on investment growth in transition economies, it has no significant effect for firms in Latin America and SSA. Consistent with this finding, Cleeve (2012) found that, contrary to expectation, corruption showed no clear relationship with FDI inflow in SSA (Cleeve, 2012). He notes, however, that FDI is commonly linked with bribery and corruption in most of SSA (Egger and Winner, 2005; Ezeoha and Ogamba, 2010; Houston, 2007). It is worth noting that these findings relate only to investment growth (flow), but do not discuss the effect of corruption on economic growth, total factor productivity or other spillovers effects. Although studies on SSA that specifically measure the effect of corruption on T&K transfer are scarce, existing research in other regions shows that corruption adversely affects productivity growth (Lambsdorff, 2003; Rivera-Batiz, 2002). Arguably, corruption prevalence in SSA could be a contributing factor in poor T&K transfer and development.

Discussion and implications

Figure 12.1 captures the theoretical and empirical literature to present some of the factors that are influencing the weak or non-existent T&K transfer from FDI in Africa. The exploratory model indicates that government policy is central and it is expected that governments in Africa need to revisit their FDI policy framework. FDI attraction policies should no longer be independent of education and training policy and industrial policy if the expected benefits from FDI are to be achieved. In addition to corruption being able to retard the benefits that could be derived from FDI, there are institutional barriers, resulting from the fact that the institutions in SSA appear to lack the requisite capacity and capability to regulate and influence T&K development. Improving education (especially in science and technology) and HRM/HRD, KM/OL and R&D within firms (with specific emphasis on local firms and organizations) are also vital. Skill development requires firm-level commitment as well as state intervention. African governments can learn

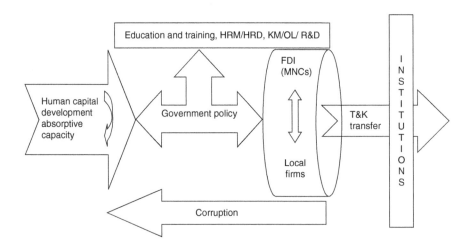

Figure 12.1 Exploratory model of technology and knowledge transfer in Africa

from the developmental state model of Singapore as suggested by Ashton and Sung (1994) and Goodwin (1997). A policy initiative towards technology development is urgent and technology transfer is integral to economic development. But T&K transfer should form part, but not be the entire technology development programme (Ofori, 1994).

African governments need to revisit their educational systems and infrastructure. Osabutey and Debrah (2012) noted that in Ghana, for example, whilst national enrolment at the tertiary level was generally growing, the investments into science and technology education by public and private universities and related enrolment figures were reducing year on year. Access to post-secondary education in Africa on the whole represents less than 3 per cent of the eligible age group – the lowest in the world by a considerable percentage (Teferra and Altbach, 2004). Teferra and Albach (2004) note that most African universities suffer from the effects of scarce financial resources, which contributes to scarcity of published materials of books and journals and essential resources for teaching. In addition, laboratory equipment and supplies for research and teaching are lacking. It can be argued that like FDI policymaking and targeting, education policymaking and targeting are not aligned to development needs in Africa. In the emerging and competitive global knowledge economy countries can only benefit from globalization if the appropriate investment in tertiary education is able to develop human capital in line with global standards. African tertiary education must produce graduates who can think globally and act locally. To do this, the tertiary institutions in Africa would need to become abreast with current existing knowledge through R&D. Having access to current databases, journals and periodicals is essential for undertaking meaningful and reliable research, but these resources are scarce or non-existent in most universities in Africa (Teferra and Altbach, 2004).

FDI policymaking and best practices

UNCTAD (2012) suggests an FDI policy framework that seeks to specifically address investment policy challenges, which also defines the role of public, private, domestic investment and especially FDI in national development. The UN Conference on Trade and Development (UNCTAD) affirms that reaping the development benefits from FDI requires an enabling policy framework that provides unambiguous and transparent rules for the entry and operation of foreign investors with sufficient regulation to lessen any associated risks. Investment policymaking should also cover measurable goals for both FDI attraction and FDI contribution to development (UNCTAD, 2012). UNCTAD (2011) also notes that countries that develop strong local skills base have a tendency to attract more FDI inflows. In addition, foreign MNCs can contribute to the local skills base through spillovers to subsidiary employees and local firms as well as active participation in local education and training institutions. The local human capital determines the quality and quantity of FDI as well as the potential T&K transfer. This also depends on FDI promotion and targeting which needs to be in sync with education and training policies, skill dissemination policies and national innovations systems

(UNCTAD, 2011). Box 12.1 discusses how the government of Singapore used FDI to develop local skills and shows that although FDI can enhance the T&K of local firms and workforce, it does so if the host country policies are right (UNCTAD, 1999).

Box 12.1 Government's role in integrating FDI and skill development

At the beginning of industrialization, the government of Singapore focused on expanding primary and secondary education to provide skills for labour-intensive manufacturing activities. To support more knowledge-intensive industries in succeeding years, FDI policy shifted to MNCs with the potential to transfer T&K to local firms and workers. To encourage foreign investors in this regard, education and training, migration and investment policies were developed with the needs of the targeted MNCs in mind. In addition, the Singapore government sought to identify and exploit opportunities for such foreign firms to contribute to local education infrastructure and the training of local workers and suppliers. This extraordinary level of policy attention and convergence allowed the country to attract FDI activities in some areas where skills were deficient by relying first on foreign workers and then alongside training local workers.

(UNCTAD, 2011)

Integrating FDI with skills development policies requires sophisticated institutional structures which are currently weak in most of Africa. The interaction, coordination and synergies between different institutions can support a self-sustaining model. Host countries themselves should be responsible for high-level specialized training and upgrading of local skills generally. UNCTAD (2012) suggests that such an approach could enhance the attraction of quality FDI and can also encourage some existing foreign and local firms to diversify into knowledge-intensive activities. There is the need for investment promotion agencies to identify skill needs of foreign and local firms, which can then be communicated to the training and educational institutions. Singapore's HRD policies were demand-driven and systematically re-evaluated and reviewed at each stage of industrial development. The reasons why such approaches are not evident in Africa could be attributed to the fact that countries in SSA have anecdotally never embarked on a development agenda that uses FDI as a key driver of industrial policy. Attempts at industrialization in Africa in the 1960s and 1970s were rather focused on import substitution and socialist policies.

Increasingly MNCs are seeking to locate in countries with knowledge in engineering, technology, organizational skills and business administration (UNCTAD, 2011). Countries in SSA seeking to use FDI to enhance skill development will need to separate long-term FDI promotion objectives from short-term ones. In the short-term expanding tax revenues and employment could mean promoting FDI in labour- or resource-intensive industries. Concurrently investment promotion should also look for opportunities to attract foreign investment most likely to benefit the economy in the future, through increased training opportunities and T&K transfers. To achieve this more incentives need to be offered to MNCs to encourage them to support local skill development and T&K transfers (UNCTAD, 2011). Perhaps countries in SSA focus on the short-term objectives to the detriment and sometimes total neglect of the long-term ones. The discussions so far lead the set of propositions that effective T&K transfer through FDI in host countries in Africa will depend on:

- Targeted FDI and technology transfer and technology development policies.
- Local firm (and foreign firm) HRM/HRD, KM/OL and R&D systems and programmes to enhance local firm absorptive capacity.
- Educational systems, technical training and R&D at national and institutional levels to enhance host country absorptive capacity.
- Reliable and well-structured institutions with the requisite capacity and capability as well as powers to regulate, monitor and measure T&K transfer.

Conclusion and implications

The chapter has reviewed the relevant theoretical and empirical literature that relates to FDI and T&K transfer and development and the expected economic growth. It has been observed that FDI inflow into Africa is not resulting in T&K transfer, skill development and capacity building the way it occurred in Singapore and continues to occur in some countries in Asia. This preparatory study identifies some relevant factors (conduits and obstacles) that positively influence FDI spillovers such as T&K transfer. The factors include poor local educational systems with particular emphasis on tertiary education, which fails to be demand-driven and lacks emphasis on science, engineering and technology required for enhanced T&K transfer and economic development. In addition, government policies need to encourage interaction between foreign and local firms with the aim of improving local capacities and capabilities. There is also the need for incentives that can encourage foreign firms to participate in local education and training. The chapter observes that in doing so, government policy needs to incentivize local firms to invest in HRM/HRD and KM/OL systems and programmes to improve their competitiveness. It is argued that corruption together with poor or void institutional arrangements were likely to adversely affect this process. FDI policymaking in Africa needs to be integrative and forward-looking as without such an approach FDI inflows may not bring the full benefits to most SSA countries.

The chapter serves as a useful link to other empirical studies by the author (and others) with the aim of bringing T&K transfer issues in Africa to the attention of researchers and policymakers. In other related studies, the author is empirically seeking to explore other factors and also develop further prepositions that can help explain why FDI is not resulting in T&K transfer and development in most of Africa. Researchers should seek to explain why countries in Africa have not been able to successfully follow some of the examples seen in most parts of Asia over the last three to four decades. Our knowledge and understanding needs to improve in this regard because the pace of globalization poses huge challenges to African economies. Policymaking is crucial because arguably what worked for some countries in the 1960s and 1970s may not work for SSA today in view of the changing global business environment. However, a lot of lessons can be learned from decades of experiences from countries such as Singapore. There is the need for further and in-depth country and sector studies to improve our understanding of the issues surrounding FDI policymaking and T&K transfer in Africa. If Africa's potential in international business is to be fulfilled for the benefit of investors and host countries then policymaking which integrates both short-term and long-term benefits with emphasis on national development agenda is required.

References

S. Adams, 'Foreign direct investment, domestic investment, and economic growth in Sub-Saharan Africa', *Journal of Policy Modelling*, 31(6) (2009) 939–49.

A. Akinlo, 'Foreign direct investment and growth in Nigeria: an emperical investigation', *Journal of Policy Modelling*, 26(5) (2004) 627–39.

S. Anokhin and W. S. Schulze, 'Entrepreneurship, innovation and corruption', *Journal of Business Venturing*, 24(5) (2009) 465–76.

D. Ashton and J. Sung, 'The State, Economic Development and Skill Formation: A New Asian Model?' *Working Paper 3, Center for Labour Market Studies*, (Leicester: Leicester University, 1994).

E. Asiedu, 'Policy reform and foreign direct investment in Africa: absolute progress but relative decline', *Development Policy Review*, 22(1) (2004) 41–8.

E. Asiedu, 'Foreign direct investment in Africa: the role natural resources, market size, government policy, institutions and political stability', *World Economy*, 29(1) (2006) 63–77.

E. Asiedu and J. Freeman, 'The effect of corruption on investment growth: evidence from firms in Latin America and sub-Saharan Africa, and transition countries', *Review of Development Economics*, 13(2) (2009) 200–14.

O. F. Ayadi, S. Ajibolade, J. Williams and L. Hyman, 'Transparency and Foreign Direct Investment into Sub-Saharan Africa: An Econometric Investigation', *The 11th International Academy of African Business and Development (IAABD)*, (Lagos, Nigeria: University of Lagos, 2010).

A. B. Ayanwale, 'FDI and Economic Growth: Evidence from Nigeria', *African Economic Research Consortium Paper 165, Nairobi*, (2007).

J. Bessant and D. Francis, 'Trasnferring soft technologies: exploring adaptive theory', *International Journal of Technology Management and Sustainable Development*, 4(2) (2005) 93–112.

M. Blomström, S. Globerman and A. Kokko, 'The Determinants of Host Country Spillovers from Foreign Direct Investment', in N. Pain (ed), *Inward Investment, Technological Change and Growth*, (London: Palgrave, 2001), pp. 34–65.

E. Borensztein, J. De Grigorio and J.-W. Lee, 'How does foreign direct investment affect economic growth?', *Journal of International Economics*, 45(1) (1998) 115–35.

Boston Consulting Group, *The African Challengers: Global Competitors Emerge from the Overlooked Continent*, (Boston, MA: Boston Consulting Group, 2010).

E. Cleeve, 'The Determinants of Foreign Direct Investment to Sub-Saharan Africa: A Review', *The 8th International Conference of the Academy of African Business*, (London: IAABD, 2007).

E. Cleeve, 'Political and institutional impediments to foreign direct investment inflows to Sub-Saharan Africa', *Thunderbird International Business Reveiw*, 54(4) (2012) 469–77.

N. Cloete, T. Bailey, P. Pillay, I. Bunting and P. Maassen, *Universities and Economic Development in Africa*, (Cape Town: Centre for Higher Education Transformation (CHET), 2011).

N. Crespo and M. P. Fontoura, 'Determinant factors of FDI spillovers – what do we really know?', *World Development*, 35(3) (2007) 410–25.

A. Daghfous, 'An empirical investigation of the roles of prior knowledge and learning activities in technology transfer', *Technovation*, 24(12) (2004) 939–53.

Y. A. Debrah and G. Ofori, 'The state, skill formation and productivity enhancement in the construction industry: the case of Singapore', *International Journal of Human Resource Management*, 12(1) (2001) 184–202.

Y. A. Debrah and G. Ofori, 'Human resource development of professionals in an emerging economy: the case of the Tanzanian construction industry', *The International Journal of Human Resource Management*, 17(3) (2006) 440–63.

P. J. DiMaggio and W. W. Powell, 'The iron cage revisited: Institutional isomorphism and collective rationality in organisational fields', *American Sociological Review*, 48(2) (1983) 147–60.

J. H. Dunning, *Multinational Enterprises and the Global Economy*, (Wokingham: Addison Wesley, 1993).

C. Dupasquier and P. N. Osakwe, 'Foreign direct investment in Africa: performance, challenges, and responsibilities', *Journal of Asian Economics*, 17(2) (2006) 241–60.

C. O. Egbu 'Knowledge Management in Construction SMEs: Coping with the Issues of Structure, Culture, Commitment and Motivation', ARCOM Sixteenth Annual Conference, Glasgow Caledonian University, (2000), pp. 83–92.

P. Egger and H. Winner, 'Evidence on corruption as an incentive for foriegn direct investment', *European Journal of Political Economy*, 21(4) (2005) 932–52.

K. Elmawazini, P. Manga and S. Saadi, 'Multinational enterprises, technology diffusion, and host country absorptive capacity: a note', *Global Economic Review*, 37(3) (2008) 379–86.

K. Elmawazini and S. Nwankwo, 'Foreign direct investment: technology gap effects on international business capabilities of Sub-Saharan Africa', *Thunderbird International Business Reveiw*, 54(4) (2012) 457–67.

Ernst & Young, *It's time for Africa: Ernst & Young's 2011 Africa Attractiveness Survey*, (London: Ernst & Young, 2011).

A. E. Ezeoha and E. Ogamba, 'Corporate tax, sheild of fraud: an insight from Nigeria', *International Journal of Law and Management*, 52(1) (2010) 5–20.

P. Figuereido, *Technological Learning and Competitive Performance*, (Cheltenham: Edward Elgar, 2001).

I. Finlay and S. Niven, 'Characteristics of effective vocational education and training policies: an international comparative perspective', *International Journal of Vocational Education and Training*, 4(1) (1996) 5–22.

X. Fu, C. Pietrobelli, and L. Soete, 'The role of foreign technology and indegenous innovation in the emerging economies: technological change and catching-up', *World Development*, 39(7) (2011) 1204–12.

S. Girma, 'Absorptive capacity and productivity spillovers from FDI: a threshold regression analysis', *Oxford Bulletin of Economics and Statistics*, 67(3) (2005) 281–306.

J. Goodwin, 'The Republic of Ireland and the Singaporean Model of Skill Formation and Economic Development', *Working Paper 14, Centre for Labour Market Studies*, (Leicester: Leicester University, 1997).

R. Griffith, S. Redding and J. V. Reenen, 'Mapping the two faces of R&D: productivity growth in a panel of OECD industries', *The Review of Economics and Statistics*, 86(4) (2004) 883–95.

J. Hellman and D. Kaufmann, 'The Inequality of Influence', in J. Kornai and S. Rose-Ackerman (eds), *Trust in Transitions*, (New York: Palgrave Macmillan, 2004).

D. Houston, 'Can corruption ever improve an economy', *Cato Journal*, 27(3) (2007) 325–42.

S. H. Hymer, *The International Operations of National Firms: A Study of Foreign Direct Investment*, (Cambridge, MA: MIT Press, 1976).

A. Isaksson, T. H. Ng and G. Robyn, *Productivity in Developing Countries: Trends and Policies*, (Vienna: UNIDO, 2005).

A. K. Jain, 'Corruption: a review', *Journal of Economic Surveys*, 15(1) (2002) 71–121.

B. S. Javorcik, 'Can survey evidence shed light on spillovers from foreign direct investment?', *The World Bank Research Observer*, 23(2) (2008) 139–59.

S. Khanna and K. G. Palepu, 'Emerging giants: building world-class companies in developing countries', *Harvard Business Review*, 84(10) (2006) 60–70.

T. Khanna and K. Palepu, 'Policy shocks, market intermediaries, and corporate strategy: the evolution of business groups in Chile and India', *Journal of Economics and Management Strategy*, 8(2) (1999) 271–310.

C. C. Kwok and S. Tadesse, 'The MNC as an agent of change for host-country institutions: FDI and corruption', *Journal of International Business Studies*, 37(6) (2006) 767–85.

S. Lall, 'Reinventing Industrial Strategy: The Role of Government Policy in Building Industrial Competitiveness', *QEH Working Paper Series*, (2003).

S. Lall and C. Pietrobelli, *Failing to Compete: Technology Development and Technology Systems in Africa*, (Cheltenham: Edward Elgar Publishing Ltd, 2002).

G. J. Lambsdorff, 'How corruption affects productivity', *Kyklos*, 56(4) (2003) 457–74.

R. Li-Hua, *Technology and Knowledge Transfer in China*, (Aldershot: Ashgate, 2004).

J. Li and K. Nimon, 'The importance of recognising generational differences in HRD policy and practices: a study of workers in Qinhuangdao, China', *Human Resource Development International*, 11(2) (2008) 167–82.

E. G. Lim, 'Determinants of and Relation between Foreign Direct Investment and Growth: A Summary of Recent Literature', *IMF Working Paper WP/01/175*, (2001).

R. Lucas, 'On the mechanics of economic development', *Journal of Monetary Economics*, 22(3) (1988) 3–42.

K. N. Lumbila, 'What Makes FDI Work? A Panel Analysis of the Growth Effect of FDI in Africa', *Africa Region Working Paper Series*, (2005).

J. Macrae, 'Underdevelopment and the economics of corruption: a game theory approach', *World Development*, 10(8) (1982) 677–87.

S. Makino, T. Isobe and C. M. Chan, 'Does country matter?', *Strategic Management Journal*, 25(10) (2004) 1027–43.

S. Makki and A. Somwaru, 'Impact of foreign direct investment and trade on economic growth: evidence from developing countries', *American Journal of Agricultural Economics*, 86(3) (2004) 795–801.

S. Managi and S. M. Bwalya, 'Foreign direct investment and technology spillovers in sub-Saharan Africa', *Applied Economic Letters*, 17(6) (2010) 605–08.

P. Mauro, 'Corruption and growth', *Quarterly Journal of Economics*, 110(3) (1995) 681–712.

D. Miles, *Constructive Change: Managing International Technology Transfer*, (Geneva: International Labour Office, 1995).

F. Mmieh and N. Owusu-Frimpong, 'State policies and the challenges in attracting foreign direct investment: a review of the Ghana experience', *Thunderbird International Business Review*, 46(5) (2004) 575–99.

J. Mongay and D. A. Filipescu, 'Are Corruption and Ease of Doing Business Correlated? An Analysis of 172 Nations', in S. Harris, O. Kuivalainen and V. Stoyanova (eds), *International Business: New Challenges, New Forms, New Perspectives*, (New York: Palgrave Macmillan, 2012), pp. 13–26.

D. C. North, *Institutions, Institutional Change, and Economic Performance*, (Cambridge: Cambridge University Press, 1990).

D. C. North, 'Economic performance through time', *American Economic Review*, 84(3) (1994) 359–68.

S. Nwankwo, 'Renascent Africa: rescoping the landscape of international business', *Thunderbird International Business Reveiw*, 54(4) (2012) 405–09.

G. Ofori, 'Construction industry development: role of technology transfer', *Construction Management and Economics*, 12(5) (1994) 379–92.

E. L. C. Osabutey and Y. A. Debrah, 'New Perspectives on Foreign Direct Investment and Technology Transfer in Africa: Insights from the Construction Industry in Ghana', *12th Annual Conference of the International Academy of African Businesss and Development (IAABD)*, (Edmonton: IAABD, 2011).

E. L. C. Osabutey and Y. A. Debrah, 'Foreign direct investment and technology transfer policies in Africa: A review of the Ghanaian experience', *Thunderbird International Business Reveiw*, 54(4) (2012) 441–56.

E. L. C. Osabutey, R. B. Nyuur and Y. A. Debrah, 'Human Resource Development in Construction', in G. Ofori (ed.), *New Perspectives on Construction in Developing Countries*, (London and New York: Spon Press, 2012), pp. 229–52.

H. Pack and K. Saggi, 'Inflows of foreign technology and indigenous technological development', *Review of Development Economics*, 1(1) (1997) 81–98.

K. E. Paprock, 'National human resource development in the developing world: Introductory', *Advances in Developing Human Resources*, 8(1) (2006) 12–27.

M. W. Peng, D. Y. L. Wang and Y. Jiang, 'An institution-based view of international business strategy: a focus on emerging economies', *Journal of International Business Studies*, 39(5) (2008) 920–36.

V. Pucik, 'Strategic alliances, organisational learning and competitive advantage: the HRM agenda', *Human Resource Management*, 27(1) (1988) 77–93.

A. B. Raiden and A. R. J. Dainty, 'Human resource development in construction organisations: an example of "chaordic" learning organisation?', *The Learning Organisation*, 13(1) (2006) 63–79.

F. L. Rivera-Batiz, 'Democracy, governance, and economic growth: theory and evidence', *Review of Development Economics*, 6(2) (2002) 225–47.

P. Roberts and R. Greenwood, 'Integrating transaction cost and institutional theories: Toward a constrained-efficiency framework for understanding organisational design adoption', *Academy of Management Review*, 22(2) (1997) 346–73.

P. M. Romer, 'Increasing returns and long run growth', *Journal of Political Economy*, 94(5) (1986) 1002–37.

K. Saggi, 'Trade, foreign direct investment, and international technology transfer: a survey', *The World Bank Research Observer*, 17(2) (2002) 191–235.

D. Sahal, 'The Form of Technology', in D. Sahal (ed.), *The Transfer and Utilisation of Technical Knowledge*, (Lexington, MA: Lexington Publishing, 1982), pp. 125–139.

W. R. Scott, *Institutions and Organisations*, (Thousand Oaks, CA: Sage Publications, 1995).

J. Stewart, 'The current state and status of HRD research', *The Learning Organisation*, 12(1) (2005) 90–5.

J. E. Stiglitz, 'Some lessons from the East Asian miracle', *The World Bank Research Observer*, 11(2) (1996) 151–77.

R. A. Swanson, 'Human resource development and its underlying theory', *Human Resource Development International*, 4(3) (2001) 299–312.

K. Sydhagen and P. Cunningham, 'Human resource development in Sub-Saharan Africa', *Resource Development Intenational*, 10(2) (2007) 121–35.

D. Teferra and P. G. Altbach, 'African higher education: challenges for the 21st century', *Higher Education*, 47(1) (2004) 21–50.

Transparency International, *The 2011 Corruption Perception Index*, (Berlin: Transparency International, 2012).

UNCTAD, 'Foreign Direct Investment and the Challenge to Development', *World Investment Report*, (Geneva: United Nations Publications, 1999).

UNCTAD, *Best Practices in Investment for Development: How to Integrate FDI and Skill Development – Lessons from Canada and Singapore*, (New York and Geneva: United Nations, 2011).

UNCTAD, *World Investment Report: Towards a New Generation of Investment Policies*, (New York and Geneva: United Nations, 2012).

S. A. Wahab, R. C. Rose, J. Uli and H. Abdullah, 'A review of the technology transfer models, knowledge-based and organisational learning models of technology transfer', *European Journal of Social Sciences*, 10(4) (2009) 550–64.

S.-J. Wei, 'How taxing is corruption on international investors', *Review of Economics and Statistics*, 82(1) (2000) 1–11.

World Economic Forum, *The Africa Competitiveness Report 2011*. World Economic Forum, the World Bank and the African Development Bank, Geneva, (2011).

K. Zhang, 'How does foreign direct investment affect economic growth?', *Eonomies of Transition*, 9(3) (2001) 679–93.

13
New Venture Internationalization and the Cluster Life Cycle: Insights from Ireland's Indigenous Software Industry

Mike Crone

Introduction

The internationalization of new and small firms has been a long-standing concern of researchers in international business (Coviello and McAuley, 1999; Ruzzier et al., 2006). This topic has been re-invigorated over the last decade by the burgeoning literature on so-called 'born globals' (BG) or 'international new ventures' (INV) – businesses that confound the expectations of traditional theory by being active internationally at, or soon after, inception (Aspelund et al., 2007; Bell, 1995; Rialp et al., 2005). Until quite recently, this literature had not really considered how the home regional environment of a new venture might influence its internationalization behaviour. However, a handful of recent studies have shown that being founded in a geographic industry 'cluster' can positively influence the likelihood of a new venture internationalizing (e.g., Fernhaber et al., 2008; Libaers and Meyer, 2011).[1] This chapter seeks to build on these recent contributions by further probing the relationship between clusters and new venture internationalization. Specifically, taking inspiration from recent work in the thematic research stream on clusters (which spans the fields of economic geography, regional studies and industrial dynamics), the chapter explores how the emergence and internationalization of new ventures might be affected by the 'cluster life cycle' context within which they are founded. This issue is examined through a *revelatory* longitudinal case study of Ireland's indigenous software cluster. The study investigates the origins and internationalization behaviour of 'leading' Irish software ventures but, in contrast to many existing studies, it seeks to understand these firms within the context of the Irish software cluster's emergence and evolution through a number of 'life-cycle' stages.

The empirical case study highlights differences between the origins and internationalization behaviour of two cohorts of 'leading' new ventures, founded at different stages of the Irish software industry's cluster life cycle. These differences are attributed to two main factors. Firstly, the regional entrepreneurial environment in Ireland by the late 1990s – when the Irish software cluster had become more established – was significantly different and more favourable than that prevailing in earlier years. Thus, some of the resources that are known to be useful for early and rapid internationalization (e.g., venture capital (VC), experienced executives and supportive institutions) were relatively abundant by this time. Secondly, many of the leading firms founded in the established cluster of the late 1990s had superior internal resources and capabilities *at inception*, in comparison with firms founded in earlier stages of the cluster life cycle, due to the extensive prior experiences (primarily within the cluster) of their founding team members. Hence these firms were particularly well placed to capitalize on the improved regional entrepreneurial environment and to identify and exploit emerging niche opportunities in global software markets. Consequently, the internationalization of this latter cohort of new ventures was *qualitatively* different from that of firms founded during earlier stages in the cluster life cycle, being (generally) earlier, more rapid, wider in geographic scope and more 'multi-modal'.

The structure of the chapter is as follows. The next section reviews the most salient contributions from the (largely disconnected) thematic literatures on new venture internationalization and clusters. The case study method and data sources are then explained. The fourth section of the chapter introduces the case context before the fifth presents the case study evidence on new venture creation and internationalization at two different stages in the Irish software industry's cluster life cycle. The conclusion then emphasizes the contribution, reviews the key findings and considers the study's limitations and wider implications.

Key points from the literatures on new venture internationalization and clusters

Resource-based perspectives on new venture internationalization[2]

A key concern of the research stream on the BG/INV phenomenon has been to understand why some new ventures are able to internationalize rapidly, often to multiple global regions, contrary to the predictions of established internationalization theories (e.g., Uppsala School). Traditionally, new and small firms have been seen to face multiple disadvantages that curtail or slow their international expansion, sometimes referred to as the liabilities of newness and smallness. From the resource-based perspective (RBV), new and small firms are often portrayed as resource deficient in comparison with larger and more established firms. Thus, studies of small firm internationalization have sought to distinguish between non-exporters and exporters on the basis of their respective resource endowments (Westhead et al., 2001). This theme has been further developed in recent work on the BG/INV phenomenon, which has suggested such firms are distinguished from non-exporters and gradual internationalizers by their possession of superior resources (including various types of knowledge) and capabilities at inception and by their subsequent ability to successfully acquire and mobilize external resources (Coviello and Cox, 2006; Gabrielsson et al., 2008; Rialp et al., 2005).

Some explanations of the BG/INV phenomenon have pointed to the enabling role of structural changes in global markets or the rise of the Internet and e-business, whilst others have focused on the use of distinctive international marketing strategies and business models by these firms (Aspelund et al., 2007).

However, it is the characteristics of BG/INV founding team members and top managers that have attracted the most attention, especially in studies adopting a resource- or knowledge-based perspective. Thus, Gabrielsson et al. (2008) observe that most of the principal resources of these firms at start-up are likely to be 'embodied' in these key individuals. Importantly, these resources (including knowledge resources) have often been accumulated and developed during prior work experiences, especially overseas or with internationally active firms (Bloodgood et al., 1996; Reuber and Fischer, 1997).

Among the various types of 'embodied' resources and capabilities thought to be useful for early and rapid internationalization are knowledge of new and emerging technologies; deep familiarity with vertical markets and potential customers; entrepreneurial and leadership experience and familiarity with effective business models and organizational routines. The role of networks is another recurrent theme in studies of BG/INVs. Coviello and Cox (2006, p. 117) have observed that 'networks both generate resources and are a resource in their own right'. Several studies have highlighted the way in which BG/INVs acquire crucial resources for early internationalization from external network actors, by using the existing network ties of their founders but also by effectively developing new networks (Laanti et al., 2007; Loane et al., 2007). Finally, financial resources have been found to be important in several empirical studies of BG/INVs. Early and rapid internationalization is said to require significant 'up-front' investment, for example, to fund new product development and international marketing efforts. Thus, access to superior financial resources (via VC) has been found to distinguish firms that are 'BG (rapidly expanding into global markets) from those that are 'born international' (Gabrielsson et al., 2004). Venture capitalists may also assist early internationalization by providing reputation resources, new knowledge and additional network ties (Fernhaber and McDougall-Covin, 2009).

Insights from the clusters literature

Most studies in the BG/INV literature are silent on the geographical context for new venture creation and internationalization (Crone, 2010). In particular, the extant literature has not explored the geographical context for the resource inheritance and acquisition that is described in RBVs. However, the fact that recent studies have shown that a cluster location can positively influence new venture internationalization (e.g., Fernhaber et al., 2008; Libaers and Meyer, 2011) should encourage international entrepreneurship scholars to take a closer look at the clusters research stream, which has been one of the hottest areas in social science in recent decades. The discussion here focuses on four key themes from this literature that might provide useful insights for research on new venture internationalization.[3]

Knowledge and learning within clusters

Economic geographers' views on industry clusters traditionally drew upon Marshall's (1890) concept of agglomeration economies. Subsequent work in economic geography and regional studies has moved to a focus on knowledge and learning among clustered firms and the associated benefits for innovation and competitiveness (e.g., Keeble et al., 1999; Malmberg and Maskell, 2002). These approaches suggest clustered firms can benefit from knowledge dissemination and 'collective learning' which are fostered through various mechanisms, including flows of professionals and 'embodied expertise' through the local labour market; high rates of localized entrepreneurship (including spin-offs from existing businesses); formal and informal networking by professionals and managers and demonstration/imitation effects. More recent studies have provided a more nuanced view of the benefits of clustering; for example, Hervas-Oliver and Albors-Garrigos (2009) have shown that certain firms are better able to capitalize on the knowledge spillovers and learning advantages available within a cluster due to their greater 'absorptive capacity'.

Clusters as 'habitats' for entrepreneurship

Another strand in this research stream has explored their role as beneficial environments for new venture creation and growth. Regions differ in the way they can sustain new businesses due to the uneven geographical distribution of information and other knowledge necessary for firm formation and business success (Malecki, 2002). This point is illustrated in empirical research on successful high-technology regions in the United States. For example, Feldman (2001) identifies a 'munificent entrepreneurial environment' – comprising the availability of VC, supportive social capital and an 'entrepreneurial culture', and entrepreneurial support services, such as intellectual property lawyers – as a key component in the emergence of new biotech ventures in the US Capitol region. Research on Silicon Valley also describes the fertile entrepreneurial environment or 'habitat' as a crucial component underpinning new ventures creation and growth in that region (Lee et al., 2000). Finally, Stuart and Sorenson (2003) have argued that entrepreneurs in the US biotech industry are attracted to establish their businesses in particular locations that are characterized by a concentration of 'critical resources' such as highly skilled labour and VC. These ideas have already been adopted by a handful of studies and suggest a possible link-up between the clusters literature and the resource- and knowledge-based views of new venture internationalization.

Cluster life cycles

More recent contributions to the clusters' literature offer several potentially useful insights that have not yet been incorporated into the BG/INV literature. First, research has highlighted that clusters have their own 'life cycles' and evolve through a number of stages (e.g., Bergman, 2008; Menzel and Fornahl, 2010). Studies of cluster evolution and clusters at different stages in their life cycle have observed that the presumed benefits of a cluster location (as discussed above) may be present when a cluster is fully established but absent during the early stages of its emergence (Bresnahan et al., 2001; Feldman, 2001), and also that cluster advantages (such as agglomeration economies) may fade or even reverse if a cluster reaches maturity/stagnation (Potter and Watts, 2010). This research cautions us to consider that the alleged beneficial impacts of a cluster location for new venture internationalization may be contingent on the life-cycle stage of the cluster – an issue that forms the central argument in this chapter and a key focus in the empirical case study analysis. These studies have also highlighted the important role played by an entrepreneurial agency in seeding clusters and driving the cluster through phases in its life cycle, noting that pioneering entrepreneurs can – through their business successes – bring about a transformation in the regional environment for entrepreneurship (Bresnahan et al., 2001; Feldman et al., 2005; Mason, 2008).

Entrepreneurial dynamics within clusters

A final strand of interest in the clusters research stream is concerned with the micro-foundations of industrial dynamics. A number of 'genealogical' studies have highlighted the important role of localized spin-offs from incumbent firms in the growth of clusters (Dahl et al., 2003; Klepper, 2001). This spin-off process may become cumulative and reinforcing because most new firms are founded in the same geographical region as the firm that 'produced' the entrepreneur (Dahl et al., 2003; Klepper, 2001; Romanelli and Schoonhoven, 2001). This implies that spin-offs and other forms of 'experience-based' entrepreneurship may account for an increasing share of the total firm population over time. Since the BG/INV literature has shown that experience can be positively related to internationalization, we might expect to find more firms with the necessary experience for (early) internationalization as the cluster progresses through its life cycle. This point is taken up during the empirical case study, along with the other themes discussed above.

Method

The empirical part of the chapter is based on a *revelatory, historical and longitudinal* case study of new venture internationalization within Ireland's indigenous software cluster. This case resonates with both literatures reviewed in the preceding section, since Ireland has been recognized as an emerging software development 'hotspot' in work on entrepreneurial technology clusters (Arora et al., 2004; Roche et al., 2008) and software firms have been a focus for many empirical studies in the BG/INV literature (e.g., Bell, 1995; Coviello and Munro, 1997). A case study approach was deemed appropriate because the study sought to examine a contemporary phenomenon (new venture internationalization) within its real-life context (the Irish software cluster) and because the study was concerned with a 'how' question (Yin, 2009). Two of Yin's (2009, pp. 48–9) justifications for adopting a single case design are present, since the study is both revelatory and longitudinal.

Yin (2009) suggests a *revelatory case study* is justified when an investigator has access to a phenomenon previously inaccessible to scientific investigation. The potential relationship between new venture internationalization and the cluster life cycle was viewed as a phenomenon previously 'hidden' from investigation, and the author's prior interest in the Irish software industry (as part of another project) had generated data that subsequently became useful for exploring this issue. The study is *historical* in nature in that is focuses on past events, going back over 20 years, and relies to a large extent on archival sources. Yin (2009, p. 49) notes that *longitudinal* studies can be useful for studying how conditions change over time; this was deemed important in light of the study's interest in the cluster life-cycle context. Thus, attention focused on both the evolution of the wider cluster over time and the internationalization behaviour on two cohorts 'leading' new software ventures, each founded at a different stage of the cluster life cycle (embedded units of analysis). The *chronological analysis* allows events to be traced over time and permits causal inferences to be drawn (Yin, 2009, p. 148). This approach was used to construct an account of the overall cluster life-cycle 'story' and to draw inferences about the relationship between temporal changes in the cluster environment and the internationalization behaviour of new ventures.

The case study is based largely upon in-depth, desk-based research using a wide array of secondary data sources, supplemented by a close reading of evidence in several previous studies of the Irish software industry (notably, O'Gorman et al., 1997; Ó Riain, 1999; Roche et al., 2008; Sands, 2005; Sterne, 2004).[4] Secondary data sources included individual companies' websites, various sector-specific and general online news media and other Internet sources. Keyword searches allowed the identification of news stories pertaining to specific companies. Several published interviews with key figures in the industry, including the founders of many leading firms, were also utilized. These secondary data were originally gathered by the author between 2001 and 2003, as part of another project, and supplemented in 2009. Data were organized into a structured archive, comprising 'source files' about each company of interest, several key industry figures and various pervasive themes. Analysis was guided by theories and concepts from the two thematic literatures reviewed above.

Case context: the Irish software cluster

Ireland has been recognized – alongside other information and communications technologies (ICT) hotspots such as Israel, Bangalore (India), Taiwan and Finland – as an example of a latecomer or emergent technology region (Arora et al., 2004; Roche et al., 2008; Sands, 2005). In the Irish case, attention has often focused on the role of inward foreign direct investment, notably from the United States, in sectors such as ICT hardware manufacturing, software and pharmaceuticals (Coe, 1997; Ó Riain, 1997). However, perhaps the most interesting aspect of the Irish experience is the emergence of a dynamic, entrepreneurial 'home grown' software industry (O'Gorman et al., 1997; Ó Riain, 1999; Roche et al., 2008). This indigenous industry is distinguished by its focus on niche software product development and its high export orientation (Arora et al., 2004; HotOrigin, 2001). It has noted strengths in the areas of telecommunications, open systems-based middleware and integration web technology, e-security and secure payment solutions, e-learning/computer-based training and financial services applications (HotOrigin, 2001).

According to statistics from Ireland's National Software Directorate, the indigenous software industry underwent a significant expansion during the 1990s and early 2000s. From a base of 290 companies with 3,800 employees and revenues of IR£150 million in 1991, the industry had grown to over 700 firms with around 14,000 employees and annual revenues of €1.4 billion by 2000 (despite a number of leading firms being 'lost' to foreign acquisitions). More significantly, the indigenous industry became more export oriented over the decade, with the share of total revenues coming from exports increasing from 41 per cent in 1991 to 62 per cent by 1999 and 81 per cent of companies being involved in exporting by 1997. The United States, the United Kingdom and Continental Europe were all significant export markets by the late 1990s. Although the majority of firms in the industry are small and micro enterprises, firms with over 50 employees were always the major contributors to exports. An interesting feature of the industry's growth during the 1990s was an increase in the number of these 'larger' firms from only four in 1989 to 24 by 1995, 34 in 1998 and at least 60 by 2001. It is these 'leading' firms that are of particular interest to this study.

A cluster life-cycle perspective

In keeping with recent evolutionary accounts of clusters, the Irish indigenous software industry can be said to have progressed through a number of 'life-cycle' stages. Table 13.1 give an overview of this life cycle in four major phases from the late 1970s to the mid-2000s, highlighting the key characteristics of both the industry and the regional entrepreneurial environment at each stage. This summary has been informed by the author's own secondary research and reading of existing studies. In particular, Sterne's (2004) delimitation of five 'entrepreneurial generations' of Irish software firms was adopted. The key points to note from Table 13.1 are as follows. First, an identifiable cluster of software firms only became evident in Ireland in the early 1990s but significant pioneering entrepreneurship was talking place as early the 1970s (Ó Riain, 1999; Sterne, 2004). Some important preconditions for future success were 'accidentally' sown in the regional environment around this time. Second, the focus on niche software products only became ingrained from the early 1990s after which the industry became increasingly export oriented. Third, the industry seems to have reached a kind of critical mass by the mid-1990s, marking the start of Stage III, when the rate of new firm formation, employment growth rate and export intensity all increased. The Nasdaq initial public offerings (IPOs) of CBT Systems in 1995 and Iona Technologies in 1997 could also be seen as watershed events, due to the international reputation effects this conveyed on the cluster and the demonstration effects for budding software entrepreneurs in Ireland. Fourth, Ireland began to resemble an entrepreneurial technology cluster with apparently self-reinforcing growth dynamics by the late 1990s, with many new ventures being formed via spin-offs from incumbent firms or by serial entrepreneurs. At this stage, the Irish state ramped up its support efforts, particularly for new high-potential start-ups, an

Table 13.1 Key developments in Ireland's indigenous software industry during four stylized cluster life-cycle stages

Cluster life-cycle stage	Stage I: Pre-/Proto-cluster (1970s to late 1980s)	Stage II: Embryonic/emerging cluster (late 1980s to mid-1990s)	Stage III: Established cluster in expansionary/accelerated growth phase (mid-1990s to 2001/02)	Stage IV: External shock, rationalization and reinvention (2002 onwards)
Key industry characteristics and developments	• Small population of firms • Pioneering Generation 1 firms focused on services and custom development for mainframes • High-profile failures and asset-stripping foreign acquisitions • Some innovative Generation 2 firms but they suffered from lack of commercial experience (e.g., Glockenspiel, Generics)	• Beginnings of critical mass? • Generation 2 firms begin exporting software products • Emergence of Generation 3 firms, including the 'leading lights' of Stage III • Industry moves to niche software product-based business model • Recognized technical communities in middleware, courseware and telecommunications software	• Critical mass attained? • IPOs and acquisitions of leading Generation 3 firms (e.g., Aldiscon, CBT Systems, Euristix, Iona) • Increasing volume of start-ups, incl. spin-offs from incumbents • Internationalization of many firms and growing export intensity • Emergence of 'true BGs' among Generation 4 firms • Some examples of outward FDI	• External shock: dot.com crash and global technology sector downturn • De-listing of several key players • Rationalization and cost-cutting • Limited number of high-profile firm failures • Gradual return to growth

Developments in the regional environment (cluster habitat)	• 'Accidental' creation of preconditions for growth • University expansion plus establishment of Regional Technology Colleges in 1970s • Upgrading of national telecoms infrastructure using EU funds • IDA Ireland attracts FDI by leading US ICT multinationals • Net outmigration of graduates and skilled professionals	• State agencies slowly begin to recognize the potential of indigenous software industry • Industry-specific institutions formed (e.g., National Software Directorate, Centre for Software Engineering) • Some internationally significant development work done by leading firms (e.g., Aldiscon, Iona)	• International recognition of leading firms and Irish software cluster as a whole • State agency Enterprise Ireland develops focus on software firms, providing hard and soft supports • Establishment of local venture capital industry, abundant angel investment, inflows of foreign VC • Establishment/attraction of private-sector support firms as part of developing start-up 'habitat'	• Harsher investment climate/funding crisis • Doubts about scale of firms and sustainability of cluster • Enterprise Ireland broadens focus to other indigenous industry sectors • Some software institutions disbanded or downgraded (e.g., CSE, NSD)

Notes: Entrepreneurial 'generations' are denominated according to Sterne (2004).
Source: Author, based on own secondary research and reading of existing studies (Coe, 1997; O'Gorman et al., 1997; Ó Riain, 1997, 1999; Roche et al., 2008; Sands, 2005; Sterne, 2004).

indigenous VC industry was seeded, and elements of a private-sector 'habitat' of specialist business service firms began to emerge.

This chronological account leads to some important inferences and insights, which underpin the case study analysis that follows. Firstly, it seems neither the supportive regional environment observed by the late 1990s nor the deliberate policies and actions of the Irish State were significant factors in the cluster's initial emergence, since both developments came *after* at least two entrepreneurial generations. Rather, entrepreneurial agency seems to have played a crucial role in the evolution of the cluster by 'inducing' the emergence of a more supportive regional entrepreneurial environment. This scenario echoes several other accounts in the literature on cluster emergence, evolution and life cycles (e.g., Avnimelech and Teubal, 2006; Bresnahan et al., 2001; Feldman et al., 2005). It also suggests that a 'co-evolutionary' perspective is appropriate, since entrepreneurial activities in the software industry both influenced and were influenced by the wider regional entrepreneurial environment in Ireland.

Case evidence on new venture internationalization at different stages of the cluster life cycle

Attention in this section focuses on the origins and internationalization behaviour of two cohorts of 'leading' software ventures that became active in international markets at different times. Firms in the first cohort were founded in Stage II (late 1980s/early 1990s) and went on to become some of the 'leading lights' of the Irish cluster in the mid to late 1990s; these were mostly members of Sterne's (2004) 3rd Generation. Firms in the second cohort were founded in Stage III (late 1990s); these were members of Sterne's (2004) 4th Generation. They were successful internationally during the 2000s; several were touted as future IPO candidates before the dot.com crash of 2002 and many were nominated in the Irish Software Association's annual industry awards. The following evidence and interpretation also pays particular attention to changes in the regional entrepreneurial environment confronting these two cohorts, in order to illuminate the relationship between new venture internationalization and the cluster life cycle in the Irish software case.

New venture origins and internationalization in the embryonic/emerging Irish software cluster

Looking into the origins of the early Irish software product firms of Generation 3, it is clear that no single source of knowledge was being exploited and there was no dominant 'entry route'. The emergence of these firms can be attributed to the efforts of entrepreneurs who sought to capitalize on: (1) the knowledge and expertise they had gleaned from varied work experience in industry, academia and the public sector; and (2) the commercial opportunity presented by the newly emerging global market for software products. Many early Irish software product firms began by providing 'bespoke' or custom services to businesses, then expanded this business by making consultancy kits and subsequently packaged products (Ó Riain, 1999). Early customers within Ireland (including some foreign multinationals) provided a catalyst for these firms by commissioning

IT development projects. Other firms were created via spin-outs of the in-house software/IT divisions of firms in other industries, such as telecommunications or computer hardware, or semi-state bodies. A variation on this theme saw new firms emerge when users of software in vertical markets, such as banking and training, started ventures that capitalized on detailed market knowledge. Finally, a *minority* of firms were based on academic research, including some of the most technically sophisticated firms (Arora et al., 2004; Ó Riain, 1999). These various routes are illustrated using some specific examples of leading Generation 3 firms in Table 13.2.

Table 13.2 Profiles of three 'leading' software firms founded in Stage II

Company	Specialism	Commentary (e.g., origins, key milestones)
Euristix	Telecommunication systems software (network/element management)	Founded in 1990 by former MD of Baltimore Technologies who had a Ph.D. in telecoms engineering and experience with state telecoms company; began selling consultancy services to government and commercial clients; first significant US contract in 1993; set up US office and introduced first product in 1995; acquired in 1999 by Nasdaq-listed Fore Systems for $81 million in stocks, when it had 170 employees
Iona Technologies	Standards-based component middleware (later web services integration)	Founded in 1991 on back of EU-funded research on distributed computing at Trinity College Dublin; sold training services to fund initial product development; led industry in implementing CORBA operating standard with its Orbix product; sold minority stake to Sun Microsystems in 1994 after struggling to secure VC; opened first US office in 1995; second Irish firm to list on Nasdaq in 1997 in $60 million IPO; revenues peaked at $180 million (two-thirds from USA) and workforce at over 800 in 2001; seen as industry 'bellwether' from late 1990s
Quay Financial Software	Financial services applications (information delivery and presentation for stock, bond and currency traders)	Founded in 1987; founder had worked in New York in early 1980s; products rode wave of PC adoption in financial services in early 1990s; angel investment from Dermot Desmond; early adopters of its products were in Ireland; used reference customers to secure sales in London and New York; ultimately gained 80 customers in 23 countries after granting global distribution rights to US vendor Micrognosis in 1992; revenues reached $19 million by 1995; acquired by CSK (Japan) in 1996, when it had over 80 employees

Source: Author, based on own secondary research and reading of existing studies.

The internationalization behaviour and paths of these early software product firms are difficult to uncover in detail from secondary research. However, the available evidence tends to suggest that they: (1) internationalized gradually, having initially focused on providing custom services to domestic customers; or (2) internationalized early due to a small or non-existent home market for their products, but progressed with a narrow geographical scope, typically focusing on the culturally proximate UK or US markets. Thus, Sterne (2004, p. 65) states, 'the typical generation two company started as a service provider to *local* customers, wrote its first code as a sideline, re-positioned itself as a product developer after a few years' and generation three firms were 'characterised by product specialisation, more frequent forays into America'. Overall, there seem to be some similarities with the traditional Uppsala or stage models of internationalization, and where firms were early internationalizers, the moniker 'born international' seems more appropriate than 'born global', since their exporting generally progressed quite slowly and narrowly. Certainly, the experiences of three leading Generation 3 firms (Euristix, Iona and Quay) are consistent with this interpretation (Table 13.2).

The regional entrepreneurial environment in the embryonic/emerging Irish software cluster

New software ventures in Ireland faced a challenging regional entrepreneurial environment in the late 1980s/early 1990s and – viewed in the context of subsequent developments – this seems to have constrained or slowed the pace of their internationalization. Seen from a RBP, the new Generation 3 start-ups look strikingly similar to the 'resource-deficient' small firm of traditional portrayals; their founders typically had little capital and many had limited commercial experience, meaning they lacked the requisite financial resources and prior business experience to pursue an early and rapid international expansion strategy. However, these internal resource deficiencies were compounded by the absence of a supportive regional environment where external resources could be acquired or mobilized.

One problem within the regional environment was an under-developed labour market; there was a shortage of experienced software managers, sales personnel and, to a lesser extent, engineering talent. There was also an absence of supportive state institutions, at least until – and arguably beyond – the establishment of the National Software Directorate in 1991. Further, new software ventures had few local role models to imitate, since there was no precedent of an Irish technology firm breaking into the key US market and many firms from the early generations of Irish software had either failed commercially or been swallowed up then run down by foreign multinationals (Ó Riain, 1999). However, the most significant shortcoming in the regional environment of the late 1980s/early 1990s was the paucity of external financing options: private investors were wary of technology firms after a number of high-profile failures in the 1980s; the major banks would not lend to software firms who had no tangible assets against which to secure a loan; there was no local VC industry; and the state development agencies were not yet enthused by the software industry. The absence of external finance meant many firms began by selling consultancy and training services to generate income to support product development and had to adopt a gradualist, low-commitment approach to international market entry.

Dissimilar venture origins and qualitatively different internationalization among leading firms founded in Stage III (the established cluster)

The Irish software cluster was characterized by faster growth during the second half of the 1990s, fuelled by increasing export intensity and a higher the rate of new firm formation. Survey evidence suggests fewer than 30 per cent of the estimated 250 indigenous software product development companies in existence in 2001 were established before 1996, and almost half were less than three years old (HotOrigin, 2001). There was also a notable change in the origin of new software ventures during this phase, as spin-offs from incumbent indigenous firms became commonplace and serial software entrepreneurship was observed. Even *bone fide* new entrants tended to have founders with extensive prior experience in relevant vertical markets or technological niches. As noted above, a majority of these new ventures were niche product specialists from the outset and founded with an explicit focus on international markets. Strikingly, many of the leading Generation 4 firms founded in Stage III had characteristics that justified the label 'true born global' (after Kuivalainen et al., 2007): high export orientation (internationalization intensity); active internationally from the very outset and in multiple countries within three years (early and rapid internationalization); won contracts with major corporate customers in at least two major continental markets (bi- or multi-regional internationalization); and engaged in 'multi-modal' internationalization – by establishing overseas offices, acquiring firms outside Ireland, or forming international strategic alliances with channel partners and/or technology partners. Note that this type of internationalization behaviour was rarely, perhaps never, observed among the leading Generation 3 firms of Stage II; hence it can be seen as *qualitatively different* in terms of precocity, speed, intensity and geographic scope.

The eight cases detailed in Table 13.3 exemplify this BG tendency. All survived a global technology sector downturn as early-stage businesses and internationalized early and rapidly to distant markets and in multiple global regions, winning contracts with major 'blue chip' corporate clients. As of October 2009, three were still trading independently as 'micro-multinationals' (one publicly listed, two privately held) some 10 to 13 years after their establishment, whilst 5 had been acquired after between 5 and 12 years of independent trading. All eight firms were founded by teams (of between two and seven founders) with significant prior experience, most of which was acquired working for earlier generations of firms in Stages I and II of the cluster life cycle. The new venture origin in all eight cases was one of three types: entrepreneurial spin-offs from successful incumbent firms (including some of the leading Generation 3 firms); serial entrepreneurship or new entrants with very experienced founding teams (Table 13.3). It is suggested here that these origins and antecedents were an important causal factor behind the

Table 13.3 Profile of eight BG Irish software firms founded in Stage III of the cluster life cycle

Company (founded)	Business niche (circa 2003)	Venture origin	Known customer locations (circa 2003)	Example 'blue chip' customers (circa 2003)	Status as of October 2009
Am Beo (Mar 2000)	Rating and billing solutions for telecoms	ESO	Europe, North America	Lycos Europe, Western Wireless (USA), Sonera ZED (Finland)	Acquired by US Nasdaq-listed company in October 2005
Cape Clear (Aug 1999)	Web services integration technology	ESO	Europe, North America, South America	AT&T, Deutsche Bank, General Electric, Hewlett-Packard, Sky	Acquired by US company in March 2008
CR2 (Jan 1997)	Channel banking and card payment solutions	SE	Europe, Middle East, India, Africa, Caribbean, Oceania	Bank Muscat (Oman), LG Petro Bank (Poland), ANZ Bank (Aus)	Independent, privately owned; founders were no longer on board
Macalla (Mar 1998)	Mobile commerce platforms and solutions	ESO	Europe, North America	ING/Postbank and Telfort/MMO2 (Neth), Dresdner Kleinwort (Germany)	Acquired by US company in September 2009
Network365 (Jun 1999)	Enabling technology for mobile services	SE	Europe, North America, Asia-Pacific	Hutchinson and CSL (Hong Kong), O2, NTT DoCoMo (Japan)	Acquired by Northern Ireland company in July 2009
Norkom (Mar 1998)	eCRM solutions and customer intelligence tools	EFT	Europe, North America	HSBC, Canadian Tire Financial (Can), KPNO (Belg), ING Direct (Neth)	Independent Plc after IPO on AIM & IEX in May 2006
Openet (Jul 1999)	Telecom billing software for real-time charging	EFT	Europe, North America	Orange, Telecom Italia Mobile, Verizon (USA), TMN (Portugal)	Independent, privately owned
Xiam (Sep 1999)	Mobile middleware and application software	EFT	Europe, North America, Asia-Pacific	Vodafone, Orange, CSL (Hong Kong), Midwest Wireless (USA)	Acquired by US company in March 2008

Notes: ESO = Entrepreneurial spin-off from incumbent firm; SE = Established by serial entrepreneurs; EFT = New entrant with experienced founding team; IPO = initial public offering; AIM is the London Stock Exchange's international market for smaller growing companies and IEX is its smaller Irish equivalent.
Source: Compiled by author using information from company websites and various secondary data sources.

internationalization behaviour observed among the eight firms, since they conveyed a particular and significant 'resource inheritance' on these new ventures, embodied in their experienced founders. The resources in question were things like technological domain knowledge, managerial and entrepreneurial experience, international marketing and market development experience in a variety of countries and deep familiarity with particular vertical markets and end users – all of which might be useful for early and rapid internationalization. Table 13.4 exemplifies this point for three of the eight cases from Table 13.3. Thus, seen from a RBV, the leading Generation 4 firms were in a superior position at inception compared to earlier generations of Irish start-ups and this partly explains why they were able to pursue a qualitatively different internationalization trajectory to their predecessors.

Table 13.4 Antecedents, origin and 'resource inheritance' of three BG software firms founded in Stage III

Company	Commentary
Cape Clear	Founded by three former executives of leading Irish middleware firm Iona Technologies (cross-refer Table 13.2). Subsequently recruited three other key executives from Iona. Like Iona, it initially specialized in middleware systems built to the CORBA industry operating standard. Embodied knowledge and expertise transferred in spin-off included experience of developing and marketing component middleware products at Iona, plus experience in various managerial roles with this leading indigenous software exporter.
CR2	Founded in 1996 by Cian Kinsella and Ron Downey after they resigned from Kindle Banking Systems, an Irish banking software firm that they had previously co-founded and grown before selling it to UK Plc Misys. Kinsella gained extensive experience during his 17 years at Kindle, including product development, consultancy, customer service and sales; he had served as Kindle's Technical Director and Sales Director. Downey led Kindle into its first export market (UK in 1994) and had established Kindle's regional offices in Singapore, Bahrain and Miami as its Worldwide Sales Director in the early 1990s. CR2 appointed several experienced entrepreneurs/executives from within the cluster to its board in the early 2000s.
Openet Telecom	Established in 1999 with a pre-selected, highly experienced, senior management team of software and telecoms industry veterans, who had worked – in Ireland – for firms like Euristix (cross-refer Table 13.2), Retix/Vertel, ISR Global Telecom and Sun Microsystems. This background gave the firm a deep understanding of its target customers and emerging trends in the telecoms market. Barry Murphy, founder of Insight (a leading Irish software firm in the 1980s) and Ireland's first National Software Director (1988–96), was recruited as CEO at an early stage.

Source: Compiled by author using information from company websites and various secondary data sources.

A transformed region entrepreneurial environment in Stage III (the established cluster)

This section highlights some important contrasts between the regional entrepreneurial environment facing new software ventures in late 1990s, and that of the late 1980s/early 1990s (described earlier). The central point is that the regional environment had substantially improved by Stage III, as a result of the gradual process of co-evolution described earlier in the chapter and summarized in Table 13.1. This transformed regional environment provided many useful resources and supports for new ventures. In particular, some of the resources that are known – from the BG/INV literature – to be useful for early and rapid internationalization (e.g., VC, experienced executives and supportive institutions) became relatively abundant by the late 1990s. Thus, the new software ventures of the late 1990s/early 2000s – including those cases in Table 13.3 – were able to (externally) acquire and mobilize some of the additional resources they required for early and rapid internationalization from within the cluster. This undoubtedly encouraged and enabled several leading Generation 4 firms to pursue of a 'truly BG' strategy. Three of the many important changes in the regional environment are discussed here by way of illustration.

Development of a local VC industry

It was only around 1998/99 that private investment capital became abundant in Irish software (Ó Riain, 1999). The modern Irish VC industry was 'kick-started' by a European Union (EU)-funded Irish government programme, starting in 1996. Using matched public and private funds it aimed to stimulate investment in promising technology-based start-ups (Enterprise Ireland, 2000). Thus, between 1998 and the early/mid-2000s, VC became a dominant source of external finance for 'build-phase' indigenous software companies (HotOrigin, 2001, 2002). The example of VC provides the clearest illustration of how the transformed regional environment in Stage III influenced the internationalization behaviour of Generation 4 firms. Recall that the use of VC has been linked in the literature to the pursuit of an early internationalization strategy, as it permits firms to rapidly build channels to market, make acquisitions and fund ongoing product development. In contrast to previous generations, who struggled to raise external funds, the leading Generation 4 firms could avail themselves of a home-grown VC industry (comprising firms like ACT, Delta Partners and Trinity VC) and, in some instances, attract investment from international VCs who were now showing interest in Ireland, following the IPOs of CBT and Iona. Thus, all eight of the BG cases in Table 13.3 received VC, together securing over €100 million in 18 separate deals worth €2–15 million between 1999 and 2003. As an example of how this funding was useful for accelerated internationalization, consider CR2's £8.1m acquisition of London-based Interlink, a global provider of software for ATM and point-of-sale devices, in June 2000. This deal, which would not have been possible without VC, instantly doubled CR2's size and gave it access to an infrastructure ideally matched to its global expansion plans; Interlink was already active in India, Africa, the Middle East and the Asia Pacific (Linnane, 2000).

A maturing labour market

Venture capitalists often stimulate the 'professionalization' of start-ups by encouraging them to recruit experienced executives and appoint non-executive directors (Hellman and Puri, 2002). This became more possible in Ireland in the late 1990s/early 2000s due to the accumulation of experience within the cluster through the 1990s. Many of the leading Generation 4 firms enhanced their top management team by recruiting executives from within the cluster; a good example is Openet Telecom's appointment of former Insight Software MD and National Software Director Barry Murphy to its CEO position in 2000 (Tables 13.3 and 13.4). Other Generation 4 firms brought in experienced advisers and extended their network ties by appointing industry veterans like the former Iona CEO Chris Horn and Euristix founder Jim Mountjoy as non-executive board directors. Experienced marketing and sales executives were also becoming more common in the cluster by Stage III, and firms were able to tap into recognized technical communities, in areas such as telecoms software and middleware, when recruiting engineering talent (Ó Riain, 1999).

Enterprise Ireland's active support of software firms

Another important development during late 1990s, triggered by the international entrepreneurial successes of Generation 3 firms, was improved support from the state. Enterprise Ireland (EI), the indigenous industry development agency formed in 1997, recognized the promise of the software industry and began offering a range of hard and soft supports to 'high-potential start-ups'. EI took direct equity stakes in many of these promising new software ventures, including Am Beo and Network 365 (Table 13.3). It also facilitated firms' international market entry; for example, Cape Clear's first US presence was as a tenant in EI's 'technology marketing centre' near San Jose, California, and mobile telecoms specialists Network365 and Xiam were among the first firms to use EI's Tokyo incubator in 2001. Many Generation 4 firms also participated in EI's international trade missions or had their visits to key international trade fairs subsidized.

Conclusion

The chapter makes a contribution to the burgeoning literature on the internationalization of new and small firms, and the emerging sub-discipline of International Entrepreneurship. It adds to the handful of recent studies on the relationship between clusters and new venture internationalization, and further extends this work by exploring how the emergence and internationalization of new ventures can be affected by the cluster life-cycle context within which they are founded. This issue was examined via a revelatory longitudinal case study that highlighted differences in the origins and internationalization behaviour of two cohorts of new ventures founded at different stages in the life cycle of Ireland's indigenous software cluster. The internationalization of leading firms founded during the later established cluster stage (in the late 1990s) was shown to have been qualitatively different – that is, earlier, more rapid, wider in geographic scope and more multi-modal – to that of firms founded in the embryonic/emerging stage of the cluster life cycle (late 1980s/early 1990s). Taking inspiration from the RBV on the BG/INV phenomenon, this difference was attribute to two main factors: (1) improvements in the regional entrepreneurial environment in Ireland (including the development of a local VC industry, a maturing of the labour market and improved policy support from EI) that made it easier for firms to acquire useful resources; and (2) the emergence of a cohort of more 'sophisticated' and 'pre-experienced' new ventures – during the established cluster – that sought to capitalize on the accumulated knowledge resources embodied in their founding team members. These resources had often been developed during prior experiences within the cluster, in earlier generations of internationally active firms.

External validity is an inherent concern with all case study research, so we cannot be certain if these findings are specific to the Irish case or generalizable to other locations and industries. However, there do appear to be some parallels with the experiences of emergent technology clusters in Israel and Bangalore (Avnimelech and Teubal, 2006; Nair et al., 2007). Also, following Yin's (2009) assertion that case study research is concerned with generalization to theory rather than populations and the conceptual links made here between new venture internationalization and the cluster life cycle may have wider relevance. Overall, the chapter suggests that a more holistic understanding of the BG/INV phenomenon could be developed by paying closer attention to the geographical and historical context with which these firms emerge. A longitudinal or co-evolutionary perspective that gives greater consideration to these contextual factors – looking before and beyond the life of a single venture or entrepreneur – might be a fruitful avenue for future studies.

Notes

1. A 'cluster' is understood here as a geographic concentration of businesses, specialized suppliers and associated institutions in a particular field, which may confer competitive advantages on its constituent firms; that is, broadly along the lines of Porter's (1998) definition.
2. Due to space constraints, this section focuses on a limited selection of work. Wide-ranging reviews of the burgeoning literature on BGs/INVs are provided by Rialp et al. (2005) and Aspelund et al. (2007).
3. Porter's (1998) ideas on clusters, which will be familiar to IB scholars, are overlooked here because the diamond model has limited utility in explaining emergent technology clusters (Nair et al., 2007; O'Gorman et al., 1997).
4. John Sterne is a Dublin-based journalist who has written about the IT business in Ireland for 20+ years. His 2004 book provides an unparalleled source of insights on leading firms and entrepreneurs in the cluster.

References

A. Arora, A. Gambardella and S. Torrisi, 'In the Footsteps of Silicon Valley? Indian and Irish Software in the International Division of Labor', in T. Bresnahan and A. Gambardella (eds), *Building High-Tech Clusters: Silicon Valley and Beyond*, (Cambridge, UK: Cambridge University Press, 2004), pp. 78–120.

A. Aspelund, T. K. Madsen and Ø. Moen, 'A review of the foundation, international marketing strategies, and performance of international new ventures', *European Journal of Marketing*, 41(11/12) (2007) 1423–48.

G. Avnimelech and M. Teubal, 'Creating venture capital industries that co-evolve with high-tech: insight from an extended industry life cycle perspective on the Israeli experience', *Research Policy*, 35(10) (2006) 1477–98.

J. D. Bell, 'The internationalisation of small computer software firms: a further challenge to stage theory', *European Journal of Marketing*, 29(8) (1995) 60–75.

E. M. Bergman, 'Cluster Life-Cycles: An Emerging Synthesis', in C. Karlsson (ed.), *Handbook of Research on Cluster Theory*, (Cheltenham: Edward Elgar, 2008), pp. 114–132.

J. M. Bloodgood, H. J. Sapienza and J. G. Almeida, 'The internationalization of new high-potential US ventures: antecedents and outcomes', *Entrepreneurship Theory and Practice*, 20(4) (1996) 61–76.

T. Bresnahan, A. Gambardella and A. Saxenian, 'Old economy inputs for new economy outcomes: cluster formation in the new Silicon Valleys', *Industrial and Corporate Change*, 10(4) (2001) 835–60.

N. M. Coe, 'US Transnationals and the Irish software industry: assessing the nature, quality and stability of a new wave of foreign direct investment', *European Urban and Regional Studies*, 4(3) (1997) 21–30.

N. E. Coviello and M. P. Cox, 'The resource dynamics of international new venture networks', *Journal of International Entrepreneurship*, 4(2/3) (2006) 113–32.

N. E. Coviello and M. McAuley, 'Internationalisation and the smaller firm: a review of contemporary empirical research', *Management International Review*, 39(3) (1999) 223–56.

N. E. Coviello and H. Munro, 'Network relationships and the internationalization process of small software firms', *International Business Review*, 6(4) (1997) 361–86.

M. Crone, 'Geographical context and the emergence of early internationalizing firms: towards an inter-disciplinary conceptualization', presented at 37th AIB-UKI Conference, Dublin, Ireland, 8–10 April 2010.

M. S. Dahl, C. Ø. R. Pedersen and B. Dalum, 'Entry by Spin-off in a High-tech Cluster', Working paper No. 03–11, *Danish Research Unit for Industrial Dynamics* (2003).

Enterprise Ireland, *2000 Report: Seed and Venture Capital Measure of the Operational Programme, 1994–99*, (Dublin: Enterprise Ireland, 2000).

M. P. Feldman, 'The entrepreneurial event revisited: firm formation in a regional context', *Industrial and Corporate Change*, 10(4) (2001) 861–91.

M. P. Feldman, J. Francis and J. Bercovitz, 'Creating a cluster while building a firm: entrepreneurs and the formation of industrial clusters', *Regional Studies*, 39(1) (2005) 129–41.

S. A. Fernhaber and P. P. McDougall-Covin, 'Venture capitalists as catalysts to new venture internationalization: the impact of their knowledge and reputation resources', *Entrepreneurship Theory and Practice*, 33(1) (2009) 277–95.

S. A. Fernhaber, B. A. Gilbert and P. P. McDougall, 'International entrepreneurship and geographic location: an empirical examination of new venture internationalization', *Journal of International Business Studies*, 39 (2008) 267–90.

M. Gabrielsson, V. H. M. Kirpalani, P. Dimitratos, C. A. Solberg and A. Zucchella, 'Born globals: propositions to help advance the theory', *International Business Review*, 17(4) (2008) 385–401.

M. Gabrielsson, V. Sasi and J. Darling, 'Finance strategies of rapidly-growing Finnish SMEs: born internationals and born globals', *European Business Review*, 16(6) (2004) 590–604.

T. Hellmann and M. Puri, 'Venture capital and the professionalization of start-up firms: empirical evidence', *The Journal of Finance*, 57(1) (2002) 169–97.

J-L. Hervas-Oliver and J. Albors-Garrigos, 'The role of the firm's internal and relational capabilities in clusters', *Journal of Economic Geography*, 9(2) (2009) 263–83.

HotOrigin Ltd, *Ireland's Emerging Software Cluster: A Hothouse of Future Stars*, HotOrigin Ltd, 64 Lower Mount Street, Dublin 2, Ireland, (2001).

HotOrigin Ltd, *Ireland's Software Cluster: Innovation – The Fuel for International Success*, HotOrigin Ltd, 64 Lower Mount Street, Dublin 2, Ireland, (2002).

D. Keeble, C. Lawson, B. Moore and F. Wilkinson, 'Collective learning processes, networking and "institutional thickness" in the Cambridge region', *Regional Studies*, 33(4) (1999) 319–32.

S. Klepper, 'Employee startups in high-tech industries', *Industrial and Corporate Change*, 10(3) (2001) 639–74.

O. Kuivalainen, S. Sundqvist and P. Servais, 'Firms' degree of born-globalness, international entrepreneurial orientation and export performance', *Journal of World Business*, 42(3) (2007) 253–67.

R. Laanti, M. Gabrielsson and P. Gabrielsson, 'The globalization strategies of business-to-business born global firms in the wireless technology industry', *Industrial Marketing Management*, 36(8) (2007) 1104–17.

C. M. Lee, W. F. Miller, M. G. Hancock and H. S. Rowen, *The Silicon Valley Edge: A Habitat for Innovation and Entrepreneurship*, (Stanford, CA: Stanford University Press, 2000).

D. Libaers and M. Meyer, 'Highly innovative small technology firms, industrial clusters and firm internationalization', *Research Policy*, 40(10) (2011) 1426–37.

C. Linnane, 'CR2' (Interview with Cian Kinsella and Ron Downey), *Business Plus Online*, 1 September 2000, (http://www.bizplus.ie/bp_online/start_ups/?ns=62 (20.03.03).

S. Loane, J. D. Bell and R. McNaughton, 'A cross-national study on the impact of management teams on the rapid internationalization of small firms', *Journal of World Business*, 42(4) (2007) 489–504.

E. Malecki, 'Entrepreneurship in Regional and Local Development', in N. F. Krueger (ed.), *Entrepreneurship: Critical Perspectives on Business and Management*, (London: Routledge, 2002), pp. 329–64.

A. Malmberg and P. Maskell, 'The elusive concept of localization economies: towards a knowledge-based theory of spatial clustering', *Environment and Planning A*, 34(3) (2002) 429–49.

A. Marshall, *Principles of Economics: An Introductory Volume*, (London: Macmillan, 1890).

C. Mason, 'Entrepreneurial Dynamics and the Origin and Growth of High-Tech Clusters', in C. Karlsson, (ed.) *Handbook of Research on Innovation and Clusters: Cases and Policies*, (Cheltenham: Edward Elgar, 2008), pp. 33–53.

M-P. Menzel and D. Fornahl, 'Cluster life cycles – dimensions and rationales of cluster evolution', *Industrial & Corporate Change*, 19(1) (2010) 205–38.

A. Nair, D. Ahlstrom and L. Filer, 'Localized advantage in a global economy: the case of Bangalore', *Thunderbird International Business Review*, 49(5) (2007) 591–618.

S. Ó Riain, 'An offshore Silicon Valley? The emerging Irish software industry', *Competition and Change*, 2 (1997) 175–212.

S. Ó Riain, *Remaking the Developmental State: The Irish Software Industry in the Global Economy*, Unpublished dissertation, Department of Sociology, University of California, Berkeley, (1999).

C. O'Gorman, E. O'Malley and J. Mooney, *The Irish Indigenous Software Industry – An Application of Porter's Cluster Analysis*, Research Series Paper No. 3, National Economic and Social Council, Dublin, (1997).

M. E. Porter, 'Clusters and the new economics of competition', *Harvard Business Review*, 76(6) (1998) 77–81.

A. Potter and H. D. Watts, 'Evolutionary agglomeration theory: Increasing returns, diminishing returns, and the industry life cycle', *Journal of Economic Geography*, 11(3) (2010) 417–55.

A. R. Reuber and E. Fischer, 'The influence of the management team's international experience on the internationalization behaviors of SMEs', *Journal of International Business Studies*, 28(4) (1997) 807–25.

A. Rialp, J. Rialp and G. A. Knight, 'The phenomenon of early internationalizing firms: what do we know after a decade (1993–2003) of scientific inquiry?', *International Business Review*, 14(2) (2005) 147–66.

F. Roche, R. O'Shea, T. J. Allen and D. Breznitz, 'The Dynamics of an Emerging Entrepreneurial Region in Ireland', in P. H. C. Phan, S. Venkataraman and S. R. Velamuri (eds), *Entrepreneurship in Emerging Economies Around the World: Theory, Evidence and Implications*, (Cheltenham: Edward Elgar, 2008), pp. 9–46.

E. Romanelli and C. B. Schoonhoven, 'The Local Origins of New Firms', in C. B. Schoonhoven and E. Romanelli (eds) *The Entrepreneurship Dynamic: Origins of Entrepreneurship and the Evolution of Industries*, (Stanford, CA: Stanford University Press, 2001), pp. 40–67.

M. Ruzzier, R. D. Hisrich and B. Antoncic, 'SME internationalization research: past, present and future', *Journal of Small Business and Enterprise Development*, 13(4) (2006) 476–97.

A. Sands, 'The Irish Software Industry', in A. Arora, and A. Gambardella (eds), *From Underdogs to Tigers: The Rise and Growth of the Software Industry in Brazil, China, India, Ireland, and Israel*, (Oxford: Oxford University Press, 2005), pp. 41–71.

J. Sterne, *Adventures in Code: The Story of the Irish Software Industry*, (Dublin: The Liffey Press, 2004).

T. E. Stuart and O. Sorenson, 'The geography of opportunity: spatial heterogeneity in founding rates and the performance of biotechnology firms', *Research Policy*, 30(2) (2003) 229–53.

P. Westhead, M. Wright and D. Ucbasaran, 'The internationalization of new and small firms: a resource-based view', *Journal of Business Venturing*, 16(4) (2001) 333–58.

R. K. Yin, *Case Study Research: Design and Methods*, 4th Edition, (London: Sage, 2009).

Index

Note: The letters 'f', 'n' and 't' following the locators denote figures, notes and tables respectively.

Printed and bound in Great Britain by
CPI Antony Rowe, Chippenham and Eastbourne